The Cars of
American Motors

Also by Marc Cranswick

The BMW 5 Series and X5: A History of Production Cars and Tuner Specials, 1972–2008 (McFarland, 2010)

Porsche 928, 924, 944 and 968: The Front-Engined Sports Cars (McFarland, 2008)

The Cars of American Motors

An Illustrated History

MARC CRANSWICK

Foreword by CARL GREEN

McFarland & Company, Inc., Publishers
Jefferson, North Carolina, and London

Library of Congress Cataloguing-in-Publication Data

Cranswick, Marc.
The cars of American Motors : an illustrated history / Marc Cranswick ;
foreword by Carl Green.
p. cm.
Includes bibliographical references and index.

ISBN 978-0-7864-4672-8
softcover : acid free paper ∞

1. American Motors automobiles — History.
2. American Motors Corporation — History.
I. Title.

TL215.A45C73 2012 629.2220973—dc23 2011037358

British Library cataloguing data are available

Front cover: 1986 AMC Eagle sedan (courtesy Sean Weitzel)

Manufactured in the United States of America

McFarland & Company, Inc., Publishers
Box 611, Jefferson, North Carolina 28640
www.mcfarlandpub.com

To Valeri Wilson

Table of Contents

Foreword: My AMC Days
by Carl Green

My first encounter with AMC was in 1968 when I went to Chicago to help Dave Puhl on a project called "Phaz II," a mid-engine roadster pickup. It had been designed by Harry Bradley and was a *Rod and Custom* magazine project car featured numerous times over the one-year build. All hand-built, all steel, a really wild vehicle of that time period. The power plant was an AMC 343 V8 that had been supplied by American Motors for the project. Dave had been building some wild stuff for AMC previous to my arrival, and most were featured in *Rod and Custom* magazine. During that time with Dave, I met a number of AMC execs (including Dick Teague, VP and head of AMC Styling) who would play into my future career for years to come. After the Phaz II project, I got a call from Spence Murray to come back to California to work on his *R & C* project '36 Ford roadster, a vehicle also powered by an AMC-supplied 343 engine.

In the early '70s I opened Carl Green Enterprises in Van Nuys, at that time one of the biggest hot rod and custom car producing areas in Southern California. Almost immediately, I got into another AMC project, a hot rod Pacer. Randall American, an AMC dealer in Mesa, Arizona, had installed a monster AMC 401 into the little Fishbowl! They needed bigger tires for the traction problem, which called for body modifications to accept the huge meats. Enter Carl Green Enterprises and the CGE Pacer was born! I modified the wheel wells, blanked out the quarter glasses, built a wild wing that sat on the rear hatch, laid on a pearl paint job with some graphics, drove the car to Lake Tahoe, Nevada, to an AMC new car event to show the top AMC brass, and the rest is history. We built about 150 CGE Pacer kits and complete cars from 1975 through 1978, including a Pacer pickup that was a Dick Teague/Carl Green joint effort. Dick and I had a great relationship during that period of time and worked on many AMC "skunkwerks" projects.

Years later, in the mid–'90s I became involved in building a number of prototype SUVs on Dodge T-300 platforms. To my surprise, many of the guys I had met and worked with at AMC were with Chrysler, transferred in the Chrysler/AMC buyout. I have many great memories of the '70s and the '90s working with a great bunch of guys from AMC.

Introduction: AMC — Ahead of the Game

There were no chauffeurs at AMC, according to Gerry Meyers. The max cold a/c dial setting on Gremlin said "desert," and if a corporation could ever be cuddly, it would be American Motors. The smallest member of Detroit's once Big Four automakers had a spirit of innovation and took on General Motors, Ford and Chrysler at the height of their powers. AMC was often the counterpoint to Detroit thinking that bigger was always better.

Famous Canadian gas tycoon Colonel Thompson used a Rambler for exploring his golf course, instead of a plebeian golf cart. Colonel Thompson's daily driver was a Rolls-Royce. American Motors sold on the strengths of economy, quality and avoiding obsolescence. Little wonder a tycoon chose it as the ultimate small car! The heart of that bedrock reputation was a solid six-cylinder, but there were interesting distractions.

AMC soon gained a reputation as an oddball, left-field thinker. Detroit was well known for its small-block V8s, but what if you took one of those motors and wrapped it in a glass bubble to float down the highway? Wouldn't it be something if your automatic transmission car could leave that highway, and challenge the great outdoors without messing around with diff locks?

American Motors was often so far ahead of the curve that the value of its work only became obvious 10 to 15 years down the road, or track. AMC was early in some areas, late in others. In the latter cases, the company showed that once it got set on an idea, it followed through with success. Racing victories did come, and cars like the Scrambler, Machine and AMX delivered. Without Boss / GTO / Road Runner nameplate cachet, they had to.

By being late to the party, AMC still had something for the enthusiast, after the other guests had left the building. A mid–'70s 4-barrel 360/401ci Matador Coupe played a V8 tune from yesteryear. It was a comfort that AMC dealer Randall American could still provide a 6.6-liter V8 Gremlin in 1974, as a subcompact alternative to the Honda Civic. Those who laugh last, laugh longest. However, due to its small size, AMC experienced the problems and questions GM, Ford and Chrysler would face later on.

Detroit's automakers steadily lost market share through the '70s. How to face foreign competitors that make the most of the North American auto scene when conditions permit, and then fall back on home markets when conditions don't? Through Jeep, AMC felt expanding demand come from overseas markets, and got involved in a merger with a foreign company

(Renault). American Motors' experience showed that good vehicles could come from a French alliance. Few Jeep XJ Cherokee and ZJ Grand Cherokee owners would disagree.

In recounting the American Motors legend, primary historical resources have been studied. Special thanks should be given to the keepers of this material, Eddie Stakes, Jeni Panhorst and Craig Bond, and for their advice concerning AMC matters. I would also like to mention the assistance provided by the Chrysler archives department. Carl Green gave valuable information regarding the history and products of Carl Green Enterprises, Inc. (CGE), a treat for Pacer lovers.

With such a wide variety of vehicle types covered across several years, the insight of AMC / Rambler owners was also invaluable. We have also been treated to a mini-tour of the Rambler Ranch museum, courtesy of its founder Terry Gale. Plus, Doug Redenius and David A. Reinhardt of the Ian Fleming Foundation have kindly provided pictures of the James Bond "Astro Spiral" AMC Hornet. Last, a very special thanks to Krystal Geary for modeling the George Barris AMX-400, and to her father Mike Geary.

It would be hard to characterize an AMC vehicle as being one kind of car. Unlike its larger U.S. rivals, AMC didn't have several divisions, so it was a bit schizophrenic in having many different types of cars under one roof. Thus, one can find the puritanical A to B of Toyota, the exuberance of Dodge and luxury of Buick. If variety is the spice of life, American Motors is a jalapeno pepper!

Chapter 1

Economy, a Survival Recipe

Car of Dreams

In the early to middle part of the 20th century the American auto industry wasn't lacking in innovation or diversity. Numerous firms offered all manner of dream cars, like the Cord 812. Gordon Buehrig and the Auburn-Cord-Duesenberg group engineers combined a front drive unibody chassis with features like aerodynamic pop-up headlamps faired into swoopy bodywork, a 4-speed gearbox, and, for 1937, added a Schwitzer-Cummins supercharger to the Cord's 90-degree V8. The external flexy engine exhaust pipes would inspire car customizers for decades to come.[1]

A glamorous Cord ad from 1937 had its sophisticated female owner claiming, "Other drivers can pass my Cord, only when I let them." All this out of Indiana and without running boards. The latter unibody omission meant Al Capone's men had nowhere to stand while discharging their machine guns! However, there were more serious reasons why cars of the Cord's ilk were ill suited to their times, not the least of which was the '30s Depression. The classy Cord advert appeared in the May 1937 issue of *Esquire* magazine, and the final Cord was constructed in August of the same year.[2]

Hupmobile bought the production dies of the Cord 810/812, with a view to combine Cord style with more conventional engineering. Hupmobile's plan, in association with the assembly facilities of the Graham-Paige Motor Co., bore limited fruit. A mere 319 Hupmobile Skylarks were built by the time Hupmobile shut up shop in late summer 1939. However, capitalism's hiccup, prohibition, and the storm clouds of war only temporarily halted the public's love affair with the automobile.

Entrepreneurs and business minds inside and outside the auto industry could see great prospects for car ownership after World War II. The mood was intoxicatingly upbeat, with new models more exciting than ever. The greatest extrovert of the bunch was the 1948 Tucker Torpedo. Just after the war it was fashionable to incorporate aviation ideas into automotive engineering. One could cleave through the air more efficiently with a rounded Saab 92, even on 2-stroke power, than with the upright devices of the prewar era. With Preston Tucker's Torpedo it was like riding in the most advanced flight bomber the world had to offer.[3]

With a specification that belonged in a sci-fi comic book, the Torpedo had a rear-mounted air-cooled flat-six Bell helicopter engine, four-wheel independent suspension, a pop-out safety windshield and rigid passenger survival safety cell. The futuristic faired-in bodywork possessed a 0.30 coefficient of drag, an extraordinary figure. Fire up the monster Bell flat 6, sit at the Torpedo's controls and one had truly entered the jet age.

Things were also jubilant at the Waldorf Astoria Hotel in New York City, because Kaiser-Frazer chose to unveil their two new models at this venue in 1946. Founded on July 25, 1945, Kaiser-Frazer Corporation incorporated the assets of the moribund Graham-Paige concern and was the first new U.S. automaker after World War II. They built cars at the giant Willow Run factory in Michigan, a U.S. government–created works for the production of B-24 Liberator bombers by Ford Motor Co. during the war. This largest single production building in the world was adept at making Kaiser Manhattans in peacetime.

The future also looked bright for Willys-Overland, with the 650,000 Jeeps built for Allied use in World War II acting as a super springboard for the civilian market with its 1944/45 CJ-2 (Civilian Jeep). From the rugged nature of the Jeep to the modern luxury of automotive air conditioning introduced by the 1940 Packard, there was something for everyone, and it didn't have to come from the Big 3. "First by far with a post-war car," cried Studebaker: a little later its Studebaker Commander coupe of 1953 was designed by Raymond Loewy's studio with a low hoodline, 3.8-liter (232.6ci) 120-bhp V8, not much chrome and no tailfins.

In the immediate postwar years the Big 3 were still pushing their old prewar iron, but change was coming. The lessons from the Big 3 explained why the bright independents would soon fade into trouble, and trouble starts with the letter "T." Henry Ford correctly assumed that many people wanted reliable, basic transport at an accessible price. The Ford Model T's 15,007,033 sales couldn't have been achieved without the speedy, cost-efficient, volume-production, modern-moving, station-to-station assembly line that Henry had ushered in. It wasn't fancy, but by lowering unit cost the product actually got cheaper over time. Plus there was no waste at Ford; even the packing crates used to send complete knockdown kits overseas were used as floorboards on Model T's put together in foreign lands.

GM proved the one thing Henry got wrong, that the public can get bored with a product. After some years one should bring out something new, or at least something that looks new. Ford was tardy in releasing its Model A, so once the T's sales peaked in 1923 at 2 million plus units, it was all downhill. GM swooped in to claim the title of biggest world automaker from Ford in 1926, and Ford never regained the number one position.

Walter P. Chrysler's firm sprinkled fresh ideas like hydraulic brakes on their new 1924 Chrysler 70, the aero unibody of the 1934–37 Airflow, and the Hemi V8 power of the 1955 300C. However, the message from the Big 3 is that innovation is at most garnish for success. Large-scale production, wide sales network and frequent model turnover added up to a storm the independents couldn't weather. While 1950 was Studebaker's best year, and others were making hay, the message of survival of the fittest was clear.

The Kaiser Darrin may well have pipped the Corvette to the post of first series production U.S. fiberglass sports car, but could it be trusted? The might of GM meant the Darrin got burnt by the Chevy's Blue Flame six! Similarly the Raymond Loewy–designed Studebaker Avanti V8 fiberglass sports car had both merit and a supercharger, but teething problems with bodyshell flex, difficulty meeting orders, and rumors of Studebaker's demise loaded the dice in GM's favor. It was also a question of convenience when a new 1963 327ci Corvette lay at the Chevrolet dealer close to home.

How could a small car maker cope with changing fashion? By 1953 the stylish Kaiser

Manhattan had only been around since the spring of 1950, and now offered Hydra-Matic plus power steering as options, but no V8, and soon everyone wanted a V8.[4] Hudson could have used a V8: their 1948 Super Six was an all-new postwar design by Frank Spring with unusual "Step-Down" unibody chassis, notching up 180,499 sales. In 1951 the car became the Hudson Hornet and the original 262-cube L-head I6 was eventually kicked out to 308ci, with the $86 option of Twin H-Power, whereby the I6 received a sports cam and alloy head.

The Hornet also got 22 victories from 37 starts in the 1953 NASCAR racing season ... but that was no substitute for a V8 and a new set of clothes. The marque with two towers and two galleons for a logo had lost $6 million by mid–1954, the same year Hudson merged with Nash to form American Motors Corporation.

United We Stand, Divided We Disappear

To deal with the economic blowtorch of the Big 3, it made sense for smaller players to merge. Nash-Kelvinator's George Mason was behind the planned merger of Nash and Hudson; at $197,793,366 it was the biggest corporate merger to that point in time. An envisioned get-together between Nash, Hudson, Studebaker and Packard was also in the cards, but didn't eventuate. The latter two entities paired up in 1954, with Studebaker not letting on just how much in the red it actually was, a true case of caveat emptor.

In the subsequent American Motors combine arising from Nash and Hudson's merger,

The Frank Spring–designed "Step-Down" Hudson Hornet of 1951–54 was the last real Hudson. After 1954 Hudsons became rebadged Nash models (courtesy Lee Rehorn).

At 308ci, Hudson's L-head I6 motor with optional $86 "Twin-H power" hop-up sports cam and alloy head was good enough for NASCAR, but lacked V8 showroom appeal (courtesy Lee Rehorn).

there was relatively more Nash than Hudson. Both were well-respected brands, but sales realities dictated that the Hudson Wasp and Hornet move onto Nash platforms for 1955 MY. Hudson devotees could take some solace from continued use of the L-head I6, but precious little from the '55 Wasp and Hornet. The market greeted the claimed "all new" Hudsons with a collective yawn.

From 1954 to 1957 was a period of badge engineering, where the use of Nash and Hudson names continued, but the real shining star and hope for the future came in the form of a smart, six-cylinder, 191.14-inch-long sedan called Rambler. Historically and technically, this 108-inch wheelbase four-door hailed from the Nash side of the street. The Rambler name went back to the Thomas B. Jeffery Company, an automaker that built cars in Kenosha, Wisconsin. This firm was making cars in 1902, and also made a bicycle called the Rambler. In 1919 this company was bought by Charles W. Nash, becoming the Nash Motors Company the following year. Subsequently household appliance manufacturer Kelvinator bought Nash, forming the Nash-Kelvinator Corporation in 1937.

The 1956 Rambler carried evolved Nash styling, which had exposed front wheel wells in 1955 and now had open fender wells at all four corners. A price tag of $2,025 also got the consumer new 4-coil suspension, 12-volt electrics and an almost-new 120-bhp ohv 3.2-liter I6. This 195.6ci motor, commonly called the 196, was a 1956 development of Nash's L-head 196 which dated back to the 1930s. The 90 bhp L-head 196 ceased to be available once the '56 ohv version arrived.

The conversion from flathead to overhead valve saw the water pump moved from the left side of the engine, driven by a shaft going to the generator, to a front placement above the timing chain. Apart from more efficient airflow and more power, the switch to ohv improved durability, since the old L-head tended to overheat with long periods of heavy throttle due to hot exhaust gases having to travel through the block. While both 196s share the same lower block, crankshaft, connecting rods and timing components, one can't bolt the ohv head onto earlier Nash blocks. The right side of the block was altered in the changeover.

The '56 196 also delivered 20 lbs/ft extra torque, and cool Kelvinator-engineered air conditioning. It was handy having a company that made refrigerators in the family. Nash-Kelvinator was somewhat of a trailblazer in the field of automotive a/c, placing the hardware in the cowl and componentry in the places one would expect on a modern automobile. Prior to this, a/c condensers could be found in the trunk, with vent outlets blowing refrigerated air from the rear C pillar. Nash considered it more egalitarian for chauffeurs to receive air aid too!

Not only was American Motors' "Weather Eye" HVAC climate system considered one of the best in the industry, it also allowed the motorist to tick the a/c option for less than with the Big 3. Indeed, the entire car undercut the wares of Chevrolet, Ford and Plymouth, with a solidity born of unit construction. Fulfilling Nash/Hudson tradition, and being ahead of the establishment, your '56 Rambler offered the squeak-free ambiance of a unibody.

In 1956 AMC launched its fresh 108-inch-wheelbase Rambler family car. The 1958 Rambler shown has the highest "Custom" trim level. That was the year AMC's Edmund E. Anderson oversaw the inclusion of tailfins on the Rambler sedan (courtesy The Rambler Ranch).

Simply consult the Rambler build plate for further assurance of the soundness of an American Motors product: "This is a Double-Safe Single Unit Body." While the opposition flexed in the era of shake, rattle and roll, the Rambler's 9,000 electric welds kept things tight. Avoidance of the separate chassis, and a credo that low cost didn't mean cheap, made the Rambler somewhat of a U.S. equivalent to the fintail Mercedes. Keeping things in tune with domestic tastes were the availability of a continental kit, power-assisted steering and brakes. However, for a real power option, the Rambler had to wait for 1957.

American Motors' First V8

The first postwar U.S. car to offer a factory supercharger option was the 1954 Kaiser Manhattan. The Hudson's Twin H-Power option encompassed a rocket badge motif, but by the time Chevrolet introduced the 1955 "Hot One," everyone wanted a V8. AMC answered the call by buying 320ci V8s and Ultramatic automatic transmissions from Packard. AMC president George W. Mason had a verbal agreement with Packard concerning parts sharing where mutually beneficial. Thus from 1954 the large Nash Ambassador and Hudson Hornet packed Packard power.

The relationship soured when Packard sought high prices for its hardware; this provided the impetus for AMC's first V8. New American Motors leader George Romney directed his technical researchers to come up with a V8 in-house. As part of the plan, the engineering department hired David Potter, formerly with Kaiser Motors Corporation. In a mere 18 months, AMC had a new 640-pound V8, giving rise to an eventual family of engines displacing 250, 287 and 327ci.

Each motor possessed the same stroke, with displacement variation arising from different bores. The 250ci had a 3.5-inch bore, with the 287 and 327 resting at 3.75 and 4 inches respectively. This arrangement saved on casting costs for the '50s-style motor with deep skirt design. The 250 V8 made a 1956 debut in the smaller Nash Ambassador and Hudson Hornet "Specials," built on the shorter Nash Statesman/Hudson Wasp wheelbase. The Specials tag indicated high-level trimmings and 4bbl carburetion, but something really special was reserved for the Rambler in 1957.

AMC can lay claim to creating the world's first muscle car, with its limited run of 1500 1957 Rambler Rebels. These "Rebel" variants of the new '56 style Rambler had a jazzy silver paint job, with gold anodized decorative side sweepspear, plus a silver and black upholstered interior. However, the real magic existed under the hood with a hot 4bbl 327, the top displacement version of AMC's new V8. As if that weren't enough, American Motors gave the Rebel an injection.

As many as six special Rebels were built featuring Bendix "Electrojector" electronic vacuum manifold pressure-sensing fuel injection. This act increased rated horsepower to 288 bhp gross, and saw one Rebel Electrojector dispatched to Daytona Beach, where it proved to be the second fastest ride during Speed Week. The injected Rebel was just a tad slower than a C1 '57 Corvette with mechanical fuel injection.

Sadly, this wasn't to be a new high-performance avenue. R&D gremlins in the Electrojector system saw Bendix halt development and license out the patents to West German company Bosch. There was some irony in a U.S. company transferring this kind of tech to

For '59 Rambler featured deep-dip primer treatment, 23 percent beefier steel bumpers and 40 percent thicker exhaust metal. In recessionary times this spelled good value for consumers (courtesy J. Winfield Heckert).

a German firm, because Messerschmitt had been handy at using fuel injection on fighter planes during World War II. The Bendix Electrojector patents were a starting point for the development of 1968's Bosch D-Jetronic electronic injection, the first computer-controlled system on the passenger car market.

Chevrolet's mechanical Ramjet "fuelie" injection also hit a dead marketing end. Just 1,503 '57 Chevy Bel Airs were sold with Ramjet injection, and while fuel injection added power and better economy, Ramjet cost $500! Rochester injection lived on into the '60s C2 Stingray Vette era, but was never much more than a small block distraction. Similarly with the Rambler Rebel the 4bbl 327 was already good for 255 bhp, and the Rebel Electrojectors were converted to this carb spec prior to sale.

The sentiment was that the V8s of this era were already making power aplenty, and increased displacement plus a 4bbl carburetor were cheaper ways to increase horses. The powers that be in Detroit were also in general agreement that sports and power competition between brands wouldn't be pursued, a social and moral decision. In addition, the high-speed youth market had yet to surface; America's teenie-boppers might have liked a Rebel Electrojector, but could only spend their money on soda pops and Bobby Vee records.

In what would soon become a tradition, AMC was ahead of the curve with the 327ci Rebel. This model also introduced the public to muscle-car–style hairy handling. Rambler's independent unequal length A-arm front, live axle rear with four coil springs, and torque tube chassis were much happier with the 196 aboard. The consensus was that the V8 motor, which could be fairly called a big block given its external dimensions and heft, made the sedan a trifle nose-heavy. However, muscle car folk have always considered this an exciting challenge, using the V8's torque to "drive around the limits."

Thrill seekers would have many opportunities for fun because the AMC V8 became a regular option on the 1957 Rambler. Tick the V8 option blank and the puritanical six was replaced with a 2bbl 250ci V8 which produced 190 bhp at 4,900 rpm. The madcap 327 had a 9:1 compression ratio, but the 250ci Rambler sedan was detuned to 8:1 CR, lest the masses lose all self-control; nevertheless, 240 lbs/ft awaited at 2,500 rpm. This cut the Rambler 0–60 mph time from the 196's 16 seconds to around 11 or 12 seconds, using automatic cars for comparison, an efficient result for a late '50s 190-inch family sedan with a 4.1-liter ohv motor.

Things moved from simmer to full heat for 1958, when choosing the Rambler V8 implied a 215-horse 250ci version with 4bbl carb and dual exhausts. Thus, it was only fitting that American Motors now denote the V8 version of their family car as ... the Rambler Rebel. Enterprising owners/dealers were free to swap in the 327. In all the excitement, the average solid citizen wasn't forgotten; improvements were made to the ohv 196. For 1957, output of the 196 I6 climbed from 120 bhp to 125 bhp at the same 4,200 rpm. This 1bbl carb motor saw its compression ratio rise from 7.47 to 8.25:1, with torque rising from 170 lbs/ft to 175 lbs/ft at the same 1,600 rpm.

For the economy man who preferred to wear red socks, 1957 also saw the option of a 2bbl 196 with 135 horses. Both 1bbl and 2bbl 196 hurtled towards 127 and 138 bhp, respectively, the following model year. Right from the start, the family Rambler I6 or V8 could be teamed with automatic or manual transmission. The latter was the sensible economy/performance gearbox of choice for the 196, with the optional overdrive for the standard 3-speed manual being a coveted option.

With Rambler came an ohv version of the Nash 196ci I6, a durable and economical engine. A 250ci V8 option was available for the indulgent (courtesy J. Winfield Heckert).

Chevrolet may have had the Hot One, but in the Rambler 6, American Motors had the Sensible One. A 1956 4-

door hardtop sedan with 196 and 3-speed overdrive manual achieved a 19.1 mpg average when tested by *Motor Trend* in January 1956, and a top end of 94 mph. However, one could also choose the no-muss, no-fuss Hydra-Matic automatic. The same choices lay with the 250ci V8 motor: a manual for an early muscle car feel, or the Hydra-Matic auto.

With the V8, Hydra-Matic was considered most apt, but the version for the V8 varied from the six. Whereas 196s used the Dual-Range Hydra-Matic, V8s enlisted "Flashaway" Hydra-Matic. The latter auto was the kind found standard on Pontiac, Oldsmobile and Cadillac. Hydra-Matic was a mechanically efficient 4-speed automatic device that used its fluid-coupling nature to eke out a performance and gas mileage advantage over a torque-converter–style autobox. However, Hydra-Matic style automatics didn't shift as smoothly as torque-converter equivalents. The efficiency of the fluid-coupling–design auto saw it adopted by Daimler-Benz and Porsche into the '70s.

Overdrive manuals were also creatures of this car era. To save gas and reduce engine noise, it's desirable to have the engine spinning at lower rpm for a given cruising speed. If a motor has enough grunt, this can be done getting the output shaft from the gearbox to spin faster relative to the motor. This situation is achieved via the overdrive unit, an auxiliary gearbox sitting behind the main gearbox. Overdrive could be electrically engaged, typically via a gearstick-mounted switch. Unlike modern gearboxes with a tall indirect ratio, this achieved the same rpm-lowering goal, since overdrive could be engaged in top and second from top. On the Rambler this implied overdrive could be activated on 2nd and 3rd gears, providing the fun of five forward ratios!

The mechanical excitement didn't stop there, because the 1958 model year saw the arrival of air suspension. AMC believed in the comfort of coils for seat springing and 4-wheel springing of its '56 Rambler, so welcomed the option of self-leveling Air-Coil suspension. The system consisted of rear rubber airbags in close-spaced coil springs, tubing, and a ride-height-leveling chassis valve. Air to said valve was supplied by a single cylinder compressor, belt-driven off the engine's crankshaft pulley.

The 1958 Ramblers also enjoyed the refinement of a new recirculating ball steering system, bringing claimed reduced physical effort and more feel at speed. Welcome features, but not unique in the industry; for that, one had to observe the Rambler's reclining front seating. For many years AMC was alone in Detroit with its Nash-origin seats with adjustable backrest angles. *Car and Driver*'s David E. Davis, Jr., offered a religious explanation as to why the Big 3 enjoyed torturing domestic car fanciers in January 1979: "Maybe Nash wrecked it for all future generations of American car buyers.... The cars from Kenosha came with reclining seats, not for driving but for sleeping, and this seemed to give reclining seats a bad name forever in the strait-laced American heartland."[5]

It was OK for a liberal import like a Volvo or Fiat to have an adjustable seat, but of the domestics, AMC was unique in thinking it was preferable for one's soul to suffer than one's back! The optional recliners did go all the way back, so that the tops of the front seats lined up with the rear seat base to make a coil-sprung bed. Henry Ford would have been mortified, but it was a popular selling point regarding possible holiday road trips. Rambler reverted back to the Detroit norm when it came to trim levels, body styles and appearance revisions.

Two-Tone Paint and Fins

From the moment the new Rambler came out in 1956, the American buyer could select from the usual suspects. There was a regular 4-door sedan, with associated 4-door pillarless hardtop that looked positively natty with two-tone treatment and rear-roof-reaching sweep-spear of the "Custom" trim level. The 1956 Rambler Cross Country wagon was laudable as a Detroit load carrier with unibody construction, and American Motors announced they would have a pillarless wagon variant ready for '57. A real Detroit innovation in engineering and style.

Easy access to luggage on the wagon was helped by the sole use of a lower tailgate with exterior lockable winding handle. Thus, the rear window could be wound down to grab items sitting atop, or the interior latches could be released to drop the tailgate. The Cross Country also had a chrome luggage rack placed on the flat rear roof section, over the cargo area.

By the 1958 model year, the Rambler Cross Country wagon was only available with pillar, but that model year saw the adoption of tailfins in the Rambler's first major restyle. This was part of a move to make Rambler blend into the auto crowd. As a popular model it didn't wish to risk contention. In 1957 the rear roofband upsweep was de-emphasized by letting the sweepspear flow just horizontally, and two-tone demarcation lines didn't flow to the rear roof.

The '58 restyle was carried out while Edmund E. Anderson was in charge of design at AMC, and highlighted the fenders at both ends. The rear now had sharp, prominent and upright fins arising from the rear fenders, but the front fenders were also more noticeable and distinguishable from the hood. Quad circular front headlamps gave a more menacing stare than Rambler's previous innocuous pair of round lamps. AMC cautiously entered the era of Wurlitzer design, using the good earnings of the past couple of years to give Rambler almost all-new sheet metal.

Sensible beancounters saw that existing doors and trunk lid were carried over, so the new-style fins weren't completely at ease on what was still a boxy structure. Something smoother was the optional Borg Warner torque-converter 3-speed auto, available for the first time on both the '58 Rambler 6 and Rebel V8. In 1957 the BW auto was only available on 196-powered cars, the 250ci V8 limited to the GM-sourced Hydra-Matic if one wanted a V8 auto.

If tailfin styling didn't push your buttons, one could push the BW auto's 5 buttons. Turn the ignition key and press the amber neutral button to start the engine, with green buttons for low/D1/D2 and red for reverse. D1 stood for normal driving, where the box would run through its 3 ratios. D2 would start the Rambler off in second, aiding traction in slippery conditions. With the torque-amplifying effect of a conventional torque converter, the BW box got by with one gear less than the Hydra-Matic.

As a safety precaution, accidental depressing of reverse when moving forward would see first selected, and then reverse once the Rambler had stopped. Peak-power shift changes were facilitated by a vacuum line from the carb to the automatic's hydraulic shift valve, which was adjustment-free. Buttons for the BW auto were placed on the usual left-of-steering-column dashboard position. However, before selecting the driving range, the buyer would have to choose trim level.

Rambler selectively offered three levels for the I6 and V8 versions, starting with the

Deluxe Six, only available as a 4-door sedan. Above this was the two-tone "Super," available on the I6 and V8 and a starting point for the Cross Country wagon. Top of the range was the "Custom," bringing two-tone paint with contrasting sweepspear. Custom was the only level to feature all four 1957 body styles, 4-door sedan and hardtop, Cross Country wagon with or without pillar. One could enjoy the fancy Custom trappings with the 196 I6 and 250 V8.

The Super tag was dropped at the end of 1961, and so was the 4-door hardtop at the close of 1960 model year, but AMC made other Rambler changes too. Everything was up for '59 at American Motors. The Rambler's body was entirely deep-dipped in primer for superior rust protection, and said body's steel bumpers were 23 percent heftier. AMC literature claimed exhaust metal thickness was 40 percent greater than the previous year, and that brake lining thickness had been increased too. Windshield wipers were longer. An improved fuel filler and a slower-sipping 1bbl carb with glass float bowl were supposed to net the operator a 1.5 mpg improvement.

Rambler had anti-burst door locks from '56, padded dash and sun visors by '57 and the option of seat belts. The Rambler unibody, with front and rear energy-absorbing crumple zones, was unique in separate-chassis Detroit (courtesy Denny Schwartz).

For all the claimed revisions, '59s didn't look much different from the '58s, and this didn't bother the consumer because in the U.S. recessionary aftermath, all that "spare the wasteful restyling spending" talk played well. The 196-powered Ramblers outsold the V8 Rebels handsomely, and the Cross Country wagon established itself as the most popular variant by the close of 1958 calendar year. It should also be recorded that AMC leapt to 4th place in the auto industry on 404,446 sales as the Big 3 winced at their corpulent excesses.

The public temporarily eschewed the V8 as AMC earned a $60 million profit, being a sensible spectacular. In such times there was just one thing to do: resculpt the tailfins for 1960! The fins were smaller now and leaned over, more Batfink than Batman, and the neighbor's kid no longer thought a shark was coming when you parked along the driveway fence; going against the Detroit grain, everything was getting smaller. The Rambler sedan was down to 189.5 inches in length with less elaborate bumpers and grillwork. Weight for a V8 sedan was 3,420 lbs and if the 215 bhp 4bbl 250 was overkill, a lo-po 8.7-CR 2bbl version with 200 horses at 4,900 rpm and 245 lbs/ft at 2,500 rpm would suffice. For 1960 a curved dashpod with needle speedo was incorporated.

Before Camry ... There Was Rambler Classic

Fear not the Naderites: Rambler kept things safe with anti-burst door locks from 1956 and the option of seat belts, padded dash and sun visors by 1957. Indeed, the pillarless hardtop structure was gussied up for 1957; it had been flex-prone. Rambler was a safe place to be by 1960, the car the editors of *Consumer Reports* dreamed of at night, if truth be told. The practical aspects couldn't be argued with. The revised 1960 bodyshell had a trunk lid that opened nearly down to chrome bumper level. The Rambler 6 with base 1bbl 196 produced a useful 180 lbs/ft at just 1,600 rpm, which made the optional overdrive ratio a real tool rather than a trinket.

All this value started from $2,098, and for the extravagant, even a $2,502 Rebel Custom automatic wouldn't bust Fort Knox, but it would break 12 seconds in 0–60 mph. Rambler's shape sauntered into 1961 MY, but there were changes afoot in AMC land. First off, a name change: by 1958 AMC already had a postmerger 3-car range, and the family car that folks had been calling Rambler needed a nameplate to distinguish itself from its American Motors brethren. Thus, the sedan formerly known as Rambler became the Classic.

When one visited an AMC dealer a Rambler Classic was now requested, and this model could have a 196 I6 or 250 V8. There was no need for the Rebel V8 nametag in such refined times. The 108-inch wheelbase and 189.5-inch length were plain to see, but one innovation wasn't. If the correct option box had been ticked, the new owner might have been marshaling an aluminum block version of the 196 with 138 ponies! The six-cylinder Ramblers had always been the best handlers, given their superior weight distribution, and light alloy would make things even better.

The block of this special 196 was made of die-cast aluminum, but the motor used cast-iron liners and a cast-iron head, wider on the right side than the cast-iron block ohv 196 counterpart. An important maintenance item for the 196 ohv motors is to re-torque the cylinder headbolts at regular intervals. This is especially key on the al2 block, where liners can shift if the cylinder headbolts loosen. The factory service manual recommended

In belt-tightening times AMC made 404,446 cars in model year 1959, easing itself into 4th place in the auto race (courtesy Denny Schwartz).

re-torquing every 8,000 miles. In the interests of preventing oil leaking into the coolant passages, and down the exterior of the 196 blocks, it has proven wise to use additional cylinder head gasket sealant.

Moves to improve refinement with the '61 Classic involved placing a rubber cap joint between the Rambler's torque tube propshaft and the gearbox. The interior of the Classic was a quieter place to be, compared to previous model years, thanks to a durable new acoustical fiberglass ceiling. There was now also a handy finger tab for the glove box door. However, in spite of such changes, one fact sounded clear as a bell: the 196 sounded somewhat thrashy next to the 250 V8. The consensus of the day was that the Classic seemed classier with the V8 aboard.

This didn't stop people from buying the sensible 196; nor did it stop AMC from tinkering with the Classic. For 1962 the tailfin was finally jettisoned, in favor of a smoother curved-edge Corvair-like look. The sweepspear had been getting trimmer over time, and any chrome side decoration that remained would be more aptly termed a pinflash. The decoration was light and the wheelbase was still 108 inches, but AMC fattened up the V8 option. The 250ci V8 ended at the close of the '61 model year; by 1962 the V8 was reserved for AMC's luxury nameplate, which used the same body.

Start steadily in '62 with the 1bbl 196, 2 horses up on the American's 1bbl ohv 196, providing 127 bhp at 4,200 rpm and 180 lbs/ft at 1,600 rpm. The optional 2bbl 196 took the game onto 138 bhp at 4,500 rpm and 185 lbs/ft at 1,800 rpm. Then came a little leap to the 2bbl 327 V8 with 250 bhp at 4,700 rpm and 340 lbs/ft at 2,600 rpm. Finally, to

The 1959 196s had a revised 1-barrel carb with glass float bowl, claimed to yield a 1.5 mpg gain. These 1959 I6 Ramblers outsold V8 versions (courtesy Denny Schwartz).

beat the Russians to the moon, the $47.50 "Power-pak" option brought the expected 4bbl carb and dual exhausts for a 327 with 270 horses at 4,700 rpm and 360 lbs/ft at 2,600 rpm.

I6 cars were limited to 3.78 rear gears, but the V8s could have a 4.11 quarter-mile special or tall 2.87 mileage master as options. The standard V8 final drive was 3.54. With all the extra go for the family Rambler, rest assured that dual circuit brakes and padded dash were now standard. As part of the restyle, the windshield was higher, which was handy, given that the 327's zip required the driver to look further down the road. Chassis lubes were now at 33,000 instead of 1,000-mile intervals, and an inspector would check the Rambler interior for leaks while the exterior received high-pressure water spray.

The optional a/c kept that interior as crisp and cool as the inspector's white coat, for just $399 in 1962. If things started to look cool at American Motors it could have been due to the recent arrival of Richard Arthur Teague in the styling department. Richard Teague, a one-time child actor in movie shorts, had ambitions to be an airplane designer. California-born Teague had worked at GM on the '50 Oldsmobile Rocket project, as well as Cadillac's Advanced Design Group.

Teague became chief stylist at Packard, and it was there he showed an ability to render freshness on a budget, something that would prove invaluable for AMC over the decades

Rambler wagon introduced a lockable exterior tailgate crank handle to lower and raise the rear window. The wagon's optional "Western Motif" interior upholstery did a good impersonation of leather (courtesy Denny Schwartz).

to come. The new-looking 1955 Packard gave few clues to its 1951 origins, and Teague designed Packard's final concept car, the Predictor. The final Packard design cars were built in 1956, the last Packards with Studebaker bodies in 1958. The previous year the Packard styling department had moved to Chrysler, where due to management conflicts, Teague left to pursue non-automotive industrial design work.

Richard Teague landed at AMC in 1959, becoming its principal designer upon Edmund E. Anderson's departure, and the rest would soon be history as Teague guided some of Detroit's most individual and famous designs to fruition. Some of America's best-known models used an economy angle to become popular Americans.

Chapter 2

The Transition from Thrift

The Metropolitan—America's Mini, or a Mini American?

The small car wasn't an alien concept in America; there were a few historical precedents. Industrialist Powel Crosley Jr. had a plan involving an Indiana-built, sub–1,000-lb, 2-door convertible, retailing for $250. This little ride made a May 1939 debut at Indianapolis Speedway. While it was not an instant hit, Crosley hit pay dirt during World War II when gasoline rationing made 50 mpg economy a desirable asset. Crosley set the pace after the war with America's first volume-produced SOHC motor in 1946. In 1949 Crosley cheekily introduced America to 4-wheel disk brakes, and in the Hotshot roadster produced the nation's first sports car, which won the 1951 Index of Performance at Sebring.

Sadly, Crosley's fortunes declined from a 1948 peak of 24,871 to just 1,522 by 1952. Not even patronage from Humphrey Bogart could save Crosley as its Marion plant was sold to the General Tire and Rubber Company. A small operation, it had produced four-cylinder vehicles too little for prosperous times. Kaiser Corporation offered something larger in the guise of the 1952 Henry J, designed by Howard Darrin.

Powered by either a 134ci I4 or 161ci I6, the Henry J economy car was named after Kaiser boss Henry J. Kaiser and sat on a 100-inch wheelbase. Originally conceived as a normal-sized automobile, it was then scaled down, in a somewhat visually uneasy manner, under Henry J. Kaiser's direction. People bought the Henry J —107,000 were produced — but the usual pattern was apparent. Motoring with diminutive Henry wasn't exactly comfy, and the six-cylinder Corsair cost more than a normal Chevrolet family car.

U.S. consumers weren't that enthralled with the virtues of small, not when they had to pay more for a slower vehicle with harsher operation. However, while everyone was thinking big, Nash's George W. Mason was thinking about postwar economy cars, and the first truly successful small American car belonged to Nash, and Austin to a degree. It started in 1950 with the N.X.I. prototype display vehicle, or Nash Experimental International, created by independent Detroit designer William J. Flajole for Nash-Kelvinator. This 149.5-inch-long, 1,785-lb two-door convertible had a width of 85 inches, symmetrical door skins, and parts commonality to aid assembly-line convenience.

Anything that would make a small car easier and cheaper to produce was a boon, since little cars have a smaller profit margin. The Nash Motors–sponsored N.X.I. used a Fiat-built engine and a unibody, the latter something Nash had been familiar with since 1941. Customer clinic testing soon saw plans for bucket seats and a floor shifter shelved in favor of a bench seat and column shift, and the N.X.I. evolved into the N.K.I. (Nash-Kelvinator International). Due to cost reasons of tackling a possibly low-volume design, different in nature from other Nashes, body assembly was outsourced to Fisher & Ludlow.[1]

The mechanical side and final assembly were taken care of by Austin. The decision to use the English manufacturer was reached on October 5, 1952, and in this period Austin had merged with Morris, creating BMC (British Motor Cars) in 1952. Recent history made Austin a natural choice for a U.S.-designed, British-built small car. After World War II, Austin was in a phase of "export or die" under boss Leonard Lord. In the postwar years there was little chance of getting a new car in Britain. Economic austerity saw the vast majority of Jaguar XK120s, MG T series and Austin-Healeys exported, often to North America.

In 1946 the newly formed Austin Export Corporation had the motto "The world is our blueprint." The 1947 Austin A40s exported to America had a publicity photo taken with the banner "Austins for Dollars." The same year the Austin Princess, Sheerline and A40 were all unveiled in New York.[2] Austin's boss came up with the idea of the glamorous 95-mph A90 Atlantic of 1948–52, a 2-door convertible featuring power top and windows.[3] This last vehicle wasn't a commercial triumph, but BMC's dynamism saw it become the fourth largest automaker in the world.

Such can-do spirit was good for Nash and their little car, so the Austin A40 1.2 liter I4 / 3-speed manual power team was selected to motivate baby Nash. Naturally, a newborn needs a name, and the new small car was to be badged N.K.I. Custom, but this was changed to Metropolitan two months before the little car's March 19, 1954, launch. Given

Map light, cigarette lighter and electric wipers were stock Metropolitan equipment. The optional AM radio and Weather Eye heater were fitted to most Mets (courtesy Marc Merkle).

Nash-Kelvinator's merger with Hudson in May 1954, what was conceived a Nash was soon available in Nash and Hudson versions from both types of dealership.

The Hudson version of the Metropolitan had a Hudson grille badge, "M" logo hubcaps, a "bull's-eye" horn button design, and a plain spare wheel cover. However, the little one had Nash written all over it in terms of scaled-down closed fender well styling, plus Nash-type Bedford cord upholstery accented with leather. Indeed, the car's accent was decidedly American, which was all the more significant given the U.S. econorides of the past and the Metropolitan's current opponents. Available as a convertible or hardtop, the Metropolitan was much jazzier and plusher than the Henry J. Customers could expect a small car that thought big!

Standard items like map light, electric wipers, cigarette lighter and continental kit were not the stuff of a poverty special. Of the three U.S. market options — AM radio, Weather Eye heater, and whitewalls — the first two were really standard, given the way most dealers ordered the cars. Thus the Metropolitan was appropriately described by Nash as "milady's perfect companion on shopping trips." A 1959 brochure also stated that the Metropolitan was "Luxury in Miniature." The advertising was quite true: the Nash was loaded compared to European small cars, especially its chief rival, the VW Beetle.

The Vee Dub was just starting to make an impact in America, and at 28,097 cars, VW was the top-selling import in 1955.[4] It would be hard to imagine two more dissimilar automobiles than the Bug and the Met; even in Export spec the VW looked severe, and mechanically the two were truly at opposite ends. The Metropolitan had its water-cooled I4 at the front with a peppy get-up-and-go nature more suited to U.S. tastes. However, while the Met was almost twice as quick to sixty as the Bug, its English origins made for a pet in the city.

The Metropolitan was the first U.S. small car that was pleasant to drive. Marketing targeted the fairer sex (courtesy Marc Merkle).

England had yet to enter the freeway age, so the Metropolitan wasn't set up for highway cruising. Americans were familiar with the Met's 3-speed manual, but top gear equated to 4,300 rpm at 60 mph. The Bug was bahn-ready, with synchro on 2nd, 3rd and 4th by 1952, allowing 3,000 rpm in top at sixty. Thus, the VW exhibited less flat-four engine wear than the Met and other English inline-four-powered small cars.

Most were content to reserve their Nash Ambassadors for the highway, leaving the Metropolitan as a great second car perfectly suited to the role of runabout. For the second lot of 10,000 units, the 1955 Series II Met picked up a new gearbox with hydraulically actuated clutch, instead of the previous mechanical linkage. The Series III Metropolitan was a '56 MY car with production starting in November 1955. The Met was up-engined to 1,489cc B series Austin A50 Cambridge power, a well-sized I4 for a small car.

Polished stainless-steel side trim facilitated two-tone paint with delicious new colors: Caribbean Green, Sunburst Yellow and Coral Red. The two-tone contrast was Snowberry White. It's probably safe to assume Dr. Ferdinand Porsche never broached the subjects of two-tone paint and whitewalls with Hitler concerning the Beetle. The Metropolitan 1500 had a new grille, with the previous nonfunctional hoodscoop deleted.

Inside, be prepared for houndstooth check cloth and white vinyl trim, with a black-painted dash where the Met previously showed body color. Also be prepared to pay more for all this snazziness: the Series III Met hardtop climbed to $1,527 with the convertible at

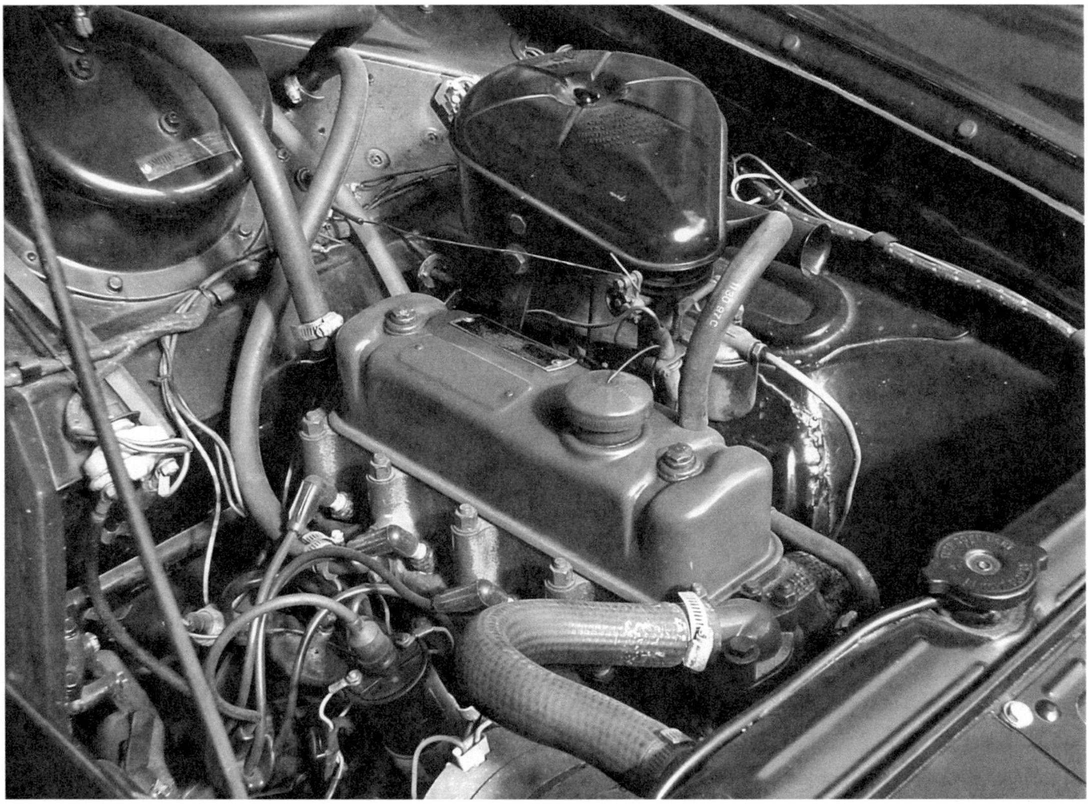

The familiar green block Austin B series 1.5-liter I4 made Metropolitan much livelier than its rival the VW Beetle (courtesy Marc Merkle).

$1,551. Slowly badge identities were fading; for 1957, Nash and Hudson grille badges were replaced with a Metropolitan "M" item. In 1958 American Motors had eliminated the Nash and Hudson tags.

The Met was built at the Austin (BMC) Longbridge factory, and it seems like another famous Longbridge-made small car followed the Met's example of throwing off the shackles of badge engineering. After 10 years the English Mini ceased to be an Austin Mini, or Morris Mini; it too simply became Mini. The Metropolitan always carried Austin Co. chassis plates, but it wasn't until October 1956 that the Met was available in England. At this point AMC allowed Austin to sell the Metropolitan in countries where American Motors had no presence.

England was as good a place as any to sell the Met, and by the late '50s, postwar recovery meant there were some local buyers. It started with the Metropolitan Series III and a brochure shot taken in the Mrs. Miniveresque English country town setting of Chipping Campden. In a bit of shutterbug sleight of hand, a reversed negative made a left-hand-drive Met look like a right-hand-drive car! The Metropolitan was retailed through Austin dealers as the Austin Metropolitan. It was an unusual circumstance for a company to make its own captive import.

Technically the Metropolitan became the first "UK" car to have a radio as standard equipment. The little Nash's extrovert two-tone Elvis style made it a low-volume curiosity piece in England. It seemed an opportunity to get U.S. style on a small scale, although in reality the Met was considered too big in the UK market, and its appearance a trifle odd.[5] Of course, the Met was off the UK sales charts in 1959, because America could use every Met it could get its hands on: 1959 turned out to be the Metropolitan's best U.S. sales year. At 22,209 units it was the second-best-selling import after VW.

It was the right car, at the right time, and that time was the rocky moment after the '58 recession. People were counting the pennies and small cars were in. As an example, observe the 1959 fourth-season episode of *The Phil Silvers Show* titled "Bilko's Small Car." Fort Baxter's Colonel Hall ordered a new Renault Dauphine, but didn't get said car at first due to the high jinks of Master Sergeant Bilko, who then hits on the idea of passing off army Jeeps as small exotic imported sports cars. The episode mentioned the virtue of good gas mileage and America's need for a small car.

The Metropolitan answered the call of duty with the revised Series IV, which commenced production in January 1959, with revisions. The Met finally got a regular external trunk lid, so owners no longer had to drop rear seatbacks to access a luggage cavity hold. There were also the additions of vent wing windows and an engine upgrade. The I4's compression ratio soared from 7.2 to 8.3:1 in October 1959, as the Met took on the Austin A55 Cambridge motor. Diamond seat cloth with white vinyl trim accompanied a 1959 price hike to $1,672.60 for the hardtop and $1,696.80 for the ragtop Met.

By 1960 the Metropolitan was available in England again, returning as Series IV cars at the friendly neighborhood Austin dealer. One difference was that the Austin tag was dropped, and the car simply sold as the Metropolitan. In May 1960 a major London Austin dealership called Car Mart Ltd. made a wedding present of a Metropolitan to England's Princess Margaret. On either side of the Atlantic the Met was pushed as something special, and this seemed linked to the car's commercial success.

In America the Met was unfurled with the following publicity talk: "It's dashing, road-hugging, exciting to drive, proudly styled, beautifully made, and it handles like a sports car." In contrast, a 1952 Willys-Overland ad for the Aero Willys earnestly extolled "Up to 35 Miles on a Gallon!"* with overdrive, and stated their I6 F-head was one of the world's most efficient power plants. American Motors knew people didn't wish to be reminded they were on a diet when losing weight!

In looks, equipment finery and ad copy, the Metropolitan was presented as something desirable, which was how Detroit sold any normal car. Preceding economy cars were described in a manner as appealing as cold broccoli. Carrying on this thinking, if a car is worthy then it would naturally have a fan club. In January 1957 the Metropolitan Club was started by AMC Metropolitan Sales Manager James W. Watson. Members had a badge affixable to their car, so they could show Met pride!

What was sauce for the goose also proved sauce for the gander as Austin promoted the mighty Met with the line, "It is a car that one never tires of driving. Extremely lively, economical, a joy to handle on the road because of its responsible manoeuvrability." Prior to the Mini and the '60s, there was nothing swinging about Austin, and the English automaker used the Met to show it had a taste for gay abandon and high spirits. However, there was some engineering exaggeration in all this.

Nash-style closed wheel wells made for insensitive steering and an inordinately large turning circle for a small rear driver. That said, AMC did market the Met for urban police force use, as an alternative to motorcycle use, and Mets were used for such duty. The Metropolitan also offered a '50s-style optimistic look to the future in the form of the Astra Gnome "Time and Space Car." Industrial designer Richard Arbib thought this was what we would be driving come the year 2000.

The Astra Gnome was based on a 1955 Met and was displayed at the 1956 New York International Auto Show, as well as on the September 3, 1956, cover of *Newsweek* magazine. Metropolitan production stopped in April 1961, although sales continued through to March '62. North American Met sales totaled 94,986, with an additional 9,400 units being sold outside North America — a solid result, and surprising in that the Metropolitan carried much the same styling throughout its run.

The concept of the very small car seemed to wane in America and Europe by the early '60s. In Europe, people were ready to go past two-stroke microcars to real small cars; in America, consumers also wanted a size up from what they understood a small car to be. Small imports like the DAF, English Mini or tiny Fiats which had profitably trickled in were not really suited to motoring American style. U.S. buyers wanted larger small cars with six-cylinder power. They had a name for this kind of car: they called it the compact, and the first one came from American Motors!

Rambler American — America's First Compact

Central to George W. Mason's postwar economy car plan was an honest family car of modest dimensions. The Metropolitan-style mobile was a fancy small car, but what Nash-Kelvinator was really cooking up was a practical compact car, a real butter-and-egg all-purpose mobile that wouldn't break the bank. It came in the form of the 1950 Rambler, which commenced as a two-door convertible. The car was a success, and more variants arrived once Korean War steel quotas loosened up. There were sedans and wagons, plus a slight 1953 restyle to boot, and then came the Nash-Hudson merger.

Newly formed American Motors gave the Hudson Jet a shot as the compact good-sense mobile. However, the Jet didn't reach the commercial altitude management hoped for. With a 105-inch wheelbase and optional 3.3-liter 114 bhp I6, with dual carb "Miracle H-Power!," the Jet was simply too much car in the same way the Henry J was too little car. There was a major refresh for 1955, but 35,000 units in 2 years equaled close, but no cigar. The happy medium would seem to reside at casa de Nash.

In the new universe of Nash plus Hudson, the Rambler compact was sold under both marques, and was restyled for '55 with open front wheel wells. However, management decided to discontinue the small Nash at the end of 1955 MY. The reasoning was that the public wasn't that into cars of this size (100-inch wheelbase). American Motors thought it had all the bases covered with the mini Met and the larger 108-inch-wheelbase 1956 Rambler family car, so AMC said bye-bye to the 100-inch-wheelbase Nash compact and its flathead 196 motor. However, even the best-laid plans are subject to change.

The snugness brought on by the 1958 recession convinced George Mason's successor at AMC, George Romney, that the Nash compact should be reintroduced to answer the public's plea for simpler motoring. So it was that the 1955 100-inch-wheelbase Nash was reincarnated as the 1958 Rambler American. Rebranded and with a new nameplate, this evolved small car carried detail changes compared to 1955. In developing the '58 American, AMC purchased '55 Nash compacts so they could be used as test mules and be made into prototypes.

The '58 American looked like a baby Volvo Amazon from behind, now that the Nash's previous closed rear wheel wells had been opened. Differences between the '55 and '58 MY versions were accommodated by tooling changes at AMC's Kenosha and Milwaukee factories. There was now a mesh-type grille with an "R" for Rambler decorative badge, and the rear taillight lenses were inverted. The flathead 196 was also back in altered form. The 1bbl 8.0:1 CR L-head no longer had its water pump driven off the generator. Like the 1956 ohv 196, the water pump was moved from the left to the front above the timing chain.

Compared to the imports, the flathead American was a veritable hot rod, establishing the AMC method for good gas mileage, which was to have a low-rpm large motor in a small, light unibody. There were 90 horses waiting at 3,800 rpm, and a meaty 150 lbs/ft at 1,600 rpm. The 196 drove through the usual 3-speed manual, with overdrive, or what was described as Flash-O-Matic automatic. The standard 3-speed came with 3.78 final drive, the overdrive and automatic with 4.11 and 3.31 respectively. American Motors bestowed some class upon the American by making its automatic a 3-speed box, not the 2-speed affairs of GM.

All this goodness in 2,500 lbs of unibody saw a clean pair of heels being shown to the opposition. *Road & Track* had the VW Beetle and Studebaker Lark down for 0–60 mph and top speeds of 28 seconds/70 mph and 21 seconds/80 mph respectively, but in March 1959 the AMC American scorched into the ledger with 16 seconds/86.5 mph. Thus, the American had an advantage over its only domestic rival of the day, and the Lark arrived a year after the American.

One serious advantage the American had over imports was 12-volt electrics. Many foreign cars still used 6-volt ignition systems well into the '60s. That was why the 2-stroke Saab placed the ignition between the front seats: to shorten the electrical path and make starting easier. Twelve-volt electrics and up-front oil filter were two '58 American refinements over the '55 Nash Rambler, which served the small car well in cold climes. How small was

Rambler American was America's first "compact" in 1958. This 1960 American Custom wagon is one of 1,430 produced, special ordered for an AMC executive. American revived the small Nash 100-inch wheelbase (courtesy Douglas Englin).

a compact car at this time? The 1958 American was 178.3 inches long, 73 inches wide and 57.3 inches high.

The American was obviously much bigger than a small import of the period like the Fiat 500, but like those imports it featured a single all-knowing circular speedo/instrument face. Unusual brevity, when most domestics carried more instruments than an aircraft. Like the imports, American Motors kept the American simple. Power steering and brakes weren't on the options sheet, because on a 2,500-lb car they weren't needed. Four-wheel 9-inch drum brakes were also felt adequate.

American Motors kept a distance between the American and the family Rambler with careful decontenting. Instead of all-coil suspension, the American got by on the usual independent front upper-and-lower unequal-length A-arms plus coils, with simpler rear semi-elliptic leaf springs tending the live axle. The American did get big brother's 15-inch wheels, so it wouldn't disappear into potholes, but the ohv 196 wasn't an option. Still, with the American being 400 lbs lighter than the regular Rambler, performance comparisons were a wash.

Sit inside the early Americans and the simple painted dash, chrome trim with passenger-side "American" script, and below-dash knee-knocker glove drawer all spelled economy car. The woven-wool cloth seating material was hardy and the Weather Eye heater kept the interior as snug as any Lincoln. A driver's door armrest could be ordered, but that would be missing the point. The American delivered elegant sufficiency at a time when Detroit was going overboard with Cadillac's 42-inch 1959 tailfins!

If the 1958 American was the correct car for the times, then the 1958 Edsel was the incorrect car. Typifying Big-3 thinking that bigger was better, and more profitable, Ford bet the public was ready for monster V8s, 161 color combinations and Teletouch automatic. So smug were management that they piled on the media hype, and embossed the Edsel's torque

The American Custom debuted midway through model year 1960 with ohv 196 I6, Custom interior and steering wheel, full wheel covers and full carpeting. The ohv 196 appeared as an optional motor in the American for 1961 (courtesy Douglas Englin).

rating on the rocker covers. Then they waited, and waited.... However, the market didn't bite, and sales went from tepid to tragic, leaving Edsel looking like it was really sucking a lemon.

There wasn't anything actually wrong with the Edsel; it was just that Ford pushed for more than the market could bear. Folks looked at the lengthy list of high-priced options, then went over to Studebaker to buy a Lark. After company restructuring and diversification, Studebaker emulated AMC by utilizing existing engine and chassis design to create the compact Lark of 1959. This new model chalked up over 150,000 sales, helping to procure a $28 million profit for the company.

As the American's only domestic rival, the Lark even carried the trump card of a V8 option, but this was of little commercial consequence. The facts show the public had gravitated away from the likes of the full-frame Edsel to the unibody Rambler American. American achieved 30,640 sales in a truncated 1958 model year, helping AMC to a $26 million profit. All this with a single model variant using one motor. Buoyed with success, in 1959 AMC saw the 25 mpg 2-door American sedan joined by a 2-door American wagon. This little unibody wagon had a market niche all its own.

At $2,145 for the American Super wagon, AMC had delivered not only good value but good balance. With a front/rear weight distribution of 52/48 percent, the wagon was ideally distributed when carrying cargo. Continuing on the might of 90-horse flathead power, the American rose to 91,491 sales in 1959 model year. If the Rambler 6 was the Camry of its generation, then the American was the Corolla, and come 1960 model choice extended to a 4-door and the option of reclining seats. The American 4-door possessed the same dimensions as the 2-door, but had a base price of $1,844.

The econofans couldn't get enough of the American, as sales surged to 120,603 in the 1960 model year. However, American motivation remained the 90 bhp 196 flathead. *Road & Track* wondered why the ohv 196 wasn't available as an option, but this and much more was on the way for '61. Starter engine for the 1961 American was the regular flathead with 90 bhp at 3,800 rpm and 150 lbs/ft at 1,600 rpm, but the optional ohv 196 changed the figures to 125 bhp at 4,200 rpm and 180 lbs/ft at 1,600 rpm. The base 196 made 160 lbs/ft by 1962. More noticeable was the American restyle.

The new 1961 American still carried the styling guidance of Edmund E. Anderson. The car resembled a cross between the Chevy Corvair, which came out the preceding year, and the Studebaker Lark. Thus, it had the full edges of the former and the boxiness of the latter, and such boxiness gave rise to the 1961–63 American's moniker of "Breadbox." That said, AMC's lil' rascal was moving away from the purely utilitarian; the new model featured a 2-door convertible.

To guard against scuttleshake, convertibles had a chassis-stiffening crossmember welded to the base of the American unibody. Ragtops were in fashion, and so too were the American's round rear lamps. Detroit's original compact now sported a curved oval instrument pod and dash in the style of a Classic. In spite of the new glitter, AMC hadn't forgotten the American's sensible side, and the expanded range encompassed a 4-door wagon. In the expansion the American shrank externally. Still riding on a 100-inch wheelbase, the Breadbox was just 173.1 inches long and 70 inches wide.

In car industry parlance the 1961–63 American was a typical reskinned car. Revised sheet metal combined with honed mechanicals equaled Breadbox. Due to American Motors' size, it started a trend that would become common in the future, especially with imported cars: shared engineering. The '62 American shared some curved looks with the '62 Classic, but also dual circuit brakes and E-Stick gearbox. With a dual master cylinder braking system, split front/rear, failure of one brake circuit meant that the car could still be stopped safely. It was standard with AMC, even on the humble American.

Long before the 1968 VW Beetle 1500, AMC slipped a clutchless semi-auto gearbox into an economy car. The '62 American had the option of the 3-speed E-Stick. This seemed like your regular 3-speed manual, except cast an eye to the driver's footwell: the clutch pedal was gone! There was a normal clutch plate, which was worked hydraulically using engine vacuum and oil pressure as the pilot snicked the shifter through the gate. American Motors had predicted the popularity of clutchless manuals, 40 years ahead of time.

As with 21st century machinery, the clutchless E-Stick was efficient, given the solid mechanical linkage, but it wasn't that smooth. However, it did save a few pennies over the torque-converter Flash-O-Matic. That said, to really save money one had to think again, because E-Stick wasn't available with overdrive in '62. For maximum mpgs, go to that trusty 3-speed + overdrive box, or in '63 MY why not experiment with Twin-Stick?

Twin-Stick was a fancy version of the 3-speed overdrive box with not one, but two gear levers! Both sticks were on the floor, not the column. On the left was a normal-looking remote shifter with a white button atop. On the right, observe a small lever. Proceed to operate the left stick as any floor shifter, then when requiring overdrive, move the small right stick. The mini stick engaged overdrive; it replaced the usual underdash lockout cable. An amber light alerted the driver to overdrive mode's presence.

The white button on the left stick was the "kickdown" button, allowing the driver to disengage overdrive and kick down to a lower direct ratio. There was some mechanical etiquette to note when operating Twin-Stick. First, one should have been traveling over 25 mph before pulling back on the small right stick to engage overdrive. It also didn't hurt to ease up on the gas when doing so. If speed fell below 25 mph, overdrive automatically disengaged and the amber light extinguished.

Normally flooring the gas pedal on a column 3-speed overdrive box knocked out overdrive, but Twin-Stick had its ergonomic white button! Just press the button and the problem was solved instantly — but not quite. Twin-Stick wasn't a box to be hurried; it couldn't be hustled through the gate like an '80s BW T5. Respect the mechanical inertia of overdrive, with its slipping in and out of direct/indirect gears. At Twin-Stick's heart lay the Borg Warner T96, with non-synchro first.

Engaging overdrive while in second (2 + OD) produced a ratio equivalent to regular third, so while one had 5 forward speeds in theory, it was more like 4 (3 + OD = 4th). However, in February 1963, *Motor Trend* tested an American 440 convertible with Twin-Stick and got 54 mph in 2nd, 78 mph in 2 + OD and 92 mph in 3rd, on a car with a 3.78 final drive. Driving 3 + OD dropped the top end to 87 mph, but also made things more civilized by reducing revs from 4,500 to 3,000 rpm.

Twin-Stick emulated the motoring fun of the 1984 Corvette's 4+3 overdrive box, 20 years early! And AMC wanted American patrons to enjoy themselves with the sporty 440H, available with front bucket seats and "Power-pack" 138 bhp 2bbl ohv 196. Consider this Breadbox a curtain-raiser to the emerging youth market, and it wasn't alone. The Chevy Corvair offered 140 bhp 4bbl Monza packs and a 180-horse turbo flat six. It was also possible to get the Buick all-alloy 215ci Trophy V8 engine on the transaxle Tempest in 1961 for $216.

Apart from two-tone paint, other options fitted to this American Custom are Flash-O-Matic auto, continental spare wheel kit, Spinner wheel covers, vent shades, AM pushbutton radio, dual OSRV mirrors, gas filler guard and backup lights. Even economy cars were trimmed up (courtesy Douglas Englin).

Weren't compacts supposed to be affordable economy cars? Proving that the road to hell is paved with great options, a loaded '63 American was a $3,500 automobile. The Breadbox offered factory a/c, which at $360 was powerful and cheaper than Big 3 equivalents. Plus, who wouldn't want his American with seat belts and reclining seats? Said buckets became more narrowly practical for '63, dropping from 26 to 22 inches wide. More practical still was the 1bbl ohv 196 / 3-speed overdrive American that achieved an event-winning 31.11 mpg in the 1962 Mobil Economy Run, but an affluent society is more interested in spending than saving.

The specter of the '58 recession was fading as Breadbox buyers loaded up their rides with power brakes, power steering and other gewgaws. The way to a dealer's heart is through the option sheet, and Detroit was learning options helped the bottom line with compacts too. The '63 American pillarless hardtop, designed to resemble a convertible with its top up, was certainly temptation. However, for classic value the consumer could always rely on the family-sized Rambler.

Classic Style 1963–66

AMC president Romney wasn't a wasteful man. Apart from coining the derisory term "gas guzzler" and predicting a new dawn of consumer awareness, he had concrete plans for a streamlined model range at American Motors. As always, plans are made in advance, so the fruits of such labor were revealed in the truly new cars AMC released in 1963–64. The '63 Rambler Classic was a 6-passenger family car that was bigger on the inside, smaller on the outside and lighter than its immediate predecessor.

The stats don't lie: comparing '62 4-door to '63 4-door, length and width fell from 189.8 and 72.4 inches to 188.8 and 71.3 inches respectively. Weight slid from 3,070 lbs to 2,948 lbs for 196 ohv cast-iron-block cars, but one figure was up: wheelbase. The Classic now rode on a 112-inch wheelbase, not the 108 inches of 1956–62. The wheelbase represents useful passenger space, and being longer implied improved roadholding and ride comfort. Carrying on the theme of real value, design sharing saved money for AMC and the buyer.

Common steel body stampings would soon be utilized by AMC's junior and senior cars, since the Metropolitan was gone and the Breadbox was in its final season. There were economies of scale in Romney's one-Rambler-suits-all approach, and the smart thinking was engineering deep. Combining separate unibody parts into single stampings, such as the "uniside" door surround, a single steel stamping that was cheaper to make and fitted better, American Motors passed the savings on to the consumer with curved side glass in the low-priced class. The curved glass, framed by aluminum extrusions, reduced wind noise. However, the Classic's new styling was making all the right noises.

Ed Anderson and Richard Teague worked on the new Classic's look, before Anderson's departure from AMC. This shape, like the American to come, was post–Corvair, placing greater emphasis on flat surfaces and sleekness. Front and rear fascias were shorter, with a concave effect. The dual-reverse-slope grille had a flat trim tab between the recessed circular quad lamps, with the name Rambler in spaced block letters. With the base 127 bhp ohv 196 and 3-speed manual power team, a top speed of just over 90 mph and 0–60 mph in 15.5 seconds could be relied on.

Rambler could indeed be relied upon, and American Motors put its money where its

American moved onto a 106-inch wheelbase for the all-new 1964 model. A ragtop body style was in the mix, and this '64 convertible was originally ordered by a naval officer who drove it around Hawaii (courtesy Rick Ennis).

mouth was by increasing its new car warranty from 12 months / 12,000 miles to 24 months / 24,000 miles. This move was quite something when most European makes could only offer a 6-month warranty and a frequent, plus heavy-duty, maintenance schedule. AMC was known for its comprehensive warranty schemes, and this quality would carry through the '70s and into the '80s.

In light of AMC's engineering and value achievements, *Motor Trend* awarded its 1963 Car of the Year title collectively to the junior and senior Ramblers. The public agreed with said accolade, lifting American Motors to 3rd place in the auto race on 480,365 sales, and if the Rambler was solid value for the American buyer, it might also succeed in Argentina. The Classic spawned a derivative that would become a legend in South America, and it had something to do with the old Kaiser.

Torino Time with IKA

Argentina wanted a car manufacturer to set up shop in their locale, creating both sturdy vehicles suited to their transport network, as well as employment. To this end, Argentina's government sent over Brigadier General San Martin to sound out U.S. automakers on the topic of producing cars in Argentina. In 1951 American companies didn't bite, feeling the

Argentine market was small beans and not worth the effort, but there was an exception. It seemed apt that Kaiser Motors Corporation would agree to the request of a military man and take a trip south of the border.

So it was that on June 19, 1955, Kaiser Corporation and the Argentine government signed an agreement involving the manufacture of cars and trucks in Argentina, creating Industrias Kaiser Argentina S.A., or IKA. The first Jeeps, another future connection with AMC, rolled off the Argentine line on April 27, 1956. Kaiser had, after all, purchased Jeep maker Willys-Overland in 1953 for $63,381,175. On the car side, IKA made the Kaiser Carabela from July 1958, a derivative of the U.S. Kaiser Manhattan.

All this "industrias"-ness occurred in the city of Santa Isabel, located in Cordoba province. Why this out-of-the-way locality? Well, Cordoba was the home province of Brigadier General San Martin, and the Brigadier General was a friend of Argentina's ruler, President Juan Peron. Sometimes it helps to have friends in high places, and IKA was soon very nicely placed, achieving 81 percent market share by 1958. In 1960 the Carabela was joined by the small IKA Dauphine, a license-built version of Renault's European rear-engined success. IKA also produced a version of Alfa Romeo's 1900 sedan.

By 1962 the Manhattan/Carabela was getting a trifle ancient; the model dated back to 1950 and Kaiser Corporation had left the passenger car game in 1955. In addition, the Dauphine and Alfa 1900 derivative were a bit delicate for Argentina, so IKA looked to American Motors and started producing the Classic under license. The CKD kits flowed southwards from Kenosha to IKA, but the Argentine firm knew it could do better. IKA wanted an automobile truly tuned to their market, something combining American ruggedness and European style. The result was the IKA Torino.

The Torino was a hybrid of the 1963 Rambler Classic and 1964 Rambler American. Starting with AMC's new common engineering designs, IKA grafted the front and rear sections of the American onto the center of the Classic's unibody, which equaled one stretched compact. However, the Rambler unibody was beefed up for Argentina. Normally the American's unibody support rails started at the front bumper and terminated at the front seats, but with the Torino they extended right to the rear.

Pininfarina were enlisted to rework the front and rear fascias, plus the interior, with classy European results. After all, while the Rambler was a solid butter-and-egg brand in America, IKA's Torino was positioned upscale for the jet set, so it should come as no surprise that Fidel Castro, Leonid Brezhnev and Moammar al Gaddafi, who had a coupe, should all have owned a Torino — even socialists like sexy! Lenin liked the Rolls-Royce and North Korea's Kim Jong Il has two '60s Mercedes 600s. Communist leaders and dictators always prefer to ride in style![6]

The Torino badge had something to do with the fact Argentina's population has a strong Italian background. So the Torino logo was based on Turin's coat of arms with a bull standing on its hind legs, like a Ferrari, only more macho. In keeping with the Torino's exclusivity, one could expect to find such accoutrements as leather interior, walnut-trimmed dashboard, complete instrumentation, wood and aluminum sports tiller, leather-trimmed console and a walnut shift knob with the ZF 4-speed manual, when specified. However, what engine would said 4-speed be connected to?

The Torino's engine was an inline six, but not of AMC origins. True to IKA's background, they chose a Kaiser motor. The power plant was a development of the 230ci single overhead cam I6 from 1962, first seen in the original Jeep Wagoneer. This engine, created while Kaiser Corporation owned Jeep, was dubbed the "Tornado," intended for service in both Wagoneer and Jeep Gladiator pick-up truck. Unfortunately the 3.8-liter Tornado acquired an early reputation for overheating, and by the 1966 model year the AMC 3.8-liter I6 (232ci) was substituted in Wagoneers and Gladiators.

The reputation of the AMC 232 I6 was golden, and off-roaders really test motor durability during sand dune adventures. IKA's people would refine the Tornado for their road car purposes. There was some irony in that by 1967 one had a Jeep powered by an AMC I6, and a Rambler (Torino) structure housing a Kaiser I6! However, nametags were taking on less importance by the Torino's arrival. Kaiser Jeep Corporation sold its interest in IKA to Renault, creating IKA-Renault in 1967.[7]

The use of the Rambler unibody for Torino still occurred under license from AMC. Plus, when AMC did an upgrade, like its safety flush-fitting door handles, such work appeared on the Torino. That said, as was typical of license-based designs of this period, the Torino took on local flavor and was quite distinctive. Thus, it was with Argentine pride that the IKA Torino made its debut in 4-door sedan and 2-door coupe forms, on the morning of November 30, 1966, at the Buenos Aires Municipal Racing circuit.

The Torino's I6 was available in 3- and 3.77-liter (183 and 230ci) sizes, and naturally the engines were made in Argentina. Top development of the I6 would be the "380W," the 3.8-liter with triple sidedraft Weber 2bbl carbs. Power rating was 220 bhp gross, which was sufficient to propel the coupe shell on to 130 mph! The Tornado motor had a hemispherical combustion chamber, facilitated by the SOHC layout, and central spark plug location. IKA-Renault improved the Tornado I6 under the supervision of engineer/racer Oreste Berta, and this took the Torino trackside.

In August 1969, IKA-Renault fielded a 3-car racing team in the 84 Hours of Nürburgring endurance event. Handling the effort were Tibor Teleki, Carlos Lobosco and no less than Juan Manuel Fangio. Car No. 3 was driven by Eduardo Copello, Oscar Mauricio Franco and an American driver known as Señor Larry! The No. 3 car achieved 1st-in-class honors and would have won the race outright, if not for a technicality. The No. 3 Torino received a 5-lap penalty for not returning to the pits to fix the exhaust.

The Austrian-held race was keenly followed in Argentina, in spite of the time difference, and garnered the Torino many kudos. After winning the Marathon of the Route of Nürburgring, IKA-Renault cashed in on the Torino's racing success with three high-performance editions. The GS coupe, TS coupe and TS sedan used a 200 bhp gross version of the 3.8-liter I6 with dual Holleys. Development of the triple 2bbl Weber 3.8-liter I6 was suspended. During 1973 the former Kaiser engine was upgraded from 4 to 7 main bearings for greater smoothness and durability; displacement choices of 3 and 3.8 liters existed, and the motor was now called Torino, instead of Tornado.

After 1973–74 the Torino's fortunes mirrored those of AMC. The fuel crisis saw more demand for and availability of smaller, fuel-efficient front-drivers. This implied a greater presence of the Renault component of IKA-Renault, and by 1976 the Torino was the only non–Renault offered by the concern. Indeed, the Torino's TS, TSX model level designations were Regie Renault in nature. With fuel consumption in the teens, the luxo rear-drive 6-cylinder Torino became more and more a niche vehicle for the well-heeled.

Coexisting with the local Renault 4, 6 and 12 programs, the Torino entered revised

Base power plant on the '64 American was still the 90 bhp L-head 196, but this car was specified with the optional ohv 196/auto power team. A 290 V8 dual carb installation was a subsequent modification (courtesy Rick Ennis).

phase-2 form during 1976–78. In 1976 came the arrival of the TSX coupe, and in 1978 the top version of the Torino became the Grand Routier touring sedan. Later Torinos were longer and the sedan versions featured a full C pillar. Then, 1979–82 saw the final phase of the Torino, with further restyle and makeover wherein the well-known bull logo was replaced by the internationally recognized Renault diamond badge. After all, IKA-Renault had been renamed Renault Argentina S.A. in 1977.

At its peak the Torino was available in over 20 different versions, but by 1981 the range was scaled down to the Grand Routier GR sedan and ZX coupe. However, while pollution controls had sapped horsepower in North America, ponies still had a corral in South America. Even in 1980 the Torino sedan had 180 bhp and a top speed of 185 kph (115 mph), with the hardtop coupe's 3.8-liter I6 rated at 203 bhp. The coupe still had an official top speed of 200 kph or 124 mph.

Renault Argentina S.A. were in a quandary over how to replace the Torino. Seeking to replicate power and luxury in one of their local lines, they created the 2-liter 1982 Renault 18 TX. The 18 was also produced at the Santa Isabel factory by this stage, and in trying to emulate the Torino, Argentina was the first market to get a 2-liter R18. There was a transition parallel between this situation and the way AMC-Renault were replacing the I6-powered Concord range with front-drive I4 Renaults in 1982–83.

American's optional power steering cut turns between locks from 6 to 4.3, with associated steering ratio of 17.5:1. Either way, American was better known for solid family transportation than sports car handling (courtesy Rick Ennis).

Matters drew to a close in Argentina when the final Torino rolled off the assembly line in 1982. Almost 100,000 Torinos had been produced in Argentina, with the Classic platform utilized for 20 years. America said goodbye to the Classic origin base when the Matador departed in 1978, and after the Concord was gone the final vestige of the American would be limited to the Eagle soft-roaders. As in Argentina it would all take place amidst a Renaultization of the passenger car line.

A Change of I6 Heart at AMC—196 and 232 I6

For Rambler's Classic only an AMC power plant would do. While the hardy 1bbl and 2bbl ohv 196s were still on hand, no flathead in the senior line, the star of the show was the recently introduced aluminum block 196. This optional power plant made a tentative start in 1961, and AMC had sunk plenty of money and effort into 196 al2. There was a penchant for peculiar power plants in Detroit at the time. Engineers entered a period of experimentation, seeing what would work and sell in the new wave of '60s vehicles.

Chevrolet had an air-cooled turbo flat six in the Corvair. Buick had designed an all-aluminum 215ci V8, with and without turbo, for upscale compacts. AMC's 196 al2 represented a joint development project between themselves and the Doehler-Jarvis Division of the National Lead Company. Doehler-Jarvis made the die-cast block at its Toledo Ohio factory for AMC, and the 196 al2 was certainly thoroughly tested before the public got hold of it. The motor had a 6-year gestation period and 2 million test miles under its belt.[8]

During the R&D process the latest aviation industry technology of using cemented plastic with polarized light to evaluate static and dynamic stress points was used. One million test miles were performed at proving grounds and on the highway, but the second million were accrued using 10 Ramblers fitted with the aluminum block 196 under NASCAR supervision. The endurance test was conducted at Daytona International Speedway. There were a few differences from the completely cast-iron 196 to keep an eye on.

The 196 al2 had centrifugally cast-iron cylinder liners, with a wall thickness of 0.093 in. The cylinder liners were mechanically and chemically permanently bonded to the block, and hydraulic tappets plus full flow oil filter were supposed to be standard with each 196 al2 engine. The aluminum I6 had the special intake manifold that lifted the 196 to 138 horses, but more noticeable was the unpainted aluminum block. The latter was a hoped-for showroom glamour selling point, but the special engine wasn't available to everyone.

One couldn't get 196 al2 in an American; that model had just met the normal ohv 196. The 196 al2 wasn't available in the Ambassador, because that was a V8-only model at this time. In 1961 the new motor was optional on the also newly introduced Classic Deluxe and Super. In 1962 the 196 al2 was standard issue on the high-level Classic 400 (think Ambassador sans the V8); 58,057 Classic 400s were sold in model year 1962. With 1963 came the year of the redesigned Classic, and this was when AMC introduced a new system of chassis engine mounting.

With the revised '63 Classic the 196 al2 motor was optional on lower 550 and 660 trim levels, but standard on the 400 replacement 770 specification. However, as per 1962, purchasers of the highest Classic could order the normal cast-iron 196 as a no-cost option. It seems that some took that route, because of the 60,000-plus '63 Classic 770s sold, the number with the 196 al2 was limited to 45,998. Going into 1964 the 196 al2 could sit in any Rambler Classic using AMC's Tri-Poised Power motor-mounting method.

AMC pioneered the popularity of unibody construction and reclining seats, the latter a contemporary social moral eyebrow raiser. Mavericks rode a Rambler (courtesy Rick Ennis).

Purchasers were distracted from the idea of the aluminum 196 being optional on all '64 Classics, because the new 232 I6 was in town. As a consequence, a mere 4,939 '64 Classics were optioned with the 196 al2. Apart from engineering kudos and neighbor motoring rivalry, reduced weight up front was the reason to buy the 196 al2. The die-cast aluminum block weighed just 60 lbs, and nose weight was reduced by 80 lbs compared to a cast-iron 196 sitting in the chassis. However, there were reasons to avoid the 196 al2.

Aside from superior road-course handling and lighter steering effort, the 196 al2 brought no performance gain. It was possible to buy a normal cast-iron block 2bbl 196, which also made 138 bhp, and whereas the 196 al2 was slated as a premium-fuel motor, the 138 bhp cast-iron block 196 was designated a regular-fuel engine. Comparing the two ohv 196s, the aluminum block version had a cylinder head ⅛ inch wider on the right side, but there was a more worrisome spec difference.

When two dissimilar metals are in contact, there is the problem of electrolytic corrosion, which arose on the special 196 because the block was die-cast aluminum, but the head was cast iron. Where head and block materials differ, coolant additive mix is important to avoid corrosion. The 196 al2 required a closer maintenance eye than what most people were used to on the hardy Rambler. Low coolant was a sure way to see warping, something aluminum is more susceptible to.

The eagle-eyed owner would also have been wise to re-torque cylinder headbolts at the prescribed intervals, lest the cast-iron liners shift. All told, there was much to consider for a family car. In addition, parts data books suggest 196 al2 motors actually possessed solid lifters and partial flow oil filters as standard equipment. So it was that the 196 al2 joined the list of engines too far out in left field to be liked. Well-cared-for Classics treated according to the book saw their 196 al2s provide sterling service, but most people were looking for something easier.

The hardly unusual upshot was that many 196 al2s were swapped out for regular 196s over time, so that the survival rate of a numbers-matching 196 al2 Classic is low. The final year for the aluminum block 196 was 1964; by the late '60s Buick licensed out their 215ci alloy V8 to Rover, and Detroit sought something more conventional. With the size of the average U.S. car growing, larger displacements were enlisted, around 4 liters for the family six and 5–6 liters for the workhorse V8.

Modern thin-wall cast-iron technology was used to create a lightweight block that was very rigid, should a turbocharger be necessary. For AMC the new motor was coded Typhoon and denoted "232" on the option sheet. The 1964 232 was the start of the ubiquitous American Motors ohv I6 found in AMC cars, Jeeps and other new things even after the year 2000. To launch the legend, AMC inserted said six in a special Classic called the Typhoon.

The Typhoon blew in during May 1964 as a limited-edition Classic 2-door hardtop with "Typhoon" script replacing the usual Classic badging. The featured color scheme was Solar Yellow exterior with Classic Black roof, and grille with blackout accents. A total of 2,520 Typhoons were made. The other visual distinction was the slight Classic restyle for '64, where the previous fussy concave grille made way for a shiny flat chrome grille with 6 vertical sections of 5 horizontal ribs. The grille encompassed two oval chrome pods that housed the pairs of headlamps. Stylistically the '63 front fascia opening had been chromed in.

In 1965 the 232 was the sole Classic I6 choice, except for Classic fleet specials that were available with the smaller 199ci I6 in 1965 and 1966. In 1966 the new 199ci I6 replaced all lingering remnants of the 196 in AMC cars. The 199 and 232 I6 were completely cast-iron ohv motors. Both versions had the same bore, 3.75 inches, but varying strokes of 3 and 3.5 inches respectively. A key engineering improvement concerned the number of main bearings, which increased from the 196's 4 to the 199/232's 7.

Top: **The genuinely new '64 American had the styling influence of AMC's Richard Teague and the engineering guidance of Floyd Kishline. It was the best American yet, but interest in small cars was declining (courtesy Rick Ennis).** ***Bottom:*** **In '65 the American received the "232" option for the first time, AMC's new-design I6. However, this 1965 American 440 2-door hardtop has been modified to accept a Chevy small-block V8/Powerglide auto combo (courtesy Kevin VanArsdale).**

More main bearings meant smoother running and a longer service life. As for the cylinder head layout, there was much debate in the '60s on the merits of overhead cam layouts. Pontiac went overhead cam with their I6, but AMC, like Volvo with their ohv 3-liter I6 164 sedan, felt the gains from ohc were more noticeable on smaller sub 3-liter sizes so they chose ohv. The new 232 had 145 horses in 1bbl form, with the optional 2bbl edition having a compression ratio of 8.5:1 with 155 bhp at 4,400 rpm and 222 lbs/ft at just 1,600 rpm.

Closet misers could secretly rejoice in the 199's 128 bhp at 4,400 rpm and 182 lbs/ft at 1,600 rpm. In 1965 came the old 196's absolute end: it posted 1bbl power outputs of 90 bhp for the flathead 196 and 125 bhp for the ohv 196; thus the new 199/232 family had the advantage in all price areas. In addition, being the fair-minded fellows they were, AMC offered 232 living across the board, from American to Ambassador. All could enjoy the 232's wedge-shaped combustion chambers and extra 600cc over the 196.

Classic V8 Rumble

While all hailed AMC's sensible new six, the V8 motor was de rigueur in Detroit by the mid–'60s. American Motors' dealers were desperate for a V8 in the Classic. AMC capitulated to dealers' requests and a V8 became optional in the new Classic late in the 1963 model year. The version of AMC's V8 chosen was the 287, related to the 327, but now with bore and stroke at 3.75 × 3.25 inches respectively. The 287 V8 made 198 bhp at 4,700 rpm and 280 lbs/ft at 2,600 rpm.

The 287 nicely nestled midway between the 196/232 I6 and 327 V8; it was the only V8 size available in the Classic, pushing top speed to a genuine 100 mph and pulling 0–60 mph to under 12 seconds even when loaded with power and comfort accessories. Typifying this period in American Motors' history, the mid–'60s Classic was looking like one of the Big 3 crowd. Chevrolet, Ford and Plymouth had the goodness of 260–290 cube V8s and a/c for their growing compacts. Gone were the days of I6 poverty specials.

The 360-lb spec-sheet weight difference between an I6 and V8 Classic partly represented the fact that, unlike its Big 3 rivals, AMC's 287 wasn't a small-block V8. Plus, there were extensive technical upgrades between the I6 and V8 Classics. For the meager surcharge of $105 to jump from 196 I6 to 287 V8, one received a better electrical system, plus improved brakes and suspension and drive-train componentry. Although both I6 and V8 models had a dual-brake master cylinder system, the 287 Classic used a Bendix duo-servo instead of a Wagner servo, and 10-inch brake drums instead of 9-inch.

Wheels, tires and suspension were also significantly different, with 14 × 5-inch rims with 6.50-inch selection rubber versus 14 × 5.5-inch rims with 7.50-inch section footwear on the V8. To deal with the extra weight in the nose, the V8 Classic came standard with stiffer front springs and front 0.75-inch swaybar. However, such hardware aside, the 287 Classic was decidedly more "plow on" in practice than a 196 al2-blocked Classic. Even with the optional heavy-duty suspension kit, the V8 Classic wouldn't be as nimble as a 196- or 232-powered example.

There were also cooling system upgrades to stop the V8 from getting hot under the collar. The V8 cooling system was 19 quarts, not 10.5 quarts, with a slower-turning 18-inch-diameter 4-blade fan; the I6 Classics had a 14-inch-diameter equivalent. As was industry practice, a/c necessitated the heavy-duty cooling system with a 7-blade fan sitting on a viscous drive hub. From all this the consumer had to think carefully between the V8 lure of the 287, and the new 232, the latter promising comparable acceleration with less weight.

AMC was using the "Sensible Spectaculars" slogan to promote its wares, implying a spicy family car. Buyers set more store by Rambler's 2-year/24,000-mile warranty (courtesy Kevin VanArsdale).

The coming of the 232 motivated AMC to up-engine the Classic for '66. V8 choices now included all of American Motors' V8 line, with the 287 through to two 327s. The 250 bhp 327 was a 2bbl regular-fuel motor, whereas the 270-horse 327 was the familiar 4bbl power-pack edition requiring premium gas. The 145 bhp 1bbl 232 was the standard Classic motor at this time. The time in question also happened to be the Classic's last model year.

By 1965–66 the Classic grille sported a slim horizontal bar between its pair of circular headlamps, anodized black in '66. The style leader in '66 MY was the new Classic "Rebel" 2-door hardtop. The Classic 2-door hardtop made its debut in 1964, but the latest Rebel and 770 iterations had a sharp-edged new-look hardtop. All '66 Classics came with new wraparound safety horizontal taillights. Wagon variants had a length extension from 193 to 195 inches, boosting cargo capacity from 80 to 83 cu ft.

Changing Gears at AMC

The 1963–66 period also marked a change in gearbox fashion. With the new '63 Classic it was possible to get the clutch pedal-bereft E-Stick with overdrive. A more historically notable arrival came in 1964 in the form of AMC's well-known 3-speed "Shift Command" automatic, a torque-converter-style auto based on the Borg Warner Model 8 unit. In contrast to the column-operated Flash-O-Matic, console-mounted Shift Command encouraged driver involvement. Shift Command would be tennis socks with sporty colored trim, if a gearbox could be a sock. Flash-O-Matic would be set-and-forget knee-high white socks.

Shift Command was saying sock it to me! Both automatics had the same 3 forward ratios, but Shift Command allowed the driver to hold onto a gear. Put the stick in "1" and it stayed there; same with gear "2." In "D" the box would do a second gear start on V8 cars, and then mosey into top. Flash-O-Matic wafted through driving ranges; Shift Command allowed "2" to be held through twisting corners, keeping the engine spinning in the meat of the rev range. The same deal was occurring with AMC's manual boxes.

The worthy 3-speed manual and overdrive boxes were there alongside the eccentric Twin-Stick, but fashion dictated four on the floor. The console-positioned manual gearbox was becoming as popular as a Frankie Avalon "Beach Blanket" movie, and American Motors acceded to requests by making a 4-speed console-shifted manual a '66 MY option. Detroit was surfing the youthful tidal wave; muscle car intermediates and pony cars weren't top dog without a 4-speed.

AMC had neither a muscular intermediate nor compact pony at this stage, but there were sound engineering reasons to adopt a 4-speed. There was a horsepower race going on in Detroit, old anti-racing and power-to-weight rules were becoming old hat, the V8 was in and it was becoming more powerful. With this came a need to harness the increased power of a tuned motor, and the extra intermediate ratio helped in that respect. There was also the issue of clutch engagement and shift speed, and overdrive boxes liked to pause.

The Twin-Stick overdrive box seemed happier when it didn't have too much engine to deal with. However, trade the 196 in for a 327 and the piggyback delay of having an auxiliary gearbox in tow introduced shift lag. Plus, the shifter didn't exactly move across the gate like greased lightning. AMC recognized the problem, and to keep the small band of Rambler dragstrip devotees happy, and there were some, there was a heavy-duty clutch option for 327-powered cars with the 3-speed overdrive manual. The optional clutch could take an extra 192 lbs of plate pressure.

The real solution lay with the newly available Borg Warner T10 4-speed, an all-synchro console-mounted unit announced as an option for V8 Ramblers in the middle of 1965 cal-

This 1965 Rambler Classic Cross Country 770 wagon has a Barcelona Taupe exterior, with wheels painted Corral Cordovan. It has been nicknamed "Marge" (courtesy Patrick Roth).

endar year. The price for four on the floor was $188.10, which was quite hefty, given one could have taken the standard 3-speed and added a little more to get the practical Weather Eye a/c system for $321 instead. On the subject of options, one could have the heavy-duty springs and shocks package for just $5.05! Very cheap as options went, and typical of Detroit at the time. HD suspension of the 1950s–'70s was affordable compared to modern optional sports suspension.

The Classic and American Motors were changing; there was so much more choice—so many more gadgets to buy and a convertible option in every AMC model line going into 1966. The Classic 770 convertible became available during 1965. The additional gewgaws made sense—a tilt adjustable steering column was a good thing—but there was something else occurring at AMC. American Motors' boss George Romney was succeeded by Roy Abernethy, a person with a super-salesman's background. There was nothing wrong with the sales angle—Romney had evangelized the virtues of thrift to AMC's benefit—but the message had changed.

During the Classic's life it was plain that AMC's new boss Abernethy wanted to take AMC from niche player into more direct competition with the mainstream three. Romney had sold America its economy car; now Abernethy wanted to sell a T-Bird to visitors to AMC dealerships. American Motors had the hardware, a 270-horse 4bbl V8, Twin-Sticks and, since '63, a Twin-Grip differential, among other devices. However, a 2-door club sedan isn't as eye-catching as a 2-door pillarless hardtop, which in turn can't compete with a real coupe personal car.

Put all the toys in a luxurious coupe and such showroom eye candy would help the whole AMC range glow. American Motors had won *Motor Trend*'s Car of the Year accolade, but lacked a glamour car, a dealership magnet. A curious omission in '60s America that Abernethy sought to rectify, but what name for such a dreamboat? Recent practice would suggest something from the life aquatic. The public's appetite had been whetted by Stingrays and Barracudas, names from nature associated with big-game fishing. This pursuit implied excitement, plus the wealth that permitted such leisure time. All positive lifestyle connotations, but would the concept sink or swim at AMC?

American Motors Goes Fishing with Marlin

The Marlin coupe's genesis was tied up with a showcar called the Tarpon. This compact 2+2 fastback coupe was based on the then new and longer '64 American 106-inch wheelbase, and was intended as a sporty little number. The Tarpon fastback saw daylight slightly before the 1964½ Mustang and was warmly greeted by the S.A.E. (Society of Automotive Engineers), but there were some problems. Firstly, who was to know Ford's pony would gallop off and capture the heretofore unknown "young at heart" market?

Management's crystal ball was cloudy that day in Kenosha; all they could see were brighter prospects for a large luxo cruiser. The second problem Tarpon faced was lack of V8 muscle. At the time AMC's only V8 design was the big burly 287/327, and this power plant wouldn't fit between the fenders of the American-based Tarpon. For American Motors' boss Roy Abernethy the solution was simple: change platforms from American to Classic. Abernethy intimated to Richard Teague that it would be a good idea to use the intermediate Classic as the base for a fastback.

It seemed like wisdom worthy of King Solomon, since the Classic already used AMC's V8, and by supersizing, one got a roomier cabin. The only problem with this transition was that a fastback doesn't work as well stylistically with a larger car. It was a question of flow and proportions that Teague, as VP of styling, was well aware of, but there was something he wasn't aware of. While on vacation in Europe, Roy Abernethy instructed the Marlin design team to raise the rear roof section by one inch!

Richard Teague never really came to terms with what was technically an appearance faux pas, but could see how it transpired. Abernethy was a big man, and tested out Marlin by sitting in the rear of prototypes, whereupon his 6-ft-4-in frame encountered a lack of rear headroom, hence the raised roofline. However, roof shock aside, relations between Abernethy and Teague continued to be cordial, and yet, this wasn't the only bit of contention to surround Marlin's styling. Which company was first with the shape, AMC or Chrysler?

Yes, the '56 Chrysler Norseman showcar set a precedent, but the Dodge Charger said hello in 1966, after the Marlin, so who was really first? The 1966 Dodge Charger's designer, Carl Cameron, said his inspiration came from the 1949 Cadillac fastback, so one should regard visual similarities as mere coincidence. That said, history will always reserve a place for the Rambler Marlin as the first American fastback intermediate of the '60s. American Motors proclaimed the Marlin's arrival on February 10, 1965, with the fastback unveiled in dealerships on March 1.

Thus, Marlin made a mid-model-year intro with a starter sticker of $3,100, at a time when an upmarket Rambler Classic 770 2-door hardtop could be yours for $3,063. As the image flagship of the AMC family, Marlin was introduced with many expensive items as standard equipment. This was in contrast to the situation of Ford's Mustang release, where the only thing included in the base price was air in the tires! However, in a Marlin one could expect front seat belts, full coil spring construction for seat squab/back, a redesigned version of AMC's famous Weather Eye heater, and probably the best brakes in the industry.

On the 1965½ Marlin one could count on the stopping power of a Bendix tandem master cylinder dual-circuit braking system, with Series "E" 11.19-inch power-assisted front disks and 10-inch non-servo rear drums—generous equipment at a time when Detroit sold a lot of cars with marginal swept brake area. The Corvette made the change from all-drum to all-disk in 1965, so Marlin was well up to the mark as a road car, in spite of not being specifically high-performance directed. Those front disks had serious 4-piston calipers. Nor was Marlin underdone under the hood: the standard motor was the 232 I6. Still a very new power plant, the ohv 3.8-liter Typhoon six made 155 bhp and 222 lbs/ft at 1,600 rpm in 2bbl form, with Carter WCD carburetion. In a preview March 1965 article, *Motor Trend* felt the 2bbl 232 might be the best choice, being lighter and newer than the 287/327, but the public decided differently. Only 2,005 Marlins were ever specified with the 232 I6, so a Marlin 232 with console Twin-Stick would be an amusing rarity.

Fewer than 6 percent of Marlins were ordered with the Twin-Stick, and although gearbox choices for 1966 also encompassed normal 3-speed column manual, 3-speed column auto, 3-speed column overdrive manual and a 4-speed floorshift, the masses mostly preferred the console-mounted Shift Command 3-speed auto. Thus, the 270 bhp 4bbl 327 and Shift Command auto were the most popular power team. With said combination, Marlin had the same scat as, say, a Pontiac Grand Prix with 389 V8. Zero to sixty in 10 seconds made it a banker's hot rod, if you will.

Marlin delivered equal performance with less displacement, since it was a smaller, lighter intermediate. Typical of AMC ordering the Classic and Marlin seemed to straddle the compact and intermediate classes. Length/width/height for Marlin were 195/74.5/54.16 inches on the Classic's 112-inch wheelbase, while the Grand Prix was 213/79/54.5 inches on a 120-inch wheelbase. Given that the extra length was mostly stylistic overhang, the Pontiac's 600-pound weight penalty didn't mean increased interior space over Marlin.

Henry Ford II coined the term "personal car" for the original 1955 Thunderbird, and another description for fancy two-doors was "specialty car." Critics and cynics claimed the term referred to the fact such special cars cost more than the normal cars they were based on, and with their swoopy bodystyles could be used for fewer tasks than regular sedans. However, American Motors' print advertising pushed Marlin's practical side: "How to tell a Marlin '66 from any other sports fastback? Put your family in it."

Thanks to Mr Abernethy's insistence on extra interior space, AMC could truthfully claim that Marlin, even with buckets, could seat six in comfort. Rambler was after all a family brand, but there was also room for sport. At around 3,500 lbs with 327 and auto, Marlin wasn't as bulky as other intermediates, so there was no need to fear corners. Low-profile 14 × 7.35-inch 2-ply rayon tubeless tires could be optioned, along with heavy-duty suspension, and there was '66's four on the floor. Thus, people started thinking Marlin might make it on the track. After all, AMC did claim on debut that the Marlin was designed to cheat the wind.

The Hess brothers entered a Marlin in the 1966 24 Hours of Daytona, but the car failed to finish. Plus, the facts revealed that the Marlin and '66 Dodge Charger didn't exactly set the track alight in NASCAR. However, brighter achievements shone through in drag

A deserving winner of the *Motor Trend* 1963 Car of the Year title, family Rambler had features like curved side glass and shared body panels between junior and senior lines (courtesy Patrick Roth).

racing. Detroit was still in its anti-racing mental state at this time, but there was some informal support for dealerships that dabbled in the 1,320-ft sprint, giving rise to one memorable Marlin. Preston Honea of Norwalk, California's, Bill Kraft Rambler had been campaigning a special Rambler American with a monster AMC V8.

The dealer famously bored out the Ambassador's 327 to 418ci and added 4 carbs on a custom intake manifold, placing the motor in a '64 American. Praise be to the enlightened dealer speed shops that looked at engineering problems and saw solutions! Was the 383 big block really too big to fit in a Dart? It was, until the enterprising folks at Mr. Norm's Grand Spaulding Dodge came up with a pair of nifty heat deflector shields for the 383's exhaust manifolds.

A Mopar anecdote provides an intro to the well-known "Hemi Marlin" drag racer. Preston Honea was working for Bill Kraft Rambler, and the dealer offered him a brand-new Marlin as the basis for a drag racer, feeling it would generate more interest than the sober Classic. To win on the strip, one needed displacement and high-end power, and in the '60s that meant Chrysler power. Thus, the "Bill Kraft Rambler" (Marlin), successor to the "Kraft Rambler" (American), used a 1965 426 Hemi with 12.5:1 CU, aluminum heads and fuel injection. Hilborn injectors were utilized on the fuel injection, an accurate way to handle methanol enrichment when the nitrous was activated.

Structural mods were made to get the Marlin ready for serious launches. The front chassis frame rails were continued one foot past the point where the rear lift bars attached to the body's tubular frame, the place where the rear swaybar was affixed. The Hemi Marlin wheelbase was also different from stock by 8 inches. The rear wheels were set 12 inches forward, and the front axle was now 4 inches closer to the front bumper. If the Hemi Marlin wanted to entertain the crowd with a wheelie, it could!

Unseen hardware included Rambler front hubs with early Ford front spindles machined to accept said hubs. The rear differential came from a 1957 Pontiac, and Pontiac rear brakes were included with Bendix drum brake linings; no front brakes were fitted. Although the car was recognizable as a Marlin, Hilbig Fiberglass supplied the front fenders, doors, bumpers and hood. Plexiglass side windows also helped kill the kilos. Normally a Marlin carried an upscale hood ornament showing a leaping Marlin fish, but hood ornaments seem superfluous on drag racers, so the Hemi Marlin substituted a mid-hood-mounted forward-facing hoodscoop instead.

The Cragar 8/8 magnesium rims were hard-to-miss period pieces, and "Flash-O-Matic" signage was on the rear fender, but the stock BW Flash-O-Matic auto wasn't present. Sitting behind the 426 Hemi was an also Chrysler-sourced Torque-Flite automatic with Hurst console shifter. All the work to transform a brand-new 1965½ Marlin into an early Funny Car was done by Blair's Speed Shop. The idea of a Rambler racer with shock value was brilliant. The Marlin wasn't a common sight on '60s streets, and when was the last time you saw one whose front flipped forward to reveal a 426 Hemi?

Preston Honea's friend Lefty Mudenbach was first to give the Hemi Marlin a trial run, and it achieved a 10.31-second ¼-mile at 138 mph straight out of the speed shop. So it was that the Hemi Marlin surpassed the 112-mph trap speed set by the 418ci '64 American "Kraft Rambler" at Fontana. Preston Honea campaigned the Hemi Marlin from 1965 through to mid–1966. It eventually got into the 9's with a 138.9-mph trap speed recorded in 1965, and a 9.83-second ¼-mile at 135.33 mph in 1966.

Mr. Honea then left Southern California for St. Louis, where he raced the "Executioner

Dart"; the Mopar lure was hard to resist. The Marlin also did some good in stock car racing. Roy Haslam used a Marlin for Super Stock in Victoria, Canada, as well as America, winning the July Cup and recording 3rd in the championships. Contrary to popular opinion, the fishy fastback was also an initial winner for AMC. The big coupe landed 10,327 sales in a truncated model year. In 1965, American Motors suffered a 3-week U.A.W. (United Auto Workers) union strike, but still managed a $5.2 million profit for the year.

Marlin was pulling its weight, and as AMC's first auto celebrity chariot no doubt drew folks into dealerships across the land, which did no harm to American or Classic sales. Plus, being so closely based on the latter, the Marlin was hardly a rash exercise. In keeping with the '60s fashionability of all things nautical, American Motors hoped two showcars would get the public hooked on AMC. In 1965 the "Black Marlin" did the show circuit accompanied by comely-looking young ladies attired in sailors' outfits. Consistent with its name, this Marlin had a black exterior.

Continuing with the *Gilligan's Island* flavor, 1966 saw the "Tahiti Marlin" star at the North American International Auto Show in Detroit. The exterior was Fireflake Blue and the interior featured "Bright South Seas Floral" upholstery with matching throw pillows. Both showcars could be driven, but weren't put into production. American Motors was more concerned with the real '66 Marlin. With the opening fanfare waning, AMC got serious with a realistic Marlin, base price of $2,601.

Marlin descended to the lower sticker price through decontenting; much of what was standard became optional. By the mid–'60s chrome trim was losing its showroom luster, so the '65 American/Classic/Ambassador had the option of black vinyl roof trim. By 1966 black vinyl trim was on the Marlin options list and involved covering the roof, trunk lid, and C pillar surround. The last trim area was new to Marlin in '66. The '66 Marlin powered on with the same intro power plants, but 232-engined fastbacks now came with a standard front swaybar. A swaybar a day, kept Ralph Nader at bay!

Matching the Classic, Marlin sported a central horizontal grille bar in black anodized finish. The 4-speed floor-shifted manual and dash-mounted tach were new '66 options that made Marlin fun to play with, and if one wasn't old enough to play with the real thing, why not a Marlin toy? In keeping with Detroit tradition, dealer promotional models were trotted out as a guide to what was new in the product line in any given model year. Such items are now a collectible part of the classic car hobby, and more valuable if the box has been retained.

A detailed 1/25-scale dealer promotional Marlin was made under license from AMC by Jo-Han in 1965 and 1966. By the end of the '66 model year, with a new-shape Marlin awaiting, thousands of surplus old-shape models were given away to children's hospitals, orphanages, etc. One more thing worth playing on Marlin was the in-car audio. Only 221 Marlins were bought without a radio, but over 50 percent chose their Marlin with an AM/FM mono tuner, skipping the starter AM radio.

Discerning acoustic buffs could specify a "Duo Costic" rear speaker and "Vibra Tone" speaker system at a time when stereophonic sound was still a novelty. Something that wasn't sounding good was Marlin's '66 model year sales, which had declined to 4,547 units. The luxo personal car market was a tough area, given that models like the Thunderbird and Riviera soaked up what disposable income was out there, and there was the problem of an American Motors badge lacking prestige.

Thus, one can also imagine the marketing trials and tribulations of AMC as it promoted a luxury personal car under the Rambler economy car banner. So it's understandable that for '66 the Rambler Marlin was rechristened the AMC Marlin, more evidence of Mr. Abernethy's trying to break from that economy-car image. Indeed, period perception of the AMC brand was embarassingly recalled in 2002 by none other than Mitt Romney, son of former AMC supremo George Romney.

Mitt Romney committed a political error in one of his Massachusetts gubernatorial campaign TV ads. In the commercial Mrs. Romney recalled their courting when Mitt Romney cruised around in a "goofy-looking car." Although the car in question wasn't specifically named as being a brand-new Marlin fastback, Mitt Romney added insult to injury by saying he was embarrassed to drive the car in high school. While one can understand that peer-group pressure would have made young Romney more comfy driving a fastback Mustang, his political rival was much less charitable.

Democrat Shannon O' Brien made political hay out of Romney's admission, using it to show how out of touch the rich kid was with blue-collar working people. While young Romney may have been blind to the Marlin's virtues — after all, how could he have seen them while hiding in the Rambler's glove box from the school bully?— AMC was wise to the image deficit. A sign of what the company was going to do about it was shown with the 1966 Marlin II showcar.

The Marlin II was a '66 Marlin with the front end borrowed from the AMC Ambassador luxury car. The Marlin II was made for the personal use of Richard Teague, and was sold in 1967. And well might Richard Teague have wanted Marlin II, because he was behind the move to shift Marlin from the intermediate Classic to the full-size Ambassador platform for 1967 model year. Teague's reasoning was excellent: if one is going to have a big fastback, then base it on the longer Ambassador.

AMC was ahead of the curve in making its luxo car a retrimmed version of the family Rambler in 1962–64. The Classic and Ambassador shared a 108-inch wheelbase in 1962, and a 112-inch wheelbase in 1963–64 (courtesy Mary Brancato).

For Teague it was all about the proportions: a long roof section, which Marlin had, needed a longer hood, which the Ambassador had, to keep everything balanced. Thus, for '67 Marlin moved onto the Ambassador's 118-inch wheelbase and adopted this luxury car's visage. Another important change for '67 was Marlin's adoption of AMC's new senior-car range open driveshaft with 4-link fettled rear live axle. So say goodbye to the torque tube, and hello to what was essentially an all-new Marlin.

The '67 Marlin measured up to true intermediate stats of 201.5 inches long, 78.4 inches wide and 53.8 inches tall for the most realistic 6-passenger coupe in auto history. It was stylish in there too, because Marlin received the new Rebel dashboard molding, but with two large circular dial faces. The Rebel used a strip speedo instead. Round dials went with the almost obligatory Shift Command console automatic; Marlin was almost a muscle car! The new exterior was Marlin modernized.

Fashion had moved on to broad rear haunches, less chrome and fussy detailing, and Marlin complied. From the rear ¾ angle Marlin's original character lines were there, but all smoothed over. The optional roof/tail vinyl trim was still available and at $99.50 was a Marlin trademark, but there was no vinyl trim around the C pillar this year. The roof/deck vinyl seemed to pour over the Marlin's body like chocolate sauce, and combined with the reproportioned flowing sail panels, made the new larger rear window look more rakish.

The rear fascia taillights with horizontal ribbing and bumper complex were very integrated. Indeed, the Marlin's rear bumper was flusher-fitting than that item on the '67 Rebel or Ambassador. Increasing the Marlin's sense of size was the absence of the recessed rear-deck Marlin chrome logo badge seen in 1965 and '66. The front was mostly pure Ambassador, with classy GTO/Mercedesesque stacked circular lamps. The grille was a sporty black anodized version of the Ambassador DPL dual turn signal lamp "rally light" edition. Even the Marlin's hood ornament was redesigned, so it seemed less obtrusive.

AMC's new finned turbocast wheel covers were suitably late '60s up-to-date, and seemed worthy of Boadicea's chariot. We will never know if an AMC designer was inspired by the Bond flick *Goldfinger*, where the Aston Martin DB5 impaled the poor hapless Mustang convertible with its knock-offs, but a Marlin with the turbocast covers looked sharp. Mr. Teague said the '67 Marlin was the best looking of the tri-year fish fastback's run, and the new shape made a strong case. However, styling is subjective, whereas performance is objective, and the '67 Marlin was the fastest Marlin to date.

Gentlemen ... We Have a New V8

A paltry 355 Marlins in 1967, the final model year, carried the 232 I6 between the front wheel wells; what people really wanted were AMC's new 290 and 343ci small-block V8s. By this stage a U.S. car maker was nothing without a good small block. Big blocks were revered, but it was the small-block V8 that got the groceries and starred in SCCA Trans Am races. When most buyers studied an option sheet, they skipped the poverty six and premium-fuel big blocks, selecting sensible engines like the Chevy 283 and Ford 289 for their intermediate sedan or wagon.

By the mid–'60s American Motors' big-block 327 wasn't making the numbers one would have expected for a motor of such heft. There was also a need for a modern V8 to complement the new and effective 232 I6. Have no fear, AMC was preparing a jewel of a small block for Mr. Mainstream, and the genesis of the new 290/343ci V8 had something to do with the Ford GT40 by way of England. English design engineer Len Bailey had worked at Austin, racing team BRM and Daimler; he was even offered a job with Nash-Kelvinator when the U.S. company visited Austin concerning the Metropolitan project.

The Nash position was declined, but Bailey's first serious work in America came with AMC, working on their new small-block V8 motor. Len Bailey gave an interesting insight into the behind-the-scenes development of the engine: "I began working for a chap called Dave Potter at American Motors, Detroit, who was in overall charge of engine design. We started drawing up plans for an all-new V8, Dave overseeing production engineering at Kenosha, Wisconsin, and the design team in Detroit. Finally, we got the engine running but, in the meantime, Dave had suffered a heart attack."[9]

Bailey then went to Ford and a team that cooked up the Mustang concept car of the early '60s, and on to the Ford GT40 sportscar program. It was with the GT40 that Bailey encountered Roy Lunn, a person who would figure greatly in the creation of AMC's cross-over Eagle range of the 1980s. At Ford there were differences between Bailey and Lunn over the GT40, with the former eventually doing much aerodynamic work to get the GT40 to work on the track.[10]

Like Ford, AMC was trying to expunge the old fuddy-duddy image with all things light and sporty. The new 290/343 V8 had its distributor and oil pump mounted on the timing gear case. While completely new, the 290/343 did keep the 4.75-inch bore center of the 250/287/327 family, so that existing boring machinery could be utilized, which saved money. AMC's new V8 was a hydraulic lifter design, and the 1966–70 era AMC small block was the "short-deck" edition.

The 290/343 had a rectangular exhaust port cylinder head. The 290 used a small valve head (1.787-inch intake / 1.406-inch exhaust) with bore/stroke dimensions of 3.75 × 3.28-inches. The starter 9.0:1 compression ratio 290 had one 2bbl Holley carb and gross outputs of 200 bhp at 4,600 rpm and 285 lbs/ft at 2,800 rpm. The optional 290 4bbl sported 225 ponies. By 1967 the larger 343 motor was at hand, with big valve head (2.025-inch intake / 1.625-inch exhaust) and dimensions of 4.08 × 3.28 inches. The 343 kicked horsepower up to 235 bhp, with the super pursuit 10.2:1 compression ratio premium-fuel Carter AFB 4bbl version making 280 bhp at 4,800 rpm and 365 lbs/ft at 3,000 rpm.

The 280-pony 343 was 10 horses up on the final 327; it was the biggest and most potent motor American Motors had on the shelf. The 1967 model year was the first time Marlin had access to what was denoted the "Typhoon" V8. The Typhoon tag seemed reserved for any new motor that blew in! Marlin could be fitted with either the 290 or 343 in any of the aforementioned 4 states of tune. The 287/327 were consigned to the annals of history. With the most potent 343, the Marlin was a low 17-second ¼-miler, dipping into the high 16s if the 4-speed manual was chosen over the autobox.

The '67 Marlin 343 HO 4-speed was a swift cruiser that tipped the scales at over 4,000 lbs. Thus, there was no doubting the efficiency of a small block that could whisk this much luxury to sixty in 9 seconds flat, but was it enough? Anything AMC could do, the Big 3 could do bigger, and they had some optional "war games" motors which were more explosive than a Soviet missile. American Motors were leaders in economy, but always a few steps behind in realizing performance variants.

Inside Rosie, Adjust-O-Tilt/Road-Controlled power steering, console Flash-O-Matic auto and air conditioning, along with electric windshield wipers, all qualified as luxury items in the early '60s (courtesy Mary Brancato).

How uneasy some Rambler devotee management must have felt at the thought of a 300-horsepower 12-mpg 4,200-pound coupe emanating from the frugal doors of Kenosha! However, while these poor souls anguished in guilt, '67 Marlin buyers savored the good life. They enjoyed Ambassaor DPL trim, minus the two throw pillows, because sporty intermediate coupe drivers preferred to throw a shift, not a pillow. Also note that Marlin was moved into the Ambassador brochure for '67, no longer promoted on its own. Standard equipment included a safety collapsible steering column, with AMC's new smaller '67 three-spoke sports steering wheel attached, but nothing, it would seem, could turn around the Marlin's fortunes.

Just 2,545 people chose a Marlin in 1967, and the model didn't return for '68. Big 3 competition and the booming pony-car market froze out poor Marlin, forcing American Motors to put the nameplate on ice. However, the passing years have been kind to Marlin, with rising interest in the fastback. The styling of the 2004 Chrysler Crossfire was unquestionably influenced by the Marlin. Pro baseball's Florida Marlins used a custom '66 Marlin convertible for parades and on-field ceremonies at Dolphins Stadium. The special car had only a driver's seat, with the remaining space for team mascot "Billy the Marlin" during the 1997 world championship season.

The Marlin benefits through its great parts interchangeability with the Classic in 1965–66, and the Ambassaor in '67. So bumpers, front fenders, hood, dashboard and trim can often be swapped. On the 1967 Marlin it's easy to exchange the 290/343 motors for one

The top version of AMC's first V8 design is present. The 4-barrel 327ci motor had external dimensions commensurate with a big block. It put out 270 bhp to whisk the Ambassador from 0 to 60 mph in under 10 seconds (courtesy Mary Brancato).

of the later 390/401 V8s. Also, in spite of a track change from 58.5 to 60 inches in 1969, identiacl mounting points and coil spring locations for the rear suspension imply that later model differentials can be substituted. Thus, '67 Marlin performance can be hotted up appreciably.

It has frequently been mentioned that AMC should have done the Tarpon instead of the Marlin. However, that might have achieved similarly moderate results. Chrysler did such a strategy with their '64 Barracuda. A speedy conversion turned the Valiant compact into the fastback Barracuda, beating Mustang to the showroom in the process, but it didn't work. Chrysler had a nifty small-block 273ci V8; AMC did not. V8 options aside, even though AMC's American-based Tarpon was prettier than Chrysler's compact fastback, it too would probably have wilted under the blowtorch of Ford marketing.

Ford had the television and print ads, and the Mustang paced the '64 Indianapolis 500. An early Barracuda with the Formula S pack was able, but the public liked the cut of Mustang's jib, and that's the auto they went for. Pushing an I6-only Tarpon, with the baggage of the Rambler economy brand, against the 289 V8 Mustang would have been a hard road to drive. AMC avoided this direct encounter with mighty, and somewhat devious, Ford.

In the past there was a tendency to either canonize or demonize a nameplate, but in retrospect many of these judgments seem questionable. *Car and Driver*'s use of the term "pariah" in relation to Marlin was most likely done for shock value. After all, this journal did match up the Pontiac GTO and Ferrari GTO, with contentious results. Given the Marlin was a fastback version of AMC's senior cars, it's safe to say that if one likes the Classic or Ambassador, the Marlin will appeal. Diplomacy often requires an Ambassador.

American Motors' Goodwill Ambassador

By the late '50s, American Motors had the small and family car segments sealed, but what of the high end of town? There were the big Nash and Hudson remnants, pre-merger designs that were increasingly becoming outmoded in terms of efficiency, road behavior and fashion; something had to be done and fast. The solution was to go brand-new, discard the senior cars of yesteryear and design a new luxury car based on the 1956–57 108-inch wheelbase Rambler unibody.

Thus, there would be a markedly different Nash Ambassador for '58, but also a companion Hudson Rebel. AMC designers did a Hudson edition for Hudson dealers, in the same way the Bentley T series would accompany the Rolls-Royce Silver Shadow. However, at the 11th hour, AMC's boss George Romney decided it made more sense to have one luxury model. The final Nash Ambassadors and Hudson Hornets were slow sellers; sensing the public were tired of their image, Romney took the command decision to discontinue the Nash and Hudson marques at the close of the 1957 model year.

For '64 Classic and Ambassador adopted a filled-in, flush, smooth front chrome grille, after the debut concave style of '63. Rosie has the comfort of AMC's Airliner reclining front seats (courtesy Mary Brancato).

That said, Nash tradition won out in that there was an Ambassador for '58, but it was called "Ambassador V8 by Rambler." This sleight of hand deep-sixed Nash and Hudson, as well as keeping the economy Rambler name at a safe distance. The distancing was wise because the reborn Ambassador was rather close to the family Rambler. The 1958 Ambassador rested on a regal 117-inch wheelbase. In plain terms it was a 9-inch stretch of the 108-inch Rambler, with the added length occurring from the cowl forward.

The Ambassador's unibody offered no increase in passenger or luggage accommodation, and its styling mirrored that of the revised '58 Rambler, but ... it had additional presence! The extra length of the front ⅓ of the 3-box shape seemed to create an altogether different beast from the standard Rambler. The Ambassador's visage was more imposing and somewhat menacing, because the Rambler's grid grille was replaced by a fussier mesh rectangle-sectioned equivalent with a beefy "V" bar trim chrome overrider linking the Rambler's bumper guards and covering slim rectangular turn signals.

In the horizontal space between the Rambler's quad lamps, the word Rambler was replaced by Ambassador. The longer word, in closer-spaced block lettering, made the Ambassador appear wider than the Rambler, even though it wasn't. While the Ambassador sedan of 1958 was 200.63 inches long, its width of 71.3 inches and 57.75-inch height were equal to a Rambler sedan. However, all the frightened driver of a Crosley could see in the rear view mirror at night was that V grille and blazing quad lights, which seemed full-size enough to make any economy car move over or hide in a ditch!

Being Rambler-related, the Ambassador could, and did, call on the 4 body styles of the shorter car. That involved 4-door sedan, 4-door pillarless sedan, and two 4-door wagons, one with and the other innovatively sans pillar. Trim levels were also Rambler-like and covered plush and plusher. Starting with the two-tone-effect Super, Ambassador skipped Deluxe and finished with Custom. Custom level bestowed the expected sweepspear, which looked almost like a lethal weapon and added to the car's sense of length.

The sweepspear was also a little marketing identity concealer, in that it obscured the "Rambler Ambassador" badges that were within the pointy end of the spear on the front fenders. Marketing wanted to keep the Rambler part quiet, and Ambassador's new emblem helped. Instead of Rambler's stylized hubcap "R," the Ambassador featured an eagle head upon an American flag shield. The logo was a pleasant sight for following motorists looking at the 4-door sedan Ambassador's standard continental kit.

The Ambassador was all about equipment, of which it had more than ordinary Ramblers. Although much of the stuff wasn't exactly Ambassador exclusive, the Ambassador did come with more standard equipment and was more likely to be found at dealerships loaded. Thus, expect a standard electric clock, as well as dual front and rear ashtrays; plus, this was the venue to try out all of American Motors' luxuries. The Ambassador seemed the appropriate place to push the buttons of the Borg Warner automatic control panel, although one could specify the 3-speed manual or overdrive boxes as alternatives.

Ambassador wafted along like a cloud on AMC's optional Air-Coil suspension. In the 1950s, luxury thinking didn't involve any notions of sport. There may very well have been a road under the car, but buyers of luxo transport didn't wish to know it was there, so how about a little music? American Motors achieved a surprisingly good acoustic result by combining the air-conditioning vents, at the dashboard ends, with the radio's speaker grilles! And front occupants would be sitting comfortably thanks to AMC's 5-position adjustable backrest.

With over 3,800 lbs to haul and a hefty $400 surcharge compared to the Rambler 6, one would expect suitable engine compensation, and AMC delivered with their 327ci 4bbl V8 which produced 270 horses. This power plant, an Ambassador exclusive, was a production version of the motor in the limited run '57 Rambler Rebel. At this time the off-the-peg Rebel was only available with the smaller 250ci V8, so Ambassador offered real distinction, as well as 0–60 mph in under 12 seconds.

Initially Ambassador was the domestic luxury upstart of its day. It quickly made its name on quality, and the hewn-from-granite-block solidity of Rambler unibody construction. Ambassador kept the opposition in the frame, and moved into 1959 with a modest restyle. In common with the family Rambler, AMC's stylists massaged the rear door skin and fender line so that the body flowed more gradually into the tailfin. It had all looked a mite abrupt in '58.

For '59 the designers gave Ambassador a reduced-fuss grille, revised sweepspear and stainless-steel-trimmed C pillar with the eagle emblem. Bigger visual changes were in store for 1960, where once again the Ambassador kept in synch with the 108-inch-wheelbase Rambler. This meant new fenders, taillights, bumpers, revised A pillar and windshield, rear window, hood, and trunk lid, a lower roofline and egg-crate grille. Like those on the Rambler 6 and Rebel, the tailfins were tilted over and less obtrusive. Ambassador entered 1960 with the same quartet of body styles.

AMC's "Airliner" reclining bucket seats arrived in 1960, and since we were entering the jet age, AMC made available not one, but two 327 V8s! The existing 4bbl high-compression 9.7:1 327 made 270 bhp at 4,700 rpm and 360 lbs/ft at 2,600 rpm, this was joined by a lower-output 327 with 2-barrel carb and 8.7 CU. Whereas the 4bbl 327 was a premium-fuel engine, the 2bbl 327 ran on regular and made 250 bhp at 4,700 rpm and 340 lbs/ft at 2,600 rpm.

Both hi- and lo-po 327s shared the same cylinder head design, but the piston top differed between them. For '60, American Motors retuned the Ambassador's suspension for greater handling, pacifying existing wallow. Ambassador had some suspension differences compared to Rambler from the start. Although using existing 4-corner deep-coil springs and a torque-tube chassis, Ambassador added a standard front tempered-steel swaybar. To cope with the Ambassador's weight and power, 10-inch ribbed drums lived at each corner, providing stronger braking than on a Rebel.

Once again, the Ambassador wasn't intended as a road-course racer, but was considered better balanced than the V8 Rebel. The added length did positive things for weight distribution, and the 327's torque helped turn understeer into neutrality. The Rebel had a weight distribution of 57/43 percent; the Ambassador sedan changed that to 56/44 percent, with the wagon the best balanced at 55/45 percent. In this era, getting the power to the ground was a problem. Detroit was fitting bigger and more powerful V8s to their rear-drivers, and with the tire technology of the day, a second gear start was the only way to get moving in slippery conditions. People liked the rear-engined winter traction of the VW Beetle for this reason.

During the late '50s and early '60s, the size of the U.S. car made some options practically mandatory. The Ambassador wasn't that big by full-size standards, but for a 200+-inch, almost 4,000-pound vehicle with a cast-iron V8, power brakes, power steering and auto transmission were necessities, not luxuries. That said, Ambassador's modest U.S. large-car size, high-com-

Chairman Romney brought shared wheelbase economies of scale. However, with changing tastes for big extravagance, AMC's new boss Roy "Ad Man" Abernethy pushed Ambassador onto a 116-inch wheelbase for '65 (courtesy Mary Brancato).

pression 4bbl 327 and optional overdrive 3-speed box could get 25 mpg in turnpike cruising. Thus, there were indeed rewards for manual labor. However, a '61 restyle proved to be a somewhat harder sell.

Edmund Anderson oversaw an unusual redesign of the Ambassador for its final year to a 117-inch-wheelbase format. The grille was trapezoidal, with the front headlamps floating séance-style in a body-color-keyed panel. The front fenders arched downward and forward of the hood's leading edge. AMC marketing declared the new appearance as being "European style," and it certainly represented ongoing attempts to distance Ambassador from the family Rambler. The American Motors faithful weren't overly taken with the European look, and Ambassador sales were on the decline.

There were no hardtop Ambassador variants in '61, and there seemed little need for them, given that the economic climate favored micro rides. AMC was spending money to distinguish a luxo nameplate that wasn't selling from its 108-inch-wheelbase sales winner. It was more waste than Mr. Romney could stomach, so for '62, Ambassador moved onto the trusty 108-inch wheelbase, sharing a body with the family guy's Rambler. American Motors was the first Detroit firm ever to downsize a nameplate.

With the '62 Ambassador, American Motors adopted the European method of model hierarchy: use the same body, with the buyer moving up the ladder in trim and power. To avoid confusion, the normal 108-inch Rambler was designated as the Classic, using I6 power exclusively in '62. The Ambassador would only use V8 power, and carry special trim like the eagle-on-American-shield logo. The '62 Corvair style Ambassador was sold as the "Rambler Ambassador," Rambler being a byword for solid success by this stage.

So confident were AMC management of their image that Ambassador carried the block capital letters RAMBLER large and clear beneath its unique front crosshatch chrome grille. A motorist would only discover something was up when the Ambassador overtook him, the 327 V8 burble clearly belonging not to a Classic. A side view would display an "Ambassador" cursive script badge on the front fender and special hubcaps bearing the Ambassador logo. The downsized Ambassador, 200 lbs lighter than its predecessor, was good for a 110-mph-plus top end with the Power-pack option and 3-speed manual.

The sportsman didn't want to guide a sea barge through lanes, so the 190-inch length gave a greater feeling of control. The new top-of-the-line "400" version offered optional front

The Big 4 had their luxo nameplates, Deville, Continental, Imperial, and with AMC it was Ambassador. Rosie has 2 remote-control exterior side rear-view mirrors (courtesy Mary Brancato).

vinyl buckets, but a floor shifter was yet to arise from the console. One couldn't specify economy E-Stick on Ambassador; that just didn't suit the luxo image. Fewer model and ordering permutations also made financial sense for a small player like AMC. The shared Classic/Ambassador body continued with the all-new 112-inch-wheelbase platform from 1963.

AMC had great award-winning material to use, so '63's Ambassador had the curved side glass, pushbutton door handles, and reduced-stamping unibody that shaved a claimed 150 lbs off the 1962 108-inch-wheelbase car, introduced simultaneously on Classic. For '63 American Motors replaced the clap-hands windshield wipers of '62 with parallel wipers that eliminated a missed swept area in the lower center of the glass, but the differences between Classic and Ambassador were hard to see.

The horizontal grille trim bar had the word Ambassador, small and in the center, instead of Classic. There was an Ambassador hood badge motif at the leading edge, Ambassador logo hubcaps, and generally fancier trimmings, but AMC in the final hours of Romney had no place for Detroit showmanship. After all, one can't see a car's styling when driving behind the wheel, but AMC's generous greenhouse meant outward visibility was clear. To see something unique to the Ambassador, just lift the hood.

Ambassador was the only senior American Motors vehicle with V8 punch; it offered AMC's own 287/327 V8s in the usual power levels. Have 2bbl or 4bbl with Walker muffled duals; the choice was yours, along with three new trim levels. Gone were terms like Deluxe and Custom: AMC was once again ahead of the pack by introducing numbers. On Classic it went 550, 660 and 770 at the apex. With Ambassador the starter Super was now the 880, and next was the Custom/400 replacing 990.

Top: A '65 Rambler Ambassador 990 convertible with 4bbl 327/auto power team and Atlantis Aqua Metallic exterior. Airliner seats, a/c and front/rear bumper guards are present. This model is one of just 2,065 built in model year '65 (courtesy Joe Howard). ***Bottom:*** For real glamour a fastback coupe trumps a 2-door hardtop, and that mid–'65 fastback in AMC showrooms was called Marlin. Think of it as Mr. Abernethy's T-Bird (courtesy Lee Greenawalt).

In 1962 a 2-door pillared sedan variant was added to the Ambassador range — this version also featured in the new '63s — along with practical 4-door sedan and wagon variants. Given the AMC senior shell could house 6 in comfort, the question whether the Ambassador offered enough plushness was best put to one's ego or neighbor, rather than that inner voice of reason. Cadillac had powered seats, but not the fun of Twin-Stick or the chance of 20 mpg cruising.

Going into 1964 the shared senior body concept continued, but the 327 was once again the standard Ambassador motor. During the latter part of the '63 model year the Classic received a 287 V8 option, so to maintain the Ambassador supremacy it used the 327 engine exclusively. The new 2-door hardtop body style was available on Classic and Ambassador, known as 990H on the latter. To further underline the Ambassador's AMC position there were no more base 880s in 1964. This was the last year of the shared Classic/Ambassador 112-inch wheelbase. Under Roy Abernethy's direction, Classic continued on the 112-inch platform for '65, whereas Ambassador moved up a size.

Playing along with mid–'60s prosperity, Ambassador now lived on a 116-inch wheelbase, and looked markedly different from the Classic. Teague's people gave Ambassador a more imposing, blockish, big-car look with squared-off three-box sections; even the bumpers were seriously square. The new face shone with stacked circular quad lamps, recessed a mite in chrome box bezels. Between the stacks lay a wide-open grille with center divider, easily achieving a sense of width. Chrome Ambassador lettering was on the leading edge of the driver's side of the hood. At the rear were vertical taillights.

Team Teague made Ambassador appear full-size, but as in 1958–61, the extra size was achieved purely ahead of the cowl! Therefore, the big Ambassador didn't possess one iota more livability than the comparatively meek-looking Classic; ho-hum. However, for economy fiends, AMC gave Ambassador a six-cylinder base engine for '65, the first time an I6 was available since the nameplate's 1958 rebirth. Chevy, Ford and Plymouth had base sixes in their 6-passenger family cars; so too would AMC.

Buy a new Ambassador and it would arrive with the 2bbl 155 bhp 232 I6. The 198 bhp 287 V8 and 250/270 bhp 327s were optional. In another first for the post–'57 era, Ambassador was now available in a 990 trim ragtop. Thus, body styles covered 2-door sedan, hardtop and convertible, plus 4-door sedan and wagon. The entry-level 880 2-door sedan with 232 and 3-speed manual had a base sticker of $2,512, but this variant turned out to be the least popular, with most buyers savoring more lavish versions.

It would appear there was method in Abernethy's madness because Ambassador sales increased from 18,647 in 1964 to over 64,000 in 1965! The public preferred fancy to plain, large to medium, and considered a real luxury car to be more than an uptrimmed version of an intermediate, however good that base was. Abernethy's sales background allowed him to correctly recognize that in the mid–'60s America wasn't ready for the one-size-fits-all approach to luxury.

With this revelation under its corporate belt, AMC went wild for '66, trinketing up Ambassador to the shiny limit. The front grille was revised to emphasize the forward-projecting horizontal chrome band; it was dubbed the "V-line" motif. Twin chrome rectangular trims were positioned on the leading edges of the front fenders, flanking the stacked lamps. At the rear, Ambassador's vertical lights appeared more prominent because new rear styling featured wraparound safety taillights.

High-level '66 Ambassadors got two bands of horizontal chrome ribbing that covered the full width of the trunk lid and extended onto the taillight lenses. In keeping with the Classic hardtops, the pillarless Ambassador 2-doors had a reshaped roofline. There was a crispness to the top now, aided by a curveless rear window. Wagons also varied: the Ambassador and Classic received new roof panels and a longer tailgate area. Thus, the Ambassador wagon rose in length from 197 to 199 inches, and matched the Classic's cargo increase to 83 cu ft.

Stylewise, black vinyl roof trim became optional on pillarless American, Classic and Ambassador for '65, and Ambassador's power convertible top was available in black, white, aqua or blue. By '66, Classic and Ambassador convertibles had a standard power top with new flexible glass rear window. One could raise or lower the top/window with everything zipped up. The convertible material was a vinyl coated nylon, and there was plenty of material in American Motors' new flagship, the DPL. Two doors and three letters for an Abernethy swansong.

AMC had priced the big 116-inch-wheelbase Ambassador competitively from the start; for '66 the price of the entry-level Ambassador 880 2 door sedan was cut to a mere $2,404, but this variant was of little import. Those seeking value stuck with AMC's bestseller, the 232-powered Classic. However, to fuel excitement in the boardroom, American Motors effected a 1966 debut for the Ambassador DPL, the most lavish 2-door hardtop Ambassador available. The DPL had the new-style hardtop roofline, and was designed to tackle Plymouth's VIP and Ford's LTD luxo rivals head-on.

The DPL was certainly well equipped, leaving nothing to chance in competing with the Big 3. Included were the AMC 287 V8, reclining front seats, extra-deep-pile carpeting, additional foam-backed vinyl trim for the dashboard and interior in general, plus big teeth! To stand out from the crowd, and thus avoid Detroit's occupational hazard of falling between the cracks, Ambassador DPL adopted super-luxo wool broadcloth for seating center and interior side trim panel surfaces. The pattern of such material was houndstooth, with said teeth being conspicuously large and bold.

American Motors was sinking its fangs into the luxury large-car segment to the tune of over 71,000 Ambassador sales in 1966. Fido the DPL was an attention grabber, but beware of those options — they could very well chase one out of house and home! The DPL's starting point was $2,860, but once one added power brakes, power steering, power windows, dash console, Twin-Grip differential and so on, the final tab would rest well above $4K. In the finest Detroit tradition, it was unlikely an Ambassador DPL existed with no power steering and the Ambassador's standard 10-inch Bendix duo-servo drums. Dealers would spec up ordered cars to at least the ¾ point.

However, what would a DPL be without vinyl-trimmed roof and rear seat reverberating speaker? The DPL's myriad controls lurked on a dash molding with 3 circular swivel a/c vents, if this option was specified. AMC had been using this dash style since the '63 new-wave seniors, the dash getting a more defined control-center hooding with separate recessed circular gauges since '65. AMC also wasn't scared to keep their 327 4bbl V8 in a holding pattern. In spite of the '60s' warming power race, the top 327 made exactly the same power and torque at the same rpm as in 1958!

American Motors' restrained 244-degree camshaft and 1.78-inch intake and 1.40-inch exhaust valves were common across the 287/327 line, and limited the worth of the top 327's 9.7 CU and 4-barrel carb. The quirky thing was that AMC allowed the owner to push that V8 in the DPL, with the new optional 4-speed manual console shifter. Cadillac or Lincoln never permitted that, and it spoke to the Ambassador DPL's intermediate origins that one could get a 4-speed in this class of car.

For '66, American Motors gave Ambassador longer shocks and revised springs to improve ride comfort, which was very important in the higher circles the car was moving in. However, 1966 would be the final outing for AMC's torque-tube chassis. It was also the year Rambler was expunged from the nameplate, the sizable one now only answering to the name AMC Ambassador. It would also seem that American Motors was experiencing mixed fortunes. Specifically, despite rising Ambassador sales, AMC's total declined to 279,225 units.

By this stage American Motors had built upon their reclining-seat car bed with an inflatable mattress option! Sadly, this provided little comfort as the company slid to 9th place in the sales race, hardly as spirited as a 327 Ambassador with 4 on the floor and optional 3.54 rear ratio. Perhaps AMC had forgotten itself. Maybe the solution lay with the car that made the company's name.

Rambler American — 1964

Greatness was expected of the '64 American. When a company has a reputation for being a small-car leader, with 6 years of unbridled compact success, a new model has to be better than good. AMC's new American for '64 was a larger, more confident economy car. The little Rambler moved up from a 100-inch, onto a 106-inch wheelbase, and was incorporated into American Motors' shared unibody program. Thus, it made structural use of some aspects of the senior line, like doors. AMC was the only company in postwar Detroit to employ body commonality between small and large passenger-car lines.

Ad copy writers could call the '64 American all-new, and not be prosecuted for misleading and deceptive conduct, but a truer description would be a new body with evolved mechanicals. That new body was pure Teague, Richard Teague having become design VP in 1964, and showed great styling restraint. The car was an example of uncomplicated industrial design, minimal decoration and the first AMC car with Teague's favorite tunnel port headlamps. Placed on the driver's side of the horizontal-ribbed grille was a rectangular plaque bearing the word "Rambler" in efficient block capitals.

It was the quiet nametag that could be trusted, and to make sure there were no nasty surprises, AMC's Floyd Kishline oversaw engineering improvements that were sensible rather than spectacular. Retained was American Motors' tried and tested independent unequal-length control arms with high-mount coils front, with semi-elliptic leaf rear suspension and live axle, but changes made for enhanced ride comfort.

The '64 American had 4-leaf springs rearwards that were now longer, 52 inches, versus the previous 45-inch units. Their deflection rate was 91 pounds per inch, as compared to 117 lbs/inch in '63. Similarly the spring rate at the front was reduced from 114 to 69 pounds per inch. A longer wheelbase and softer springs meant a more grown-up car ride, but the chassis lacked adventure. The American's front roll center had been raised, as had the rear static roll rate. However, there was no standard front swaybar, and steering choices involved a standard 6 turns lock-to-lock worm-and-roller manual, or optional 4.3 turns lock-to-lock powered recirculating ball system.

In Mustang it was all optional; in Marlin it was all standard. The intermediate Marlin's base $3,100 sticker included front seat belts, full comfort coil seating and revised AMC Weather Eye heater (courtesy Lee Greenawalt).

Six turns was a lot of arm twirling to experience road feel; the alternative was quicker but vaguer boosted steering. Still it was a sign of confidence that American didn't carry any fancy pretentions. The undemanding chassis would get mom and pop to the store and back, and if junior borrowed the keys, the worst that could happen was the small Rambler understeering to safety. The power presentation involved variations on the hardy 196, and even the most potent didn't make an American hot rod.

As always, the 90 bhp flathead 196 was the American's starting point, progressing through the 1bbl 125 bhp ohv 196 to the top 138-horse 2bbl ohv 196. With no power increase over the Breadbox days, AMC chose to stick with 9 × 2-inch drums at all four corners. This equated to a drum swept area of 235 square inches, and brake lining stopping at 139.52 square inches, even though the new American was a little bigger. Braking was modest, but then again power was modest. The American was a modest kind of car; that's what made it famous.

Junior wasn't concerned with the 2bbl 196 American's 20+-second ¼-mile; he was grinning because a clairvoyant had told him the American would soon get the hardware necessary to make it a road warrior. As things stood, the American buyer was now in charge of a 2,600-lb vehicle that measured 177 inches long, 68.5 inches wide and 54.5 inches high. All body formats were in evidence, which covered 2- and 4-door sedans, a 4-door wagon, and a fancy convertible, plus 2-door hardtop. Trim levels set up some distinctions.

Although AMC's excellent new 232 I6 was Marlin's base engine, the 4bbl 327/automatic combo fitted to this 1965 Marlin proved the most popular. Roy Abernethy was right: austerity was over (courtesy Lee Greenawalt).

The lower-level 220 and 330 took care of the 2- and 4-door sedans and 4-door wagon. The upscale 440 could be chosen on the 4-door sedan, 2-door hardtop and convertible. As with the Breadbox, the sporty bucket-seat 2-door hardtop was denoted 440H. The range commenced with the rudimentary $1,907 220 2-door sedan, topping out with the $2,346 440 convertible, of which 8,907 were constructed in 1964. Something for everyone, perhaps, but the American got much more appealing with the '65 arrival of the 232 option.

Moving into '65, one could stay faithful to the 90/125 bhp flathead/ohv 196, or be adventurous and specify AMC's new 3.3/3.8-liter Typhoon six. At the heavy-hitting end of the spectrum, this entailed the 2bbl 155 bhp 232 with those respectable 222 lbs/ft of max torque. Enough to strike fear into the hearts of all those I6 Mustang secretary specials! Compared with the 2bbl 196, the 2bbl 232 dropped the American's ¼-mile time by over one second.

The stylized fish logo served as the Marlin's hood ornament, and had connotations of affluent leisure activities befitting the coupe's status (courtesy Lee Greenawalt).

The new 199/232's contribution to American performance had as much to do with refinement as improved speed. New wine in a new bottle made for a more discerning palate, a better compact. Choose the big "232" on American and the car was fitted with wider 9-inch drums. In place of the 9 × 2-inch drums came the same brakes one would find on a '63 Classic I6. Front stoppers were now 9 × 2.25 inches; rear ones rested at 9 × 2.5 inches, which took brake lining area to 153.76 square inches.

The extra brakes brought a tangible improvement, maintaining the American's balance. There was also a slight styling revision to front and rear fascias for '65. The American's grille went from unbroken horizontal ribbing between the tunnel port headlamps, to 4 sections of 6 horizontal bars in the cleaned-up style of the '64 Classic. One could look cool and keep cool, with the aid of the convertible's power top and air conditioning, but only if one stuck to the 196. Curiously, the Typhoon I6's additional 3 to 4 inches in length over the 196 meant that '65 Americans with factory-fitted Weather Eye HVAC had to rely on the 196.

The need for nose space to fit an a/c condenser and the 199/232 six brought a restyle for 1966. The front and rear of the American were made over and the car grew to 181 inches in length, although the unibody's center section was unaffected. This was enough to allow a 199/232 American to have a/c, and very necessary to boot, because the 199 had replaced all 196 iterations by the start of the '66 model year. American's face still sported circular lamps, but housed in square frames with rounded edges. As a sign of the influence of U.S. car styling at the time, this chrome-traced, "dumbbell"-shaped grille outline was adopted by the 1968 European Ford Escort.

An American Rogue

At the rear, American featured a concave fascia below the trunk lid, an appearance the model would retain until its demise, as it would keep its new top trim designation. The American was the model that pulled the carpet from under the Big 3; it was a bit of a rogue, all told. So it should come as little surprise that AMC christened their range-topping 2-door hardtop as the Rogue for '66. The American range was reordered into 220, 440 and Rogue. Rogue had replaced 440H, with two-tone flash!

The top Rogue enjoyed the distinction of having its roof, plus rear deck, painted a contrasting color. A chrome cursive-script Rogue badge also graced the leading edge of the front fenders, and that wasn't all. One could specify the humble 1bbl 199 and 3-speed manual power team on Rogue, or choose a more appropriate 2bbl 232 and Flash-O-Matic auto combo, but there was more. In late 1966 model year the American was granted exclusive rights to AMC's new small-block V8, which made its debut in 200 bhp 2bbl form.

To showcase the new lightweight V8, which weighed 85 lbs less than a 287, AMC planned a run of 1,700 290ci V8 Rogues. The feature exterior color scheme was metallic Sun Gold, with glossy black for the Rogue's contrasting roof and rear deck. The base price for this sport compact was $2,668, and the cover charge included the recently AMC introduced BW T10 4-speed console shifter. From here options abounded to both personalize one's Rogue, and rid the American of its dour, puritanical image; after all, it was a rogue.

By 1966 the American's stock spring rates were 80 and 91 lbs/inch front and rear respectively. Heavy-duty suspension raised those figures to 99 and 102 lbs/in front/rear to complement the standard 0.81 in front swaybar. To this it was advisable to add the front-disk

For '66 AMC turned down the base price on Marlin to $2,601. Black vinyl body trim was now optional, covering roof, trunk lid and C pillar surround. Now the base Marlin 232 came with a standard front swaybar (courtesy Joe Howard).

brake option, the sort one would find on an Ambassador or Marlin, as well as optional oversize 7.35 in (187 mm) front section 14-inch tires. The also optional power steering's 4.3 turns lock-to-lock was necessarily speedier, and the meatier tires provided more weight and feel to counter typical domestic over-assisted steering.

Nearly there, from grocery getter to road-course racer via a couple of option blanks. AMC was readying its 4bbl 225 bhp premium-fuel 290 as a follow-up. A total of 8,718 2-door hardtop Rogues were sold in model year 1966, with 623 290ci cars built in '66. American Motors hadn't taken leave of its senses; it was belatedly giving folks what they wanted: compacts with flair and spirit. It was nothing new compared to what was happening at Ford and Dodge showrooms with the Mustang and Dart. All of a sudden Gran Turismo meant more than economy runs.

Welcome to the American's increasingly schizoid life. On the one hand, purveyor of an alternative to a 289 Mustang; and on the other, still the standard-bearer for domestic economy cars. In spite of the length increase to 181 inches, American Motors could, and did, claim their '66 American was still the shortest new domestic automobile money could buy. Plus, AMC data stated American's turning circle was a tight 36 feet. This was a car one could still see the corners of when parking, and the hardtop's outward visibility put many to shame.

The American was increasingly occupying a middle ground between imported minnows and domestic sharks. The base 3.3-liter I6 and 3-speed column manual said economy with an American accent, as the little sedan whisked past Volkswagens with a negligible gas mileage penalty. With overdrive, overall economy reached 20 mpg. In real-world driving one would have to pretend there was an egg under the gas pedal of small-engined imports, and pray at the merest hint of an incline, to better that figure.

All work and no play makes Jack a terribly dull boy, so for 1967 the American received a 343ci V8 to complement the 290 motor. That was the first year for the 343 at AMC; it was available across all model lines. The American no longer enjoyed the new small block exclusively, but it was the model that let the fun flow most freely. As the smallest and lightest AMC vehicle, the 4bbl 343's 280 horses and 365 lbs/ft had the best opportunity to make a good impression. With 4-speed manual an American 343 V8 was a sub–8-second 0–60 mph car.

Over 100 AMC patrons chose a 343 American in '67. There were 55 American 440s purchased with the 343, 58 in Rogue format. Seven American ragtops had the 343, the convertible having ascended from 440 to Rogue trim level for '67. The only year the 343 was available in the American was 1967, the final year for the convertible variant. It didn't matter much to AMC that the American was being re-emphasized back to homely status; their star for '68 was the new Javelin coupe and plenty of those would be bought with a 343.

The tide of fashion was turning against convertibles; fewer wanted them, and there were those rollover safety concerns as well. Like other cars sold in North America, the American was ready to be federalized for '67, with changes directed at clean air and safety. AMC's newish I6s and V8s were already emissions-clean for the time being, but American did adopt an energy-absorbing collapsible steering column, a more crash-friendly steering wheel, extra interior padding, four-way hazard flashers, and locking seatback latches on 2-door variants.

American switched from a strip speedo to circular faces for '67. A large-sized speedo appeared smack-dab in the center, just as in the '58 American, with fuel and coolant temp gauges on either side and turn signals outwards of them. There were warning lights for when

This is a '67 Marlin with 2bbl 232 I6/column-shift automatic power team. It is currently one of only two Marlins in Sweden (courtesy Johan Lindersson).

either battery charge or oil pressure got critical, but there were also omissions. The 5-digit odometer went around the clock every 100,000 miles, but there was no tripmeter that one could reset for each journey to help make notes and keep tabs on gas mileage, a common act for econofiends.

The American's vacuum-operated windshield wipers and lack of a parking brake warning light were harder to live with as frugality measures. Electric wipers and a parking brake warning light were optional. Therein lay the philosophy distinction between U.S. and imported small cars. In size and power the American would have matched up with a Peugeot 504, Triumph 2000, Rover 2000, etc. Even then it was a hard comparison because even these Citroën DS league executive cars would be outgunned by AMC's 232. However, the American lacked the classy chassis and standard fitments of these imports.

In truth, one could option up a Rogue to overcome the base American's poverty fixings, and still have a healthy saving over a luxo European import. If one was swearing at, instead of by, the AMC 3-speed manual, then the 3-speed automatic overcame that irksome non-synchro first. The automatic also gave the performance benefit of torque amplification over the manual, with minimal gas mileage penalty. Auto was available on those imports, but it stymied their small-displacement engines, and the Citroën DS's semi-auto seemed like a stepping stone to the real automatic which AMC already had.

American also offered a very sound a/c system. The optional aircon outlet grille was nicely faired into the lower, middle part of the dash, with associated control panel underneath. The 3 large swivel a/c vents were the kind one would see on a senior 1963–66 AMC car. Out of the imports, the Toyota Corona, of shovel-nose fame, had an optional factory a/c system that was good, but placed its 3 vents on the passenger glove-box door — not ideal for air distribution, and a sign that the imports were behind the eight ball in the world of climate control.

With American the good stuff was designed in, not added on, and since a/c needs stiffer front springs and cooling system upgrades, a factory system made more sense than a dealer-installed aftermarket unit. Indeed, be grateful for what came standard on a '68 American 220. The bounty included an ashtray, door armrests, padded sun visors and glove box. OK, there was no cigarette lighter and the stock bench seating plus rubber floormats were unglamorous, but if one were duck hunting, wall-to-wall carpeting would be ruined by muddy boots.

Once out on the highway, looking for adventure, the little imports seemed born to be mild. American had a psychedelic rainbow of 128 to 225 bhp, with the top option in '68 being the 4-barrel 290 V8. However, American was still the sensible one in 1968; AMC offered the cheapest U.S.-produced wagon, and American adopted those federally mandated side marker lights: more visible meant more safety at night. Stylewise the sedan's roof contour was slightly sleeker and the rear window was now flat. A squared-off sedan C pillar and altered grille were also effected.

On uptrimmed American 440s and Rogues, new stainless steel decoration highlighted the car's profile between fender arches and beltline, commencing at the front amber side marker and finishing at the rear red one. No 343, no convertible, and in '69, no American! For 1969 the American was redesignated "American Motors Rambler." Going into '69 the American/Rambler seemed remnant-like. The only model in AMC land that lacked the company's flush-fitting safety door handles, it looked quite sad sitting on blackwalls with base tinfoil hubcaps, and to top it all off, it was deemed Rambler!

The 155 bhp 2-barrel 232 I6, with air filter decal proudly stating the longevity and extra smoothness coming from 7 main bearings. Power steering pump and a/c compressor are items drawing power from this 232 (courtesy Johan Lindersson).

Surely only old people who cheered when Edsels ran out of gas would be impressed by the name Rambler. Regardless, the compact was improved for '69, taking on legally required front outboard shoulder seat belts and head restraints. The head restraints were useful if one paid the extra $216 for the 232/automatic power team, because by econo standards that I6 was fiery and could get a pensioner into the 18s ... with whiplash! Plus, as a sign of how devilish the American had become post–Romney, one couldn't order disk brakes on I6s, not even the tire-frying 145-horse 232.

The '69 American did have an alternator with transistor regulator as standard; so too a new translucent battery case. It was the final year for the American, but AMC had something special up its sleeve. True, there was plenty of room under the hood for the 199/232 and more. Preston Honea's "Kraft Rambler" 418-cube American showed how much more. This car's motor would have given that little old lady from Pasadena a heart attack, featuring quad carbs, Isky 505-A camshaft, transistorized ignition and a final drive ratio that allowed the American to hit the 8,200 rpm redline in top when crossing the ¼ mile.

SC/Rambler—From Economy Car to Super Car

By the late 1960s every Detroit automaker wanted a halo Super Car. Super Cars represented the ultimate performance vehicles one could order up, all the finest hardware a company offered in the one car. To be a real Super Car a special kind of speed was required, acceleration so explosive that an Allstate Insurance man would spontaneously combust at the thought of the sizable insurance premium he could slap on your chariot. That was pretty fast, and since AMC was a latecomer to this speed hedonism concept, they called on a specialist.

AMC knocked on the door of Hurst Performance Products and asked for something special. It had to be memorable: in 1968 Hayden Proffit ran a Rebel "Funny Car" that set records at 6 different drag strips. AMC's chosen base was the humble American; they took this iconic econobox to Hurst and told them to come up with a stock car. The "stock car" terminology begat the "SC" part of the new '69 SC/Rambler. Specifically, AMC wanted their hot American ready to roll in the NHRA's (National Hot Rod Association) F/Stock class, feeling this would be a good showcase for the best of AMC.

That's exactly what the SC/Rambler, or Scrambler to use its street moniker, was. Hurst subsidiary Hurst Performance Research Inc. took the most serious American Motors parts and bolted them onto the American in Hurst's new facility near Detroit. All the exciting stuff from AMC's 1968 AMX 390 2-seater sports car was shared with the American. AMX was Javelin-derived, and Javelin was American-based, which made Scrambler a Vette's worst nightmare, according to the law of transitivity.

The Scrambler didn't much care for laws like speed limits, or for fashionable good taste, given the way it was liveried. However, the most revered fast cars usually have wild plumage. The first thing that caught the eye on Scrambler was likely to be a contest between the Rambler's body decals and hoodscoop. The original plan was to homologate Scrambler for F/Stock, which meant 500 cars, and those first 500 were hard to miss.

The color scheme for the Scrambler was red, white and blue. This was very patriotic, and the style was reminiscent of the similarly decorated Dodge "Thunder Charger" featured in the 1967 NASCAR-oriented movie called *Thunder Alley*, starring Fabian. However, AMC was justified in using the look because their logo had red, white and blue, plus they were American Motors, after all. The Scrambler's profile was dominated by red: American Flag Red covered three-quarters of the side down to mid-wheelarch level. The color block was outlined with black pinstriping.

Marlin's vinyl trim seemed to flow over the exterior like Bosco chocolate syrup. This Marlin was originally purchased new at a Florida dealer called "Clearwater Rambler" on October 16, 1967 (courtesy Johan Lindersson).

Down the center of the

Marlin always shared the Rambler senior-style dashboard, including the new-design Rebel/Ambassador '67 molding. However, '67 Marlin enjoyed the sporty distinction of circular instrument faces. The a/c on this column-shift automatic car is an aftermarket unit (courtesy Johan Lindersson).

car AMC went one better than racing stripes, sanctioning a 12-inch-wide arrow in American Flag Blue that started at the hood's leading edge and pointed into the forward-facing hoodscoop. Just before the arrowhead the Scrambler's motor displacement was stated in bold red 6-inch-high script: "390 cu. in." Atop the actual hoodscoop, on each half were the 4-inch script "AIR," also in red letters, so bystanders were left in no doubt what moved the Scrambler, or how fresh air induction would help it move down the ¼ mile. The 12-inch-wide black-pinstriped blue band continued over roof and trunk lid, with a black grille and matte-black rear fascia serving as cosmetic bookends.

The Scrambler's rims were 14 × 6-inch stamped steel items, painted blue and wrapped in Goodyear Polyglas E70 Widetread Redlines. SC/Rambler and Hurst badging was on the front fenders behind the wheel wells and on the rear deck. The interior was relatively reserved, and plush compared to Road Run-

Marlin was always roomy. By 1967 length was 201.5 inches, so AMC wasn't joshing when it said the whole family could be accommodated by the big coupe (courtesy Johan Lindersson).

ner and stripped racer standards. There was full nylon carpeting, and this plus the American vinyl seating surfaces and interior side panel trim were charcoal.

The buckets reclined, which was welcomed, but the red, white and blue headrests were less so. That was the odd thing: at the tail end of the '60s one would have expected people to like how the Scrambler looked, like a Hot Wheels car come to life, or something that would have transported the Beatles to their Yellow Submarine. But no, the public considered the get-up rather extreme. It could be that the silent minority never really liked cars like the Judge or the Dodge Swinger 340, thinking them over-ornamented, but they dared not admit it.

It was easier to voice their umbrage when AMC was at hand, since it was a soft target. The powers that be preferred the sleeper look and bided their time until the '80s monochrome Mustang arrived. However, the Scrambler's mechanical ingredients made it swift enough to make an '82 Mustang look like it was going back to the Model T! The heart of the matter was a 6.4-liter small-block V8 called the "AMX 390." This was the ultimate, most powerful edition of AMC's new V8 produced thus far, making a 1968 debut in the company's swinging 2-seater AMX projectile.

The AMX 390 didn't have tunnel port heads, or the SOHC layout that Ford didn't put into volume production, or a solid lifter format to annoy one at a burger joint drive-through. What it did have was 315 bhp at 4,600 rpm and a confidence-boosting 425 lbs/ft at 3,200 rpm. A cast-iron ohv engine with 10.2 CU and one Carter 4-barrel imbibed the juice. Nothing temperamental that would overheat, and enough torque to keep a 302 Z/28 Camaro off the streets. The small block was pleased as punch to push through its 5,000 rpm redline as one person-handled the happy Hurst console shifter.

That Hurst shifter was attached to the BW T10 4-speed manual, the Scrambler's only gearbox choice. The steering-column-mounted SUN tach instrument counted up to 8 grand, complementing the car's standard 120-mph speedo, allowing shifts to be timed to perfection. Yes, it could take the shift strain: Scramblers came standard with 10.5-inch clutch plate and AMC's Twin-Grip limited slip differential. The shoebox was also delivered with a 3.54 final drive, which limited top speed but complied with the car's mission statement.

OK, it isn't Barry Goldwater's Stetson, but you could wear one in a Marlin. Roy Abernethy gave the order to raise the rear roofline 1 inch when Richard Teague was away on vacation (courtesy Johan Lindersson).

In the right conditions a Scrambler could achieve nigh on 14 seconds flat for the ¼ mile at over 100 mph, and zero to sixty in 6 seconds. Independent testing showed the Scrambler to be at least one-half second quicker to sixty than the final Lamborghini Miura, and to have still been even with the Italian car by 100 mph. "So what?" you say:

Detroit iron was known for being quick off the line; what made the Scrambler special? That would be price: at $2,998 one didn't have to be a third-world despot to own a Scrambler.

AMC not only undercut Lamborghini, Ferrari and Maserati, they also undercut the Big 3, coming up with an American-style Super Car without the killer price. For a whisker under 3 grand, AMC included the low-volume 390 with expensive touches like forged steel crankshaft and connecting rods, special lightweight pistons and tri-metal bearings for the mains and rods. Compared to the 343 V8, the 390 was stiffened at the pan rails. How did they do it for the money? With American Motors one got the same performance for $750 to $1,000 less.

AMC had long undercut the Big 3 on feature and model prices, but the Scrambler must have specially benefitted from the freeze on American styling changes. It cost money to do annual sheet-metal alterations, and such wouldn't make a Scrambler move faster. Model cachet back then also counted for something, in the way badge cachet does today. American Motors would have had trouble charging Super Bee or Road Runner prices, because of the reverence shown to the established players.

At this hour, one could get a GTO, with a mere 2bbl 400! That was fine, since the Goat's reputation preceded it, but AMC had to compete on substance, so each and every Scrambler had to be 100 percent winner, no filler. Thus, the only option that could be lavished on Scrambler was an AM radio, for the princely sum of $61.20. Dual adjustable racing-style rear-view mirrors and vacuum-controlled-valve functional hoodscoop: all included. Tromp the throttle and the Carter carb mixed the gas with outside air. There was no charge for real cold-air induction at American Motors.

Forget grandpa's muscle car with the monster engine, bench front seat and 4-wheel drums; the Scrambler came with the best brakes AMC had on its shelf. The very same Bendix 11.2-inch front disk / 10-inch drum power-assisted failsafe tandem master cylinder braking system that was optional on Ambassador was standard on Scrambler. Indeed, although muscle-car lore was built on the intermediate, it was the compact that was the best home for high performance. Put the same hardware in a car 500 pounds lighter and it will accelerate, brake and steer in superior fashion.

The Scrambler was a great exponent of less-is-more, and in spite of its F/Stock aim it had the goods to be an all-arounder. It borrowed AMX traction bars to limit live axle movement under load, and the part of the chassis floor the rear suspension was attached to was reinforced. Ride settings were firmed up to AMX sports-car standard, and generally the American live axle was positioned off-center to counter acceleration tail squat and braking nose dive. That last feature was designed into American for '64, but it took Scrambler to do something with it.

The Scrambler surprised with the seriousness of its standard spec. AMC gave the multi-colored marvel "fast" manual steering, with a ratio of 20:1 and 4.8 turns lock-to-lock. By '69 the American/Rambler came with manual steering possessing 5.25 turns lock-to-lock, or optional power steering with 4.3 turns. The standard steering was down from the previous 1968's 6 turns, but still felt like trying to change direction on an oil tanker. The power steering was much quicker to respond, but gave the helm little feel. Thus, the Scrambler's steering was relatively quick and the most apt for this instance.

At the time, enthusiasts preferred manual steering for accuracy and enhanced feel. Add this to the Scrambler's E70 tires and something unusual was afoot. Non-boosted steering

Chief stylist Teague suggested moving Marlin onto the longer 118-inch Ambassador platform for '67. This allowed a more graceful, flowing roofline, along with the better proportions of Ambassador's longer hood (courtesy Johan Lindersson).

with the equivalent of 195/70 rubber on a 6-inch-wide rim was atypical for the late '60s. The stock American/Rambler had 4-wheel 9-inch drums with brake-swept area of 254 square inches; the Scrambler moved that number to 371 square inches. Out of the box, the Scrambler meant business.

Scrambler's complete spec gave it an edge over hot Detroit iron of the era, which had a lot of engine, but four on the floor and special brakes were optional. The Scrambler accorded to European practice of having the high-performance version as manual only. In contrast, many drag-strip activists prefer an automatic, and an auto was usually optional on comparable U.S. Super Cars. Thus, the Scrambler was the car one could enjoy on the way to the drag strip, and underlining its road-car credentials, the second batch of 500 Scramblers made had a more restrained exterior.

For 1966 MY American's length was increased to 181 inches. American could now take the new design 232 I6 and a/c under its longer hood. This was also the first year American could be V8 optioned (courtesy Marc Merkle).

Exterior scheme "B" was quieter than "A," with body-length red and blue stripes on the lower part of the profile, so

Top: In '64 the new American started with a 90 bhp flathead 196 I6, but the '69 AMC SC/Rambler's 315-horse premium-fuel 390ci V8 was something else. This special American represented a joint venture between AMC and speed guru Hurst Performance Research, Inc. (courtesy Eddie Stakes). ***Bottom:*** Mies van der Rohe, when commenting on the over-ornamentation of 19th century architecture, said that less is more. AMC didn't subscribe to this thinking with Scrambler, whose exterior graphic scheme "A" was outlandish in the extreme on the first 500 and last 512 Scramblers (courtesy Eddie Stakes).

the user could work that ergonomic Hurst console shifter discreetly. However, the final 512 Scramblers went back to the game "A" exterior, loud colors and all. Such livery made Scrambler easier to spot at speed, which was very important by 1969. At the start of the decade, going slow was cool. Folks were shocked by American's otherworldly fuel economy, recording a winning NASCAR-supervised 51.281 mpg (U.S. gallon) in the 1960 Pure Oil (Company) Economy Trial.

By the late '60s a car showed its prowess with power, not thrift. Take the Baja 500, a grueling Californian desert endurance race: in July 1967's Baja 500, an American raced by Spencer Murray and Ralph Poole completed the event in a record 31 hours. It was just as well Scrambler came with a heavy-duty cooling system, plus NASCAR-style hood tie-downs and locking pins and cables. There are times when a pit crew needs quick and unfettered access to an engine bay. In the desert a vehicle's engine is put through high loads, and axle bearings wear out as churning axles fight fine sand.

The Baja 500 would show what AMC was made of, and for 1969 the company signed up actor James Garner's "American International Racers" (AIR) team under a 3-year contract. American Motors supplied AIR with 10 new Scramblers, which were then rally prepared. Ground clearance was raised — Goodyear tires on 15 × 10-inch rims kept the cars out of ruts — roll cages fitted and the window glass was removed. The engines used were 410 bhp blueprinted versions of the AMX 390, and they were fed by a 44-gallon tank included with each Scrambler.

With a taller-than-stock final drive, these Scramblers could do 140 mph. Eight of the 10 were entered in the passenger car category, the other two were converted to all-wheel drive and competed in the Experimental class. On June 11, 1969, 7 Scramblers managed to finish the race. Three of the 2-wheel-drive cars made it into the top 5 of their class. The two all-wheel-drive Scramblers managed first and fourth in class, with the winning car piloted by Bob Bondurant and Tony Murphy.

The American's good PR was also added to when the AMC factory team achieved 2nd, 3rd and 5th, plus the Manufacturer's Team Award, in the 1968 Shell 4000 Rally of Canada. Thus, the American started very low-key, and finished with racing glory and glamour. In the '67 model year, Rogue production ran to 4,249 2-door hardtops and 921 convertibles; numbers held steady at 4,765 hardtops in '68. In American's final year, 3,543 Rogue hardtops were built, with 1,512 hard-core Scramblers.

If the full-size Scrambler proves elusive, then the Johnny Lightning model should be more accessible, since over 125,000 have been made. The 23,768 Rogues showed the new path AMC embarked on in the 1967–74 era: more youthful, more oddities, but contrary to management claims, still shadowing larger domestic rivals. This meant the end of the Rambler nameplate. Regardless of how many colors were heaped onto it, the name didn't spell sexy. Thus, the Rambler brand died with the American in '69. On the day of June 30, 1969, the final Rambler left Kenosha; 4.2 million had been built since 1950. However, the American would return in altered form ... with a sting in its tail!

CHAPTER 3

Being One of the Big 4

A Time to Rebel

Strange coincidences abound in the world of cars. Industrial designer Raymond Loewy was known for restrained economic design that avoided waste. He claimed to have been the first to use the term "compact" in relation to auto design, and American design icons don't come much more famous than Loewy's 1920 Coca-Cola glass bottle, something that is still with us today.[1] On the other side of the ledger, AMC was the first U.S. automaker to make the compact car popular in America. Like Loewy, AMC wasn't big on excess, and so it was with some irony that American Motors applied Loewy's famous Coke-bottle style to the profile of its new '67 intermediate called Rebel.

Could a 3,500-pound mass of steel and glass do justice to the reputations of AMC and Loewy? In its defense, the Rebel was very trim by contemporary intermediate standards, and the range did start with the 145-horse 1bbl 232 / 3-speed manual power team sourced from the American, and no one ever called the American a gas hog. Coke-bottle styling was being used on cars everywhere; AMC was staying abreast of fashion and came up with their first family car with style that rivaled function. It was enough to make passersby do a double take. Was that really a Rambler badge?

It did say Rambler on the leading edge of the hood, and on a trunk-lid plaque: the intermediate-size "series 10" Rebel was from the house of American Motors. Body styles available were extensive: 2- and 4-door sedan, 2-door hardtop and convertible, plus family-duty 4-door wagon. The 2-door sedan had a slim B pillar and was only available in the Rebel's opening '67 model year, its role made practically redundant by the stylish hardtop. The convertible was stylish and short-lived too.

A victim of federal safety regulations, and public taste that increasingly favored closed-top motoring, the Rebel convertible was available in 1967 and 1968 only. In 1967 the ragtop's availability was limited to the upscale SST trim line, a position it shared with the hardtop. As per Rambler tradition, the Rebel undercut its Big 3 rivals across the board, and the Rebel SST convertible followed suit. The AMC ragtop was a rare bargain in that only 1,686 '67s were made, and it came with a powered top and a glass rear window.

Trim levels for the Rebel started with the basic 550, went through the 770 and finished with the SST, which was exclusive to the hardtop and ragtop initially. In the convertible's swan-song '68 MY, the open-top Rebel was available in 550 spec starting at $2,736 in I6 form, and peaked in V8 SST guise for $2,999. The latter was the most expensive Rebel made by AMC,

The 1970 Rebel Machine was AMC's high-performance followup to the '69 Scrambler. Being based on the intermediate Rebel with mechanical upgrades, "The Machine" could be classified as an American muscle car or "Super Car" (courtesy Tom Guarr).

and 1968 would be the last time an American Motors designed ragtop was produced. A total of 1,200 1968 Rebel ragtops ran out the door, 377 of which were 550 trim cars, and the remaining 823 SSTs.

Whichever Rebel one selected, Rambler's family car now rode on a longer wheelbase, up from the Classic's 112 to 114 inches. The Rebel's length was also a couple of inches up on its 1966 predecessor. A 2-door hardtop had a length of 197 inches, width of 78.4 inches and height of 53.5 inches, weighing in at 3,500 lbs with manual transmission and no options like a/c. This AMC upsizing put pressure on the Rambler braking hardware, the stock 9-inch drums having the same 254.4-sq-in swept area as in '63. Thus, judicious use of the standard 3-speed manual column shift brought welcome engine braking in mountain road driving.

Front disks could have been specified, but in the last years of the '60s the Big 3 were getting the public used to the idea of power front disks, so the Rebel's standard non-power drums, even by 1970, rubbed the consumer's brake linings the wrong way. This plus standard vacuum wipers showed the gulf between AMC and the Vengeful 3. Thus, at first glance the Rebel may have appeared better priced than its rivals, but a typical showroom Rebel ordered the way Joe Public wanted was closer priced. In action an automatic Rebel hardtop with base 232 took a casual 17-plus-second saunter to sixty, topping out around 95 mph. Fuel economy on regular with 3.15 rear gears was 14 to 19 mpg.

So Rebel didn't compensate with incredible gas mileage, but there were reasons to stick with the six; for starters, try easy servicing. There was so much room around the 232 in the Rebel engine bay, one could really stand in there with the motor! Thinking of cars with hard-to-get-at spark plugs and firewall-buried distributors was enough to put a smile on the dial; sensible Mr. Rambler knew a car couldn't move fast in a shop. Weight distribution was also commendable thanks to the 232, with the hardtop equaling 53.4/46.6 percent. It made sense to order the heavy-duty suspension with firmer springs and shocks that cost $7.80, as well as a front swaybar because I6 cars didn't come delivered with one.

Options on the 232 Rebels were limited: one couldn't have a 4-speed or $90.60 power front disks, or non-power disks for that matter. Such items were reserved for Rebel V8s over the entire 1967–70 run. True, AMC was on an economy drive, and with declining market share in the Abernethy years saw it strive for belt-tightening. On the "To Do" list was a reduction in ordering permutations, and a target of cutting operating costs by $27 million in 1967. There was also a wish to bolster the AMC dealer network and increase the number of dealers.

So a 3-speed manual and 155 bhp 2bbl 232 were the pinnacle of excitement for I6 drivers. Obviously anyone wanting real fire in the belly would have optioned the 200-pony 290 and taken things from there. The extra could be harnessed thanks to AMC's newly introduced senior-car-line rear suspension. The torque tube was deceased; long live the Rebel's new 4-trailing-arm link, coil-sprung rear end with torque arms and Detroit's ubiquitous live axle. The front end stayed loyal to American Motors' unequal-length control arms and high-mount coils.

AMC's dashboard molding could have used a style update, and this was done for '67 with a safety dash that grouped all instruments and HVAC controls within a hooded binnacle. Very neat, and one could take in the strip speedo's entire 0–120 mph sweep through

Rebel Machine's 340 bhp 390ci V8 was unique to Machine, and would prove to be the most powerful motor ever fitted to an AMC production car. Compared to the normal 325 bhp '70 390, Machine's motor had a special medium-rise intake manifold, freer-flowing exhaust manifold and special heads (courtesy Tom Guarr).

the 10-and-2-o'clock spokes of the 3-spoke AMC sports steering wheel. Vertical heater and defroster slider-type levers were on the left, and in air conditioned cars, two round circular swivel vents were in the upper middle of the dash, with audio speaker grille to the right above the glove box.

AMC introduced an energy-absorbing collapsible steering column across the board in '67. The Rebel incorporated this, and the chance of the newly optioned 4bbl 343 V8. This power plant had 280 bhp and cost $90.65. It had a jolly crescent outline decal with a checkered flag sitting above the numerals 343 within a fez-shaped frame. There was nothing square about the new Rebel, but American Motors still worked in down-to-earth goodies. The ceramic-coated exhaust was a longtime AMC industry exclusive, as was deep-dip rust-proofing.

Yes, Rambler Deep Dip made one look askew at Impala salesmen wanting to charge extra for rust protection. By 1968 AMC introduced flush-fitting, recessed safety door handles on all its cars, except American, and Rebel had non-slip footwell pedal covers. All the above proved that even pipe smokers can be groovy! The new Rebels were among the 229,058 cars American Motors chimed out in 1967. The Rebel was sharing factory space with the luxo Ambassador, specifically the West Assembly Line in Kenosha, Wisconsin.

The Rebel was also built in Canada at the AMC Brampton (Ontario) plant, as well as overseas. The Rebel was assembled in various countries, where it was sold as a large luxury car. At the time Europe had few cars in the Rebel's size, power and weight class, so Rebel was over there taking on the pricey European makes. Back home, Rebel only carried the Rambler name in its first model year, but overseas Rambler Rebel had no marketing drawbacks. Indeed, away from home, American cars had a special cachet due to rarity and were priced accordingly.

In the UK market a new '56 Rambler Six priced out at 2,071 pounds sterling, while a Jaguar 2.4 Mk I sedan was just 1,431 pounds sterling. These were the days when Detroit made the biggest and most powerful passenger car engines in the world, so U.S. cars had the edge in acceleration and outright speed. When it came to power assists, climate control, automatic chokes and other modern conveniences, Detroit was still setting the pace by the late '60s. Thus, even though American Motors was battling in 10th place in America in 1967, in foreign markets the Rebel was still the epitome of the modern mass-produced U.S. sedan.

Citroën had France's big car, De Gaulle's DS; Renault did not, so for those wealthy few on the continent who didn't want an Opel Admiral or Mercedes 250S, Renault assembled the Rebel under license in Haren. Renault had performed the same licensed arrangement with the previous Classic, which it sold and promoted through certain Renault outlets as the Renault Rambler. At that moment, and continuing on into future times, Belgium was something of a hub for the popularity of American cars in Europe.

Along the same lines the Rebel was also assembled by VAM (Vehiculos Automotores Mexicanos) in Mexico City, and by AMI (Australian Motor Industries) in Port Melbourne. In keeping with France, and even more so, laws in countries like Mexico, Australia and South Africa favored local vehicle assembly and high local content from domestic parts suppliers, and were anti-imports. So imported luxury cars were discouraged via import quotas and/or stiff tariffs. Naturally, the affluent minority in such countries didn't buy Rebels with three on the tree, 4 wheeled drums and hose-out interiors; neither did many American buyers back home.

A Change with Chapin

In July 1967 *Mechanix Illustrated* did an interview piece with AMC's new CEO, Roy D. Chapin Jr. Chapin succeeded Roy Abernethy, becoming the company's boss on January 9, 1967, at the age of 51, formally stating the 1964–66 period of direct competition with the Insurmountable 3 was over. A new strategy of speaking to the atypical U.S. buyer was instituted, but AMC employed a different niche model compared to foreign automakers.

The Europeans and Japanese catered to niches outside the Big 3's orbit, areas they weren't interested in covering. American Motors chose instead to offer differentiated models within existing recognized car-size classes, playing to their strengths of quality and frugalness in the U.S. idiom. Searching for ways to promote AMC without breaking the mold or bank, American Motors became an early exponent of the special edition model. The new '67 Rebel was promoted with a genuinely limited run of 3 upscale-spec Rebel theme wagons.

The wagons were cosmetically different and carried the names Briarcliff, Mariner and Westerner, each with a visual get-up and sales availability that reflected their names. Briarcliff was sold in the east and southern areas, with Matador Red exterior paint and simulated black camera grain side-panel trim, plus regal decorative medallions. The Rebel Briarcliff wagon had a black antelope grain vinyl interior; 400 units were produced. For coastal areas, the Rebel Mariner wagon had a nautical air.

If Captain Birdseye had a wagon, it would be a Mariner wagon. This Rebel came with Barbados Blue exterior and imitation bleached teakwood effect panels, complemented by narrow black horizontal stripes and a shipshape anchor medallion. Inside, landlubbers enjoyed a two-tone blue-hued cabin, with anchor and star motif decorations for dark blue

The first 1,000 Machines had a red, white and blue color scheme, which then became a $75 option. Many at the time considered the tricolor livery a trifle garish (courtesy Tom Guarr).

suede seat bolster panels, white piping and broad horizontal pleated inserts of medium blue antelope grain vinyl. Six hundred Rebel Mariners set sail from Kenosha.

Finally, the regional Rebel wagons were completed by the Midwest and southwest Westerner. Five hundred of these wagons were sold west of the Mississippi River. On the outside the Westerner sat in the corral with Frost White paint and simulated tan leather panels, plus pony express medallion. Inside the Westerner moseyed into town with Stallion Brown vinyl on the seats and door panel trim, which according to AMC resembled richly tooled leather, and white antelope-grained vinyl. Since it was vinyl trim, the antelope was left to play at home on the range, without a discouraging word from early environmentalists.

The regional nameplates were placed on the rear fender, with model medallions on the C pillar. On the mechanical side all three came with the same hardware: a 200 bhp 2bbl 290 V8, automatic, power steering, power drum brakes, power tailgate window, pushbutton radio, heavy-duty suspension, the new three-spoke sports steering wheel, fender-to-fender carpeting of the cargo area, AMC's unusual lockable hidden compartment, adjustable reclining seats and the expected roof rack. So these wagons were truly loaded, and the 343 was optional for those into serious wagoning.

It was little surprise that the Mariner proved most popular out of the run of 1,500 regional wagons. As holiday areas, the Pacific and Florida coastal areas were places a wagon would be needed, and where people would have the leisure time to notice a special ride, one that appealed to certain buyer tastes. Selling cars was becoming more profile-targeted by the late '60s. Before, it was a simple case of two cars in the garage to go with the two TV sets and refrigerator; now, both buyer and car company had an agenda.

A non-red, white and blue Machine, in Big Bad Green with flat black hood section (paint code 8A) present on non-tricolor Machines. This Rebel Machine spent 20 years stored in a barn before finding freedom (courtesy David Durst).

AMC and others were livening up their products. The Rebel name said it all: Classic sounded conservative and staid, but Rebel implied wrestling a bear, climbing a cliff and hang-gliding all in one day! Forget about economy Rambler; Rebel was the car for you, it was the car for today, as AMC's 1967 print ads gently suggested: "The 1967 American Motors — Rebel — The Now Cars." After reading that suggestive ad copy, one gazed at the aggressively driven square-jawed Rebel hardtop with road stones and dust flying. Mobil Economy Runs were out of sight and out of mind.

This was part of Mr. Chapin's plan, too: differentiated youth and a new top trim designation, SST. SST — Super Sport Touring, Super Sonic Transport, you call it — sat above the 550/770 and initially covered just the hardtop and convertible. With SST one received sports-type equipment as standard, the 200 bhp 2bbl 290 V8, and the stiffer springs and shocks of the HD suspension which lifted spring rates from 118/96 lbs/inch to 135/110 lbs/inch front/rear. AMC's reclining bucket seats with front fold-down armrest and "Goodyear Wide Tread" tires were also part of the SST experience.

SST could be combined with Rebel's deluxe trim, which comprised adjustable headrests, checkerboard fabric and vinyl seat bolsters, plus two DPL-style throw pillows, adding woodgrain inlay for the 3-spoke steering wheel. Choose the optional 4-speed and premium-fuel 343 and you would think that was it for a Rebel hardtop, but more lay at your local AMC dealership. Beyond factory options, there were dealership performance kits like a sports camshaft with competition lifters, to answer criticism that normal 290/343 valve-train components were too lightweight beyond 5,000 rpm, leading to undignified valve float.

Dealer kit goodies also included a cold-air intake and a madcap 4.44 final drive! Even more far out was the SST's drag-racer-style dashboard-mounted tachometer, a small circular add-on perched at 2 o'clock, ideally in the driver's line of vision and optional on V8 Rebels alone. Extroverts could also add a body-length racing stripe, a broad center flanked by two narrower sections that started at the hood's leading edge, went over the roof and trunk to rear bumper level on the driver's side.

The console-shifter-only SST could be a tiger with stripe decal. The driver-side SST grille badge classed it as a sports intermediate; the NHRA-AHRA classed a Rebel SST 343 in E/SA, G/SA drag-racing categories. In 1967 the drag strip was the place to be. It was a sign of the times that extreme 4.44 rear gears might live on the family Rambler. There was good sales publicity to be had on the ovals and the strip; thus AMC Performance Activities Manager Carl Chackmakian set up a $1 million deal with Grant Industries president Grant McCoon.

The result of the agreement was the Grant Rambler Rebel Funny Car for NHRA X/S Experimental Stock and Super Experimental Stock classes, to show AMC could swing with the best on the ¼ mile. To the car's credit, American Motors' own small block was utilized; the 343 V8 was bored and stroked out to 438 cubes, courtesy of Amos Saterlee. The car had a 122-inch wheelbase and a chrome moly steel tube chassis. Using a GMC 6/71 supercharger and Enderle fuel injection with 1,200 bhp on alcohol and nitro methane made for an 8.11-second pass at 180.85 mph!

With the public's attention gained, Grant Industries brought out the 1968 Grant Rebel SST in AMC racing colors of red, white and blue, and there was also the '68 King Rebel blown-fuel Hemi-powered beast. The 1967 Grant Rambler Rebel was initially driven by "Banzai" Bill Hayes, and then by Hayden Proffit. This early car was red with blue racing stripe and white stars. It was Proffit who clocked the 8.11-second run, and went on to drive the '68 Grant Rebel SST. The Ted McOsker–owned King Rebel was driven by Ron Rosenberry and achieved 9.58 seconds at 148.02 mph.

Having achieved their profile-raising objective, American Motors got out of drag racing at the end of 1968. Interest was accumulating in pony cars and the SCCA Trans Am road circuit racing that involved them, so that's where AMC decided to place its racing dollars. This kind of activity seemed to be taking over from drag racing as a news story. Rebel's tale continued with a promotional hardtop coupe called the Rebel Raider. The 1969 Rebel Raider 2-door was a regional hardtop; 300 were made and sold in the New York and New Jersey areas, coinciding with the New York City Auto Show. Like the regional wagons, the 2bbl 290 V8 / auto power team was standard issue, along with black upholstery and black carpeting; black was also the color chosen for the front grille and vinyl roof.

The Rebel Raider also came with a sports steering wheel, AM radio, power steering and power brakes for $2,699. However, the most illuminating aspect of the Raider was its exterior color selection. The Rebel Raider was the first model to feature the famous AMC Big Bad colors. The outlandish shades of Big Bad Green, Orange and Blue made their debut on the Raider, and were then introduced on the AMC Javelin and AMX in mid–'69 MY. AMC was something of a Big 3 corporate raider of its own, carving into view with its successful new pony car, which provided money for freshening up the Rebel.

For the 1970 model year, Rebel received its first major restyle, and the SST trim level was now available on 4-door sedan and wagon. For '70, Rebel sedan and hardtop were two inches longer, had a new grille with black plastic insert, new-look full-width rear bumpers on sedan and hardtop, and new roof panels on sedan, hardtop and wagon. The hardtop now had a reverse–C pillar outline, and the wagon's luggage rack was longer that year, necessitating the roof change. As usual on Rebel wagon, choosing the optional 3rd row of rear seating provided the side-opening tailgate as standard equipment.

Rebel sedan and hardtop had different rear-fender sheet metal, with the former afforded reshaped rear doors. The 232 I6-powered Rebels now moved around more gracefully thanks to a standard front swaybar. Yes, AMC was still loyal to vent windows, but was that a bad thing? Domestic car practice ensured that if one didn't choose a/c,

The Machine's hood-mounted tach was partly due to necessity. There was no place in Rebel's strip speedo instrument display for a rev counter. Liberal usage of Machine decals underlined the humor of the era (courtesy David Durst).

then the intermediate buyer was left with two fresh-air vents to admit cool air, which weren't effective. In a non-a/c intermediate, vent windows were your friend.

The Rebel's dashboard molding was subtly altered for '70, the instrument hood extended further to shield gauges from obscuring sunlight, and the former circular dash vents were now rectangular with vertical slats. The standard 3-speed column manual was all synchro, but somewhat wasted on the bucket-seat-equipped SST hardtop. It was more logical to order the console-mounted Shift Command auto on the SST hardtop, since autos had better resale and the console shifter now had a neat wild-west pistol-handle-shaped grip.

By the start of the '70s, what AMC could afford to do was starting to be limited by its size. What changes were rolled out for its intermediate were modest next to what Chevrolet could do on a Chevelle, or Ford could work with its Torino, but the smallest member of the Big 4 strove on. Rebel's side structure was stronger on the sedan and hardtop for 1970, and the SST's buckets endeavored to introduce integrated head restraints that didn't block out all the rearward vision, which was an industry problem at the time.

By '70 MY, one could get SST trim on hardtop, sedan and wagon, with simulated exterior woodgrain trim on the SST wagon. With Rebel, one was also getting an intermediate a little smaller and lighter compared to Detroit's big players. A 1970 Rebel measured 199 inches in length, with width and height at 77.2 and 54.5 inches respectively. A 3-speed manual 145 bhp 232 hardtop weighed only 3,110 lbs, a V8 automatic wagon 3,310 lbs, according to AMC's manufacturer info. Trunk capacity on the '70 Rebel was down from 18.2 to 18 cu ft.

The only heavy thing about the '70 Rebel was its new 325-horse 4bbl 390ci V8 engine option. The 390 was more motor than the Rebel needed, or Consumers Union would recommend. No, the sensible choice was a wagon with the newly introduced 2bbl 304 210 bhp V8, but there would be plenty of time to be sensible later. Unknown to most was that 1970 would be the pinnacle of performance, not just for AMC but for Detroit in general. Pollution controls had been knocking on the door since 1966, an air pump here, a transmission-controlled spark there, but the trend to 1970 had always been up.

Emissions-mindful cams and recurved ignition aside, 1970 still had premium-fuel V8s and high compression ratios, but it was all about to end. The 1970 model year was the peak for power outputs and the '71 Boss 302 Mustang would remain a prototype. It wouldn't be until the mid–'90s that a 300 net horsepower small-block V8 would again be available. In 1970, AMC made its most powerful engine ever offered in one of its production cars. The special 390 sat in a unique 2-door hardtop, a swan song for the U.S. Super Car called ... The Machine!

Up with That Rebel Machine

In Detroit, sporty cars had 2 doors only; the concept of a sports 4-door was alien. American Motors planned an ultimate Rebel intermediate, originally intended to be a real street sleeper. In June '68 AMC was thinking of a black Rebel 2-door hardtop with black wheels, like the '65 Black Marlin show car. There was going to be minimal ornamentation, no stripes, no scoops, nor aerofoil wing like the Super Car opposition, but it's always an automaker's prerogative to change its mind. When the 1970 AMC Rebel Machine hardtop made its

The Rebel Machine was a chariot that could get one into the 14s. Like Scrambler it was jointly developed with Hurst, although the latter's name was left out of media hype. The Machine faced stiff competition from very powerful Big 3 rivals (courtesy David Durst).

debut on October 25, 1969, at the NHRA's World Championship Drag Race Finals, held in Dallas, Texas, the new coupe was highly motivated and decorated.

In the tradition of Scrambler and its racing cars, the Machine was presented in red, white and blue. The main exterior color was Frost White, paint code 25A; the central hood section was Electric Blue, coded 6B, with contrasting red, white and blue bunting. Red and blue stripe reflective graphic decals were utilized, with the three colors finishing across the trunk lid, and being repeated at the base of the front grille aperture. The Scrambler spirit lived on in the Machine's interior, albeit in more discreet armrest form among the 284,326 1967–70 Rebels made.[2]

The Machine's black interior contained a standard console-mounted 4-speed BW T10 manual transmission, and thus, standard bucket seats. There was also a center cushion and armrest included for the front buckets, with said vinyl armrest in red, white and blue. This exterior and interior combo applied to the first 1,000 Machines constructed, whereupon the "Red-White-and-Blue Machine Package" became a $75 option. Frost White was still the standard no-cost base color, but other solid colors were available past that first 1,000, and the Machine's center hood section was now flat black, paint code 8A.

Three Machines were known to be made with the Frost White exterior and flat black hood section, a particular collector rarity. After the initial 1,000, the Machine's red, white and blue striping was dropped from the stock equipment list, but the use of stylized "Machine" script decals continued. Such "Machine" decals were exhibited on the front fenders behind

The Rebel range was stylistically updated for '70 MY. Two-door hardtops gained a reverse-slope C pillar. Note the 15-incher "Machine" sport slot rims, optionally available across the 1970–72 AMC line, except for Gremlin and Hornet (courtesy David Durst).

the wheel wells, on the passenger side of the trunk lid, and on the interior's passenger-side dashboard. *Hot Rod* magazine didn't think this was too classy, saying the Machine had more identity markers than Peter Fonda's bike in *Easy Rider*, but today all the trimmings add to the Machine's collectibility.

Standard equipment on the Machine was a 340-horsepower 390ci V8, the ultimate example of AMC's small block in bhp. The motor distinguished Machine from other Super Car intermediates. First, it was the only one using a lightweight small block. Second, at 3,817 lbs, the Machine had a power-to-weight ratio equal to other Super Cars, and unlike some that started with tepid base engines, the Machine only came with one choice: the best!

The Machine's output was quoted in gross horsepower (1970 would be the last year the industry collectively stuck to this measure), and came in at 5,100 rpm. Maximum torque was 430 lbs/ft at 3,600 rpm, compared to the 325 bhp 390 one would find in an AMX of 1970 vintage. The 340 bhp edition was unique to the Machine and had a new medium-rise intake manifold and new exhaust manifold, plus special heads. Both versions of the 390 had 0.45-inch valve lift on the intake and exhaust sides with a 266-degree camshaft. Due to stricter pollution control the Machine's 390 and AMC's other hi-po engines were down from a 10.2:1 compression ratio to 10.0:1.

The stock Autolite 4bbl carb on Machine was a 690-cfm unit, and for those who only used their car at the drag strip, or didn't fear smog inspections, there was an AMC dealer-listed high-performance "Emissions Devil" kit that involved heavier-duty valve springs and dampeners, 0.477-inch valve lift and a 302-degree camshaft. That took the 390 beyond 340 ponies, and so did H.L. Shahan. It was common during the muscle car's heyday for the engines of cars submitted for magazine testing to be breathed on, or hotted up.

Machines called in at H.L. Shahan's speed shop in Tulare, California, prior to testing, where heads were shaved 0.030 inch to raise compression, the carburetor was re-jetted, ignition timing altered and the transmission linkage inspected. This was all rather sedentary compared to the staged exercises masterminded by Jim Wangers. Let's face it: no GTO available to the public could do 0–60 mph in 4.6 seconds, but it was a nice dream. Thus, we can say the mid–14 quarter mile the Machine achieved in press was slightly optimistic, but rely on no worse than high 14s. The Machine was as swift as the Mercedes 300 SEL 6.3, but only cost $3,475.

Even if one added a few options — by choice, not necessity, because the Machine was mechanically complete — American Motors delivered a bargain. As always with AMC, the Machine came standard with stuff optional on rivals, and still cost less. Along with standard 4 on the floor (the Judge GTO started with 3), the Machine had a Borg & Beck semi-centrifugal dry-type heavy-duty clutch. No need to pay extra for a dual exhaust system or the Bendix 11.2-inch front disk / 10-inch rear drums found on AMC's best cars of the era. No extra cost for the handling pack either.

The Machine rallied forth with 0.94-inch front and 0.95-inch rear swaybars, and 1.19-inch-diameter telescopic sport shocks. The Rebel's normal front unequal length control arm, rear 4-link trailing arm, and 4-coil layout was retained, but said coils were stiffened to the tune of 141 and 125 pounds per inch front and rear respectively. The Machine had raided the AMC parts shelf, and found the Rebel wagon's rear springs to be very acceptable. Connecting all this to the road were new-design 15 × 7-inch "Mag-Styled" steel rims, with tires being top-shelf E60 Goodyear Polyglas white-lettered items.

The 15-inch "Machine" rims had oversize brake-cooling slots and were optional on AMC's big cars during 1970–72; they were not available only on Hornet and Gremlin. These rims had a press-on one-use trim ring designed not to fly off in the heat of battle, and therein lies their problem. The rings can be a trap for mud and debris, which in wet climes can hide and promote rust that will weaken the rim. In addition, a set of these authentic 15-inch rims goes for big money due to rarity, something to consider when assessing the completeness of a Machine for restoration.

A couple of items expected from a Super Car of this era were functional fresh-air induction and a hood-integrated tach; the Machine had both, standard. Both items lent credence to the consensus that the Machine was a more refined Super Car than the Scrambler. The hoodscoop was wide and low with two forward-facing openings to admit cool, dense air. Floor the gas pedal and the usual vacuum-activated solenoid opened the scoop flap to let in that sweet air. There was a rubber underhood gasket sealing the air cleaner housing off from warm engine-bay air.

The rear part of the scoop, in the driver's line of vision, had a raised, blended-in housing for the 8-grand tach. This unit was OK as such devices went, but as expected, it could fog up and at night the illumination wasn't well placed. Fun, but not especially functional, hood tachs reflected the fact that family intermediates weren't designed with sports instrumentation in mind. It was up to the new wave of pony cars to put the tach in the instrument cluster.

With equipment, the Machine's stock HD cooling system was welcome; the space-saver spare, not so much. There were mechanical options that could enhance your Machine. The $105.30 power steering was an essential, since the standard manual steering involved an awkward 6 turns lock-to-lock; power steering dropped this to 3.2 turns. Power assistance denied the driver road feel, but 6 turns was impossible for sports maneuvers on a big car.

Unlike its rivals, AMC didn't permit manual steering with the quick ratio, although the popularity of same was waning as most went for power steering.

Even as late as 1970–71 there were some old-school types that were ordering their cars the old-fashioned way, with zero trim, manual steering, non-boosted brakes, no a/c, and the most powerful engine available with trash-can hubcaps. This could be done on the Machine, but most dealers carrying a Machine would have ordered one with the $84.20 power disk front brakes. Final drive ratios were performance oriented, the stock 4-speed car coming with 3.54, and make that 3.15 if the optional automatic was chosen.

The only other factory option was the $10.40 3.91, which was used in magazine tests, but given the 390's torque a shorter ratio may not have helped in the ¼ mile, and an automatic might have been as good as the 4-speed. The 3.91 was too busy for a daily driver, but dealers offered ratios as short as 5.00. From the factory the $43 Dana Twin-Grip limited slip differential maximized traction, and fanatics could go to certain dealers for a no-spin Detroit Locker-type differential. As with the Scrambler, audio was optional; an AM pushbutton radio was $61.60.

The Machine's standard 4-speed came with a Hurst shift linkage, and the same shifter handle length as on AMC AMX and Javelin. As per the Scrambler, the Machine was jointly developed by AMC and Hurst, but by the time the model was released there was no mention of the Hurst connection. Roy Chapin may have declared "Let's go racing," but by the end of 1970, events were overtaking Detroit. There was renewed interest in small cars, and AMC had one of those in 1970. Super Cars were becoming caricatures of themselves: the 1970 Mercury Cyclone Spoiler GT had a stylized "gunsight" grille emblem!

The colorful late–'60s personal car era was coming to an end. Buyers still wanted something sporty, but interest in special mechanical componentry wasn't as great as it used to be. Plus, to be sporty by the early '70s, it wasn't enough to tack hoodscoops onto a brick-shaped intermediate with a hot V8. The underlying shape had to be sexy, which explained the rise of the pony car over the performance intermediate. Intermediates with all the fruit weren't cheap; bang for buck dictated that junior look at a compact-based pony first. Any given power team would yield more in a smaller, lighter car. As champions of value it behooved AMC to have a pony in its corporate stable. The Rebel Machine sold 1,936 or 2,326 units, a disputed figure, but pony cars sold in the tens of thousands, sometimes even more.

But first, an experiment.

AMC's Fab Four

An increasingly sophisticated auto market saw a need to investigate specific model proposals early on; plus, under AMC's post–1966 strategy, the company wanted to test out niche thinking. The upshot of this was American Motors' summer of '66 Project IV cars, a quartet of showcars that indicated where AMC was going. Roy Abernethy was still at the helm at this time, and stated Project IV's more advanced take on consumer taste. This exercise really did show what AMC would be up to for the next 15 years.

First, detailed demographic study would be seen on AMC's Pacer. AMC stood out in Detroit during this time and the ensuing decade, as a company that wanted to know what people wanted ahead of time. GM, Ford and Chrysler in 1966–81 weren't as innovative as in earlier years; they just reacted to negative circumstances, with a lag. Project IV vehicles were smaller than the cars AMC was putting out in 1966. Small wasn't exactly "in" at the time, but it soon would be, and AMC would reassert its Detroit dominance in this area.

One of the Project IV cars was called Cavalier, but there was nothing cavalier in its attitude to design. The Cavalier harked back to Romney's thinking on waste minimization, with interchangeable panels and parts. The right front fender and left rear fender were identical; so were the hood and trunk lid. The front and rear bumpers were the same too. The Cavalier's four doors were exactly the same as well. All this spelled reduced tooling costs, and as the littlest member of the Big 4, that meant something at AMC.

The Cavalier's strong horizontal lines, flat surfaces, minimal overhangs and blockish face were all visual hints to the 1970 AMC Hornet compact. In keeping with Project IV, Cavalier had slim pillars for excellent outward vision, and a concealed rollover bar to fend off feared federal roof strength testing. Project IV's Vixen 2-door fastback appeared subcompact in size, a sleeker precursor of the '70½ AMC Gremlin. The Vixen's proportions suggested a truncated Cavalier, very telling of imminent AMC practice.

Other Vixen qualities were appearance-directed. There were 4 sail-panel-style slots parallel to the C pillar window arch, but these didn't do much to alleviate the rear blind spot. Vixen also had a functional hoodscoop, bright yellow exterior, lattice rims and some exterior panel interchangeability. The fastback's grille, with rectangular trim section, looked like the one introduced on the '75 Hornet. As a visual statement, Vixen wasn't unlike the '79 Spirit fastback. However, the remaining two Project IV show cars were of greater immediate importance to AMC.

Project IV had two heavyweight backers in Roy Abernethy and Detroit financier Robert Evans. Evans purchased 202,000 shares in American Motors, appointing himself chairman in June 1966. These two were foursquare in favor of AMC's having a pony car. The millionth Mustang arrived in 1966 and competitors were scrambling to bring rivals to market. In Project IV it was the AMX II that was relevant to the pony-car cause. It was a study that had risen from the ashes of the Tarpon fastback.

Initially AMC thought it could rustle up something on the cheap using existing chassis and sheet metal building blocks, but early on it was realized this style-conscious segment hungered for something truly fresh! By late 1964 Richard Teague had already directed young AMC designer Robert Nixon to commence work on what would become the AMC Javelin 4-place pony car. AMX II showed what AMC wanted with Javelin. The overall front view reminded of the Buick Riviera, which spelled personal car. Look closely at the nose and there was a resemblance to the Porsche 914; the Javelin would be sporty.

AMX II's profile was rather close to that of the 1964½ Mustang, and that was the target. Other touches on the show car were nice but incidental. AMX II had AMC-style front and side curved glass, spacious trunk and V-shaped rear window to complement the rear deck. A notable safety feature was the tri-colored taillighting: accelerate and it was green, with amber for deceleration and red for braking. AMX II wasn't burdened by exterior trim.

There was an initial plan to make Javelin's unibody in fiberglass. Automotive fiberglass parts specialist Dow Smith Inc. made 3 prototype bodies for the project. However, AMC had concerns over the structural integrity of the plastic bodies, and possible future federal crash testing. The decision to go with a conventional steel unibody meant some modifications, and the body became slightly shorter. To productionize Javelin, it was also decided to substitute easier-to-make front and rear fascias. That said, design boss Teague was pleased with the final result, saying 90 percent of AMX II had made it through. He also expressed the feeling that Javelin was the first AMC vehicle to come through where the designers were 100 percent satisfied with the outcome, seeing no need to redraft.

The project took 18 months from start to finish, with Javelin getting management's green light in April 1966, and a subsequent September 26, 1967, debut to rave reviews. So that was the teenage drive-thru hamburger crowd catered to, but AMC had an upmarket companion model that would take the fight right to Chevrolet's flagship. After a shaky start, the Corvette gained Chevy's small-block V8, respect and the position as America's only volume-produced modern 2-seater sports car, but where there was a will there was AMC.

The remaining member of Project IV was AMX, a show car that had its genesis in an October 1965 direction by Richard Teague to Advanced Design Chief Chuck Mashigan to create a special two-seater. By January 1966 a plastic metallic-orange full-scale mock-up was displayed to the S.A.E. by American Motors' management in Detroit. As with Tarpon, the reception was positive, so Teague requested a functional steel prototype to be created. The AMX show car was hand-built by Vignale in Turin, Italy.

The AMX had the most far-out mindset of Project IV. This was a 2-door 2-seater hardtop coupe with a pair of auxiliary rumble seats and no A pillar! A pillars get in the way of seeing out, and AMC was always looking far into the distance, so AMX did without these front posts. The cantilever roof did have inner structural members that gave rollbar protection. Rumble jump seats were an old prewar concept, until one placed them in this futuristic buggy and called them "Ramble Seats"! These seats were part of AMX's breath of fresh air.

With convertibles on the decline, AMX showed a new way to bring the outdoors indoors with an unusual vent system. The AMX had 3 vent slots on either side of its hood to admit fresh air; with the rear window angled open, this created an effective through flow of air, even with the vent-wing-devoid side windows closed. Plus, the open rear window served as a protective weather awning for those sitting in the snug Ramble Seats. The hood also had 4 canted slots towards the front to aid engine bay heat extraction.

AMX excited in other ways, with shell leather bucket seats, full-length center console and ribbed rocker panels decorated with brushed aluminum. Side exhausts were in vogue at the time, and the Vignale AMX had real dual-exhaust outlets discreetly placed at the rear of the rocker panel just ahead of the rear wheels. The exit rectangle slots were flush. AMX also had the big 15-inch, 5-petal mag rims seen on Cavalier and AMX II. Tires were asymmetrically sized, with the rears being bigger in footprint. The tires had a blue stripe which went with the AMX's profile blue body striping.

The silver-blue metallic AMX had dual gas tanks, with two flush circular gas filler doors on both sail panels. The AMX's visage was conventional, suggesting something that could be easily productionized. There wasn't a smooth nose or concealed headlamps, just a conventional grille. However, the nose was aggressively V-shaped, with headlamps recessed for protection and the round driving lights mounted low in the flush-mount integrated bumpers. A button opened the hatch-style doors, which wrapped into the roof to make for a larger entry/exit opening.

At the rear, AMX had full-width taillights covered by a chrome-appearance metal mesh that turned transparent when the lights were on, letting the red brake lights shine through. As shown in publicity photos with either the petal mags, or AMC's new turbocast wheel covers,

A '68 AMX SCCA B production racer allowed Ike Knupp, Bob Spooner and Dick Durant to be Midwest Champions in 1969, 1970 and 1971 respectively. AMC's Javelin-based 2-seater provided stiff opposition for the plastic Chevy (courtesy George M. Stragand III).

there was a small AMX plaque on the passenger side of the grille. When it came to names, Javelin was a product of AMC's marketing types, found with the aid of computerized questionnaire survey research notes. The pony car was originally to be called Rogue, but that ended up being reserved for upscale American compacts.

There was even an intellectual property tussle because there happened to be an English automobile called Jowett Javelin, but AMC won out. Arriving at the AMX name was much quicker and simpler: Richard Teague thought it up! AMX stood for American Motors Experimental, and the Vignale-built car was the star attraction when it made its debut at the New York International Auto Show in April 1966. It subsequently toured the U.S. and Canada from June 1966, as part of the AMC Project IV cavalcade.

AMX fired up everyone's imaginations; it was the most popular of the Project IV chariots. AMC's Robert Evans was particularly fond of the Vignale AMX and his feeling, shared with all who saw it, was that this was one show car that just had to be made. As a show car, AMX was 179 inches long, 72 inches wide and 48 inches high on a 98-inch wheelbase. All this was much smaller than Mustang; the stats spelled Corvette rival! To make AMX a reality it would have to be Javelin-derived.

The bean-counters broke out the collective abacus and figured AMX could swing it if a truncated version of the Javelin unibody, along with the pony's rear window, trunk lid, taillights and rear bumper, were utilized. In fact, a once-mooted name for AMX was Javelin II, so close were the two cars in the cause of reducing tooling costs. Compromises aside, AMC did unveil the production AMX at the Daytona International Speedway on February 24, 1968.

AMX was a courageous act for little AMC; it was a real two-seater at a time when GM management tolerated the Vette only because of PR. With Ford and Chrysler, the pony car was as far as they wanted to go. The difference between GM and AMC was that everyone at Kenosha was behind the 2-seater. However, the two leaders supporting AMX and Javelin weren't around to see either car released. Roy Abernethy's 5-year tenure as boss was over at the start of '67, and Robert Evans was replaced by William Luneburg as AMC president. Even so, the genie had been let out of the bottle!

Sharpening the Javelin, 1968–70

There were April showers in Detroit when the Mustang was launched in 1964, but the rain only fell on Ford's competitors. Companies like Chevrolet, Pontiac and Plymouth soon launched new or revised cars to compete in the great pony-car derby. The last pony car to join the corral was from Detroit's last independent, AMC. American Motors was working on Javelin while the pony scramble was taking place, and the lag time resulted in their entry's being very refined. AMC's pony had windows that would roll down completely, safety flush-fitting door handles and the chance of reclining seats.

There was a completeness to the Javelin that made Mustang and the GM F-body siblings seem raw. Those companies had more money, most of which was spent on big hi-po motors that thrilled teeny-boppers and excited ad copy writers. On release, the Javelin didn't have this, but it did have the cleanest-looking exterior styling. As with the new '67 AMC senior cars, Javelin was universally judged attractive, even overseas. Oddly, Javelin was completely normal-looking by long-hood/short-deck pony standards, but didn't look like any of the Big 3's stuff.

The Javelin didn't have tunnel port headlamps, but it had flush-fitting chrome bumpers front and rear, plus that unibody. The unibody was at the heart of Javelin; AMC had it, GM did not. The GM Camaro/Firebird had a partial unibody with front subframe, but with Javelin it was all in one, like the dashboard. Javelin's interior had a one-piece injection-molded ABS plastic dash with optional tach that lived in the instrument cluster, not on the hood. The Javelin's '68 arrival occurred amid safety reforms: the only sharp thing permitted was style; the rest had to be foamed up.

The new Javelin came standard with 4 seat belts (Nash had been offering seat belts as early as 1952), deep-dish three-spoke sports steering wheel with 3 horn buttons recessed into the spokes, energy-absorbing steering column, padded dash and sun visors, and 4-way hazard lights. The dash gauges were recessed for safety; so were the buttons for the washer/wiper and headlamps. Even Weather Eye's triple slider panel lived in a recessed cut out at the lower left extreme of the dash. Javelin's American compact-based engineering was a safe bet too.

If Mustang's success was underwritten by Falcon mechanicals, then Javelin could rely on American's front unequal length control arms with high-mount coils and rear leaf springing. However, those Javelin leafs were 53 inches long and 2.5 inches wide, compared to 52 inches and 2 inches on American. I6 Javelins and Americans shared the same 9-inch drums; V8s had the 10-inch drums standard with AMC's front disk option only available on 8-cylinder models, as per any American Motors range. All of which was elegant sufficiency given Javelin's opening motor choices.

Steady characters were pleased with the base 145-horse 8.5 CU 1bbl 232 I6. However, in the Age of Aquarius, there weren't many steady types, so most selected the optional 200 bhp 2bbl V8. This 290ci motor had 9:1 compression and was content to sip regular gasoline. Whether one went for the 232, or paid $105 extra for the 290 V8, AMC had the measure of regular Mustangs. The starter Stang came with a mere 200ci I6, and Ford's small-block was no tougher than the AMC 290. After this were two premium-fuel V8s for Javelin.

Trade up to the 4bbl 290ci 225 bhp V8, or race on to the 4bbl 343ci unit with 280 horses. Also feel liberated enough to spend $25.90 on real duals, for that super-menacing street sound. The more efficient exhaust system was only available on the 4bbl 290 and 343, and was essential to fuel those Speed Racer dreams. And there Javelin hit a brick wall. The more powerful 390 would come on stream once AMX arrived; until then, buyers could amuse themselves with gearbox choices, unless a Javelin 232 was at hand.

Holding firm to Roy Chapin's mantra of cutting costs through fewer permutations, I6 Javelins could only have a column shift. Whether it was the standard 3-speed manual or optional $188.15 Shift Command auto, the selector was on the tree, which showed that being a stone-slow greenie was boring even back in the '60s. Without a floorshift, the Javelin's standard buckets were as fun as chilled lentil soup, which suggested the optional $184.85 4 on the floor. The 4-speed console shifter was the only floor-actuated shifter available on Javelin in '68.

AMX offered a 3-motor lineup: small-block 290/343/390ci V8s. This '68 AMX has the high-comp 4bbl 343/4-speed manual power team (courtesy George M. Stragand III).

The 232-powered Javelins couldn't have a 4-speed; in North America, V8 Javelins could have a 3-speed, but only if it was on the tree ... bleah! However, all manual gearboxes available for Javelin were with synchromesh on all forward speeds. Steering choices involved a standard manual, quick manual or power steering. The stock steering was a Saginaw recirculating-ball 20:1 ratio system with 5.1 turns lock-to-lock, with the "fast" manual being 16:1 with 4 turns between locks. Most popular, and desirable, was the $86.80 "Road Control" power steering option.

The Road Control power steering had a Saginaw gearbox with integral rotary valve and Thompson engine belt-driven pump. With power steering the ratio and number of turns were down to 15:1 and 3.6 respectively; unfortunately, so too was road feel. One might as well also have chosen the Adjust-O-Tilt steering wheel option at $42.15. That was the great thing about sport compacts: they had all that choice. Ford showed the way in 1964 with a super-low stripper price advertised on Mustang, from which point the buyer would start selecting options to make the car decent.

By the time Javelin arrived, the pony base model was more complete, and car makers were moved to state the car shown in ads did have options that boosted the sticker price. For AMC Javelin that 232 3-speed base price was $2,482, which included 6.95-inch-footprint 14-inch tires, cigarette lighter, glove box lock and heater. However, for $105 extra the buyer could go supersonic with Javelin SST. SST turned the standard buckets into ones that reclined, added disc wheel trims, and, if the $99.75 vinyl roof was specified, offered black or off-white tops for a modern two-tone effect. The vinyl top covered the rear sail panels and followed the rear fender line.

If one wanted reclining seats on the rival GM F-body, then calendar days would be ticked off until 1982 arrived! This omission underlined the difference in auto-building philosophy between AMC and the Big 3. The reclining seat and independent rear suspension were things the Big 3 believed 99 percent of people didn't care about. In the meantime they saved money by leaving out the little mechanical adjuster and reclining seatback. By the time the Europeans and Japanese included reclining seats as standard equipment, it would have looked bad if the Big 3 charged extra for this feature.

Big 3 management sat out the '70s on their fixed-position buckets, waiting for the '80s to make reclining seats standard. This was no surprise because the Big 3 were the bean-counter masters of the universe. They were cost cutters par excellence that came up with the idea of putting two power window buttons on the center console of coupes, so that the passenger window button didn't have to be repeated on the driver's door panel. That act cut the button count from three to two. On the GM F-body the back ends of the front subframe might have been joined to make everything stiffer, but the 3-foot gap was left to stand. Once again, imagine the pennies saved on 3 million–plus F-bodies over 1966–81.

If all that didn't work, the Big 3 could always use their big orders to encourage parts suppliers to make their contract tenders cheaper. Giants can do that; when a company makes many cars it behaves a certain way. American Motors, as the smallest member of the Big 4, didn't have this scale of operation, so the Javelin was a different kind of pony. The Javelin owner was left to ponder the discontenting ways of other cars as he looked through the 59-degree raked windshield. Javelin's buckets had AMC's usual coil springing, like a Caddy, so the Javelin owner was comfortably smug.

There were lots of Javelin owners, too; it was initially hoped AMC's new ride would hook 45,000 prospects in its first model year, but that number ended up becoming 55,124 units. So Javelin was a hit, injecting youth and interest into the AMC lineup, with sales at American Motors up 23 percent in model year 1968. This was all very cheery after the $76 million loss of 1967, not to mention slumping to 10th place in the industry. So Javelin had to be a winner, and even though AMC had been frugal in jointly developing Javelin and AMX, new car tooling costs had to be amortized.

Numbers in '68 broke down to 29,097 base Javelins and 26,027 coupes in SST trim. To get some perspective, 107,112 Pontiac Firebirds were sold in model year '68, and 400,000 Mustangs trotted out within one year of its debut. This was a rough crowd, with bigger-budget companies fighting over the same pie. Chapin's rationalized niche plan for AMC post–1966 meant Javelin would only be available in the one coupe fastback body style; no Javelin convertible would be produced. To keep cool, select the optional Weather Eye a/c system.

For $356.20 one received two round swivel dash vents smack in the center of the dash, between the also-optional $58.25 AM radio that lived at the base and the speaker grille above. With a/c, a temperature control dial was added to the Weather Eye control panel. This was all much neater than the under-dash unit on a Mercedes 250SL, and essential in warm climes. Being ultramodern, Javelin had single-pane side windows, no vent wings. Thus, as per domestic car practice, the only way to keep the interior cool with the windows up was with the a/c running.

Having the windows up was the best way to enjoy Javelin's deluxe audio. For $191.55 the echo chamber was filled with the sounds of a stereophonic 8-track cartridge player/AM radio that brought two additional rear speakers. Eight-track cartridges were in fashion until the late '70s, when compact cassettes took over. Eight-track worked on a single spool with tape flowing in one direction. It was supposed to cope with road vibration, but like any cassette, mangled tape was a hazard. The next time you see an Andy Williams cartridge stuck in a junkyard Pinto's dash, you will know why.

On the serious side, the a/c option included the heavy-duty engine cooling system, which cost $16.05. This pack incorporated a larger radiator core and 7-blade thermo-flex fan with shroud. Choosing a/c also saw the Javelin's battery and alternator upgraded to 60-amp and 40-amp units respectively, although a heavy-duty 70-amp battery was available separately for $7.40. One of the most popular heavy-duty options of the period was HD suspension, and Javelin had two sets, applying to I6 and V8 cars. HD suspension on 232 Javelins saw the coupe get a front swaybar, not usually included, plus firmer shocks and springs for $16.05.

V8s already came with a front swaybar, so with HD suspension, 8-cylinder Javelins got a bigger front swaybar, the stiffer shocks and springs, plus 5.5-inch rims for $18.45. Option packs were really coming to the forefront by the late '60s, and for $30.64 the "Performance handling package" did what the V8 HD suspension did, but with 6-inch-wide rims. At the top was the variously named Performance package, Power-pack or Go-pack. The Power-pack title harked back to the times of optional 4bbl 327s and up-engined Americans, but by the time AMX arrived, Go-pack held sway as the familiar term. Go-pack put most of the performance goodies in one set for Javelin, and subsequently AMX.

Proving if the car at hand is Go-pack genuine needs the original window sticker or build sheet; because Go-pack was an assortment of separately available options, its presence wasn't discernible from the car's VIN or door tag. In addition, in the early years, buyers

Javelin and AMX (shown) shared a number of body parts to save on tooling costs, as well as front independent unequal length control arms and rear semi-elliptic springs/live axle suspension (courtesy George M. Stragand III).

could do Go-pack, minus some of the items commonly understood to be part of said pack. Go-pack was only available on cars with the top two V8 power plants. Thus, for $265.50 the buyer would get at least a Javelin with 343 V8, duals, power front disks, the V8 handling package, E70 14-inch Red Stripe tires and rally striping.

Normally Javelins came with a discreet profile pinstripe, but the Go-pack's rally stripe was much wider and more noticeable. Go-pack or no, the Javelin prospect had to pay extra for a tachometer. The gauge hollow for the tach was there on the molding, but in stock form was just blank. Tick the option blank and make the dealer happy to the tune of $48.05, but only if the Javelin had a V8. The 232 Javelins couldn't have that tach; their economy-minded owners just shifted to the strains of the I6.

To ponder the madness of the era, think on the cost of tach and other options, then realize that one could buy a brand-new 315-horse 390ci crate motor from AMC for a mere $160; pay an extra $8.40 and it would even come fitted with your Javelin! Whether it was base 145-pony Javelin versus base 115 bhp Mustang, or a 343 Javelin SST undercutting the upscale Cougar, by $120 and $350 respectively, the question was: why not AMC?

Javelin made a sharp impression on the sport compact scene, and moved into the '69 model year with only detail improvements. On '68s the "Javelin" script badge was on the left-hand side of the radiator grille; on '69s it was moved to the leading edge of the hood. The '69 grille now had a "target sight" decoration to lock onto road rivals. Javelin might spear a Barracuda, or whatever other game was out there. Inside, budget V8 fans were pleased to discover that the 290 now came with a standard floorshift 3-speeder.

As before, the SST came with deluxe vinyl, or no-cost extra fabric seating, but now Javelin offered the luxo ambience of woodgrain appliqué. There was a wood panel on the dash center, from the radio to over the speaker grille, as well as a vertical rectangular plank surrounding the window handles, plus a strip on the door's armrest. The trim also forested the center console. As ever, Javelin continued with AMC's trademark noise-absorbing molded fiberglass ceiling, so that the forest appliqué was peaceful and quiet.

AMC's "Pre-Set Impulse" locking system meant the doors would lock automatically when closed from the outside. However, more likely to get the pulse racing were new breathing-apparatus fiberglass hoodscoops and new-style air cleaner worth 12 bhp on a 390ci Javelin. If TV had *The Mod Squad*, AMC had the "MOD Pack." The MOD Pack was available on '69 and '70 Javelins, involving a set of the dual non-functional hoodscoops on the '69s, fake side exhausts and a roof spoiler.

The faux rocker panel side exhaust trims looked impressive. The trims were very flush-fitting with 6 sections of small horizontal vents. The effect of the 390 motor idling as gas emitted from such vents would suit an anime cartoon, and that's the only place this part could be functional. The optional rally stripe was redone for '69 and now looked like a walking stick, the handle just behind the front wheel well. Who would have imagined AMC could have dreamed up such a happening machine? On top of this, Javelin couldn't be purchased with an overdrive gearbox; imagine the MPG waste!

If you wanted mileage, buy an American 220; for action choose Javelin. So no 3-speed overdrive for Javelin, and not even an automatic option for the 4bbl 290 Javelin. With the popular 290 the standard final drive was 3.15, with 3.54 optional with the 4-speed. Start with an automatic 343 or 390 Javelin, another popular avenue, and the car came with 2.87 rear gears. That might sound sleepy, but with the 390 the passenger was glad AMC put a grab handle above the glove box on '69s; not even a tall ratio and auto could prevent two black lines from being deposited on asphalt.

A 10.2:1 compression ratio and 390 cubes wouldn't let depression set in. Optional factory available axle ratios would be provided at no charge, but habitual visitors of the drag strip and those who liked to practice holeshots benefited from the $42.10 Twin-Grip differential. AMC's LSD helped maintain control, and hard-core quarter-milers could choose from shorter dealer rear ratios. Performance-oriented dealers offered choices from 3.73 to 5.00:1, but this would cost extra. As a normal Javelin 343 one could expect low to mid–16s, dropping into the 14s with 390 motorvation.

All the above put Javelin on a par with its pony car rivals. In fact, in export markets, AMC put on a better show than the Big 3. American Motors put more effort into fine-tuning the Ramblers sold over there, because unlike General Motors, Ford and Chrysler, the smallest of the 4 U.S. automakers didn't have foreign subsidiaries to clash with. AMC achieved good results overseas through such careful model selection and preparation; remarkably, in the first half of 1967 nearly 40 percent of American cars imported into Britain were from AMC.

U.S. pony cars were best suited to European tastes out of all American cars. Being physically smaller coupes with sports pretensions, they fitted the requirement for a low-volume glamour car, which made Javelin a natural. AMC was known for supplying factory-direct right-hand-drive kits to the UK, and did so with the Javelin by the '69 model year. Javelin joined Rebel and Ambassador in the UK, with the RHD factor giving the car an automatic advantage over LHD Mustangs, Camaros, Firebirds, Barracudas, etc. It was a question of presentation.

Of all the engines on all the option sheets, they had to lay the 343 on me! However, the buyer wasn't complaining; from 232 to 390, the 343 was just right for the export buyer, and that luxury buyer would be expecting an automatic. Thus, AMC tailored a Rambler Javelin SST spec around the 343 auto power team. The luxury prospect wouldn't be considering manual brakes or a 4-speed; the one-size-fitted-all Javelin had power steering, power brakes with front disks, console, reclining seats and natty vinyl roof. This was basically a luxo version with Go-pack.

Right-hand drive Rambler Javelin SSTs forj the UK received a custom woodgrain panel to surround the dashboard instruments, and several locally sourced components like Lucas sealed-beam headlamps and Exide batteries. Above the stock Goodyear Redlines, one could sample Dunlop SP41 tires. Either way the Javelin sat on 6-inch-wide rims, but the wide-section SP41s gave greater grip in the wet. The export Javelin felt very complete, more haute couture next to Mustang's off-the-rack nature. It's understandable that AMC didn't bother with the Rogue in this market; Javelin had the bases covered.

Javelins were also built in Germany. West German coachbuilder Karmann, of VW Karmann Ghia fame, assembled the Javelin at its Osnabruck Werks between January 1969 and July 1970. In total, 281 LHD German-produced Javelin SSTs rolled out of Karmann's doors, and today one resides in the coachbuilder's museum. These Karmann Javelins can be distinguished by observing the driver-side metal door tag, which says 6979-K, the "K" suffix standing for Karmann naturally. AMC sent parts from Kenosha to Karmann to tackle Mustang in Continental Europe.

As usual, the deal was to sell high-spec Javelins to Europeans who wanted something different from their Alfa- and Lancia-owning neighbors. Enter Javelin, with a choice of 3 power plants. Given the low sales volume, Karmann kept a lid on variations, and no one in this market wanted a stripper special. Thus, the range commenced unusually with a 2bbl 155 bhp 8.5:1 CR 232 I6 and 3-speed floorshift manual power team. Next was the 2bbl 200 bhp 290ci V8, with 3-speed floorshift standard as per U.S. '69s. The 280-horse 4bbl 343 swung at the top of the tree.

Javelin and AMX also shared an energy-absorbing dashboard, with recessed safety circular instruments. AMC's Weather Eye HVAC panel was left of the steering column (courtesy George M. Stragand III).

Further interesting spec variations from the U.S. version involved the inclusion of standard front power 11.2-inch disk brakes, even with the Javelin 232. This was most likely in deference to the fact owners would be taking these cars on European freeways for an 80 mph cruise. Therefore, the inclusion of Javelin's 4 wheel drums wouldn't have been wise. As with U.S. cars sold in Europe since '68, the Javelin kept its U.S. emissions controls. However, this stopped at the basic "Engine Mod" system, not bothering with an air pump for the sole manual gearbox V8 combo (290 / 3-speed manual). West Germany didn't start clamping down on emissions until the early '70s, so no need for the smog pump.

The 343 came with standard duals to intimidate Porsche 911s at the lights. Power steering and the optional console-mounted Shift Command auto were reserved for V8 Javelins. Thirteen Karmann SSTs were assembled with the 3-speed manual, although any 3-speed manual was considered old hat in Europe by this hour. Still, during the Cold War, a gleaming new Karmann Javelin with automatic choke shone so much brighter than 2-stroke Trabants, Wartburgs and other Eastern-bloc humor. AMC fought communism with Javelin!

Much the same was done down under with Javelin in Australia. Here Javelin was part of the local assembly operation of AMI (Australian Motor Industries). Since Australia was a country with a national policy to encourage local manufacturing, there were big cost savings if a model could be made locally. By being put together in Port Melbourne, AMCs sold in Australia avoided the high import duty imposed on exotic machinery like Chevelle SS 454s and Porsches that were coming in, but were definitely not being made locally.

Australia had local representatives of the Big 3 (General Motors Holden, Ford Australia, Chrysler Australia) that made V8 gruntmobiles, albeit ¾ the size of a U.S. intermediate, and using just small-block V8s. Think of hi-po versions of the Chevy 327/350, Ford 302/351 and a tepid Chrysler 318/360, because a local Hemi I6 did the serious work in the Australian Charger. These cars were RHD; the expensive Buick 442s and Mustang 428s had to be converted from LHD. Unlike Europe, where one can drive either LHD or RHD legally, Australia forced conversion to RHD soon after a vehicle was imported.

Between the local V8s and imported U.S. V8s, AMC held the middle ground, and all on 343 power. The Australian Javelin, known as the AMI Rambler Javelin, used the 280 bhp 343 and Shift Command auto power team, plus variations from the U.S. Javelin. Enter the AMI Javelin and the dashboard looked ... unusual. The general outline of the U.S. dash could be discerned with the usual Javelin gauges, including a standard tach, but trimmed in neat vinyl. In the dash center above the radio were the ammeter, clock and oil pressure gauges of the Rally Pak.

The AMI Javelin had a strong performance bias: standard features encompassed the V8 Javelin's HD suspension and Twin-Grip LSD, along with 205 section metric footprint 14-inch radials for the 6-inch-wide rims. This was all a good 5 years before radials started to make inroads in the U.S. home market. The AMI Javelin had the right stuff to harness the 4bbl 343/auto, and in this locality, high-octane leaded juice would be available well into the '90s!

AMI Javelin SST upstaged U.S. imports with those standard reclining buckets. On the trunk lid there was a rectangular "Rambler" plaque to the left of the normal "343V" script, 280 horses pushed the auto to 118 mph, but Javelin was also setting the pace in style for Australian-built cars with the coupe concept. With the exception of the local Chrysler Charger, Australian high-performance cars were either sports sedans or sedan-based 2-door hardtops. Thus, AMI Javelin brought the good looks of a real coupe to a market where blockish shapes ruled.

The only style oddity in all this was the AMI Javelin's pressed-metal wheel covers.

A top-of-the-line '69 Bittersweet Orange AMX 390 with Go-pack, automatic console shifter and tan leather interior, plus a/c. A total of 8,293 AMXs were sold in 1969, the 2-seater's best year (courtesy Joe Howard).

They looked more at home on a base Comet or Maverick, but were locally sourced, and so contributed to the Australian content quota. AMI continued to surprise by bringing the genuine 2-seater AMX to Australia for 1970. In the history of the Australian motor industry the AMX stands alone as the only volume 2-seat mainstream V8 Australian car. The AMX also set a precedent in handling prior to the '70s' getting on a roll, with interest in tuning Australian V8 cars to handle well with good ride comfort too.

AMI simply combined their Javelin's hardware with the shorter 2-seater AMX unibody. It was easy to pour the 343/auto, power disks and other Javelin items into the locally assembled AMX. There were no 290s or 390s, no 4-speed; things were kept simple. Australia never got the Corvette, except for a tiny trickle of imports, so the AMI AMX racing around on ER70 Dunlop SP Aquajets could lay claim to being the best-handling car in the land, short of mid-engined exotica. AMI AMX made do with the Javelin's 2.87 final drive and Twin-Grip, delivering outright figures close to Javelin, but that wasn't the point.

AMI AMX was for the person who thought he had everything. The sight of a Big Bad Orange AMX with blister hood and stamped-steel 6-inch-wide sports rims made him realize he did not. The AMX was the chariot of choice to wow them at the golf club. However, the odd thing about the AMI AMX was its out-of-synch nature with the U.S. car. Blame it on logistics, but the Australian-assembled cars tended to lag by one year. In the U.S. the Javelin was restyled for '70, and the 360 motor arrived, but the 1970 AMI AMX had a 343 and the '69 body style.

The world was a much bigger place in 1970, so the select few who chose an AMI car would have been none the wiser concerning model lag. This CKD operation used mostly U.S.-sourced Rebel parts for the RHD conversion, and that was the main difference between U.S. and Australian AMCs, but over in Mexico there was greater distinction. Mexico's car industry was a strictly governed operation: back in 1962 the Mexican government had talked to the Big 4 U.S. automakers and laid down the law concerning the manufacture and sale of U.S.-derived designs south of the border.

The Mexican government insisted on 60 percent local content, placed a limit on local production levels and had restrictions on model diversity. A manufacturer could have 3 main model lines, and 2 styles within a line. However, Mexico was freer in other respects. Pollution controls were laxer and engineering latitude was greater. For example, Mexico got a 302 V8-powered Mustang II in 1974, one year before America, and this ride was as quick as a 1982 Mustang GT. The engineers didn't have to worry about a/c, which allowed them to snake the V8 in sooner.

As is normal for Latin America, road conditions aren't so smooth, so vehicles are set up with a bit more ground clearance. The interior seating materials, being locally sourced, tended to be harder-wearing and look different from materials used on U.S. market versions. The quality was also easy to see: because car production in Mexico was for a select crowd, the fit and finish of versions made were of a very high standard. In Mexico the manufacture of AMC-based vehicles was performed by Vehiculos Automotores Mexicanos, or VAM, which made the Javelin from 1968 to 1973.

Whereas the AMI Javelin was V8 only, the VAM Javelin was only powered by versions of the AMC I6. With limitations on product diversity, VAM never took on the 2-seat AMX, concentrating instead on a Jag XKE-style spec Javelin. The first VAM Javelins had a 232 I6 with 9.8:1 compression ratio, flat-top pistons and 2bbl Carter carb for 160 bhp. This engine was teamed with a standard Tremec 4-speed console Hurst-shifted gearbox. The VAM Javelin wasn't available with a 3-speed manual, or any form of column-operated shifter. However, the console-mounted Shift Command auto was optional.

The strange thing was the combo of this hi-po power team with standard manual 4 wheel drums, but in other areas the VAM Javelin was high spec. The buyer received standard reclining buckets, sports steering wheel, driver's side exterior rear-view mirror, tachometer, AM mono radio, wide footprint tires, electric 2-speed wipers and a 200 kph (124 mph) metric speedo. Again reflecting the tastes of the market and road conditions, manual steering was standard and a heater was optional.

The '69 VAM Javelin was gussied up with more standard stuff. The bucket recliners now had safety headrests, and the dash had the Javelin's woodgrain appliqué with console standard on automatic cars. Chrome accents were added to the exterior trim and the Weather Eye heater was now standard. The formerly optional heating/vent front defroster package was now built into every VAM Javelin. The gas pedal also went from being floor-mounted to firewall-mounted, and it summoned a more powerful I6.

Development of the AMC I6 was always limited in the '60s and '70s by the presence of the company's V8, but since the VAM Javelin exclusively enjoyed the six, the engineers could let rip! Predating the arrival of the North American 258ci I6, VAM engineered a special local 9.5 CU 252ci I6 with 170 bhp. VAM kept in synch with the U.S. Javelin by adopting the revised '70-shape car. The '70 VAM Javelin had a new steering column with ignition key lock, but differed in the dash.

VAM chose to put the 1968–69 dash gauges into the new 1970 U.S. Javelin's flat-panel dashboard. This new dash had a more expansive woodgrain appliqué, and less-recessed gauges. The earlier safety gauges were quite hard to read, especially with sunlight reflections. In mid–1969 AMC put a hooded shroud around the instrument binnacle, which was much made-over for '70. Javelin's gauges always seemed to run contrary to logic. There were 2 large round faces, but the one on the right was for coolant temp and gas. One might have expected the right one to have the tach, but that was placed in a small circular face at the extreme left.

In 1969 AMC used the large right dial to house a 240-degree 8K rpm tach, with coolant and fuel levels in the bottom ⅓ of the face. A clock was now in the place of the earlier tach. AMC retained the relative gauge face size and placement for '70. Moving down the interior, Shift Command autos had the pistol-grip shifter AMC introduced on its '70 model ranges, and the seatback release was moved up the seat for easier use. In 1970, Javelin, like Rebel SST hardtops, received bucket seats with integrated headrests. When Javelin came out, a pair of height-adjustable headrests ran to $49.25. A lockable cubby console was now also available between such front buckets.

Interior side panel door trims took on the padded class of '70 Rebels too. On the outside Javelin changed slightly for '70 with a new full-width dual-opening grille that now incorporated the headlamps. Turn signal lamps still resided at the outer ends of the revised flush chrome bumper, but their cutouts were now rectangular, not circular. The Javelin's rear was the same as before, save for dividing the taillight strip into 5 segments. Exterior dimensions were now 191, 71.9, and 51.6 inches for length, width and height.

Javelin was now 1.82 inch longer and 0.2 inch lower, but stuck with the original 109-inch wheelbase. On debut in '68 the Javelin had 14 solid exterior color choices; this was true for '70 too. Those Big Bad colors of 1969 had also made it through to '70. However, pollution controls were getting dreary. On release, Javelin had 2 emissions control systems. On I6s and automatic V8s there was the "Engine Mod" set up, which had thicker head gaskets, leaner carb and retarded ignition. Manual V8s had an air pump to lean out the fuel mixture on its "Air Guard."

In 1970 compression ratios were reduced slightly and larger displacement replacement motors entered, which would be typical of the whole industry in the following years. The starter 145 bhp 232 continued, but the 290 V8 gave way to the new SCCA Trans Am–influenced 304. This 304 V8 was only available in 2bbl form, 10 horses stronger than the outgoing 2bbl 290 at 210 bhp (gross). By '70 all versions of the 343 were replaced by the new 360, available in 245 bhp 2bbl and 290 bhp 4bbl editions. AMC's 390 was still at the pinnacle, producing 325 bhp in '70. The 390 now made 10 extra horses, even though its compression ratio was cut from 1969's 10.2 down to 10:1.

Nothing nasty about all that, and if one didn't fear the smog police, engines could be adjusted upwards, but things were changing. Californian '70 Javelins had a gas tank vapor emissions control system that made filling up slower than frozen molasses, which didn't augur well for the '70s. Comparing '69 Javelin 390 with '70 Javelin 390, weight was up: 3,480 lbs versus 3,545 lbs. Javelin was still a sport compact, and gas misers could now rejoice, given that AMC had made the 3-speed manual floorshift standard on the frugal '70 Javelin 232.

To get the console Shift Command autobox, the 304 option box had to be ticked, but

Top: Go-pack on AMX was limited to the top two engine options, and brought two over-the-top racing stripes. AMC included a passenger-side grab handle on '69s. With a 390 aboard, better hold on tight (courtesy Joe Howard). ***Bottom:*** In the groovy Monkee Mobile customizing era of the mid to late '60s, George Barris turned the 1969 AMC AMX into the otherworldly AMX-400 (courtesy Mike Geary and Greg Ornazian).

as before, real excitement started with the Go-pack. By this stage the Go-pack involved either the 360 or 390, both being the only motors available with Javelin's optional 4-speed console manual with Hurst shift linkage. Go-pack brought the usual power front disks, plus F70 14-inch Goodyear Redline Polyglas tires on 6-inch-wide rims. Optional were E60 tires on 15 × 7-inch rims, which would have helped Go-pack's HD suspension bring on the lateral G's on the skidpad.

The most visually arresting aspect of Go-pack was the new-for-'70 forward-facing functional dual-nostril fresh air induction scoop. As usual, such a device sealed out warm underhood air and is believed to have been worth an extra 15 to 20 ponies on top of the 390's 325 bhp. One could select the Shift Command auto on a 360/390 motivated Go-pack Javelin, which would have entailed a standard tall 2.87 final drive, but crystal ball gazers suggested otherwise. In those dying moments of high-compression 99-octane heaven, it was time to shift into high gear.

In building the ultimate '70 Javelin, power steering would be overlooked in favor of Javelin's fast manual steering, still at 4 turns lock-to-lock. The 3.91 rear gears sounded right, and Twin-Grip lsd a mandatory accompaniment with this ratio. You were on your way to a special power trip, but it was wise to seek out those 7-inch-wide rims. Even with the 2.87 final drive, auto and F70 rubber, the 390's torque was tough to tame. Getting below the mid–15s required skill, not more power.

Right out of the box, the 390's 420 lbs/ft invited wheelspin, which suited Javelin's more ferocious image. Javelin's squarer face and hoodscoop signaled greater aggression, a natural response when territory is encroached upon. In 1970, GM launched its new F-body, so Javelin would have to stay sharp to spear this predator. AMC had lots of new items for 1970 too. Apart from Javelin's new styling, there was a logo change. American Motors went from their cursive script to the new "A-mark" symbol, which incorporated the red, white and blue colors, in strong, simple geometric shapes.

AMC was in better shape thanks to Javelin and its truncated sibling AMX. In the '50s some budget versions of family cars were sold without a rear seat. Less seating implied poverty — then came the Corvette. The plastic 2-seater and imports fueled the imagination with road-course racing; the SCCA had itself recently started. However, it wasn't until 1968 that a fellow domestic came to challenge Corvette. American Motors made one of the few volume 2-seat sports cars in U.S. car history, two of which were from GM (Corvette and Fiero). After the show circuit and publicity hype, people were expecting great things from AMX.

American Motors' 2-Seater Experiment

In the '50s and '60s, when a company had a new product to promote, and they wanted people to know it had the right stuff, they went record-breaking. Some kind of endurance feat would impress upon Joe Q. Public that a new car could be trusted, and AMC's AMX was no exception. The plan was hatched in December 1967, when American Motors Performance Activities boss Carl Chackmakian enlisted the services of Craig Breedlove to show what the new AMX could do. Breedlove in turn sought the help of engine building specialist Traco Engineering to prepare the AMC V8 for the endurance test.

For Class B, Traco Engineering bored AMC's 390 V8 out to 397ci, whereupon it made 443 horses at 5,800 rpm. Another AMX used the 290 V8, the AMX's starter engine; Traco Engineering bored this small-block out to 304ci. At 304ci this V8 was within Class C's 305ci limit, and it anticipated the production 304 of the '70 model year. So there it was: Craig Breedlove, wife Lee Breedlove and co-driver Ron Dykes took such prepared AMXs to the Goodyear Tire and Rubber circular test track in San Angelo, Texas, during the first week of February 1968.

The endurance test was done before the AMX was showroom available as a mid–'68 model year entrant. The Breedloves, AMXs and company met with success, and their success made for good advertising copy. The ad ran, "Mr. and Mrs. Breedlove went for a nice, long, Sunday drive in an AMX." The homey adline placated the nervous Naderites who feared public highways would be turned into demolition derbies by youth in their hot rides. The stats showed AMX had the legs to catch Corvette: 77 speed records were broken in 3,380 miles; all told, the new '68½ AMX demolished 106 records during the exercise.

Such record-breaking was USCA and FIA approved, and the little AMX 304 ran at an average speed of 140.790 mph for 24 hours. If anyone wanted to buy a new AMX 290 and take same to Le Mans, he could be confident it would go the distance. The buyer would also be happy with what $3,245 commandeered. The AMX 290 had a number of tech upgrades over Javelin and other ponies, such as AMC's hi-po 225 bhp 4bbl 290 V8 and BW T10 4-speed power team. Don't look at the tree, focus on the console, because that's where the Hurst-linkaged four-on-the-floor stick lived.

To go with this, AMC included their Javelin tach, plus Javelin V8's HD suspension. That involved a 0.94-inch front swaybar, the kind one would subsequently find on a '70 Rebel Machine; the AMX was serious when you were. All AMXs also received mini-traction bars to guide the rear suspension through acceleration and deceleration. These traction bars were also available on Javelin as a dealer-installed option. These bars were mounted above the rear axle, being attached to a reinforced part of the chassis floor.

All AMXs also came standard with Goodyear E70 14-inch bias fiberglass belted Polyglas tires, a new design, on 5.5-inch-wide rims. The AMX was a new alternative to open-top English 2-seaters, with rugged features the imports didn't have. The 4-barrel 290 looked meek next to the muscle car crowd, but gave AMX much more straight-line acceleration than an MGB or Triumph TR5. The AMX was for the domestic car fancier who always liked the idea of an Austin-Healey. In fact, the Austin-Healey 3000 was killed off at the close of 1967 by pending stiffer U.S. car regs.

The '68½ AMX came with the same kind of all-around 10-inch drums standard on a V8 Javelin or American. However, a solid majority, 4,445 of the 6,725 AMXs sold in its first model year, had the optional $97.15 power front disk brakes. Either way, AMX could claim to be, at the very least, America's second-best-handling car. In tuning up, AMX handling was given definite priority by AMC engineers Vic Raviolo and John Adamson. The biggest aid to AMX nimbleness was the 12-inch wheelbase chop performed on Javelin to create the 2-seater.

The part of the wheelbase removed was just behind the B pillar, giving the Vette a domestic 2-seat companion for the first time since the demise of the 1957 Ford Thunderbird. Why have the "+2" part of 2+2? The token rear seats were only good for taking 2 people you didn't like around the block. AMX gave up the pretense of +2, and its standard reclining buckets had headrests that fitted perfectly in the rear floorpan curvature, once the front seats were reclined all the way to horizontal bed position.

It was cozy in the AMX, too; the sporty one had full carpeting that dealt with the whole area behind the seats, even over the intruding wheel well arches. In addition, by having the same dashboard as Javelin, the AMX's Weather Eye HVAC system was more effective, given the smaller cabin. Less was more with AMX, and Javelin power teams in a lighter body promised more go. Figure in a saving of 150 lbs, which made an AMX 390 a low 15s car at the worst.

The 390 took its AMX 390 name from use in the sportster, but was originally envisioned as a heavy-duty Ambassador engine option. At 590 lbs, it was 25 lbs heftier than the 343. Power climbed from the 4-barrel 343's 280 bhp to the 390's 315 horses, but the 390 was about more than power ratings. The 390 had quality, using forged parts, while the 290/343 made do with cast items. It was AMC's insurance policy so the low-volume 390 could be introduced on schedule without a flood of warranty claims. Larger big-end journals kept it safe at the drag strip.

The 390 could also be chosen on Javelin, and the pony had much more in common with AMX. To contain those pesky tooling costs, the AMC siblings shared front and rear bumpers, front fenders, firewall and windshield, doors and door glass, rear window, trunk lid and taillights. So which aspects of the AMX showcar actually entered production? The Vignale AMX's sail panel dual gas filler doors were included as cosmetic circular impressions with an AMX script badge in the center. As per Javelin, one filled up an AMX from behind the spring-loaded rear license plate.

Domestic stylists liked to conceal the filler, so AMX's sail panel decorations delighted while the real filler annoyed. Looking at the AMX head-on one noticed its unique open-mouthed grille; the Javelin had that central divider. The AMX's hood was also model-specific with two blisters, the sort expected to integrate with the intake carb trumpets of a V8 racer, but they weren't functional. On the Vignale AMX these hood blisters had the air vents that were a part of the show car's unusual ventilation system. However, AMX used the same ventilation system as Javelin.

Fresh air entered through the grille at the windshield's base, and exited at the rear edges of the coupe's doors. The movement from high to low pressure area was aided by manually controlled flaps under the Javelin/AMX's door armrests. Naturally the production AMX didn't have an opening rear window or rumble seat, but the 2-seater's styling suggested a cantilevered roof, even though the car did have normal A pillars.

AMX—A Lamborghini on Leaf Springs

The AMX was obviously solid, but there was a nagging suspicion that more could have been done with the concept. The car AMC showed in North America, and the one Vignale displayed on the European show circuit wowed with its innovative ways. After this, the standard equipment the real-life AMX enjoyed over Javelin, like driver-side outside rear-view mirror with internal adjuster, was welcome, but where did the exotic ride go? However, did you know that right to the end of the '60s, six-cylinder Maseratis had semi-elliptic rear suspension? So forget about the spec and know that the AMX was in fast company!

Since it was Javelin-linked, AMX buyers could choose Go-pack, which was similar to the one on the 4-seater except AMX brought suspension even firmer than that of Javelin HD equipment. The Go-pack AMX also included dual "Over The Top Roof Stripe" racing decals for that complete wacky-racer look, but only if a 343 or 390 was in the cards. There was no Go-packed AMX 290, since that wasn't a natural fit. However, the AMX had the same steering choices as Javelin. Among these the "Quick-Ratio" fast manual steering was a natural accompaniment to Go-pack, using a different pitman arm to the stock slow manual steer.

AMC's Big Bad colors added a special accent to their youthmobiles by 1969. In the company's words, "They happen on the new Javelins and AMXs, from bumper to bumper ... including the bumpers." In '69 they happened on 284 Big Bad Orange AMXs, 283 Big Bad Green AMXs and 195 Big Bad Blue AMXs. You could be the coolest cat in livery that couldn't be had on a Vette. So there were choices to make AMX very special. Plus, the AMC bean-counters had cleared it for AMX to get its own rear quarter fender panels. That meant the kicked-up rear wheel arches of the Vignale AMX came along for the ride.

In 1967, AMCs were "The Now Cars"; in 1968 they became "The Right Now Cars," as Javelin/AMX stopped Rambler from being a square. However, in the psychedelic Age of Aquarius, the kids wanted more, so they went to see Craig Breedlove. Breedlove and auto stylist Bill Moore came up with a groovy bolt-on kit for AMX, called "Breedlove AMX 600," that cost a not-insubstantial $700 over the base car. The standard front fenders melded with a fiberglass grille and partial bellypan. AMX's hood became fiberglass with real NACA ducts to admit cold air to the intake apparatus.

There was also a sail panel-mounted roof handle spoiler. The cosmetic alterations were dubbed "Aerodynamx Kit," with reference to the AMX tag. For legal road use, compromise abbreviated aluminum front bumpers were available. For 30 percent extra, one was ready to either fight crime, once some kind of superhero suit was donned, or join the NASCAR scene. However, to look fancy one needn't even have left the AMC dealership, thanks to George Barris.

Car customizer Barris got into an association with AMC, whereby customers could enjoy that far-out customized experience when buying a new Javelin or AMX. Kits were devised by Barris, involving straightforward touches that could be done in little time, under the "Instant Kustomizing" banner. Cosmetics, paint and rims, all things a dealer could handle. The kits were marketed nationwide; just walk into an AMC dealer, order a new Javelin or AMX with kit, and the car would be delivered complete with the additional work incorporated into the payment plan. Barris came up with the Javelin Bonanza and AMX El Toro.

With the AMX El Toro, Barris made use of the AMX's hood blisters by cosmetically blending 8 air intake trumpets, suggesting each bank of the AMC V8 was inhaling the same air you were. As if this weren't enough, Barris offered a more specialized AMX-based car called the AMX-400. The AMX-400 used a 390-powered 1969 AMX as a starting point, and accorded with the righteous ride one would expect from Barris.

The stock AMX had its roof chopped 4.5 inches and made use of custom roof pillars. The nose and tail were extended, making the vehicle unrecognizable as an AMX. The AMX-400 had a futuristic look typical of custom cars of the period, and the ride's hidden headlamps helped in that respect. Barris also added more elaborate faux fillers on the sail panels, but as ever, the rear license plate magic door had to open-sesame before filling her up. AMX-400 took a leaf out of AMC's own AMX II show car by having full-width taillights that illuminated green during acceleration, amber when coasting and red under braking.

For active safety the AMX-400 had full-width taillighting that shone green with acceleration, amber when cruising and red under braking. The AMX-400 had the top dog 390ci motor, and a normal AMX interior (courtesy Mike Geary and Greg Ornazian).

AMX-400 was the kind of future chariot that might have figured in films like *Death Race 2000*, and actually did feature in TV's *Banacek* in 1972. The future was the place to be; the retro ride concept would have mystified designers in the '60s. GM had recently introduced the C3 Corvette as a '68 model year newbie, and comparisons couldn't help but be made with AMX. The 2-seater thing was hard to ignore, and AMC played along.

AMX versus Vette

AMC management stated the '68 AMX wasn't in direct competition with the hallowed plastic one, but knowing what everyone was thinking, they mentioned the handy price saving if one chose AMX over the trunkless Chevy. Was it a fair comparison? Were the AMX and Makovette even real sports cars? All sound questions that people were asking at the time, because all wasn't well in Vette-land.

Based on the revered C2, the '68 C3 Corvette quickly built up a reputation for unreliability and poor build quality in its early days. Chevrolet even forgot to include the evocative Stingray name until the '69 model year, quite an oversight. With the rise of mid-engined cars, the thinking was that the Vette wasn't progressive enough, and was a bit fat. Some unkind comparisons with a 5-pound ax were made. Thus, mighty Chevrolet had shot itself in the foot, leaving the door open to AMX while it hopped around on one foot.

The base Corvette came with a 300-horse 327 and 3-speed manual. The AMX came with 4 on the floor standard, and one could choose a 315 bhp 390 and still be over a grand better off. The Makovette had a plastic body, the AMX just a steel unibody. However, the Corvette's plastic body was bolted to a steel frame, whereas AMC had planned to make a fiberglass unibody for Javelin/AMX before strength issues persuaded them to go all-steel. Even so, the AMX weighed roughly the same as the Corvette, maybe a shade less.

The Vette's domestic trump cards at this time were 4-wheel disk brakes and independent rear suspension. Factory optioning allowed AMX to go disk or drum, but if one went to certain participating AMC dealers, the AMX could be bought with 4-wheel disks. Such parts had been homologated for the Javelin's SCCA Trans Am campaign. If you knew where to go, a new AMX 390 with Go-pack and 4-wheel disks could still be delivered under the cost of a base Corvette 327. As for the rear suspension, Corvettes up to 1963 had a live axle and semi-elliptics, so AMX had that much in common.

Sitting on respective wheelbases of 98 and 97 inches, the '68 Corvette and AMX may not have seemed like sports cars next to a MG T-series, but certainly did seem so compared to a Rebel wagon, or even a Mercedes 280 SL. Technically you had to call AMX a sports car: AMC had sent homologation papers to the SCCA's headquarters so it could compete in the Production Category sports car class, and it did! For the 1969 racing season Product Development Group VP Gerry Meyers organized the AMX's challenge to Corvette, Ferrari, Porsche and Cobra.

Meyers oversaw the creation of a volunteer group of engineers called TEAM (Technical Employees of American Motors). TEAM was managed by Jim Alexander in what was an enthusiastic SCCA B production endeavor. TEAM was up against a factory-backed Corvette 327 for racing honors, but still did OK. AMC's electrical laboratory supervisor Dwight Knupp managed 5 wins, 2 seconds and one 3rd place. This gave AMX the SCCA Central Division Championship, and AMC's 2-seater was second in the National Championship.

Knupp's good showing saw AMX invited to the National runoffs, where that second place could nearly have become first. In November at Daytona, Knupp over-revved the AMX's 343 when, ironically, dodging an out-of-control Corvette. Thus, independent Corvette campaigner Allan Barker edged Knupp out for first. If the proof of the pudding is in the racing, then AMX was baked to perfection. It didn't look as swoopy as the Vette, but benefited by having a real 9.6-cu-ft trunk, instead of the Corvette's crawl space with aspirations.

AMX went into '69, with the '69 Javelin upgrades, and sold even more. The base price increased to $3,297, but sales stood at 8,293 units for the '69 model year. In what amounted to a carryover year, AMX retained its open-mouth grille with small AMX badge on the driver's side. Changes for 1970 were more extensive, incorporating Javelin's restyle with detail differences.

Previously Javelin and AMX had their turn signal lamps in the front bumper. Javelin continued with this, but on the '70 AMX the Javelin front bumper turn signal cutouts became front brake cooling apertures. AMX now had its front turn signals as two round grille lamps, just within the hood shutlines. The grille was now forward-projecting with the middle accented with 4 horizontal highlight lines and AMX script in the center. At the rear, AMX used the '70 Javelin's 5 segment taillights, where the middle one was the back-up lamp. The AMX script was on this center lamp, just where it had always been.

One of the 2,501 1970 Mark Donohue Signature Edition Javelins. This was the only production car to bear the name of the U.S. racing legend (courtesy Wayne Davis).

The Ram Air hood induction, where ordered, added to the '70 AMX's attitude, and the Javelin's rocker panel cosmetic side exhaust trim was standard on AMX this year. The interior "friends of the forest" flat-panel wood-trimmed dash didn't go with the AMX sports car flavor; rivals had moved onto engine-turned imitation trim by now. However, in 1970, AMX could still count only the Corvette as a domestic 2-seat tight wheelbase challenger, even though AMX grew for '70 in keeping with Javelin.

Originally AMX was 177.2/71.6/51.7 inches for length, width and height; due to changes made to Javelin, these numbers now read 179.04/71.57/51.4 inches. Manufacturer-quoted curb weight for the AMX 390 was still 3,340 lbs and the 97-inch wheelbase was retained. All '70 AMXs had the Scrambler-style 14 × 6-inch stamped-steel "Rally Wheels" that used to be optional. As per Javelin, one could take things higher and swap the F70 Polyglas tires for E60 ones on a 15 × 7-inch rim. AMC's new 2-spoke steering wheel was fun to grab hold of.

As with Javelin, Go-pack was still around, although only on 360/390-powered AMXs. Indeed, by 1970 the AMX only existed in 4-barrel 360 and 390 forms. Thus the '70 AMX base price of $3,395 netted 290 gross horses, 325 bhp with the 390 and 340 bhp with 390 Ram Air, allegedly. It was true that AMC had carried out engineering changes to their small-block V8 for '70. Apart from the new-order 304/360 sizes, the motor received increased deck height and redesigned heads. The tall deck turned the 290 into the 304, and the 343 into the 360. AMC kept its top 390 displacement via specially sized connecting rods and pistons.

The '70 model year head redesign involved going from a rectangular exhaust port shape to a "dog-leg" exhaust port. The area of the port was now greater, and the shape of the port floor changed from concave to convex for less turbulence. This made for a 20 percent flow improvement. AMC also increased combustion chamber size from 50–52cc to 58–59cc. The changes made by American Motors were in anticipation of stricter emissions control and pending compression drop for '71.

The Big 4's route to high performance now involved torque and the amount of air inhaled and exhaled. Thus, engine displacements went up, with more attention paid to intake manifolds/headers, less to camshaft profile. The continued availability of AMC's Big Bad colors also maintained excitement in '70. There were 114 takers for Big Bad Blue AMXs, 74 for Big Bad Green and 122 for Big Bad Orange. AMC continued to make news in the style stakes with its new Shadow Mask paint option.

By this stage in high-performance fashion, style dictated partial use of matte or low-gloss paint. The Shadow Mask $52 option, available with Big Bad colors as well, was denoted by the prefix "8" on the metal door trim tag. The hood was painted in a satin finish R-110 Low Gloss Black, code number 9372, with the treatment continuing on the side glass / C pillar outline. A ⅜-inch silver demarcation stripe separated the exterior color from the Shadow Mask zone. Shadow Mask also involved a blacked-out engine bay, with all Shadow Mask painting done at the start on the assembly line when the unibody was a shell.

In all, 982 AMXs had Shadow Mask in '70, the only year the option was offered. There were more (2,875) AMXs with the Ram Air cold-air induction option. A total of 4,116 AMXs were built during 1970, and the way the two-seater was optioned over its 3-year run says something about the desires of the time frame. For example, in '69, 619 and 843 buyers chose a 4-speed 290 and 343 AMX, respectively; 3,620 went with the 4-speed 390 power team. It seems not many bought the idea of the small-engined AMX as an alternative to small-engined imports. That crowd stayed in their MGBs.

The 390 was the most popular motor in the AMX, and it seemed like patrons were thinking of the quarter-mile and muscle-car life when buying their AMXs. In the car's '68, '69, and '70 model years 967, 1,742, and 1,056 chose a/c, but 4,958, 6,569, and 340 chose the Twin-Grip differential. Also, 376, 1,570, and 556 in the 3 respective years actually felt comfortable with the standard 4-wheel drum brakes! Air conditioning, limited slip differential — and who wouldn't bet Corvette owners of the day would have skipped the disk brakes, if they weren't already standard?

So buyers didn't choose their AMXs in true sports-car fashion; they ordered them like they would a Corvette. This showed that even in the late '60s, import and domestic buyers didn't intersect. It also seems true that many of the 2-seater AMX's 19,134 sales were conquest ones from the Corvette camp. AMX ordering also showed up some detail points: 628 1970 AMX buyers selected the Rebel Machine 15-inch rim. Visually interesting, and the wheels definitely would add to a '70 AMX's value today, if the spec could be verified by the build sheet.

Fifty-six '70 AMXs were bought with a rear-window defogger that year, but none in 1968 or 1969. This was because, curiously, the Javelin itself was unavailable with a defogger in those earlier times. Real leather upholstery became an AMX option in 1969, with choices in Charcoal or Saddle Brown available. Black and red were around by 1970. However, comfort and convenience options counted for little in the quarter-mile, for which some special AMXs were let loose. Did you have $5,994?

If money was no object, one could have a purpose Hurst-built AMX drag racer. This

Part of the MD Javelin's raison d'etre was to homologate the stronger internal 360 V8 design for Trans Am racing. This particular MD Javelin has a 390ci/4-speed power team. Note the early AM logo decal style (courtesy Wayne Davis).

model had a blueprinted 390 with Crane roller camshaft, mega 12.4:1 compression ratio, and two Holley 615 cfm 4-barrels sitting on an Edelbrock tunnel ram intake manifold. The drag-racing AMX also used Doug Thorley headers to expel hot exhaust gases. Only 52 copies of this 1,320-ft specialist were built, and the manufacturer info said it would be doing 124 mph when it crossed the ¼ mile. Drag racer Shirley Shahan achieved many Super Stock (SS) Class D records in the AMX.

Impressive and concurrent work was done with the Hurst Scrambler, but there was rising interest in the SCCA's Trans Am road-course series and the Javelin spent much time pursuing success here. The series showcased the very best of the Big 4's pony corral. These compacts loved going around corners, and it was the type of car many were buying. Thus, they identified with the racing cars. Win on Sunday, sell on Monday, the T/A series also accelerated pony road-car development via the homologation process to get better hardware on the track. If they raced it, technically you could buy it! Soon everyone was getting trackside.

SCCA T/A—Javelin versus the World!

When the Big 3's anti-racing stance softened and they started using factory-backed motorsport to sell cars, AMC offered the following retort in one of its ads: "The only race AM cares about is the human race." Cornier than the produce section of a supermarket, perhaps, but American Motors was more at home in an economy trial than a time trial. However, no truth stands forever, and AMC got tempted. Drag racing was a start, and some super AMC drag-race cars achieved notoriety.

Super Stock Javelins were sponsored by the American Motors' Dealers Racing Association. This was all well and good for the local promotion of AMC, but to go national one needed to participate in the SCCA's Trans Am series. Pony cars were the hot-ticket showroom items of the hour, so it made sense to get involved with a racing format that featured them. Plus AMC had a new pony in 1968 called Javelin, which was handy. The Trans Am series of tin-top racing showed sporting and even non-sporting cars fighting on national road circuits, in a form the public could relate to.

Even in the most extreme category, of which Javelin was a part, if a team raced with something, that item had to be publicly available to some degree. Thus, if a car did well in the races, people could infer that the brand had a good car, one worth buying over another. There were classes for the little cars, machines up to 2 liters (122ci), and the big blasters which were capped at 5 liters (305ci). The small-scale imports, like Alfas and Saabs, duked it out while domestic pony cars waged war in the 5-liter category.

Such diversity didn't exist in drag racing, and in the Trans Am series Javelin was taking on the world! A number of things were going Javelin's way. First, management was for it. Boss Roy Chapin Jr. believed that a successful Javelin would have a halo sales effect for all AMCs. So Chapin and president William Luneburg liked the concept of putting Javelin on national show. Overall the Javelin's plan was controlled by Performance Activities Manager Carl Chackmakian.

The AMC Javelin Racing Team, Inc., was instituted with Jim Jeffords as president and Ron Kaplan as vice president. Indeed, Ronnie Kaplan Engineering, Inc., prepared the Javelins of the Javelin Racing Team. The cars carried the company logo on the front fender, where "RKE" script sat over a cartoon piston and conrod. This leads to Javelin's second plus point, its engine. To do T/A, a good high-output V8 under the 305ci limit was needed. This was good for Chevrolet and Ford with their 302s, but not good for others that made their name with 400ci + motors.

AMC only had one V8, a small block, so they took their trusty 290 and bored it out to 304.3ci, the size that would feature greatly in the firm's 1970–79 cars. Normally the 290 came with a small valve head, but for better breathing the T/A Javelin used the 343/390 big valve head with a high-rise intake manifold with 4bbl carb. Suspension involved HD factory springs. This Javelin 304 was driven by Peter Revson and George Follmer during the Javelin Racing Team's launch '68 racing season.

The Javelin made its debut at the 12 Hours of Sebring, where Revson shared his car with Skip Scott, and Follmer partnered Jerry Grant in the second Javelin. Engine builder Traco Engineering of Los Angeles supplied the 4bbl 304s, which proved good enough to power the Revson/Scott Javelin to 5th in class and 12th overall. Indeed, the Javelin proved a model of consistency during the '68 racing season, setting a record by allowing AMC to be the only manufacturer to field at least one finishing car at every race entered.

By the business end of the year, Javelin was proving a quick opponent, garnering a second place from the last race. By this stage AMC was proffering almost as much power as defending champ Ford with its Mustang, Javelin 435 bhp at 7,000 rpm versus Mustang's 440 ponies. By the end of the '68 season Javelin had procured an Edelbrock-design cross-ram intake manifold of aluminum construction, that allowed two 600 cfm Holley 4-barrels to be harnessed.

The Mission Bell 250 at Riverside proved eventful, with Australian driver Horst Kwech coming first in a Mustang. Craig Fisher got third place in the T/G (Titus/Godsall) Firebird, something of a Camaro Z/28 in drag, after starting 32nd on the grid! Peter Revson's Javelin ended up being sandwiched between the two in second place. This helped Javelin finish third in the T/A Championship, behind Ford Mustang in second and the Chevy Camaro in first. The series involved mostly "time races," where placement was determined by the number of laps completed after a set time limit.

The driver could then select the 10 best results from the season's 13 races. AMC and Javelin had started strong, and good results continued into the '69 racing season. Although AMC came fourth in '69, in reality they were a moral third. Chevrolet won again, Ford was second and Pontiac came third. However, the Firebird campaigned in '69 by T/G Racing was a Canadian back-door entry. GM of Canada sold Pontiacs that were Chevrolets with altered sheet metal and Chevy hearts. Because the Chevy 302 was a technical Canadian Firebird option, T/G Racing could campaign their car in '68. The team did so again in '69, although comically, since the '68 Chevy 302 Firebird option meant T/G Racing's '69 season racer had to look like a '68 Firebird, sheet metal-wise!

Thus, AMC was just behind Chevrolet and Ford once again, with enough kudos accrued to warrant a couple of special-edition Javelins for 1970. The two cars carried the revised '70 Javelin look, the rarest being the red, white and blue-liveried Trans Am Javelins, capturing the essence of the '69 Javelin Racing Team cars. Just 100 of these loaded road cars were produced. They were advertised with the following treats: 390 motor, Ram Air hood, real exhaust duals, HD engine cooling, Twin-Grip differential, 4-speed manual with Hurst shifter, power disk front brakes, HD suspension, front and rear spoilers, F70 section raised-white-letter Goodyear Polyglas 14-inchers, 140 mph speedo and tach!

The Kenosha-built Trans Am Javelins had the 7079–7 driver side metal door tag, which implied an SST car with American Motors' new-style front buckets with integrated headrests. All this was all yours for $3,995 with a factory-quoted curb weight of 3,340 lbs. The other special '70 model year car was more numerous — 2,501 were made — but was linked with one of the most famous names in U.S. racing. The 1970 Mark Donohue Signature Edition Javelin was the only production automobile to bear the moniker of the racing legend, and like the Trans Am Javelin is certainly a collectible AMC ride of the present.

The AMC print ad for the MD Javelin said, "Donohue puts his mark on the Javelin." That 2,501 build number was no random act; this machine was a homologation model to allow the use of certain racing parts under SCCA T/A rules for the '70 racing season. Mark Donohue was an engineer, a 1959 graduate of Brown University, and he designed the rear aero ducktail spoiler which bore his name, and which was fitted to all MD Javelins. The other ingredient slated for the MD Javelin was the 360 motor. The 360 V8 was a 1970 AMC newcomer, and it would help Javelin on the track, because of its intestinal fortitude.

The racing Javelins were using a mild 308-degree duration Engle camshaft, but this wasn't as limiting as block strength, key for race durability. The AMC small-block had higher nickel content than Chevy and Ford V8s, but the homologation of the 360 motor allowed a beefier block design with thicker webbing and 4-bolt mains to be utilized. Under American Motors' special high-performance parts catalogue, a '70 360 with 4-bolt mains carried the part number 448 8937.

The MD Javelin is thought of as an SST with 360, choice of console 4-speed or automatic, dual exhausts, power front disks, E70 Goodyear Polyglas 14-inch raised-white-letter tires, and that ducktail spoiler. However, the MD Javelin can be murkier than that. Some got the 390, non–Ram Air hoods, plus even column-shift autos (and not all of them) used the Javelin SST as a base. So although the MD Javelin was also made at Kenosha, not all have the 7079–7 SST door tag.

MD Javelins could be ordered in basic or loaded specs, with Adjust-O-Tilt steering wheel and in any Javelin exterior hue, including the Big Bad colors. Looking at the individual parts making up a Trans Am or MD Javelin, one sees parts that could be applied to any Javelin. The internal house memos of AMC's Director of Advertising E.B. Brogan bear this out, by stating either limited-edition Javelin could be created, in theory, by any dealer via ordering the parts and fitting them to a Javelin. Thus, the authenticity of either rests with the original window sticker.

The Donohue connection also concerned the on-track race campaign of 1970. Chevrolet dealer and team owner Roger Penske, with Mark Donohue, had dominated the SCCA T/A series in 1968 and 1969. Penske Racing was established in 1966, and for the '70 racing season switched camps from Chevrolet to AMC. If you can't beat them, sign a 3-year contract with them and get the victories that way. Donohue, the driver who showed them how it was done in the Penske Camaro, would now be piloting Javelin.

So Penske Racing would handle Javelin, and AMC wasted no time telling the public about their coup de grace. The ad showed the new '70-shape Javelin race car with the headline, "From zero to Donohue in 3.1 years." The results weren't slow in coming, Donohue snatched 2nd in his first Javelin outing at Laguna Seca. The '70 driver lineup for Penske Sunoco Javelin was Mark Donohue and Peter Revson. Javelin's first victory occurred on June 21, 1970, at Bridgehampton, when Donohue's Javelin saw off Mustang amidst much rain.

In fact, 1970 was the most competitive year for the big cars in SCCA T/A racing. Rule changes meant a large-displacement V8 design could be used, if it could be snuck within the 305ci limit. This left the door open to the new Mopar E-bodies, the Dodge Challenger and Plymouth Barracuda, as well as a real Pontiac-powered Firebird Trans Am. The Mopar cousins used destroked versions of the Chrysler 340, while the Firebird fielded a Ram Air 303 edition of the famous Poncho 400.

The manufacturers were really digging T/A racing in 1970, pumping money into the series so competitive machinery could be developed. Chrysler offered $1 million towards the Mopar cause, and Hot Wheels sponsored the Barracuda and Challenger. Indeed, the series gave rise to valuable collector road-going 1970 model year cars like the Chevy Camaro Z/28 (350ci), Dodge Challenger T/A 340, Plymouth Cuda AAR 340, Pontiac Firebird Trans Am Ram Air IV 400 and well-known Boss 302 Mustang. George Follmer, who used to be in the Javelin Racing Team, switched to Mustang in 1970.

It was thought the use of larger engines would provide a durability edge, but the front-runners were still small-block V8 users. Mark Donohue's nemesis in 1970 was Parnelli Jones in the Bud Moore Mustang. In the battle royale that ensued, Donohue managed a first at Elkhart Lake on July 19. By the final race at Riverside, Jones was on 4 victories, Donohue was on 3. In spite of several mishaps and race repairs, Parnelli Jones's Mustang won that final race, and by doing so secured the T/A Championship by a solitary point. Javelin was in second place.

Mustang was champ again for the first time since 1967, but it had almost been 3 in a row for Donohue and a first for Javelin. In the Trans Am and MD Javelins, AMC had two SCCA T/A related cars, and for those interested in the parts that made the track cars scoot, there were the Group 19 High Performance Parts. These mechanical upgrades were for

Javelin, AMX and American, to help these cars in motorsport and satisfy homologation requirements. If one went to certain participating AMC dealers with performance bias, they could get such parts.

Note that these hop-up parts couldn't be ordered AMC factory direct; due to their specialist nature, it had to be dealer-arranged. The list of items was extensive and often involved well-known aftermarket companies, such as Edelbrock. This company made two styles of intake manifold for the AMC small-block V8. There was the high-rise aluminum R4B, designed to take one 4-barrel carb. This item could be dealer-purchased with an AMC part number cast in, 448 5729 for 1967–69 cars and 448 8409 for the '70 model year on, or from Edelbrock themselves sans part number.

The mildly mad could skip R4B and go for Edelbrock's aluminum Cross Ram STRII, which accommodated two 4bbl carbs and had a removable top half. For 1967–69 cars the correct part number was 448 6228; on '70 and later AMCs it was 448 8411. One could get the same from Edelbrock minus the part numbers. The Cross Ram STRII was designed to work with carbs up to a 650 cfm limit, and was found on the AMX Super Stock drag racers, as well as in the SCCA T/A series.

In AMC's arsenal there was an optional Holley 4bbl with vacuum-activated secondaries that could be used on the stock intake manifold as a Carter AFB replacement, part number 448 5730, or with the R4B intake manifold. With R4B the carb carried the 448 5731 part number for 1967–69 cars, 448 8410 on '70 and later. With the Edelbrock R4B a special AMC Group 19 intake manifold gasket was needed. Otherwise an air passage would be open that would trigger the automatic choke permanently. This heat-blocker gasket had the part number 448 8475 for 1967–69s and 448 8476 for '70 and onwards.

Normally the 290s and 343s that left AMC, the company that claimed it had the world's biggest engine plant under one roof located in Kenosha, had cast malleable connecting rods and nodular iron crankshaft. This was fine for everyday road usage, but racing requires forged steel versions for durability. Group 19 had 290/343 forged connecting rods, part number 448 5725, and a forged steel crank listed under 448 5728. For high-rpm operation it was also wise to enlist AMC's sb V8 camshaft kit, with sports cam, special pushrods and lifters, double valve springs, seals, keepers, retainers and studs. The kit had the part number 448 6719 for manual transmission 1967–69 cars, 448 8413 for 1970–71 AMCs. A high-performance rocker arm set with longer screw-in studs had the part number 448 7989.

AMC produced cast aluminum pistons for its stock sb V8; the company didn't make forged equivalents, but these were available on the aftermarket. AMC also didn't make free-flow headers, but did assign part numbers, 448 5726 and 448 5727, for the headers one could get from California-based companies Jardine, Doug Thorley and Bellanger. AMC also assigned the 448 5741 part number to the 8.5-quart deep sump oil pan, which was to be ordered direct from the California firms Aviad Metal and Racing Components.

A Mallory-sourced dual-point ignition system with tach drive (part no. 448 8062), or without (part no. 448 8049) was around, as was a complete high-performance ignition system, including 3-piece distributor cap and external condenser, with mechanical tach drive (part no. 448 7901) or without (part no. 448 7900). Ending ignition hardware was a Capacitor Discharge Ignition System, part number designated 448 5742.

Dave Kempton's SS/FA 390ci AMX used stock AMX 4-wheel drums; disk brakes created slightly more wind resistance, so were generally avoided in the ¼-mile. However, heavy-

For 1970, Javelin featured revised exterior styling, new 304/360 V8 engine options, an amended smooth dashboard, and oversize front buckets with integrated headrests (courtesy Wayne Davis).

duty rear drum brakes were listed in Group 19, with part numbers 448 5736 and 448 5737. Heavy-duty front disks with hub and calliper listed under part numbers 448 5732 and 448 5733. For $1,000 AMC had rear disks; such were available for Camaro Z/28 and Firebird too under homologation provisions, with hub and calliper (part numbers 448 5734 and 448 5735).

There were 15 × 8-inch American Racing Equipment–made rims available, just like the Javelin Racing Team cars wore. The special brakes and alloy rims could be obtained through Ronnie Kaplan Engineering, the company preparing the Javelin Racing Team racers. One couldn't be serious without the positive locking differential, part number 448 6997, and for drag racers there were AMX traction bars listed for Javelin (448 5582) and American (448 5753). There were also extensive homologation SCCA T/A aerodynamic aids.

A fiberglass front spoiler mounted via brackets to lower fender braces and a center bracket: this was for 1968–70 AMX with part number 364 1522. Outside Group 19 a stainless steel front spoiler (899 2553) was an alternative for 1968–70 Javelin and AMX. There were two rear trunk-lid wings; version 1 was coded 899 2357, had no metal end plates, and was problematic, which gave rise to version 2. The latter was a Group 19 fiberglass wing with metal end plates, and was height adjustable. It had two metal stands with 2 sets of holes drilled in to set the 2 height positions.

The version 2 wing was the one fitted to the 1970 limited-edition red, white and blue Trans Am Javelin, but the ducktail spoiler on the '70 MD Javelin was a non–Group 19 part. So was the 1969–70 Javelin roof spoiler, just a normal accessory part. In all the wonderment of Group 19, some reality needs to be considered. How many owners of a brand-spanking-new '68 Javelin would tear down their 290 or 343 to fit forged engine parts?

One could enjoy the SCCA T/A races without wishing to turn the daily driver into a road-course warrior. The red, white and blue Javelin Racing Team jacket was available for $9.95 retail, $6.50 wholesale if one knew a dealership buddy. Wear the jacket, have some popcorn, chomp on a Red Hot, maybe even affix a Sunoco decal to the Javelin's rear window? Why make sacrifices when Donohue was doing the winning for you? The rear disk brake conversion was ⅓ the cost of a well-specified V8 Javelin SST!

Only a few hundred Edelbrock Cross Ram intake manifolds were made for AMC cars, and practicality wasn't on your side. Fit the Edelbrock R4B on a V8 with stock air-cleaner housing, and the hood wouldn't shut! With Edelbrock's Cross Ram STRII intake manifold, there was no hole for a heater hose, or for a brake booster line. Technically with the Cross Ram there was insufficient vacuum for power brakes. This was no problem on the Cross Ram using Super Stock Javelins; usually they had drag-racer drums, and drums have a natural assistance making boost nonessential. However, most folks wanted power brakes, and if vacuum wipers were fitted it behooved one to have been afraid, very afraid.

Instead of building a 7,000 rpm screamer, one could select the $168.40 390 V8 and keep the sensible Carter AFB. Eight-inch-wide racing rims and an adjustable-height rear wing might also have been overkill for the road — although the latter would have been priceless to lean on, as your Corvette-owning neighbor pulled into the golf club parking lot. The Group 19 parts that AMC and others offered, plus the T/A series cars, generated a mystique that was advertising gold.

Typical of the period was a Mustang Boss 302 ad that described the ecstasy of dropping a gear in the 4-speed box, flooring the gas and letting the jewel of a small block spin as the Boss 302 showed its "handling on rails" quality in a turn. Some companies familied up their ads by showing a young couple with their new pony car, and AMC/Wells, Rich & Greene used the Mr. and Mrs. Breedlove angle. However, the Naderites weren't placated by foam-padded dashboards, safety switches and seat belts for long. They read between the lines and considered all the above an open invitation to the nation's youth to treat the public highway as a racetrack, which some did.

In present times, Group 19 parts are rare and valuable. Items come across will most likely be kept "new in box" as period examples of the zenith of the domestic high-performance era, too historically significant to fit to an actual car. This is probably all for the best; AMC didn't provide an air cleaner to go with the Cross Ram intake manifold, and aluminum intake manifolds were notoriously cold-natured, driveability-wise. Some things are best admired from afar, like a mid-engined sports car.

The AMX/3: Modena Meets Kenosha

By the late '60s things were moving to the mid-engined format in the sphere of ultimate cars. Before this the racing world had seen front-engined designs overtaken by those that placed the motor in the middle, and now it was happening with road cars. The Lamborghini Miura made Ferraris and Aston Martins seem old-fashioned, and soon most manufacturers had a mid-engined car in production or being planned. Remember the Fiat X1/9 and Porsche 914? Daimler-Benz was working on a 4-rotor Wankel-powered model called C111. All these cars had a 2-seat, 2-door layout, what one expected in a mid-engined machine.

The domestic automakers were also working on such a design, even though muscle and pony cars were their main game. GM had something called Astro II, a mid-engined design influenced by the Mako Shark show car in terms of general styling. This design was expected to be the next Corvette at some point in the '70s. After all, the current Vette's chassis dated back to 1963. This proposed car never saw production, and the Corvette stayed front-engined through the troubled '70s GM had to endure.

Ford was expected to deliver a great mid-engined ride. The company had the Le Mans-winning GT40, and even offered 7 examples of same to the public in sanitized road-car form. In 1967 one had the chance to buy an uptrimmed, exhaust-muffled GT40 Mk III for $20,800.[3] For this outlay the GT40 was fitted with a "detuned" 302 that made 335 bhp, at a moment when the 2bbl 302 in Mustang had 223 gross ponies. Good, but still a mite raw, so Ford worked on a more civilized Mach II, and there was also a GT70.

Ford of Europe's Boreham competition department came up with a true road-going version of the GT40, that would be comfy and might have challenged the Lancia Stratos in '70s rallying. However, U.S. Ford management took one look at the GT70 and said bury it! This was because they were cooking up a deal to sell the De Tomaso Pantera through Lincoln-Mercury dealerships across the land. Old Henry gave the Pantera the 351 and his blessing. However, right under the Big 3's noses, AMC was getting ready to unveil its mid-engined sports car first!

If the original AMX showcar of spring 1966 promised much, then the AMX/2 suggested AMC was ready to blow everyone out of the water. The AMX/2 was shown in the spring of 1969, seen at the Chicago and New York International Auto Shows. Resplendent in an intoxicating iridescent red, the AMX/2 announced AMC was in the ultra-car race too, with something that would debut in the '71 model year. The swoopy 2-seater sat on magnesium rims, 15 × 8.5-inch front and 15 × 9.5-inch rear, wearing Goodyear Blue-Streak rubber. The AMX/2 was enigmatic; it didn't give much away.

For '70, Javelin length rose from 189.2 inches to 191 inches. The increase was fitting because 1970 would prove to be the zenith of the performance era. The rocker panel exhaust outlets were decorative, but visually welcome (courtesy Wayne Davis).

The facts on AMX/2 stated a 171.5-inch length and 105-inch wheelbase, a mid-engine placement and some mechanical suggestions. There were two hood impressions and two backlights; this Noah's Ark approach was the reason for the AMX/2 moniker. The car would have all-independent suspension, all-wheel disk brakes and driver-controllable spoilers. As expected, a horizontal-mounted radiator would sit in the nose; the smooth-front AMX/2 was a "bottom breather." Water hoses traveled from the radiator rearwards, under the center console, to the amidships V8.

C pillar scoops would admit air to the carb/intake manifold. Specific info was scarce: yes, a V8 with transaxle was intended, but which AMC V8 and transaxle? It was known the steering gear and front suspension would be AMC passenger car sourced, but the rear suspension was a mystery, the only noise being hub carriers with elongated fingers connecting to control arms. The AMX/2 was 43 inches high; the Ford GT40 was 40 inches, hence its name. The AMX/2 was 70.4 inches wide; the GT40 was originally 164.6 inches long with a width of 70 inches.

Signs were that the AMX/2 would be livable, and that it would be placed in production. The remaining vagueness was because AMX/2 was a big model, not a real functioning device. The darkly tinted windows concealed an interior that was no more than 2 headrests and the top section of a steering wheel, all one would notice at a glance. The gas tank wasn't real; neither was the engine. However, that green plastic pretend engine suggested that AMC was thinking of a Wankel engine for the AMX/2.

The Wankel aspect was like the Mercedes C111, but there was no gullwing in the AMX/2 decoy, and like a plastic duck the AMX/2 drew attention from the real car AMC was working on. The whole project started from an idea by AMC's Product Development Group VP Gerry Meyers. Meyers set up a competition between American Motors' styling department and Italy's Giorgetto Giugiaro, to see which side could come up with a better mousetrap. In Kenosha versus Modena Team Teague won out in November '68, with their work displayed as the AMX/2 while the technical side was done.

AMC's stylists had finished the look of AMX/3 by the time AMX/2 was on show in February 1969. To develop the engineering side and build AMX/3, AMC sought help from a number of parties. Karmann's coachbuild price was too high and Pininfarina was busy. Richard Teague was a fan of Pininfarina's flowing designs, and AMX/3 looked as good as anything the Italians had cooked up. Pininfarina suggested AMC should knock on the door of talented, but financially shaky, designer/coachbuilder Bizzarrini.

Giotto Bizzarrini knew a few things about ultra-cars: he had worked for Enzo Ferrari and had done the 1962 Iso Rivolta and 1963 Iso Grifo. The Isos were acknowledged as great designs and excellent road cars, and being U.S. V8-powered Italian hybrids, they had a natural flow on to the AMX/3. The racing Grifo was sold as the Bizzarrini GT America. Bizzarrini was known for the use of parallel wishbone independent suspension with pivots designed to yield a low horizontal roll axis. It was safe to assume AMX/3 would handle OK with its front and rear swaybars.

The AMX/3 used AMC-sourced front suspension spindles, balljoints, unequal length control arms, plus steering linkage and Saginaw steering column and box. Rear suspension was listed as unequal length control arms with aluminum-cast suspension uprights. Coils were used all around, with twin coils/shocks per side at the rear. As expected from AMX/2, the radiator was in the nose, and AMX/3 had two thermo fans. The engine proposed was the 390ci AMC V8 rated at a "Machine" spec 340 horses.

The use of a high-torque V8 caused AMC to seek out a strong transaxle. This led them to Italian company OTO Melara, who specially designed an aluminum-cased transaxle with Porsche-type synchromesh, capable of withstanding the Rebel Machine spec 430 lbs/ft. The layout was the 4-speed gearbox, then the small-block V8 ahead of the rear axle line. Driveshafts with Rzeppa style constant velocity universal joints were used too.

The AMX/3 had exterior dimensions of 175.6-inch length, 74.9-inch width and 43.5-inch height. This implied more interior space and legroom, plus an engine that could stay in the engine bay. In the Swiss Hemi 426–powered Monteverdi Hai, the U.S. V8 big-block actually lived inside the cabin. The motor snugly sat between the 2-seater's buckets, under a nicely trimmed engine cover. The AMX/3's use of a small block, and the car's length, allowed the 390 V8 to be completely in the engine compartment, with a full-size spare tire.

The AMX/3 shown to the press and in magazines had a B.F. Goodrich Space Saver. Either way, the spare sat above the gearbox and behind the 390's air cleaner. The rear engine deck lid was partially glass, so ⅔ of the air cleaner was visible. Driver rearward vision was also good for a mid-engined car. The raised-rear central spine of the AMX/2 was gone, replaced by a well-sized double-glazed concave pane that was part of the large flip-back engine deck lid. There was a single row of functional air louvers on the deck lid to expel engine heat, once again not as fancy as the twin sets on AMX/2.

AMX/3 wasn't as futuristic-looking as AMX/2, but it was an attractive sports car with more curves than the Pantera, along with AMC's sensible flush-fitting door handles, the

American Motors had concrete plans for a 2-seater mid-engined sports car using its most powerful V8, and worthy of the AMX tag. The AMX/2 was a 1969 show circuit teaser to whet the public's appetite (artwork by author).

very normal dashboard with provision for full Weather Eye HVAC, and even well-designed, subtle side marker lights. The AMX/3 looked so production-ready it might already have been in dealerships, which was the goal all along. The 24-gallon gas tank was situated on the rear left driver side, filled from a flush circle flap on the sail panel. For good weight distribution the battery was placed on the rear right passenger side.

Weight distribution on the AMX/3 was 43/57 percent front to rear. The coupe had a 66-degree-angle windshield and looked very trick, but Richard Teague admitted many years later that no formal aero wind-tunnel testing was done in the modern '80s idiom. Teague mentioned a front spoiler wasn't on AMX/3, since they weren't in fashion; this contributed to the front end's going light at speed, once again not unlike a Pantera. Look back to early Panteras, Miuras and the Ferrari 365 GT4 Berlinetta Boxer: these mid-engined cars also lacked front spoilers.

As these designs, or their successors, moved into the '80s, the aero aid was incorporated and lived up to its name by spoiling design purity. The often-seen AMX/3 wore rear 1970½–1973 Pontiac Firebird–sourced taillights turned upside down. It was common for Italian ultra-cars of the time to use Fiat lighting parts. The Lamborghini Miura used front headlamps from the Fiat 850, while the luxury Ferrari 365 GT4 2+2 used taillights from the same Fiat.

Mr. Bizzarrini went to the same Fiat for round rear taillights for AMX/3. Richard Teague wasn't crazy about these units; after all, you can put lipstick on a Fiat, but it's still a Fiat. Thus, AMX/3 number 5, the last car Bizzarrini built, used GM-sourced taillights. Teague ended up personally owning this yellow-exteriored number 5 AMX/3. The other interesting thing back there was a pop-up flush-mounted panel spoiler, which would arise at speed to increase downforce and stability.

Similarly subtle at the front, between obligatory electrically powered pop-up headlamps, was an automatically opening letterbox port to route fresh air to the AMX/3's interior, since you wouldn't be driving with the windows down on the Autostrada. Top speed on unregulated European freeways would be 160 mph. This was the figure touted for an AMX/3 weighing 3,090 lbs, and powered by the 340 bhp 390ci V8. That would have made the AMX/3 on a par with the Maserati Bora V8. AMX/3 acceleration with mooted 3.45 rear ratio was in the mid–5-second bracket for 0–60 mph.

In this league of thrust, AMX/3 needed super brakes, and it had them. Inner-vented 4-wheel Teves-sourced disk brakes were there with ATE calipers. Two-piston brake calipers were used at the front, with two single-pot calipers for each rear wheel. To make sure AMX/3 was legit, Bizzarrini took the semi-unibody, his chassis description, to the old Nürburgring, where the AMX/3 pulled 145 mph on one straight in top gear fourth, with the 3.45 final drive.

AMC, not taking any chances, hired BMW to test out AMX/3, fine-tune the suspension settings and make suggestions. The West German firm had a test track in northeastern Munich, a computer test bed that simulated the Nürburgring, and the AMX/3 was also put through its paces by BMW's engineers and test drivers in the Bavarian Alps. This was the acid test for durability-trialing the AMX/3's hardware, and Kenosha's coupe came through with flying colors, naturally.

The wheels and tires chosen for AMX/3 were Italian Campagnolo cast-magnesium 15-inchers, 6.5 inches wide at the front, 9 inches wide at the back. The VR-rated Michelin X tires were sized 205/70 front and 225/70 rear. Unknown to AMC at the time (Richard Teague even said they worked on AMX/3 unaware of the Pantera), BMW was working on a mid-engined 155 mph 2 seater gullwing sports car of its own. This gullwing, powered by a turbo version of the BMW 2002 engine, had safety car touches and would be shown in 1972. Perhaps the German engineers took some inspiration from AMX/3?

However, the Pantera would be the AMX/3's chief domestic rival. The cars were similar, both being steel-monocoque mid-engined V8s, but their differences suggested one was better off with AMC. The Pantera used a ZF transaxle; AMC chose the OTO Melara transaxle because they thought the ZF unit was too weak for their 390. Performance between the two was similar; the AMX/3 was more powerful, but larger and heavier. U.S. buyers would have appreciated the AMC's supersize.

Pantera's technical side was handled by Italian Giampaolo Dallara, the AMX/3 by Bizzarrini, but AMX/3 benefited through AMC's project input. The Pantera was good, but raw, not quite finished at launch. The interior layout was worthy of Salvador Dalí, and those Italian idiosyncrasies reminded one this wasn't a Ford. With AMX/3, another 4 inches were added behind the rear wheels to permit larger mufflers. The Pantera was badged a De Tomaso, the AMX/3 an AMC, and the American consumer would have quickly seen why.

In spite of killing off in-house designs in favor of the Pantera, Henry was still beaten to the punch by one day. In the unveiling of America's first mid-engined machine, the AMX/3 was presented at the Rome Hilton hotel in Italy, one day ahead of the Pantera. Even though they didn't let on, AMC's people must have known the Pantera was imminent. Starting from an idea in July '68, here was the result two years later.

Nineteen seventy was the year when you decided if you were in or out. Monteverdi was in: the Hai made its debut at the Geneva Autoshow in March 1970, but Mercedes got cold feet. In the Daimler-Benz boardroom that year the gullwing MB C111 missed going into low-volume production by just one vote. They were worried about the Wankel engine: would the C111's halo glow be worth the outlay and probable loss of money on each car sold? Conservative management buckled and retired to their compact diesel taxis to eat porridge!

Unfortunately AMC had to give up plans to make the AMX/3 too. The idea was to get Bizzarrini, who specially reopened his little factory, to make 24 1971 AMX/3s, with a showroom price of $10,000. Sadly, a number of factors worked against this happening. The coachbuilder price was always a problem, but equally so were pending federal regs like impact bumpers. The AMX/3 shown at the Hilton had painted steel bumpers, but giving the car the necessary 5 mph bumpers proved difficult.

Richard Teague said the technology for 5 mph bumpers that wouldn't ruin the car's look wasn't there at the time. GM was testing soft bumpers on New York taxis during this period, and the fruit of their research was the 5 mph front bumper on the 1973 Corvette. AMC didn't have the money to tackle this problem, and America lost out on a new AMX/3 with a real 6.5 cu ft trunk, which the '73 Corvette didn't have. Mercedes ended up making 13 C111s for their own uses, BMW built 2 gullwing Turbos, and Bizzarrini produced 5 AMX/3s. Bizzarrini made an initial 2, with 3 more cars before the project was wound up.

In the end, AMC turned over the rights to the AMX/3 design to Bizzarrini, who sold a few AMX/3s under the moniker Bizzarrini Sciabola in Italy. One more AMX/3 was assembled from parts at a later date by a private party, making 6 AMX/3s created in total. If AMX/3 had arrived in the '71 model year it would have had the new 401ci V8, AMC's 390 replacement, which wouldn't have affected performance from the projected AMX/3 390 figures.

The Pantera went on to become the top-selling car of its type in North America, before the fuel crisis struck and Lincoln-Mercury cast out poor Pantera in '75. Interest in this kind

The Javelin held to the pony car trend of puffing out sheet metal on an existing platform to create a bigger, more imposing car. Richard Teague didn't exactly see it as an advance, but marketing loved it! This special order '72 Javelin AMX was originally purchased by an AMC zone manager, and had SCCA Trans Am period features like a lead loaded and balanced racing body and Cross Ram STRII intake manifold for the homologated 360. The Findlay, Ohio, car was ordered in D7 Trans Am Red with functional cowl induction, 3.15 Twin-Grip, Go-pack, Rally-Pac, automatic, power steering, power disks, 15 in rims, AM/FM radio and rear window defogger (courtesy Eddie Stakes).

of ultra-car was on the decline by the mid–'70s. The small specialist firms suffered falling sales, and Detroit wasn't making the high-output ohv V8s that they and Formula 5000 racing had relied on for years. This left the scene to the Italian establishment that used in-house engines.

Exotic mid-engined sports cars have been around since the AMX/3, but with its demise and Ford's ending the De Tomaso deal, so closed the chance of ordering an ultra-car from the local neighborhood dealer, via Italy, for reasonable money. In the history of American cars the AMX/3 is still the only one of its kind that can truly claim to be of U.S. design. AMC would continue to make sporting cars after 1970, but that side now rested with the Javelin pony car. Domestic 2-seaters were now confined to plastic Chevys.

The Humperdinck Javelin, 1971–74

It's hard to quantify the halo effect of a car. The AMX brought a good measure of publicity to American Motors, no doubt about it. The 1968 *Playboy* magazine Playmate of the Year, Angela Dorian, was presented with a brand-new pink 290ci AMX 2-seater. This car had Miss Dorian's vital stats displayed on a plaque on the dash; she subsequently had the plaque removed and the AMX repainted black. At the other end of the spectrum, Barry Goldwater, arch-conservative Arizona Senator and presidential candidate in the '64 national U.S. election, also owned an AMX.

In the early '70s, folks turned to sport compacts to beat the rising cost of motoring. This purple and white striped '73 Javelin 304 V8 resides in the National Automotive and Truck Museum located in Auburn, Indiana (courtesy Frank Gilbert).

Regardless of one's modesty of attire, AMX was the "in" car of 1968, and the Industrial Design Institute awarded AMX "Best Automobile Design" that year. Everyone, it would seem, was happy to show AMC a little sugar, but the bean-counters soon grew restless. The '70 model year had its woes; a strike in the fall of 1969 contributed to the posting of a $39.8 million loss as well as a reduced number of AMX sales. In addition, the pony car craze seemed past its peak and AMC boss William Luneburg considered axing both AMX and Javelin!

AMC had a number of family-car-type new releases in 1970 and 1971, so sporty rides seemed extravagant. The changing economic times were no doubt a big reason why the AMX/3 project was canned. Nevertheless, there was a new Javelin for '71, nicknamed "Humpster Javelin" on account of its noticeable fender arches. To this point Javelin had always looked low-key, but now it was the most outlandish-looking pony.

There had been a trend since 1968 of puffing out ponies; the cars of this segment were lengthened on existing wheelbases with wilder sheet metal. This was done with the '71 Javelin too, although the car did grow an honest inch to a 110-inch wheelbase. Richard Teague wasn't as pleased with the styling of the '71 Javelin, compared to the purity of earlier versions, saying it was a move initiated by marketing to stay abreast with Mustang et al. However, he did concede that the '71 Javelin was more of a scene stealer.

Richard Teague still felt strongly about the need to continue the 2-seater AMX, so much so that he made a '71 AMX 2-seater prototype/study car based on his own silver-blue '68 AMX. Teague added the hump fenders and Trendsetter side exhaust covers to persuade management to reconsider, but Luneburg said no dice. On the face of it, AMX sales were a drop in the bucket, but Teague felt the Javelin-based 2-seater brought positive publicity to the marque.

The official AMC line was that customers visiting AMC showrooms wanted an AMX with 4 seats, hard to imagine given that was Javelin's job ... blame it on those bean-counters! Thus, for the next 4 years, Javelin and AMX were both 2+2s; varying only in terms of trim, performance options and cosmetics, they shared the same unibody now. Compared to 1970 the Javelin's length went up from 191 inches to 191.8 inches and its width rose from 71.9 inches to 75.2 inches, with a manufacturer-stated weight increase of 61 lbs.

The Javelin's front track remained 59.3 inches, but rear track increased by 3 inches to 60 inches. Javelin had a unique, tougher look compared to before. Those fender bulges were Can Am sports car-inspired. On a racing low-slung sports car with limited suspension travel, such bulging fenders are needed to house big wheels. However, on the '71 Javelin, the wheels are quite far away from the bulges. Function followed form, but no matter, it looked cool. Richard Teague referred to the bulges as blister-type fenders; they were the work of AMC stylist Eric Kugler.

The Javelin's new interior set it apart from the pony crowd even more: '71 brought a divided dash with curved control center for the driver. It predated the 1973 Pontiac Grand Am's dash, and set a new standard in pony-car ergonomics. The Weather Eye panel was now in the middle of the dash, in front of the shifter. Previously specifying a/c brought 2 outlets; now there were 4 ideally placed vents, which improved system effectiveness. Paying $120 over the base $2,879 1971 Javelin allowed the owner to move up to SST trim level. The price of Javelin a/c was now a hefty $399.

By gaining altitude to SST level, the dash took on imitation burled walnut trim; a/c made things chilly, but others only thought you were really cool with AMX. On sports AMX the walnut was replaced with imitation engine-turned metal, like that used in the 1970½ Pontiac Trans Am. The '71 divided dash plus metal-effect cladding made the dash seem NASA-designed. A spacesuit and helmet were more appropriate for AMX than racing overalls! Javelin didn't hide its light under a bushel. The SST badge was now located in front of the rear side marker, and 360/401 engine badge callouts were behind the front side marker if one ticked off the big motor options.

The new Javelin had more than appearance: it was the first to become SCCA T/A champ, achieving such under the watch of Penske Racing Enterprises. Roger Penske and Mark Donohue came close in '70, and 1971 would see them reach the pinnacle in a series that was already feeling the pinch. In 1971 Mark Donohue commented on the stiff cost of Trans Am racing, saying the old '70 racing Javelin totaled at least $62,000 given its specialized hardware and the preparation of a quality outfit like Penske Racing.

The rulebook had been loosened for the 1970 season, which meant more mods and greater series costs. Ford and Chrysler had pulled out official support at the close of the 1970 season, figuring the kudos weren't worth the money. AMC reasoned a motorsport profile was still good for public product perception, so they continued. Roger Penske used only one driver for '71: Mark Donohue in the #6 Sunoco Javelin was enough. The pre–'71 racing Javelins were offloaded to the Roy Woods Racing–run American Racing Associates (ARA).

Apart from the new sheet metal to reflect the current Javelin, the '71 Sunoco Javelin sported engineering developments that couldn't be seen by race fans. There was a new dry sump lubrication system for 1971, new induction and exhaust, as well as Mark Donohue aero input for the road and race Javelin. The basic '71 Javelin shape was done by the time Donohue came on the scene, but he influenced the design of AMX's fiberglass hood, which was part of the windshield-base-fed cold-air induction system, plus the front and rear AMX spoilers.

Donohue also suggested AMC engineers put more anti-dive into the front suspension, as well as use better balljoint hardware. The Humpster Javelin was a better shape aerodynamically: it was slipperier but with more downforce where necessary. Compared to 1970 the Javelin's air drag was cut from 390 lbs to 365 lbs. Front lift was up from 335 lbs to 380 lbs, rear end lift was -80 lbs in 1970 and was now +45 lbs. So the '71 Javelin could reach higher top speeds on the straights, and maintain grip in the corners.

Penske Racing winter-tested the '71 Sunoco Javelin at California's Ontario Motor Speedway. If you want to see how this venue looked at the time, the opening scenes of the 1971 movie *Evel Knievel* starring George Hamilton show the track. During testing at the Speedway it was recorded that the '71 Javelin AMX rear spoiler was worth 100 lbs of downforce, handy when trying to use the power of the Traco Engineering–built small-block V8.

To avoid the initial mistake Chrysler made with Charger in NASCAR, Mark Donohue advised AMC to make the Javelin AMX's grille flush for improved airflow. The '71 Sunoco Javelin was built in Philadelphia, and track success came fast. After 8 races Donohue had achieved 6 consecutive victories, the only opposition coming from George Follmer in the Bud Moore Mustang, plus Peter Revson in the #68 ARA Javelin. Mark Donohue attained 7 race wins in 1971, which made him series champion as well as giving AMC the Manufacturer's Championship for the first time.

With a professional concern like Penske Racing, success was bound to come, and Donohue was the Trans Am driver's champ for the third time. Javelin continued on its winning way through the '72 racing season. Former Javelin Racing Team driver George Follmer in the aptly numbered #1 ARA Javelin brought home the bacon. The ARA Javelin was supported by AMC dealers, with Follmer securing the Driver's Championship and a second Manufacturer's Championship for AMC.

Javelin had achieved all that could be gained from the Trans Am series, and AMC celebrated with a special limited run of 1973 Javelin Trans Am Victory Editions. These well-optioned cars had large Trans Am Victory Edition decals on the front fenders, which read "SCCA 1971–72 Trans Am Champs." The cars had AMC's 14-inch sport slot rims with E70 raised-white-letter tires and space saver; if only the SCCA's series could be inflated with a gas can! By 1973 the manufacturer exodus from Trans Am racing and the series' escalating costs saw the big car ranks opened to foreign makes for the first time. However, no matter, Javelin had done the T/A series!

By this time buyers were more interested in style than speed, so in stepped the Pierre Cardin appearance package in the '72 model year. American Motors was getting into tie-ups with designer labels and fashion icons, and adding the Pierre Cardin pack to Javelin or Javelin AMX jazzed up the Humpster even more. The Pierre Cardin interior involved stripes of Chinese red, silver, plum and white on a black material background. This profusion of color transpired on the seating surfaces, door trim panels and headliner.

A total of 4,152 Pierre Cardin Javelin/Javelin AMXs were made, a popular option given its restriction to cars with Trans Am Red, Snow White, Stardust Silver, Diamond Blue and Wild Plum exteriors. That said, 12 Pierre Cardin-specified cars left Kenosha with Midnight Black exterior in 1972, and contrary to press info releases, the Pierre Cardin pack was still available in '74. The presence of Pierre Cardin can be discerned from the Javelin's door tag:

Top: During 1972–74 the 255 bhp (SAE net) AMX 401 with Go-pack was one of the few genuine remaining examples of the domestic high-performance car. A 1973 automatic example is shown. Between 1971 and 1974 AMX shared Javelin's 2+2 body (courtesy Jim Stokkeland). ***Bottom:*** The 304ci automatic Javelin, like this 1974 car, was the sensible choice in a motor lineup that still extended from 100 bhp 232 I6 to 255 bhp 401 V8 (courtesy Scott Wilhour).

the last letter would say "W" in 1972 to indicate Wellington vinyl and "S" on '73 and '74 cars for Uganda vinyl.

However, by choosing the right power teams, one could marry panache with performance. It may have been the '71 model year with motors taking a compression ratio gulp for low lead, but it was all still in the pantry. Ecofiends still had an ally in the base 232, which "sported" an 8.0:1 compression ratio and 135 gross horses. To cope with tightening emissions, AMC introduced their 258 I6 and 401 V8 for '71, and these were two of the best power plants in the business. The new 4.2-liter I6 wasn't far from the 2bbl 304, and one had to go 360ci to gain a real advantage.

The most powerful engine AMC made was the 330 bhp (gross) 401 V8. Max power arrived at just 5,000 rpm, with a goodly 430 lbs/ft at 3,400 rpm. The motor was redlined at 5 grand, had cast-iron 4-into-1 headers, and with it there was no performance loss compared to the 390, in spite of a compression ratio drop to 9.5:1. Zero to sixty was 6.5 seconds, exactly the same as 390ci Javelins, which suggested the 401 was more potent since the new car weighed more. In 1971, a period of transition, automakers were switching from gross to net figures.

Net flywheel readings are more honest, since they are taken with manifolds and ancillaries attached. For '72 AMC dropped the CU again, for tightening emissions, and quoted all motors in net S.A.E. terms. Thus, we now enjoyed the 100 bhp 232, 110 bhp 258 and 150 bhp 304. The 2-barrel 360 was rated at 175 horses, the 4bbl 360 had 195 bhp and punched out to 220 ponies with optional duals. The top 401 4-barrel with duals now delivered 255 net horses and had a compression ratio of 8.5:1, which meant it could now avoid premium gas.

Don't cry: the 401ci Javelin could still make the tires fry! In spite of the ratings game and easing of one's ecological conscience, the sacrifice was a 0–60 mph time of 7 seconds flat, and that could be relied on until the end of '74 MY in AMC's stabilized smog motor lineup. Javelin still had the performance factor, and this was recognized by the Alabama police force. In many countries, the police like to use a hot car to deter road users from breaking the law; Alabama state director of public safety Colonel Walter L. Allen bought this reasoning, which led to an AMC trial.

A trial sample of 401ci 4bbl Javelins were brought in and fitted with full HD law enforcement equipment. State troopers then proceeded to use the Javelin 401s and record the results. After 11 weeks and 22,000 miles, the log revealed Javelin 401 had a 95 percent-plus police officer approval rating, so the force decided to let Javelin be with them! Seventy Javelin 401s were purchased in 1971, 62 in '72, to clock up 70,000 miles per annum and to be sold at police auction to the public once 120,000 miles had accrued.

AMC had maintained its reputation for quality; one doesn't want to pull over with vapor lock when chasing a moonshiner into Dead Man's Hollow! You also needed good brakes, and AMC always had those, but there was a new system for '71. There was a change from Bendix to Kelsey Hayes 10.9-inch vented front disks and 10-inch rear drums, available boosted or non-boosted. AMC's automatic door-locking Pre-Set Impulse system continued to be available. The setting knob was under the armrest. In '72 came notable engineering changes like the adoption of optional Torque Command auto.

The '71 Javelin's console auto shifter was an aircraft throttle-type bar, but was still attached to the old BW Shift Command autobox that had design origins in the Ford empire. This old design, with brake bands that had to be adjusted periodically, was replaced by the quick-shifting Chrysler Torqueflite auto that used clutches, not brake bands. This modern unit was sold in AMC vehicles using the Torque Command description. AMC made the Torqueflite switch across all model lines in the '72 model year.

There was also the touted arrival of 1972's "Zero-Lash" balljoint front suspension upper pivot. AMC literature described the move to a one-piece ball/stud, which was claimed to be stronger, tighter-sealing, and able to retain a set tolerance for longer. Back in the '70 model year, AMC had changed from having one balljoint and trunion to two balljoints. This later design can be retrofitted to earlier AMCs by drilling one hole in the joint plate so the second balljoint can be bolted to the lower control arm. The imaginatively named Zero-Lash 1972 change involved going from a two-piece to a one-piece balljoint "socket assembly."

Also in 1972, I6 Javelins became available with AMC's front disk brake pack; previously this option was reserved for V8 Javelins. That year AMC also stated it was using quieter and longer-lasting cylindrical rocker arm bearings on its I6s and V8s. American Motors was also getting Javelin up to speed on federal regs. The '72 Javelins had standard side-impact door beams, and Javelin was ready to meet the January 1, 1972, requirement of inertia-reel front and rear outer seat belts, with attendant lamp/buzzer warning against non-usage.

Strangely this was a time when pony cars were doing well; their death had been foretold, but sales were steady in 1972–74, and even picked up slightly. In a trend accelerating with the fuel crisis, people were moving to smaller rides, and before downsizing happened for real, the switch was being made to subcompacts, compacts and ponies. People wanted a smaller, easier-to-handle vehicle with lower running costs to fight '70s inflation. Ponies fitted the bill, but they were changing.

Buyers wanted their cars well equipped. In '71 the SST outsold the base model 17,707 to 7,105; thus AMC dropped the latter at the close of '71. This left Javelin SST and AMX, and interest in AMX was rising. Note that AMC eliminated the SST tag by model year '73, so call it "lux" for reference ease! Buyers weren't as obsessed with powerful engine options, but were seeking out the top performance version for the complete package it represented. The reason such versions like the Camaro Z/28, Firebird Trans Am and Mustang Mach 1 351 were increasingly sought was that as the general level of performance was falling, these were the last refuges for enthusiasts. They had the most handling and power as emissions and economy took their toll.

There was also an image reverse sleeper factor in the '70s. It wasn't cool to run around in dog-bowl hubcaps and primer anymore; a nice ride had to look fast. Thus, it all came together in cars like the AMX, as people sought out the few remaining examples of the "tuned" road car. These top-dog versions, which used to be a small percentage of the mix, now rose to prominence. In 1971 2,054 AMXs were sold, in '72 this figure was 3,220 units and in 1973 5,707 Javelin AMXs went out the door.

With the boring factors biting harder, it was ironic that the public wanted the "hot" versions even more. The wider fan base for the American performance car — let's not use the terms muscle or pony by 1972/73 — was shown by AMC's making the 304 V8 the AMX's base engine for '72; in 1971 it had been the 360, but the AMX and its ilk were now more family racers. Cruise securely at 80 mph, negotiate twisting mountain roads, go buy a toaster at Sears: you could do it in an AMX.

The 4-seat AMX had the look: standard ducktail SCCA T/A rear spoiler, optional chin front spoiler, red, white and Sunoco blue "AMX" badge on the fine chain-mail mesh flush front grille and sail panels, plus contrasting hood T-stripe decal. The wider rear track of the latest Javelin aided the macho quotient, as did the option of Rebel Machine 15-inch rims in 1971 and 1972. However, the AMX wasn't just a show pony. The man who raced it also owned a Javelin AMX.

In advertising, AMC referred to the Sunoco Javelin as "THE STORM," and Mark Donohue also personally owned a new-shape '71 401ci Javelin AMX. He made modifications to this car to raise its level of active safety. There was a 13-inch padded sports steering wheel, fast steering courtesy of shortened steering arms, 7-inch-wide front rims with E60–15-inch tires, and 9-inch-wide rear rims with G60–15-inch tires. The front suspension was adjusted to reduce toe steer, and stiffer lower control arm pivot bushings were employed.

The front springs and all 4 shocks were stiffer than the suspension on a regular Javelin AMX with Go-pack, and Donohue's car did have the optional front spoiler, although he admitted this was largely a cosmetic item. A normal AMX was able to register 0.7 g lateral acceleration on a skidpad; on the Penske Racing skidpad, Donohue's modified Javelin AMX recorded 0.8 g. However, the racing Sunoco Javelin pulled 1.4 g in testing at the Ontario Motor Speedway.

These readings show the going rate for 1971 sporting cars, as well as the gulf between road and race cars. Donohue's AMX had cowl induction, and this item plus Go-pack were much-vaunted options. Go-pack, as with the first Javelin, was only available with the top two motors, the 360 and 401 V8s. This AMX spec option involved handling and appearance, and the following items: HD suspension, 14-inch sport slot rims with raised-white-letter FR70 tires, Twin-Grip differential, HD cooling system, power front disks and Rally-Pac instrumentation.

The Rally-Pac instrumentation brought two additional readouts for oil pressure and battery charge, at the top and bottom of the extreme left gauge respectively. In the extreme right gauge there was what AMC dubbed "Tick-Tach," an unusual clock superimposed on a rev counter; both were circular with the outer tach reading up to 8 grand. There was a great desire up to the '80s to place a large timepiece in car instrument clusters. Often the optional tach would replace the clock, but here AMC let the driver have the best of both worlds. One would never shift late again!

The 1971–74 Javelin had 3 recessed gauges in round-edged square frames. The center gauge was the speedo, and it would read up to 140 mph with Rally-Pac instrumentation. The extreme left gauge of all Javelins had coolant and fuel readouts at 3 and 9 o'clock respectively. Floor the gas and the top 6,573cc V8 would make the fuel gauge go south fast, accompanied by a nearby sucking sound. That household vacuum sound was the cowl induction.

Cowl induction wasn't part of Go-pack; it was a separate option that tied in with AMX's fiberglass hood, and was only available on 360 and 401. The 1971–74 AMX's cowl induction is technically the most effective form of fresh air induction to have, and was used by Corvette around this time. Natural airflow patterns suggest a low-pressure area at the base of the windshield, where air shoots forward from the glass. However, to work effectively, the aperture taking air in must be close to the windshield. Those inside the industry have admitted that placing a reverse scoop further away from the glass was done for style.

On 1971–73 360- and 401-powered AMXs the cowl induction involved a flapper assembly on top of a breather, and triangular metal shield inside the hood between the fiberglass and lower metal frame. At the entrance was a metal grate, with the triangular baffle forcing air into the flapper. Up to mid '71 model year (August 1970–February 1971), cowl induction was dual snorkel, then becoming single snorkel in nature, with the base having an emissions unit on the single snorkel.

Regardless of the presence of cowl induction, the quoted power of the V8s remained unchanged. By late in the '74 model year the AMX switched from fiberglass to regular steel hoods, AMC having run out of the former as '74 Javelin production ran late, going into November 1974. Cowl induction could be dealer-fitted as well, and was a worthwhile option, given that fresh air induction on various muscle and pony cars produces lower elapsed times.

AMC made slight visual changes to the Humpster in its first 3 years. The non–AMX '71 Javelins had a coffin nose molding within the front grille. The inner grille outline was shared by Javelin and AMX in 1971 and was rather Lancia-like. AMX kept this shape for its remaining life, but on the '72 Javelin it became a mouth outline with injection-molded plastic crate trim piece inside. Also, 1972 saw the adoption of "C"-shaped profile decal on SST; that year Javelin was the most fashion-conscious AMC vehicle with the greatest number of exterior color choices, 15.

In 1973 the SST's grille gained a new crosshatch insert with rectangular driving lamps. The 1971–74 AMX always had round driving lights, but such grille lamps were new to SST. The '73 model year also saw a fat-thin-fat SST body profile decal that accentuated the Javelin's hump fenders. The same year also saw the ditching of the 1971–72 pagoda roof, where the 5 choices of vinyl roof covering were in 2 panels separated by a raised center section. This

With 150 bhp, 245 lbs./ft. 2bbl 8.4:1 compression ratio 304 and automatic transmission, a '74 Javelin recorded 0–60 mph in 11.2 seconds and the quarter mile in 17.3 seconds at 83.1 mph; under the watchful eye of *Motor Trend* magazine in their April '74 "The Fearsome Foursome" pony car report (courtesy Scott Wilhour).

vinyl roof trim was sometimes specified on AMXs. The '73 and '74 model year Javelins were available with full vinyl roof.

At the rear there was a taillight change for '72 to a full-width slot-style unit with chrome grid overlay. The change applied to Javelin and Javelin AMX, but especially suited AMX with its ducktail spoiler, where the red brake lights resembled rocket-ship flames! This style only lasted one model year; for '73 Javelin changed to 4 TV-shaped taillights, squares with rounded frames. Once more this applied to AMX too, which during 1971–74 sometimes had the rear fascia area trimmed. The blackout trimming on the upper rear bumper and around the taillights was done using tape, not paint.

With Javelin one could count on a standard center console and bucket seat vinyl-trimmed interior, but for how much longer could pony car fans count on Javelin's being around? (courtesy Scott Wilhour).

Australia was a place where Javelin lagged behind on style changes. Local company AMI was always playing catch-up when assembling AMCs down under. The 1970 AMI Javelin was in fact the U.S. '69 model year car, and the 1971 AMI Javelin was the revised '70 model year U.S. car, not the Humpster. However, the 1971 Australian AMI Javelin did have the U.S. Humpster's 110-inch wheelbase, which was odd given the '70 sheet metal. AMI had discontinued the 2-seater AMX at the close of the 1970 Australian model year.

Therefore, the sole Javelin choice in Australia for '71 was a U.S. '70-shape 2+2 type coupe ... with a 390! Yes, even though America had moved on to the 401 mill, Australia was still using the 10:1 compression ratio 390, this still being a leaded-gas-only market at the time. As the sole Javelin V8 choice, AMI had replaced the 343 with the 390 for '71, and in so doing created the largest-engined locally assembled muscle car the country had ever seen.

Thus, the '71 AMI Javelin 390 had bragging rights over the local Holden Monaro GTS 350 and Ford Falcon GT 351, even though it wasn't as quick as those cars. Indeed, the fastest-accelerating Australian car on record was still the 6-cylinder Hemi Charger R/T by Chrysler Australia. No matter; the AMI Javelin 390's 325 gross horses were sufficient, and luxury buyers were content with the model's automatic-only status.

The Javelin's 6.4 liters may not have matched the accelerative efficiency of the 4.3-liter Hemi Charger, but the combo of high-compression V8, automatic and 2.87 final drive made AMI Javelin the Economy King of the high-class segment. The '71 AMI was a soothing amalgam, wearing the stylish 14 × 6-inch slot rims one would find on a sport spec '71 U.S. Javelin SST, but not having that car's automatic aircraft bar shifter. AMI was also still using the older Bendix 11.2-inch solid front disks.

A further oddity was AMI's dropping the reclining seat, which had been fitted to their previous shape Javelin and AMX (1969 U.S. model year appearance). New shape introductions didn't quite meet up with normal U.S. model year dates, and organizational inertia meant AMI got with the Humpster Javelin program in the '73 model year. AMI once again offered a single automatic luxo/sport SST version, and this '73 AMI Javelin wore front and rear fascias one would find on a U.S. '72 SST.

Thus, the '73 AMI Javelin had the Humpster's front grid grille, and the 1971–72 pagoda 2-section vinyl roof. There was no AMX version of this AMI Javelin, AMI last doing AMX when it assembled the U.S. '69-shape 2-seater in 1970. AMI crated over the low 8.5:1 compression ratio 401 4-barrel as a replacement for the toxic 390, pairing it with the Torqueflite Torque Command auto.

With the previous AMI Javelin 390, the AMC small-block V8 set a record as the largest and highest horsepower rated engine to be inserted into an Australian-built car. The latest AMI Javelin 401 set a new record for the largest mill fitted to an Australian passenger car, but it wasn't the most powerful. The smog fighter nature of Detroit's latest big-inch V8s meant the 401 was trumped on bhp by less tightly controlled local Holden Monaro GTS 350s and Mad Max *Road Warrior* Ford Falcon GT 351s.

That said, the Humpster Javelin's front fender "401" callout badge was new to Australia, and brought more street cred than a gong-sized medallion. The low compression ratio also meant it could be filled up with regular, rather than super leaded. Plus, the AMI Javelin 401s were complete in standard spec, which hinted at their real market. Power steering, power front vented disks, Torque Command, Adjust-O-Tilt steering wheel, reclining seats, trunk lid luggage rack, radio and 8-track audio, laminated windshield, rear window defogger, locking gas filler cap and more satisfied buyer needs and desires.

One didn't even have to pay extra for a/c, or for the sporty 14 × 6-inch SST slot rims wearing ER70–14-inch radials. You got the lot, standard, with vinyl roof and none of the import duty one would associate with a more expensive Jaguar or Mercedes, which were the Javelin's real rivals in this country. AMI was still using the 2.87 final drive they had always used, which suited the Javelin 401's cruising nature. Inside AMI was sticking with the old 1970 pistol-grip shifter, which raised the question: were Detroit's annual style/trim changes really necessary?

The AMI Humpster interior also had the lockable storage "between-the-buckets" cubby as standard equipment, plus full Rally-Pac instrumentation, but in bizarre surrounds. AMI had lifted the center section of the Javelin AMX's dash panel, 3-gauge instrument cluster and surrounding engine-turned metal finish, and placed it in their own flat panel non-angled dash. This dash was similar to those on earlier AMI Javelins.

Yes, one got the ammeter and oil pressure gauges, plus Tick-Tach, and just enough of the metal trim to surround the top and sides of the outer gauge faces, then the trim abruptly stopped! To the right was a separate small panel with toggle switches for a/c temp and fan speed, with remaining HVAC controls in a panel to the left of the instrument cluster. Unfortunately the absence of the real Humpster dash meant the a/c blower/evap core was a rectangular after-market box-type unit sitting under the dash.

AMI did include the new-style Javelin '72 model year sports steering wheel, which replaced the 2-spoker "Machine" unit seen on U.S. '71 Javelins. So there it was: a Humpster for the Southern Hemisphere and very exclusive too. Just 40 would be built that year for Australia, with 8 for New Zealand. For a quality RHD-assembled American car without the import duty, AMI's Rambler Javelin 401 was hard to beat. They still honored the Rambler name down under.

South of the border, down Mexico way, VAM took the Latin American Javelin to new heights. The firm was ready with a Humpster Javelin for 1971, no lag, and a super-duty I6. VAM engineers had created a 4.6-liter version of the AMC I6, the same year American Motors got to 258ci or 4.2 liters. This Mexican I6 had a compression ratio of 9.5:1 and output of 200 bhp (gross). Combine this with standard 4-speed manual and standard front non-power disks, and the 6-cylinder-only VAM Javelin set a new benchmark for AMC I6 performance.

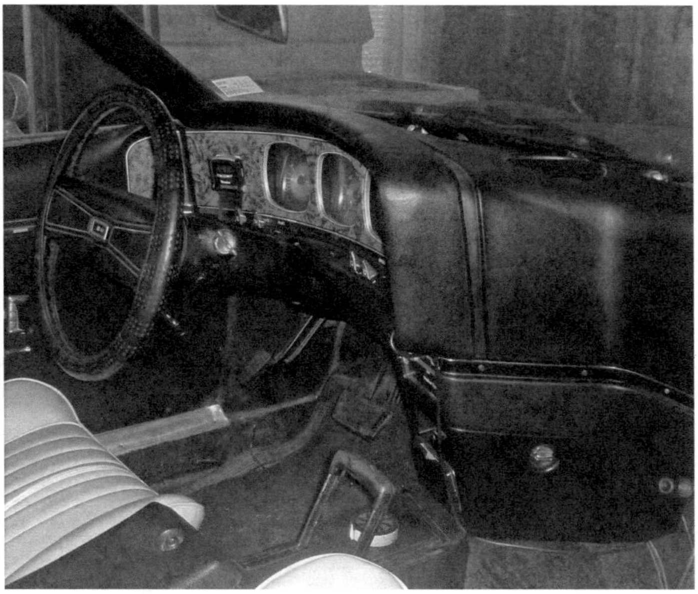

Humpster Javelin brought a new wraparound, cockpit-style dash. The absence of dash vents signifies this as a non a/c car. The '72 Javelin, like other AMCs, changed from Shift Command to Torque Command auto (courtesy Scott Wilhour).

Even as late as 1973 the U.S. Javelin only offered 4-wheel manual drums as standard, and it wasn't until the '74 model year that the U.S. Javelin got non-power front disks as stock equipment. However, some very early '71 VAM Javelins used the outgoing 252ci I6, rather than the new 282ci I6. Of course, being from a metric-oriented country, the super six was denoted "4.6," and had 4.6 fender callout badges in the locations one would find 360 or 401 badges on U.S. Humpster Javelins.

As in Australia, the existence of a single Javelin version saw a blend of sports luxury. Standard was the 4-speed and 4.6, but so too were woodgrain dash appliqué and demi Rally-Pac instrumentation. Like the AMI Humpster Javelin, it had the higher 140 mph speedo in 240 kph metric, a record high for a VAM, and the Tick-Tach rev counter. However, it was missing Rally-Pac's ammeter and oil pressure gauges, and these weren't even options.

In some equipment areas the VAM Javelin was lacking. AM/FM radio, 8-track player, dual exterior remote controlled side mirrors, Adjust-O-Tilt steering, a/c, shoulder portion seat belts, interior hood release, tinted glass and lighting group weren't available; neither were reclining seats on any 1973–75 VAM Javelin. It could be this was related to Mexico's restrictions on accessory importation, to maintain local content percentage goals and the integrity of Mexican industry.

A reasonable course of action would be to have a new VAM Javelin fitted with a locally available aftermarket a/c unit on purchase, and probably dealer-fitted. As a further luxurious flourish, and to take advantage of a pony car blind spot, VAM offered round C-pillar porthole opera windows on Humpster Javelins, most unusual. Aside from this, VAM Javelin continued as expected, taking on the grid grille insert and rear fascia chrome grid taillight overlay, at the same time as the '72 U.S. Javelin.

The '72 VAM Javelin also adopted the Torque Command auto, and if one did specify the optional automatic, then power steering was thrown in too. VAM raised the bar even higher, making power front disks standard in 1972. The '73 model year saw the VAM Javelin adopt the '73 U.S. Javelin look of mesh grille with rectangular driving lamps, plus the TV-shaped quad taillights.

Sadly, VAM stopped making the Javelin at the end of the '73 model year. With a wish to introduce Gremlin and Matador Coupe in Mexico for '74, old Javelin had to make way. Mexican restrictions on model lines meant VAM couldn't make them all. Unknown to VAM, they had reached their zenith with Humpster Javelin, which turned out to be the most popular VAM offering of all time. In spite of no AMX version, no Pierre Cardin, the Mexican public said yes to Humpster.

The VAM Javelin didn't actually have a designated trim level, but it was an SST in spirit. The 1971–73 VAM Javelin's shape was a winner in this export market, and the also style-oriented Matador Coupe didn't manage to replace Humpster in the public's imagination. Sports fans were also increasingly digging Javelin at home. SST and AMX sales dropped only slightly between 1973 and 1974; the figures were 25,195 and 5,707 versus 22,556 and 4,980 respectively. The fall in sales was minor given the apocalyptic nature of '74 car sales amid the fuel crisis and ensuing recession.

Somehow things had played back into AMC's hands by 1973–74. When Humpster came out it was clear GM's money meant their F-body represented pony car best practice. For ultimate handling, power and other fine details, the resources of the giant GM were hard to match. The Mustang slowly deflated after 1970, and Chrysler was past its prime too. Then came a sea change, and Javelin was back by default.

SST Javelins eschewed the AMX's metal-finish trim and Tick-Tach rev counter, in favor of burled walnut paneling. As per pony tradition, sport compact spec was up to personal preference (courtesy Scott Wilhour).

As industry leader, GM took on bumper law, emissions and other challenges head-on. In the short run this added weight and length to the F-body, the engines had less moxie, and weight distribution, handling and acceleration were negatively affected. By 1973 the writing on Ford's wall said Mustang II, since their heart wasn't really in Mustang I anymore. By now Chrysler was doing some serious moping, and then there was Humpster.

AMC triumphed by doing nothing; inactivity was their friend. Their engines were

Although Javelin/AMX were selling well in 1973 and 1974, AMC decided to pull the plug on the pony at the end of the '74 model year. It was felt the pony car market was at an end, and resources were being marshaled for the new Pacer (courtesy Scott Wilhour).

holding court; indeed by 1973 the 255 bhp AMC 401 4bbl knocked out Pontiac's 250 bhp L75 455 4bbl. In 1974 Camaro Z/28's hi-po 350 made 245 bhp, AMX 401 still equaled 255 horses, and Mustang? In 1974 Mustang II Mach I was pleasant, but with a 2bbl 2.8 V6 as a shining beacon, there was little hope for this pony against the AMX stallion.

AMC also had a novel way of handling the 5 mph bumper issue: it did nothing! AMC was incorporating retractable bumpers on all its cars, bar static-bumpered Javelin. They didn't say anything about it when announcing their '74s, but AMC decided this model year would be curtains for Javelin. The chief reason for stopping the coupe was the cost of designing some real 5 mph bumpers. As with AMX/3 the money needed to do the job right was better spent elsewhere.

Need AMC's size be mentioned? The firm had spent big to tool up for '74's Matador Coupe, and pennies would also have to be saved for the upcoming Pacer. Nothing concentrates the mind on priorities like an inflationary recession. Pony-car-wise, only GM would still be in there come 1975. Collectors were breaking their piggy banks to snap up and hoard zero-mile '74 Camaro Z/28s and AMC AMXs. The Javelin AMX 304's '74 model year price was $3,299, $300 more than the 232ci base Javelin.

There were no visual changes from 1973 to 1974. The '73 Javelin had gained beefy rubber bumper guards as standard equipment. It was a 5 mph bumper stopgap measure that didn't affect Javelin's looks like the rubber baby buggy bumpers on the '74 MGB. Javelin's length increased from 191.8 inches to 192.3 inches, but there were no other dimension changes. Starting weight for a manual Javelin 232 was still 2,950 lbs, and Javelin still offered the best trunk in pony land: 10.2 cu ft with a full-size spare was a miracle.

Javelin sales in the final 2 years may have been aided by the increased showroom traffic

AMC was experiencing from its small cars during the energy crisis. Having more people visit an AMC dealer did no harm. Through it all Javelin carved out an image as the easiest AMC car to understand, since fast coupes with long hoods and short decks are an easy sell, but even here Javelin was affected by AMC's somewhat oddball position in American life.

Many liked Javelin's look, but didn't realize it was an AMC! And whereas Mustang helped Steve McQueen fight crime in 1968's *Bullitt*, Humpster Javelin was the ride of Bradford Dillman's character in the 1975 horror film *Bug*. Somehow the idea of someone mind-melding with mutant cockroaches didn't seem like such a stretch with an AMC in the garage. Even with the popularity of 235,497 sales in 1968–74, including 15,961 Humpster AMXs, poor Javelin still got AMC typecast. If E.T. had driven a car it would probably have been an AMC!

Buzzin' Hornets, 1970–74

The past is the past; what have you done for me lately? AMC may have started the compact revolution, but the time had come to farewell the American, and create a new standard-bearer for small cars. The Big 3 had their compacts with the formidable Chevy Nova, Ford Maverick and Plymouth Valiant, but no one was going to give AMC a freebie because of history. So it was that American Motors embarked on a 3-year program costing $40 million for their next compact.

This new ride was called Hornet, because AMC had a right to. There had been the real Hudson Hornet of 1951–54, and the badge engineered Nash-based Hornets leading up to the new 1958 Rambler Ambassador. With Hudson being in the '54 AMC merger, the firm was able to revive the nameplate. It was convenient because car names that sounded like silverware had given way to things from the animal kingdom. A hornet couldn't maul like a cougar, but it could give a nasty sting!

In the Hornet, AMC had a compact that was designed, not simply styled. Inspiration was taken from the Project IV Cavalier show car. That was the design that set much store by strong, crisp horizontal surfaces and body panel swapability. Indeed, Teague's team of efficient designers gave Hornet front and rear bumpers from the same stamping. Hornet had a forceful, blockish appearance combined with the styling fads of the moment.

In spite of modest 179.3-inch length and 70.6-inch width dimensions, it was proportioned along the long-hood, short-deck lines so loved at the time. Front and rear fascia details weren't unlike a 1st-gen Camaro. Hornet was sensible; the form didn't hurt function, but there was fun too. Hornet was the first AMC under the Chapin niche-fits-best strategy, where American Motors would offer something a little bit different, like quality.

Apart from AMC's cool ball-bearing-actuated ashtray, Hornet established an industry first with internally reinforced guard rail door beams. A compact is also different when one can option something foreign to a Caddy or Lincoln: reclining buckets! Hornet wasn't an econocan; it was a small car, one that proved a good fit. The Hornet set a world auto record for spawning 4 successful car design spin-offs.

Hornet suited AMC, the public, and *Motor Trend*, the magazine declaring Hornet *Motor Trend* Car of the Year 1970. It could all be yours for $1,994; that was the bait advertising price for a basic 199ci I6-powered 3-speed manual 2-door Hornet sedan, or call it a notchback. There was also a 4-door version, and if one chose the Hornet SST, then the 232 I6 would be standard equipment.

Top motor for the Hornet in 1970 was the 304 V8, and the sedan could be trimmed up with a/c, powered drums or front disks, electric clock, vinyl roof, power steering, fancy wheel covers and so on. Hornet was well received on debut, and in spite of a labor strike affecting '70 AMC totals, the new sedan attained 92,458 calendar year sales and 101,092 for the model year. The 199ci I6 was discontinued at the end of the '70 model year, but AMC had lots of new items for Hornet in the pipeline, including a new hero Hornet.

'71 SC/360 and Sportabout

A high-flying Hornet would boost the range's image, and that implied a powerhouse Hornet. However, with high-performance car sales waning, and insurance company premiums for such rides becoming prohibitive, there was a problem. Some of the final 2-seater '70 AMXs were still on dealer lots by the summer of '71! Thus, AMC's third and final dedicated performance model would be different in nature from the Scrambler and '70 Machine. No wild exteriors and extrovert scoops; think low-key, think sensible.

The new version was Hornet SC/360, where SC stood for Super Coupe rather than

The '71 Hornet SC/360 succeeded Scrambler and Machine to be the third, and final, of American Motors' performance car trilogy. This SC/360 has been modified with Machine 15-inch rims and red, white and blue livery (courtesy Eddie Stakes).

stock car and 360 signified 360 V8 cubes. AMC's advertising line said it all: "Introducing a sensible alternative to the money squeezing, insurance-strangling muscle cars of America — The Hornet SC/360." Yes, this was a quick ride even your mother would approve of; just say Rambler made it! Behind the blurb lay slide rule-confirmed calculations that equaled no extra money for the insurance companies.

With a formula observing horsepower, displacement and power-to-weight ratio, the insurance company would heap a 25 percent loading onto any vehicle deemed "high performance," but they didn't figure on the variable factor of Hornet. The basic 245 bhp 2bbl SC/360 avoided the surcharge with no problem, and it was no coincidence that Chevrolet's '71 Nova SS 350 also had 245 horses. As for the SC/360 with optional 285 bhp 4bbl 360 V8, that was right on the limit; better inquire within before starting payments on that one.

A Hornet SC/401 was also considered, but rejected by AMC due to likely breach of the insurance limit. It should also be considered that the 401 was a premium-fuel '71 motor, but the two 360s were both regular-fuel, and even the 4bbl 360 had a sensible 8.5:1 compression ratio. Gross quoted horsepower ratings aside, AMC was on its best behavior with this smogger. The opening 2bbl SC/360 with 3-speed manual was only $2,663, which placed it $40 under the '71 Plymouth Duster 340.

For the pennies the SC/360 came with D70 14-inch Polyglas tires on 6-inch-wide sports slot rims and a discreet profile rally stripe incorporating the SC/360 script. To match the

Hornet's front and rear bumpers came from the same stamping. By giving rise to Gremlin, Concord, Spirit and Eagle 4×4, Hornet was AMC's most commercially significant car of the '70s (courtesy Alexander Ortiz).

exterior color chosen, the stripe could be in red, black or white. The SC/360 also had a painted-red rear deck panel between the taillights. AMC also stung the Mopar crowd with its Hornet emblem. There was a Hornet badge in front of the front-fender Hornet chrome script, this item being available on other 1970–72 Hornets. Plus, on the optional locking gas cap, the Hornet emblem slid to one side when one inserted the key.

One item unique to SC/360 in the '71 Hornet range was the 360 motor. This power plant had bore and stroke dimensions of 4.08 inches and 3.44 inches respectively. Wisdom at the time said smaller displacements in the same block were sweeter to rev, making the 360 a happier Hornet choice than the 401. The hi-po 4bbl 360 had the Autolite 4300 1RA4 4-barrel carb with 1⁹⁄₁₆ in primaries and 1¹¹⁄₁₆ in secondaries. With stricter emissions, one of the few ways to boost a motor was to get more air in, and more air out, so AMC introduced a new bigger sweep design exhaust manifold.

Special performance items like the 0.477-inch lift/302-degree duration Emissions Devil cam kit, transmission oil cooler and Detroit Locker differential were still dealer-available. The special intake manifold/carb kits available from certain AMC dealers and parts suppliers, like Edelbrock, were also still listed. However, legally these leftovers from drag racing and Trans Am series days were for non-public highway use, and the SC/360 got by just fine without them.

General year-to-year improvements in car tech meant these compact performance smoggers were as quick as 1960s intermediates with optional V8s. A 4bbl SC/360 did 14.8 seconds at 94.63 mph for the ¼ mile when tested by *Hot Rod* magazine in December 1970 at Orange County International Raceway, with the optional $237.85 Shift Command auto. A Shift Command 4bbl SC/360 was group tested by *Motor Trend* in January 1971, doing the quarter in 15 seconds at 94 mph with 0–60 mph in 6.7 seconds.

The 4-speed manual Dodge Demon was slightly quicker than the SC/360, but wasn't anywhere near as frugal as the Hornet's 13–17 mpg range. With the optional power front disks fitted, costing $84, the SC/360 braked from 60 mph to rest in 124 ft. Performance compacts had great overall ability; *Motor Trend* was very pleased with the SC/360 fitted with handling pack. By this stage cars submitted to magazines weren't tweaked, adding to their street cred.

The Mopar 340 could do more in a Duster or Demon than a Cuda. The Maverick Grabber was eventually up-engined from a 250ci I6 to the 210 bhp 302 V8, and along with its Mercury Comet GT twin, was a pleasant machine. If one really wanted an intermediate, the 1970 Olds Rallye 350 could also limbo under the insurance bar, but it wouldn't be as quick as a little 4bbl SC/360. The 4-barrel 360 was included in SC/360's $199 Go-pack, which provided the visual, functional fillip of an arrowhead hoodscoop designed by aviation firm Rockwell Corporation.

The Go-pack-equipped SC/360 would be the last AMC with genuine forward-facing Ram Air, its mechanics involving the usual flapper and vacuum actuator. Go-pack also entailed a dual exhaust system, HD suspension, tachometer and raised-white-letter tires. On Shift Command cars a 3.15 final drive was standard, 3.54 optional. The 4-speed with Hurst shifter was $204.90, and with it came the chance of a 3.91 final drive. The 4-speed had a new 11-inch clutch.

AMC's across-the-board available $111 variable-ratio GM-sourced Saginaw power steering had just 3.3 turns between locks, a desirable option along with the infinitely adjustable

This '73 Hornet sedan with 100 bhp base 1bbl 232 I6 and column-shift Torque Command auto was originally sold by New Jersey AMC dealer Greenbrook American (courtesy Alexander Ortiz).

front reclining vinyl buckets. Even though the SC/360's pollution controls meant no vacuum advance under 30 mph and lean carb settings, the small rocket could do a lot for you. One would have expected the Hornet SC/360 to be very popular — AMC envisioned 4,000 sales in model year '71— but sadly it didn't happen.[4]

Hate the game, not the player: in the deflated fast-car market, SC/360 could only manage 784 unit sales in its one and only model year. AMC weren't putting a lot of marketing effort the SC/360's way, and it didn't help that so many pocket rockets were competing for their slice of the key lime pie. Chevrolet also pulled the Nova SS 350 from its line at the close of 1971 after 7,016 cars had been sold. Bad news for automakers then, good news for collectors now, because rarity increases value.

In all, 206 2-barrel Hornet SC/360s were sold, 187 automatics and 19 with the 3-speed manual. The other 578 SC/360s had the 4bbl 360 which made 285 bhp at 4,800 rpm and 390 lbs/ft at 3,200 rpm. The 4bbl version broke down to 249 automatics, 23 with the 3-speed manual, and 306 with the 4-speed manual. Items like the SC/360's glove box decal are on the list of reproduction parts, but a Hornet SC/360 cannot be faked. The Hornet SC/360 was only available as a 2-door notchback with the body code VIN 7106–1, with the final digit "1" being SC/360 unique, so beware the clones!

All SC/360s were assembled on the east line at Kenosha. Figures for its weight range from 3,057 lbs to 3,300 lbs, but the real heavyweight '71 commercial impact lay with the new AMC Hornet Sportabout. The Sportabout was a 4-door Hornet wagon variant, that had its genesis in an earlier Javelin wagon show car. The Sportabout was Detroit unique, a small, practical hold-all with liftback rear door, not a conventional tailgate.

Sportabout was built on Hornet's 108-inch wheelbase and rang true to Chapin's philosophy of doing what Detroit didn't. The figures showed it worked: in model year '71, AMC made 244,758 vehicles; 123,304 of those were Hornets and 73,471 Hornets were Sportabout SSTs. The Sportabout was only offered in SST spec, and the little lugger benefited from the 232's being the Hornet's new base engine, although it went better with AMC's new 258 I6.

In 1971 Sportabout also helped make a greener society with electric power. That year a concern called the Electric Fuel Propulsion Company offered the Electrosport. Based on converted Sportabouts, this electric wagon could get the job done for urban dwellers, and would take just 45 minutes to fill up at proposed fast-charge stations. However, Sportabout's voltage was seriously upped in 1972 with the introduction of the 175 bhp (net) 2-barrel 360 V8 option for Hornet.

The SC/360 was no longer, but one could still have a 360 between the suspension towers and build a mean wagon. A '72 Sportabout could be equipped with 360 V8, the newly introduced Torque Command auto, fast manual steering, HD suspension, power front disks, and for that sleeper look, simulated woodgrain exterior side paneling. Usual Hornet fare, but from late 1971 Sportabout enjoyed an optional roll-back sunroof cover, to accent the little wagon's lifestyle flavor.

Sportabout also had the style about town with the '72 Gucci appearance package. As part of innovative ways to spread the Hornet word, AMC entered into cross-promotional tie-ups with designer icons and fashion labels, something soon copied by the rest of Detroit. The Gucci interior was available on Sportabout only in '72 and '73, when 2,583 and 2,252

***Car and Driver* declared Hornet hatch "the styling coup of 1973." One could take all that style camping, thanks to AMC's optional Hornet hatch tent (courtesy The Rambler Ranch).**

were sold, respectively. The Gucci Sportabout had Gucci's signature red and green trim colors on well-padded beige-upholstered seating, plus interior door trims with red and green pinstriping.

Gucci Sportabout had exterior Gucci logos on the door panels, and the package was limited to 4 exterior colors: Snow White, Grasshopper Green, Hunter Green and Yuca Tan. Indeed, when it came to trim, 1972 was limited to the SST; the base Hornet was discontinued at the close of 1971, with SST now offering so much more for a few additional pennies. It was a bargain that brought rear-seat armrests and ashtray, cigarette lighter, full carpeting, locking glove box, under-dash package tray and custom steering wheel.

With '72 came a time of range rationalization, and Hornet was down to half the number of '71 iterations. However, there was more choice because apart from Gucci Sportabout, AMC introduced 2 further packages. One was the sports-appearance "X" package, a response to the successful pack of the same name introduced on the '71 Gremlin. Hornet X was a 2-door sedan to start with, bringing the expected rally striping, sport slot steel rims with wide oval rubber.

If you thought Hornet X was devilish, then be prepared to repent for the '72 Hornet Rallye. The Rallye was a more serious X and included front buckets, front disks, HD suspension, fast manual steering, full-synchro 3-speed manual floorshift and sports steering wheel, all as standard equipment. A Hornet Rallye with 360 was a '72 SC/360 in all but name, but here's a surprise: Hornet X and Rallye weren't hits.

It says something about the decline of the sporty car in the early '70s that a Sportabout 232 was everyone's friend, but Hornet X and Rallye met with cool response. Hornet X continued to be offered, but Rallye ended at the close of the '72 model year. No, the Rallye's special lower-body decal stripes didn't sway the public, nor did the Hornet's revised wrap-around taillights; what people wanted was quality guaranteed. This was delivered by AMC's new super warranty, the Buyer Protection Plan (BPP).

BPP set a new industry standard in coverage width and depth, which really meant something at a time when the woes once a car was brought home could be most trying for domestics and imports, especially domestics. BPP was in tune with the new wave of "stick it to the man" consumer activism, giving prospects another reason to choose AMC. In the '73 model year the successful Hornet adopted a fourth body style, the Hornet hatchback.

Hornet hatch answered the call for real coupes; 2-door hardtops just didn't satisfy like they used to. As per Sportabout the hatch involved a liftback mechanism — a top-hinged, counterbalanced hatch panel on gas struts, to be precise, one that predated the 1974 Mustang II fastback. Designers were discovering that hatch was a coupe's ally, blending perfectly with profile outline, adding a new dimension in practicality.

Still on a 108-inch wheelbase, Hornet hatch had a cargo-boosting fold-down rear seat, something the GM F-body would have to wait until 1982 to receive! Indeed, with that rear seat folded, and a 2bbl 360 V8 optioned up front, the Hornet hatch turned into a 2-seater with AMX flavor. Choosing the X pack helped with that sensation: by '73 Hornet X was only available on the Sportabout and hatch. Matching Javelin, AMC deep-sixed the Hornet SST at the end of '72 too.

The Hornet hatch was a critical success; *Car and Driver* certainly admired it and declared the coupe "the styling coup of 1973." AMC used that quote in their print ads, which helped move 40,110 '73 Hornet hatches out of AMC showrooms. No mean achievement to sell a

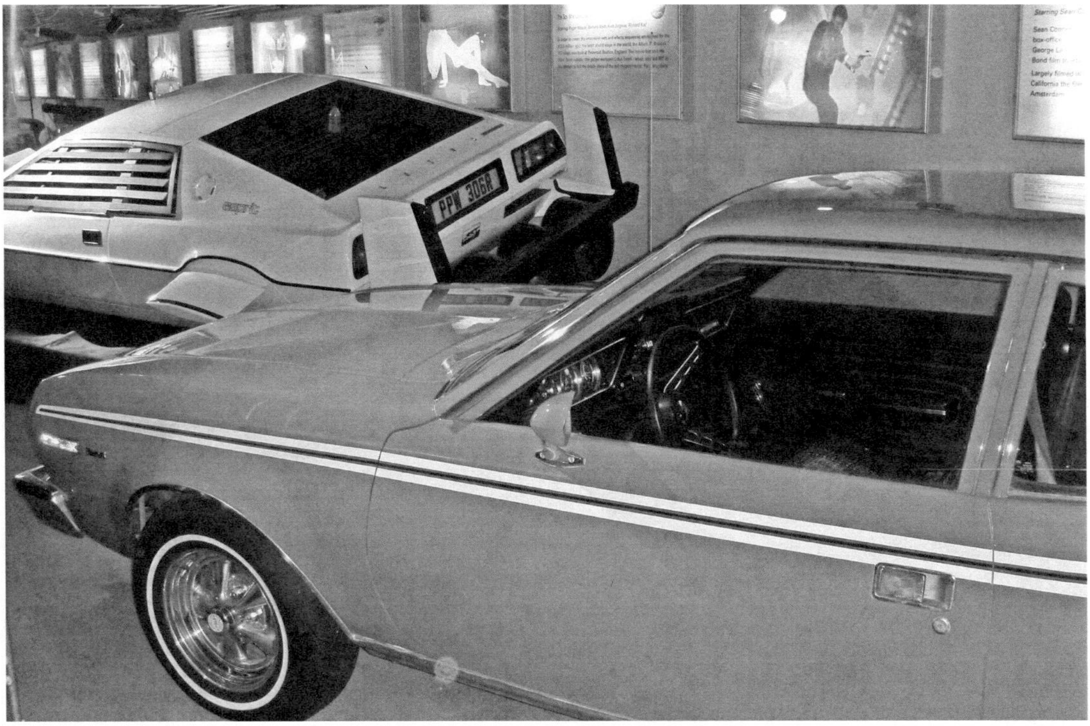

In *The Man with the Golden Gun*, Bond pursued assassin Francisco Scaramanga, who was driving the new '74 Matador Coupe. Note the Bond Lotus Esprit submarine from *The Spy Who Loved Me* (1977) (courtesy Doug Redenius and David A. Reinhardt).

new coupe on looks in '73, given the new federal 5 mph front and 2.5 mph rear bumper law. While others, especially imports, were losing face with some very tacked-on trimmings, the 3,031-pound Hornet hatch looked neat.

OK, Hornet wasn't as cleanly styled as before, and the grille was more ornamented now, but the 5 mph bumper integrated well with 2 choices. Accept the standard 5 mph bumper with 2 vertical rubber bumperettes, or go for the optional recoverable 5 mph bumper. The latter was visually distinguishable by a horizontal rubstrip. This could be supplemented by looking under the "Protection Options" in the '73 Hornet brochure and selecting the also-optional 5 mph recoverable rear bumper, putting one's Hornet beyond the law. Quite natural, since AMC was always an outlaw!

With front and rear energy-absorbing bumpers, Hornet was ready for the worst supermarket parking lot bumper-car game. In 1972 Hornet adopted the ad slogan "A Tough Little Car," and it never seemed more appropriate than now. The only downside to the re-bumpering was extra size: '73 Hornet had redesigned grille, hood, and front fenders to blend with the 5 mph bars, changing the car's length and width to 186 inches and 71 inches, respectively.

Inflation was bringing on unwanted sticker price increases to $2,298 for the 2-door Hornet notchback and $2,449 for the hatch. That was the price of being tough, and what were the tough wearing? The answer was hard-wearing denim, or at least something that looked like denim. For '73 AMC got into another fashion attraction with their licensed

Levi's blue jeans interior package. Levi Strauss and AMC, two American icons made for a good fit!

The Levi's pack was tailored to include denim-like seating surfaces and door trim panels, copper rivets as seatback buttons and on seating cushions too, red Levi's tabs and denim snap-off cargo pouches. If this was a bit frantic, one could retire to Sportabout's latest deluxe pack. Unquestionably upscale, D/L brought woodgrain exterior trim panels, roof rack, air deflector and individual reclining front seats in luxo Scorpio cloth.

The Name's Hornet ... AMC Hornet!

It was apt Hornet was showing such flash, because AMC was going to Hollywood! Yes, AMC vehicles would be featured heavily in the upcoming 1974 James Bond movie *The Man with the Golden Gun*. Star of the show, apart from Roger Moore, was an AMC Hornet X hatch that did an amazing "Astro Spiral" 360-degree barrel jump that was 100 percent real, not computer generated. It all started at Cornell University in America.

Specifically the Astro Spiral concept had a home at the Cornell Aeronautical Laboratory (CAL). At CAL the director of the Transportation Division, Bill Milliken, was an authority

The rear seat into which Sheriff J.W. Pepper was flung post–Astro Spiral jump. The whole stunt was done in one take with no problems. The Bond Aston from *The Living Daylights* (1987) is nearby (courtesy Doug Redenius and David A. Reinhardt).

on the handling, stability and behavior of cars and planes. CAL employee Ray McHenry was testing a computer program predicting the motion of a car on irregular surfaces. To judge the program's predictive ability, McHenry contacted the All American Hell Drivers, based in Buffalo, New York, and run by W.J. Milligan Jr.

It was Milligan who dubbed the stunt Astro Spiral, and the first tests were done on the concrete apron adjacent to CAL in upstate New York. Bill Milliken encouraged tests of the Astro Spiral at CAL, and soon the stunt would be taken on the road. Milligan's J.M. Productions Hell Drivers toured county fairs, events and meetings as The American Thrill Show, an AMC-sponsored affair using vehicles manufactured by said company.

Thus, it was at the Houston Astrodome on January 15, 1972, that the Astro Spiral made its public debut as part of the Hell Drivers' program. In front of an ecstatic crowd of over 66,000 people, Chick Galiano did the Astro Spiral jump in a six-cylinder Humpster Javelin. The stunt entailed jumping off one ramp at around 42 mph, doing a 360-degree barrel roll in mid-air, and landing on another ramp to a cheering crowd!

For optimal weight distribution, I6 Javelins were chosen. Six examples were used, stripped with no options, and with heavy-duty front suspension parts and welding to cope with the landing. The Hell Drivers toured during 1971–75 and in addition to the Astro Spiral Javelin, there would be Gremlins and Hornets driving on two wheels, as well as Matadors, 1971–74 AMXs and eventually Pacers as support vehicles. Some of these stunt cars still exist in Buffalo, N.Y.

It was stunt coordinator W.J. Milligan who suggested using the Astro Spiral stunt in *The Man with the Golden Gun*, to Bond franchise boss Cubby Broccoli. Milligan's Hell Drivers had been involved in the 1971 Bond movie *Diamonds Are Forever*, where stunt man Joe Williams drove the red Ford Mustang Mach I of character Tiffany Case, which did stuff like scoot around, infuriate police in a parking lot, jump and exit an alley on two wheels.

The Man with the Golden Gun was set in Thailand, and the fun started when Bond dropped into a Bangkok AMC dealership and the driver's seat of a '74 Hornet X 360 hatch with Torque Command automatic and dealer-installed 14 × 6-inch Cragar S/S rims. Bond did this because he wanted to pursue evil assassin Scaramanga and his sidekick Nick Nack. In the Hornet's passenger seat was recurrent Bond movie character Southern Sheriff J.W. Pepper, who was evaluating said Hornet when Bond happened by.

The Hornet X had the VIN A4C037N317300, with its 360 V8 making the usual 2bbl's 175 bhp at 4,000 rpm and 285 lbs/ft at 2,400 rpm using 8.25:1 compression ratio. As it happens, 1974 was the last year one could insert a 360 into the Hornet; such automatic Hornet 360s had a 3.15 final drive standard, with 3.54 rear gears optional. It was sufficient for Bond and Pepper to give spirited chase of Scaramanga in his Matador Coupe. The Thai police were also pursuing in AMC Matador sedan cop cars. At the time, Thailand's police used Japanese patrol cars, so chalk up the Matador's presence to artistic license and AMC's sponsorship of the movie. In chasing Scaramanga, Bond had to jump a Thai canal, which is where the Astro Spiral and Hell Drivers' Loren "Bumps" Willert came in. The Hornet would leave the first ramp, disguised as a damaged bridge, do the 360-degree roll, and land on its wheels on the other end of the broken bridge, as the computer predicted.

With the CAL simulation program, 7 tests were conducted in advance. It was calculated that success entailed a Hornet X and driver with combined weight of 1,460.06 kilos would leave the first ramp at 64.36 kph, with 15.86 meters between the two ramps. The computer program also specified ramp length, and suggested teak wood would be optimal for ramp construction. The special Astro Spiral Hornet had a centrally mounted steering mechanism, so the center of gravity would be in the middle.

As with the Hell Drivers' Astro Spiral Javelin, all nonessentials were junked to minimize the Hornet's weight, but safety was essential. As a precaution an ambulance with paramedics was on hand, as were 2 divers and a crane to winch the Hornet from the canal should things have gone wrong, but they didn't. Bumps Willert got it right on the first take. Cut and print!

The scene was captured with 6 cameras rolling, and afterwards Broccoli gave the go-ahead for a set champagne celebration. What a day for poor J.W. Pepper: after enduring the Hornet X's smashing through the showroom glass, and the mid-air barrel roll, the movie scene post-jump showed him flung into the Hornet's rear seat! James was shaken, but not stirred. The Astro Spiral shows and the Bond movie led to CAL selling plenty of their computer programs.

The Other Urban Cowboy

Years before John Travolta decided dancing in an urban environment with cowboy boots and a neckerchief was a good idea, AMC planned a small pickup truck called the Cowboy. The Cowboy prototype was based on an early SC/360 with 4-speed, but don't get the idea AMC wanted to elbow out El Camino on the wagon trail. This Cowboy was intended to take on the small Japanese imported pickups that were kicking up dust by the early '70s.

The Cowboy would have been most commonly specified with a 100 bhp detoxed 232 I6 and 3-speed manual, but even this would have provided more pep than the exclusively 4-cylinder opposition. Cowboy could have occupied a niche between the little and big trucks. The Cowboy proto started the trail with a '71 Gremlin face, with altered grille bearing the Jeep logo, Jeep being in AMC's domain by this hour.

Subsequently AMC stylist Jim Alexander substituted a Hornet visage. The Cowboy's unibody construction influenced the future Jeep Comanche, but it didn't have 4×4. All-wheel drive wasn't considered for Cowboy; the extensive changes needed for that would be saved for the '80 Eagle. Sadly, AMC Cowboy never reached production. With Hornet, Gremlin, and Sportabout, and Hornet hatch imminent, AMC already had plenty of body styles based on their compact.

The 1974 Annual Report put out by AMC had an AMC Sportabout as one of the cover vehicles, and well it might, since Hornet was underlining AMC's bottom line. Hornet production soared to 133,468 units in 1973, and 186,275 in the extended '74 model year. With the production lines flat out stamping Hornets and Gremlins, there was no room for poor Cowboy. The prototype rode off alone into the sunset.

It might also be noticed that the '74 Sportabout on the Annual Reports cover had the recoverable 5 mph rear bumper. The formerly optional 5 mph front and rear bumpers were now standard on all '74 Hornets. The front 5 mph recoverable bumper's distinction of having a full-width horizontal rubstrip was dropped. All '74 Hornets had a pair of vertical black bumperettes front and rear, just like the '74 Javelin. The changed rear bumper meant Hornet's rear license plate now lived between the taillights, and one day soon AMX would be on that rear deck!

CHAPTER 4

Big and Small — Gremlin to Ambassador

Matador Tames Big 3 Bull ... Ole!

It was most likely with the recent experience of AMC's '60s rise and fall by the small car in mind, that *Motor Trend* stated the continued need for an American Motors family-sized car: "They still need an intermediate-sized, good performing luxury sedan."[1] This entailed ongoing development and manufacture of AMC's Rebel class car, but it wasn't called Rebel anymore.

Classic and Rebel joined the list of unfashionable tags, allowing AMC to introduce their 1971 Matador. Names like Capri, Matador and Barcelona had that Mediterranean flavor of exotic jet-set travel that was now in vogue, but in substance the '71 Matador was mainly a revised '70 Rebel. There was a new chrome grille, convex instead of concave face, a new interior, and detail alterations, but AMC's intermediate continued on a 118-inch wheelbase.

Thus, the Matador carried over the Rebel's 4-door sedan/wagon and 2-door hardtop body styles. The practical wagon still offered the option of third-row reverse seating and side-opening tailgate. Better still, Matador wagon could morph into a 2-seater with snap-in carpet and rubber cargo mat to cope with heavy family duty.

Matador and all other AMCs were available with a Low Fuel Warning System introduced the previous year. The system varied in application, but basically involved a small rectangle cutout in the middle of the fuel gauge at the ½ full point. This was covered from behind by a piece of red tape, and the warning light flashed rapidly when 2 gallons were left. The option had its own wiring harness and Chrysler-sourced sender unit. Of the 2 new '71 AMC engine options, one would make that light flash sooner.

Ode to the 401

It certainly wasn't the new 258 I6, which could be teamed with the Shift Command auto for sensible souls. The Devil urged one to check the 401 V8 option blank. AMC's 401 replaced the 390 and was first listed as a "factory experimental" V8 block with 4 bolt mains in AMC's high-performance parts catalogue in late 1968.

Between 1971 and 1978 the intermediate Matador was American Motors' family car, replacing the 1967–70 Rebel. A 1977 360-powered Matador wagon is shown (courtesy Pascal Cicchella).

This 401 V8 was used by Craig Breedlove in his supercharged, fuel-injected AMX Bonneville Salt Flats racer. A GMC Roots blower and Hilborn injectors were utilized on this AMX. In '71 the 401 was the top motor in the latest "Machine" package. Following from the '70 Rebel Machine, the Matador Machine was a high-performance parts pack that involved a 4-barrel 360 or 401, genuine duals and heavy duty suspension. As with Rebel, the Matador Machine came only in the 2-door hardtop body style.

As part of the major 1974 revisions, all Matadors got this new 3-instrument pod dash molding. The presence of 4 dashboard vents marks this wagon out as having a/c. AMC still offered the cheapest a/c on a domestic family car, costing $473 in 1975 (courtesy Pascal Cicchella).

The 15-inch "Machine" rims were still available, and the 2-door body appeared the same, but the red, white and blue livery was absent, as was the hoodscoop/tach. There were few takers for the Matador Machine: with hot cars on the decline, fewer than 50 were sold in the model's sole model year, 1971. In 1971 one could team the 4-barrel 360 and 401 with a 4-speed manual, but as part of power team pruning, the only manual '72 Matador was the 3-speed 232.

Fear not, because the 401 lived on. Its presence was signified by 401 fender callout badges on Javelin, Matador and Ambassador. Dimensionally it kept the 390's bore, 4.165 inches, but raised stroke from 3.57 in to 3.68 in. Still a low-volume performance motor, the 401 carried on the 390's forged crank and connecting rods. Taking up no more external space than a 290/304, the 6.6-liter small-block bore a raised "401" on the block's side.

Looking for a replacement for your high-mile 2-barrel 290? AMC offered a "Service Replacement" Multi-Displacement block based on the 1970–71 design AMC small-block V8. This was a 401 casting, bearing the 401 casting number but sans the "401" raised block script. The unit came with a 360 V8 bore and thicker deck, so a 343 to 401 short or tall deck could be cooked up on demand.

The AMC V8's high nickel content meant a hard block and little of the dreaded "core shift," but it wasn't all good. The best 401s to have are those from before mid–'71. These tall-deck versions have the better dog-leg exhaust port, plus the larger exhaust valves introduced later in model year '70. This involved an increase in the exhaust valve size concerning the big valve 343/360/390 head from 1.625 in to 1.68 in. Dog-leg plus the larger exhaust valve led to AMC's claiming 50 percent better exhaust side flow.

AMC revised its exhaust manifold to take advantage of the improvements, and the result could be seen on vehicles like the '71 SC/360 Hornet. It should also be noted that early 401s retained the 50–52cc combustion chamber size, and with it a higher 9.5:1 com-

The 360 was the biggest V8 AMC had for a passenger car post–'74. It made 140 bhp and 278 lbs./ft. in 2bbl '78 model year form, by which stage it was Matador wagon's standard engine (courtesy Pascal Cicchella).

pression ratio, which would drop to 8.5:1 at mid-year. These later 401s have thinner head castings, larger coolant passages and more elaborate rocker arm arrangements, all of which makes them harder to port.

The 401 was near the displacement limit for a small block, with little more to bore. As per the 390 V8, AMC recommended a mere 0.020 inch as an overbore, just to be safe. The motor's lubrication system also had problems. Oil makes its way up the front of the block to supply the lifter galleys, tending to neglect the rear crankshaft bearings, and the distributor's drive gears tend to see rapid wear. This, along with the 401's cooling system issues, makes it understandable how some ordered 4bbl 360s with duals and 285 bhp and 220 lbs. ft. of torque, compared to the 401's 330 and 255.

So a good maintenance schedule of regular coolant and oil changes benefits a 401. Today's aftermarket also offers solutions to the original design flaws, and 500 ponies isn't out of the question for a streetable ride. In the past, religiously followed maintenance was a given in the police force, and 401-motivated AMCs were popular cop cars. There were some Ambassadors and Matador wagons on the force, but most were 1972–74 Matador sedans.

A Matador 401 with HD suspension was a speedy 125 mph quality pursuit vehicle. As with the Alabama state trooper Javelin 401s, officers placed more faith in a Matador with Buyer Protection Plan than a Big 3 equivalent. When you're chasing bad guys through Demon's Canyon, you want to come out the other side in one piece! Matador police cars could be seen on the small screen, driven by LAPD's Malloy and Reed in *Adam 12*. Matador could also be seen in the Canadian-set 1978 police siege movie *Tomorrow Never Comes* starring Oliver Reed and Raymond Burr.

In real life, Matador was a favorite of the LAPD, the L.A. County Sheriff's Department, and other agencies like the military police. Rental fleet Matadors were the first to switch over to Torque Command autos late in the '71 model year. This may have been true for other fleet users like the police too. During this period AMC was also using a different kind of carb to get the job done, the Autolite Motorcraft 4000 series.

The Autolite Motorcraft 4-barrel was of Ford origin, and was the first carburetor to have an annular discharge booster venturi. This involved a ring of several discharge holes high in the venturi, making for better fuel atomization and suck-in vacuum. The design allowed smaller jets to be used for improved economy. By the time AMC was using the Autolite 4bbl, it was the 4300 version.

AMC stopped using the Carter 4bbl in '69, bringing in the Autolite 4300 on its V8 cars and Jeeps for '70. All Autolites used by AMC had automatic choke action, and the accelerator pump was mounted vertically inside the fuel bowl. An exclusive quirk of Ford and AMC Autolite applications was the use of a thick spacer as a vacuum or EGR valve connection. To work out the specific vehicle application details, consult the aluminum identification tag on the carb's air horn screw.

AMC cars and Jeeps carried a 4- and 5-digit tag sequence, respectively. The Autolite's efficiency made it a NASCAR fave, and AMC had some NASCAR presence too. In 1969 AMC entered the NASCAR Grand Touring series in association with Warren Prout. Jim Paschal was doing the driving, and not much happened. However, in the 1970 racing season, Paschal nabbed a victory in the Grand Touring series.

Fast-forward to 1973 and Roger Penske was in charge of an AMC factory-backed NASCAR effort, with drivers Mark Donohue and Bobby Allison. The team's weapon was the

Matador 2-door hardtop, a.k.a. "The Flying Brick," on account of its less-than-streamlined aerodynamics. Not to worry: on January 21, 1973, at Riverside, Mark Donohue attained victory in the Winston Western 500 while driving the aforementioned Flying Brick.

Such a solid result was needed by the smallest member of the Big 4. It was hard work not getting lost in the Big 3 crowd. AMC promoted their intermediate with a "What's a Matador?" ad campaign, humorously alluding to the fact the average Tom, Dick or Harriet might not know AMC was still in the inter business. By the end of '73, folks probably knew about Matador, but in case they didn't AMC released a much revised car for '74.

The latest range was dubbed "coffin nose" Matador, since the '74 sedans and wagons had a forward-projecting middle hood, grille and bumper section reminiscent of the classic Cord 810/812. In the '70s Detroit was fondly recalling the glories of the prewar era, so AMC said why not? AMC's family midsize had had pairs of circular headlamps since '63, but now Matador had one round headlamp per side, with inner amber turn signals, also round.

The rear fascia was also amended, now sporting 4 taillights per side. These changes coincided with the introduction of 5 mph recoverable shock absorber bumpers front and rear on Matador as required by '74 federal law. In '73 the optional recoverable 5 mph bumpers were a Hornet/Gremlin exclusive at AMC. The old-school styling provided interesting ways for designers to disguise impact bumpers. Observe the 1973–74 Pontiac Grand Am's example.

Matador was living up to its solid citizen status by incorporating safety and pollution changes. There was a new 3-point seat belt setup with that mandatory Interlock device, a logic sequence computer that made sure front occupants wore their belts. V8 motors now had induction-hardened exhaust valve seats, so AMC's I6s and V8s were good to go on low-lead and even no-lead gas.

A 3-drivebelt accessory system on V8s made the handling of ancillaries neater. Matador in all its forms could now be specified with the industry's current miracle: the radial tire! Matador's suspension settings were retuned to ride and handle well on radials. As before, Matador's roadability could be improved with the optional handling pack comprising HD springs, shocks and a rear swaybar.

Matador wagon offered the convenience of a side-opening tailgate and humongous 95.2 cubic feet of cargo space. That figure included 8 cubic feet of secret sub cargo floor compartment (courtesy Pascal Cicchella).

This pack was found on police Matadors, and was included in the optional Trailer Towing Package, which had adjustable air shocks for the rear suspension. For style, Matador featured a new "Bravado" vinyl roof material to complement the 15 possible exterior colors, 9 of which were new for '74. On wagons the optional woodgrain exterior appliqué was also of new finish, and the shape of the paneling was also altered.

Matador's interior was

Matador wagon's optional 3rd row rear seating came with a nifty powered rear tailgate window under the Convenience Options (courtesy Pascal Cicchella).

much changed for '74 too, with a new dashboard containing 3 round-edged square pods for the instruments. The AM-FM stereo radio/tape player, when specified, was now integrated within the dash. Combination AM-FM stereo radio/tape player audio systems came with 4 speakers and 4-way volume balancing. Music played would be better heard because '74 Matadors came with AMC's Extra Quiet Insulation Package as standard equipment. On AMC vehicles this entailed underhood sound deadener material, cowl panel insulation, front and rear floor insulation, rear shelf panel and rear wheel well insulation, plus full undercoating.

These were good value stock items, and if optional a/c was purchased, Matador would get 4 adjustable dash vents, 2 in the center and 2 at the outer ends. The 1974 Matadors also carried new seating material, and the interior door panels were restyled too. It was a comprehensive makeover, and the '74 Matador represented the typical 6-passenger, rear-drive intermediate family car that was at the volume core of Detroit, and what it did so well.

In the dying days of the pre-downsized era, Matador had length, width, and height dimensions of 216, 75.7, and 54.7 inches on a 118-inch wheelbase. This practical sedan weighed 3,670 lbs, not much in the overall history of the automobile, but a heavyweight once OPEC declared war on humanity! That 3,670-pound curb weight reflects a car with the base 232 / 3-speed full-synchro manual power team, which ran with 3.08 rear gears.

By this time that 232 was available only in 1bbl 8.0:1 compression ratio form, producing exactly 100 bhp at 3,500 rpm and 185 lbs/ft at 1,800 rpm. How could anyone accuse you of being a gas hog in one of these? It required 24.9 gallons to fill the tank on the Matador 232 sedan, and the 1-barrel carb made sure the no-lead was sipped like a saint! However,

Sadly, not even Hyde Park, Mediterranean-flavor Barcelona seat trim or the solidity of the "Big Car" ride could halt the exodus to GM's new downsized full-size rides (courtesy Pascal Cicchella).

if one wanted to drink like a fish, the 255 bhp 4bbl 401 was still on the table, and it's the one the police still fancied.

Sadly, 1974 was the final MY for the 401 in Matador, or any AMC car for that matter. Part of the reason for this was the fuel crisis and recession, which caused reduced sales of big-motored cars. However, the 401 was still in demand for police Matadors, and the withdrawal of the 401 from the normal car line helped AMC honor law enforcement Matador 401 orders. The 401 continued to be available in AMC's Jeep line.

Between 1975 and 1978, AMC 360/401 V8s used the updated Autolite 4350 4bbl carb. The 401 dropped to a 215 bhp rating during the 1975 model year, and was emissioned down to 205 ponies for '76. That was the heat a cop's Matador was packing. The coffin-nose police Matador 401s weren't as well regarded as earlier Matadors. The added length and weight impaired handling, and there was a feeling that reliability had declined. Law enforcement agencies subsequently switched orders back to the Big 3 and their new downsized wares. However, some police Matadors continued to serve and protect into the mid–'80s!

Matador wagon supplied 38.5 inches of headroom and 39.6 inches of legroom in its rear compartment. Plenty of room for the kids on that trip to Wally World (courtesy Pascal Cicchella).

Even though AMC's senior cars were reaching an evolutionary zenith, the public in the '74 gas crunch and earlier were seeking out smaller, thriftier rides. The compact was everyone's friend again, as well as a new domestic segment started by AMC called subcompact. With an unusual name and small exterior, this was the kind of ride people were signing up for as larger cars gathered showroom dust.

Gremlin—AMC Reinvents the Small Car

Back in 1959 small cars were in vogue. To be big, you had to be small; this attracted the Big 3 like sharks going to a feeding frenzy. The compacts came and smote the imports, and Detroit was back on top. Then small cars weren't fashionable any more, so the compacts got fancy and begat the pony car. AMC brought out a real honest-to-goodness new '64 American compact, at which the public yawned. However, even though Detroit and the small car went their separate ways, one small car was still alive and well in America.

Volkswagen was going to make Beetles at a defunct Studebaker factory, with its New Jersey U.S. corporate headquarters nicely complementing things by 1962, but it didn't happen. U.S. parts suppliers didn't bite: they weren't going to bother providing a competitive contract price for a little car that wasn't going to sell much, or so they thought. However, the Beetle did end up selling big. In 1959 Carl Hahn took charge of VW of America, enlisted Doyle, Dayne & Bernbach Inc. to supply snappy advertising, and the rest is history.

The adverts whimsically extolled the Beetle's virtues of dependability, frugalness and an aversion to fads that would leave more of one's money in the wallet where it belonged. Under this veneer of mirth, VW of America engineered a business model that had a lot to do with the process of buying. There was a substantial inventory of spare parts, a strong network of authorized VW dealers with trained technicians, and dealership selling behavior that was controlled by HQ.

The Big 3 put the product before the process: whether one would buy one of their models rested on the specific appeal and qualities of that model. The manufacturer then pushed as much stock onto the dealer as possible, leaving the consumer to play hunt-the-discount as dealers tried to offload supply. VW's method had the actual car as only one link in the chain. Thus, by blending advertising, product perception, after-sales care, and dealer

On April 1, 1970, American Motors released the first domestic subcompact. With their tardy Vega and Pinto, the April Fools' joke was on GM and Ford (courtesy Jo Wilson).

stock levels they were able to engineer the Beetle into people's default small-car choice, in spite of the product's shortcomings.

In 1960 Beetle sales broke the 100,000-unit barrier in North America, in 1963 200,000 was exceeded, with 300,000 sales per annum passed in 1967.[2] The Bug peaked with 423,000 Beetles sold in North America in 1968. Part of this meteoric rise was due to VW's rigorous plan, which sent shade-tree-mechanic favorites Morris Minors and DAF Daffodils to oblivion. The other was the public's desire for a truly small auto.

AMC's cartoon Gremlin character was found on the front fenders, and plastered all over AMC dealer showroom glass. The Gremlin was a goblin associated with aircraft mechanical problems during World War II (courtesy Jo Wilson).

Back in the late '50s, the Big 3 studied the Bug on their road to the compact. Future U.S. Defense Secretary Robert McNamara canned the Edsel and instructed the Ford folks to examine Beetle when he was running Henry's workshop. Detroit wanted to know whether the Beetle was any good. By the late '60s, Detroit didn't care if the Beetle was any good; they just wanted to be like it. Detroit was rectangular, fast and flash; Beetle was round, slow and minimalist. The counterculture revolution dictated that the square should copy the hippie!

Somehow the clockwork toy presented to Hitler had become a trendsetter. GM redid its strategy, pushing the new Vega as a thoughtful small car. Management said it would achieve a heretofore unseen level of quality in a highly automated factory. The Vega's advertising also showed the mental sea change. Print ads had a cute cartoon orange Vega, in front view, with said front obscured by 5 license plates reading 1971 to 1975. The point of this was to say GM was out of the obsolescence game; in Chevrolet's words: "Chevy's new little car: If you like the 1971, you'll like the 1975."

So GM claimed there would be no change for the sake of change. This bit of blasphemy probably worried some execs and dealers: why would anyone trade in on a new '72? And what of the mid-model-year freshen-upper? Children were going to starve! Over at Ford they were getting equally Scrooge-like: Lee Iacocca was pushing his people to come up with their 2,000 pound/2,000 buck small car, to be called Pinto.

The whips weren't being spared at Ford, while Chrysler was relying on its captive import Colt cars derived from a linkup with Mitsubishi. However, all this was for nothing, because in the 3-way race to come up with America's first modern, domestically designed and built supersonic subcompact, the winner was American Motors! The company decided to hang superstition and present their new little car, the Gremlin, to AMC dealers on Friday the 13th, with a public release on April 1, 1970.

The April Fools' joke was on the Big 3. Vega and Pinto would debut later as '71 cars; meanwhile, AMC sold 28,560 Gremlins in what remained of the 1970 model year. AMC dealers were very pleased: the public had given Gremlin the thumbs-up! AMC had a slight head start on the others since Gremlin, in true AMC money-saving tradition, was Hornet-based. That said, it should also be noted that Pinto was somewhat of a truncated Maverick itself.

As a truncated Hornet, Gremlin could accept any motor AMC's compact had on the books, but Gremlin would have to wait until '72 for a V8 option. American Motors' ads made much of the fact Gremlin came with larger, more powerful engines than its subcompact rivals (courtesy Jo Wilson).

Originally the Hornet link was going to be even stronger. Initial plans involved a 12-inch wheelbase chop on a Hornet, creating a short notchback with the moniker Wasp. However, this wasn't that snazzy, and Richard Teague convinced management that if their new subcompact was going to survive once GM's and Ford's designs were out, Gremlin had to be distinctive and stand out from the crowd.

Distinctiveness was definitely achieved, courtesy of Gremlin's sharply angled rear end. That rear view was new, but the front was familiar. Gremlin and Hornet shared front fenders and bumpers, with the two distinguished by Gremlin's open-grille front fascia and hood with slight power bulge. Hornet's hood had a subtle center crease and fascia with round parking lights, rather than Gremlin's rectangular equivalents. There were also humorous decorative touches linked to the Gremlin name.

"Gremlin" is defined as an imaginary goblin-like creature, blamed for military aircraft problems in World War II. AMC did a cartoon figure to go with the myth, and this character was on the rear-deck gas filler cap, as well as in the form of small front fender badges until the end of the '71 model year. The image was also shown decal large on dealership showroom windows as an attention grabber. Gremlin was designed under the leadership of Richard Teague, but AMC's Bob Nixon was also on the team.

Bob Nixon joined AMC as a 23-year-old and did the first formal Gremlin car sketch in 1967. That early rendering showed a sleek-looking economy car. In reality, the front of Gremlin, and Hornet, may well have been taller than stylistically desired, since there was a need to accommodate the upright AMC I6. However, early small-bumper Gremlins showed that good appearance was an objective. The rear ¾ top-down pose displayed a lower fascia panel lifted from the '64½ Ford Mustang.

The Beetle firmly placed function before form. Richard Teague alluded to this when, comparing scale profile outlines of VW and Gremlin, he remarked, "It looks like the Hindenberg next to a GT40."[3] This was no exaggeration: the Gremlin was only slightly longer than Beetle, 161.2 inches versus 158.6 inches, but much shorter in height, 51.8 inches against 59.1. Gremlin was about as short as one could go with a modern wedge-shaped look.

The public caught their first glimpse of the general shape at the 1968 New York International Auto Show, where the AMX GT showcar was displayed. This concept ride was like a slightly shorter real-life Gremmy, with a '68 AMX nose. The '70½ Gremlin structure was unique looking and very sturdy. There were few window openings, and a liftback window extending only halfway down the rear fascia. A subsequent proto–Gremlin, the "Voyageur," made on the chassis of a '70 model, had a complete pull-out rear deck drawer.

The Hunt for Black Beetle

Having a liftback and floorshift manual was very import-like at the time—think Renault 16—but Gremlin power was very American. Gremlin's base engine was AMC's 7-bearing I6, and a small car needed a strong unibody to cope with the twist of a 3.8-liter engine, or even a 3.3-liter one. Indeed, it could be said AMC had not one, but two 2-seater cars in 1970. One was the AMX; the other was the '70½ Gremlin Business Coupe, America's lowest-priced domestically built automobile.

Gremlin had such decontenting as a 2- instead of a 3-gauge dash pack—therefore no clock—but Business Coupe went further. The rear Gremlin bench was missing, and the rear window was fixed. For your $1,879 there was a 1bbl 128 bhp 199 I6/3-speed column manual power team, non-boosted 4-wheel drums and 13-inch tires with 6-inch footprint. This was the import fighter Detroit had to have, specifically targeting traveling aluminum siding salesmen who liked to save a buck.

Sadly, there were only 872 takers for the Gremlin Business Coupe in '70; obviously aluminum siding was on the way out by this time! The other 27,688 '70½ Gremlin buyers went for the Highline 4-seater with functional rear hatch window. Paying $45.35 extra for the 145 bhp 1bbl 232 motor automatically nabbed one the 3-speed floorshift manual, useful for power-vaulting past Beetles and asthmatic Valiants at traffic lights.

The $43 Twin-Grip LSD was available on Gremlin too. Gremlin 232 was a small-car hotshot to fear, out-accelerating an expensive fuel-injected Saab 99 in *Car and Driver* testing. *Mechanix Illustrated*'s legendary "Uncle" Tom McCahill thought well of Gremlin 232 when an automatic example clocked 0–60 mph in 11.9 seconds and touched 100 mph at Daytona Speedway. McCahill's famous quote was much used in publicity blurbs: "On a dollar for dollar basis, I rate the Gremlin the best American buy of the year."

Top: **Borrowing its dash from Hornet, Gremlin had HVAC controls the ancient Beetle and other small imports could only dream of. The Beetle was very much a *Bismarck*** AMC **sought to sink (courtesy Jo Wilson). *Bottom:*** With the **199 econo six discontinued at the end of '70, engine choices for '71 were the 135 bhp 232 I6 and new 150 bhp 258 I6. Gross ratings, perhaps, but plenty to trouble Vega GT and Pinto Rallye (courtesy Jo Wilson).**

Small-car buying prior to the gas crunch involved more than just fuel economy. Low initial purchase price, low maintenance costs, resale value, convenient size and gas mileage were in the mix. It was a time when "U-Service-It" maintenance was an encouraged selling point. For example, '71 Pinto was available with a beginner's toolkit ($29), master toolkit ($45), and instructional servicing manual for $2. Thrown in was a Swiss Army knife-style key-shaped gadget that could act as a screwdriver, ruler, feeler gauge and spark plug gapping tool.

Ford weren't the only ones using self-service bait to liberate a few more dollars from buyers of economy cars. In truth, the "one tool fixes all" didn't work that well, and the service manual had the mystery of a Nancy Drew adventure. Pollution-controlled cars of the early '70s were tough to tune at the best of times. On the subject of fuel economy, AMC put forward a choice unique among small cars: a big engine.

As mentioned, Gremlin was exclusively I6-powered, whereas the other cars, import and domestic, used small four-cylinder engines. The results held true to an old maxim: a heavily worked small motor is a thirsty one. Vega and Pinto came with 2.3 and 2.0 OHC I4s, the Japanese were similar, and VW used their tiny air-cooled flat four. Gremlin didn't drink much more in real-world driving, with a big acceleration advantage as big-six compensation.

In January 1971, *Consumer Reports* published the outcome of the acid test, Beetle versus Gremlin. A manual 4-speed VW Super Beetle did 0–60 mph in 20 seconds and the quarter mile in 21.5 seconds at 62 mph. The Gremlin 232 with 3-speed manual floorshift and 2.73 rear gears chirped its tires to record equivalent figures of 13 seconds and 19.5 seconds at 72 mph. So the Gremlin was obviously fleeter of foot, but what of gas mileage?

Consumer Reports' economy figures for Super Beetle were in the 17–29 mpg range, for Gremlin 12–24 mpg. Not much thirstier, considering it's a 1,600cc flat four against a 3,800cc I6, and the bigger AMC gas tank meant one was going to make fewer gas station stops than with Beetle. Gremlin's gas tank was twice the size of the Beetle's at 21 gallons, giving a much longer cruising range.

On price, Gremlin had a slight edge over Beetle: $1,879 versus $1,880. However, even properly equipped, Gremlin was still in front on value. *Consumer Reports'* Gremlin 232 manual cost $2,100 and weighed 2,634 lbs; VW Super Beetle 117 (sunroof with vinyl trim) retailed for $2,139 and tipped the scales at 1,978 lbs. Plus, in spite of the MacPherson front suspension upgrade, Super Beetle's ride comfort ranked very low.[4]

This '71 Gremlin was sold new with light blue exterior and blue interior. Today the exterior is yellow and the seats sport yellow and black vinyl covers, custom made by Automotive Interiors of Belchertown, Massachusetts. The car's front grille and roof rack have gone from chrome finish to black (courtesy Jo Wilson).

Objectively, the "The Little Cars" test had shown Gremlin to offer more car for the money than Beetle. AMC delivered more crush safety, style, interior space and a better performance/economy combo for the same money. Gremlin could also be more kinds of car than even Vega, whose automatic gearbox option was the $168 2-speed Powerglide. Two speeds mated to an I4 motor didn't promise good performance or economy.

Gremlin offered the BW 3-speed Shift Command auto for $200.95, much more civilized. Gremlin's interior could also be dressed up with the $19.95 Interior Appointment Package, in-

Arizona AMC dealer Randall American was a speed shop that offered a 6.6-liter V8 "401-XR" engine swap for Gremlin during 1972–74, as well as complementary options to turn the subcompact into the ultimate street or strip car (courtesy Mike Randall).

volving under-dash storage shelf, glove box door and light, plus cigarette lighter. The $49.95 Custom Interior Package brought carpeting, more luxurious door panel/seat trim and custom steering wheel. Or maybe you wanted things sporty? In that case there were $89.90 front buckets, $23.55 HD suspension and B78 14-inch tires, along with $11.65 quick ratio manual steering.

For '71 AMC formalized the sports Gremlin with the $300 "X" package, an appearance/sport collection of useful things. To get X, one needed to start with a 4-seat Gremlin. The pack included profile spear body decals, color-keyed front fascia panel with blacked-out grille insert, Javelin-derived buckets, Goodyear Polyglas D70 tires on 14 × 6-inch slot rims with space-saver spare, engine-turned instrument trim panel and the upscale Custom Interior Package.

The X pack also included a painted lower rear fascia panel, the same color as the profile spear stripes, that carried the car's engine size in fancy Euro metric, e.g., "3.8 litre" or "4.2 litre." Raised-white-letter tires were optional, as were spoke sport rims. With insurance and inflation biting, Gremlin X was now part of the junior, junior performance car scene. Before the little guys were things like Plymouth Duster 340 and Hornet SC/360; now below such machines were the mini racers.

AMC's '71 Gremlin X ad showed that in the real-life Hot Wheels crowd, Gremlin was the least toylike. Up against Vega GT, Pinto Rallye, Maverick Grabber and Comet GT, Gremmy came with fatter rubber on its new-design slot rims, a wider track for more poised handling, and most importantly for America, more standard power. The 199 I6 was toast at the end of the '70 model year, so Gremlin X came with a 135 bhp 232 as standard, with the new 150 bhp 258 I6 optional. Both figures reflect gross bhp.

Gremlin X hit the spot: it was a sales winner and Gremlin marched on to a 76,908 '71 model year total. The price of a 4-seat Gremlin had risen from $1,959 to $1,999 in '71, management feeling the 2-grand level was of psychological importance. All seemed to be going swimmingly well for Gremlin, and AMC, this being one case where the subcompact hadn't eaten the compact. There was an industry feeling any new entrant wouldn't dent VW sales; it would just eat into the maker's own compact sales.

Maverick's sales were considered reduced by Pinto's presence, but it seemed doubtful if Gremlin affected Hornet. Gremlin and Hornet were different in character, in spite of mechanical similarity; hence the relative failure of Hornet X next to Gremlin X. Gremlin may not have reduced Beetle sales much, but it probably roped in new buyers that ordinarily wouldn't have gone this small. There were examples of people choosing Gremlin over 4-cylinder Pinto and Vega because of the big six.

So thank Mr. Teague for making Gremlin different, and thank the optional '71 rear roof deflector for keeping Gremlin's rear window sparkly! However, there were problems concerning quality. The January '71 *Consumer Reports* test highlighted the quality gap between import and domestic, but it also heralded the coming of the Japanese. Datsun PL 510 and Toyota placed first and third on test respectively, with superior fit and finish to the domestics.[5] VW Super Beetle recorded a record-low 11 defects; Pinto was at the opposite end of the scale with 30 defects.

In what would be normal for the next 30 years, GM's new Vega was attractive, a good small car with novel features like an aluminum-block I4 with linerless bores; it placed second on test, but was defect-prone and recall-ridden: good design, poor execution. Test Gremlin was also no prize, coming with 23 defects, such as poorly fitting doors and a glove box door that was supposed to be there, but wasn't. The trouble with Detroit was that when a model was selling hot, which Pinto, Vega and Gremlin were, the aim was to get the cars flying off the assembly line into showrooms ASAP, where it was up to the dealers to right the wrongs.

The VW Super Beetle was alone in offering a 24-month/24,000-mile warranty and

Gremlin's rear deck gas filler cap was an often-stolen piece of industrial art. For '70s medallions, AMC was the King of Bling (courtesy Donnie Solomon).

free 6,000-mile diagnostic inspections. Gremlin took the hint and made '72 the year of quality. Firstly, the Gremlin Business Coupe was history. The 2-seater had moved up to $1,899 in '71 and sold 2,145 copies that model year, making a 3,017 total over an 18-month period. Its job was done, and Gremlin was established, so Business Coupe exited stage left at the end of '71.

The 1972 Gremlin came with a rear window that could be opened, fold-down rear seat and electric wiper-washer system as standard equipment. It was also available with some new upscale options like a fabric sunroof, Adjust-O-Tilt steering on column-shift automatic Gremlins, flip-open rear windows, AM/FM non-stereo radio, removable front door storage pockets, and more mechanically. Gremlin was now available with front disk brakes and a full synchromesh 3-speed manual floorshift.

Group 19 American traction bars were items that could be fitted to Hornet and Gremlin, and in '72 and '73 they were a formal option. Due to the similarity in AMC car chassis, Javelin's '72 Zero-Lash front suspension balljoint was introduced on Gremlin, too, according to AMC brochure material. The transition from a two-piece to a one-piece balljoint socket assembly was supposed to improve durability. New-design rear brake cylinders were aimed at reducing lockup.

The hardware upgrades were related to Gremlin's being in AMC's new '72 comprehensive Buyer Protection Plan warranty, an attempt to restore American Motors' quality reputation back to what it was in halcyon Rambler times. Therefore, the revised-body-color front fascia of '72 Gremlin was a face one could trust. Trust the public did, as Gremlin sales climbed to 94,808 units, 10,949 of which had a V8.

Yes, AMC were first with a U.S. subcompact, and before the four-cylinder Vega and Pinto came, truly did have "the best gas mileage of any production car made in America," according to AMC. Now AMC became the first to offer a subcompact with factory-fitted V8. Once again in AMC's own words, "An optional 304 V-8 package that goes. Wow does it go." Even with the modest 2bbl 150 bhp (net) detoxed 304, the 2,746-pound Gremlin V8 could do 0–60 mph in 8.5 seconds.

No factory VW could sprint that quickly; nor could Vega, Pinto or MGB. V8 Gremlins received larger front brakes and a front swaybar normally only included with the I6's HD suspension. The only thing that shone brighter than the V8's performance was Gremlin's standard "Luster-Guard" triple-coated, baked-on acrylic enamel finish. This was another sign of quality. At $2,153, not even the Big 3 had an answer to the V8 Gremlin; it was the cheapest high-performance car in the country.

First with a domestic subcompact, and first with a V8 option for same. The $2,153 '72 AMC Gremlin 304 was America's most affordable speedy car. A 1974 Gremlin X 5-liter is shown (courtesy Donnie Solomon).

The 6.6-Liter Gremlin, 401-XR

Gremlin V8 buyers could choose the sleeper look of the optional Custom Trim pack, which included profile rally stripe, wheel covers, roof rack, rear roof air deflector, scuff molding and bumper guards. Alternatively, they could decline hiding their V8 under a bushel and select the X pack, which in this case carried a "5 litre V/8" script callout. There was another choice: fit the 401ci V8 to Gremlin! Who on earth would do such an act? The answer was AMC dealer Randall American, located in Mesa, Arizona.

Grant Randall's dealership was a known speed shop, but in dropping the AMC 401 motor into the subcompact's engine bay, they surpassed all other speed shops by having the biggest engine in the smallest car, for the lowest price! In truth, the groundwork was done when AMC created the Gremlin 304, the little car getting cross-member and engine mount changes to take the small-block V8, as well as HD suspension. Randall's Performance Director Ed Beard said the engine swap was easy if one started with a Gremlin 304 base car, given that externally the 304 and 401 V8s were the same.[6]

Randall tried for endorsement of the Gremlin 401 project from AMC, and they got unofficial support and 30 401ci crate motors. The engine received was the usual 255-horse smog-safe 401 with 8.5:1 compression ratio, but since Gremlin was so light its performance was unusual. Place an order at Randall, come back 2 weeks later, and for $2,995 you would own a Gremlin 401-XR 3-speed floorshift manual. This car could do 13.9s at 105–107 mph according to Randall, and there was no reason for doubt.

There was also no reason to stop there. Randall would outfit the 401-XR with options like Torque Command auto, which fortuitously had just arrived at AMC, or BW Super T10

Even with just 150 net ponies, the 2bbl 304 could zip Gremlin to sixty in 8.5 seconds. The 304 continued as a Gremlin option until mid–'76 (courtesy Donnie Solomon).

4-speed, headers, front disk brakes, Twin-Grip and normal Gremlin luxo options like a/c. AMC's a/c package brought HD radiator cooling, 50-amp battery, 51-amp alternator, tinted glass and power steering to deal with the added weight over the front wheels of a/c.

The V8 engine itself contributed to the nose-heavy nature of Gremlin, and the anticipated understeer. Uncle Tom McCahill described the Gremlin 232 as having "fast and easy" handling. Having a big six in a short-wheelbase car spelled much plow on through corners, with abrupt transition to oversteer should engine torque be exerted. Not a problem: in the dying seconds of the "hawt" streeter scene, the Gremlin 401-XR was there to be built up with sports cam, high-rise intake manifold, bigger carb, new gauge pack with 160 mph speedo and rear axle ratios from 2.87 to a very short 5.58:1.

Randall would do all that for you, and it spoke to the nature of those pre–Prius times how seriously built-up a car could be, and still be considered a street machine. Such a Randall-modified car was tested at Lions Drag Strip in Los Angeles by Steve Collison of *Car Craft* magazine, who drove said car from Arizona to L.A. for testing, averaging just under 10 mpg on high-test.

This Gremlin 401-XR was a 4-speed machine with Hurst Super Shifter, 850 cfm Holley 4bbl, Edelbrock aluminum intake manifold, Iskenderian #310 hydraulic cam, Accel distributor with 38 degrees of advance at 3,000 rpm, AMC differential with 4.44 rear gears and Ed Beard design rear pinion snubber. Tires were Inglewood G60-14 Pos-A-Traction Torque Sixty items on 14 × 7-inch E-T rims.

The 1⅝-inch tubular exhaust headers let out the exhaust gases, and a Schiefer Rev-Lock diaphragm clutch helped transmit the 401's power to the rear axle. The vehicle weighed 2,820 lbs with a half tank of gas, and recorded a 12.22-second pass at 115.97 mph![7] This may have been deemed a road car, but it was a handful. The 401's torque made for much movement of the small block on its engine mounts, and difficulty engaging and disengaging cogs at high revs in spite of the special clutch. Should have chosen that Torqueflite box!

According to Mike Randall, 20 streeter 401-XR Gremlins were built, with one dedicated strip machine as well, over the 1972–74 period. All examples were converted Gremlin 304s. AMC provided the final hurrah in Woodward Avenue's twilight. With the formal Trans Am and drag racing strip times mostly over, AMC was more concerned with down-to-earth matters, like interior space and impact bumpers.

Gremlin Surfs the Small-Car Wave

There wasn't a great deal of space in a Gremlin, especially for rear occupants. *Consumer Reports* had a nice way of describing living arrangements back there: "The Gremlin's rear seat is large enough for children or for adult contortionists."[8] All the small cars tested were rear-drive, even the Japanese ones. For efficient internal space packaging in a small car, front drive was required, and only practiced by the English and French at the time.

Limitations observed, AMC still tried to make amends, reshaping and positioning Gremlin's front seat in model year '72 to give more thigh clearance between seat bottom and steering wheel. In model year '73 Gremlin's rear bench was redesigned to liberate more legroom, but what can you expect in a sub–170-incher? Realistically, if more space was needed, Hornet and Matador were there; for parking ease and tight urban spots, there was Gremlin. Plus Gremlin still had a smaller turning circle than VW.

Friends of fashion were interested in Gremlin's Levi's trim pack, available for '73 just like Hornet. The advert was nearly correct: "Levi's Gremlin, with seats of the pants." It wasn't possible to use actual denim due to fire hazard. Spun blue nylon was used instead, and as per Levi's Hornet, a nice blue hue adorned door trim panels, map pockets, carpeting, headliner and sun visors. Burnished copper denim rivet buttons, orange stitching and red Levi's logo tabs maintained authenticity.

A Levi's trademark emblem decal on the front fenders was hard to miss, as was Gremlin's optional 5 mph recoverable bumper system. Normal Gremlin bumpers were beefed-up 5 mph front and 2.5 mph rear items, in compliance with '73 federal dictates. Hornet and Gremlin were the only AMCs to allow the buyer to be '74 bumper ready! Optional was AMC's 5 mph shock-absorbing front and rear recoverable bumper system.

The '73 Hornets and Gremlins with the recoverable bumpers had special VIN details. On the sequence after the letter denoting which engine was fitted, there would be the digits "00." This way insurance companies could give owners who chose the recoverable system a lower premium, just by checking the chassis number. Recoverable bumpers meant less low-speed impact damage, and smaller repair claims.

These "free-standing" bumpers had no beauty panels covering the gap between body and extended bumpers. Gremlin's dimensions now stood at 169.4, 70.6, and 52.3 inches for length, width and height. The change also raised weight to 2,831 lbs. More welcome additions were Gremlin's optional floor-mounted Torque Command auto, soft-touch dash knobs, and the use of international symbols for the instrument display.

In model year '73 the Torque Command auto was only available in floorshift form, and there were changes with rear axle ratios. The 2.37 econoaxle, introduced on the 232 automatic power team in '71, was discontinued at the close of the '72 model year. The standard axle ratio on I6 Gremlins was now 2.73, and 2.87 for V8s. This was no big deal to most who just wanted a small car, and many did, taking Gremlin sales to a new high of 122,844, with 11,672 being 304 powered.

The Gremlin X continued to be popular, and had its decorative stripes redone for '73. The profile spear stripe was ready to kick up over Gremlin's rear fender openings. So popular were Gremlin and the X version that the stripes were redone for '74 too. For '74 Gremlin had its two horizontal sail panel indentations replaced by 4 vertical sloping ones not unlike the Project IV Vixen's canted roof vanes. The new-style '74 X "hockey stick" spear stripes followed Gremlin's window line and then swept up onto the sail panel, highlighting the indentations.

The 5 mph recoverable bumpers were standard in '74, along with a floorshift 3-speed manual, and weren't exactly cosmetically liked. They made Gremlin look more rugged, but purists yearned for the neater '72 look. AMC wasn't worried, since the actions of OPEC made Gremlin even more popular. People wanted small and frugal to combat inflation and soaring gas prices.

A vehicle with a long range was a good way to avoid long gas lines. The alternative was to buy a Mercedes 240D diesel compact and fill up where the truckers did, thereby avoiding the dreaded lines. The only problem with that route was that diesel cars were a real bear to start in cold weather. In some parts of the country you would be at the mercy of block heaters, glow plugs and thinner engine oil. So avoid the expensive diesel import, and rely on Gremlin 232 to get you to work on time!

Oddly, Gremlin V8 sales rose for the third year in a row to 14,137. Even in a fuel crisis, folks were wanting their Gremlin with the 2bbl 8.4:1 CR 304. Demand for the 150 bhp Gremlin V8 heralded the start of a trend where buyers wanted uptrimmed and up-engined smaller cars. The '74 model year marked Gremlin's best-ever result: 171,128 of the little 2 doors were delivered. The big number was partly due to AMC's extending their '74 production year into November. This was to avoid fitting catalytic converters, necessary for the stricter '75 model year pollution regs.

In all the excitement, Gremlin's Levi's and X packs continued, and both included the refinement of AMC's Extra Quiet Insulation Package. The '74 X pack came with a larger, color-contrasting rear fascia panel that now reached under the rear bumper. There was also a new version to aspire to, called Gremlin Rallye-X. Rallye-X involved starting with a Gremlin X, and added functional driver performance aids.

The front disk brake package was Rallye-X included, as was a front swaybar if a 304 car wasn't already at hand. Instrumentation changed to the Hornet's 3-dial display, so that a tach could be installed in the extreme right gauge. The instrument panel received blackout trim, which also covered the steering column, and there were readouts for oil pressure and battery charge. A nifty leather-wrapped sports steering wheel worked standard power steering.

AMC surfed the small-car-loving energy crisis wave in 1973–74. Just as in the late '50s, they had the cars Americans wanted, as the economy experts (cartoon by author).

By '74 a Gremlin could feature an AM/FM stereo radio with 4 speakers, and a rear window defogger. You might have wanted to option up the brakes, since stock Gremlin stoppers were still 4-wheel non-boosted drums. However, there was one item not on Gremlin's option list: space! Many would have thought that for a few pennies extra, they would have been able to buy a loaded, full-size sedan with a premium-fuel V8. A couple of years earlier that would have been possible. AMC still made one of those land yachts in 1974. The full-size car was still called Ambassador. In spite of the close Matador connection, Ambassador had a special air as it made options standard on big cars.

AMC's Final Full-Size—Ambassador, 1967–74

As part of fitting in with the groovy generation, Ambassador adopted a stylish new Coke-bottle body for the '67 model year, which it largely shared with the new midsize Rebel. The move was a good one since it brought with it AMC's new open driveshaft, 4-link trailing arm rear suspension chassis, giving the 118-inch wheelbase Ambassador a degree of roadability the nameplate had never known.

Whenever an Ambassador out-wheelbased its smaller cousin, the extra length was in the front, and in this case added grace to the profile. Ambassador also sported differentiated front and rear fascias. That front was shared with the '67 Marlin and involved vertical stacked headlamps flanking a grille with sharp central horizontal divider and a pair of round parking lights. Rear taillights were also distinguished from Rebel, Ambassador's being slim rectangular units with center vertical divider. There was even a hint of a tailfin!

The style-conscious took their final opportunity to sample the Ambassador ragtop. The 1967 model year would prove to be the last year for AMC's full-size convertible; just 1,260 Ambassador DPL convertibles were sold that year. Ambassador's 2-door sedan body style was also shown the garage door at the end of '67. As per the equivalent Rebel 2-door with pillar, there was little need for the variant, given the 2-door hardtop's existence.

Management wanted to curtail permutations and rein in cost, so '67's 880/990/DPL range was simplified to 1968's Ambassador/DPL/SST trim levels in the 3 body choices of 2-door hardtop, 4-door sedan, and wagon. SST was the new top trim level and guaranteed V8 power, starting with the 290. The plain '68 Ambassadors were available in hardtop and

In the words of American Motors, "The 1969 Ambassador — An automobile for the price of a car — with air conditioning standard." On the recommendation of advertising exec Mary Wells Lawrence, a/c was made a no-cost delete option (courtesy The Rambler Ranch).

sedan, but mid-level DPL could be chosen on all three bodies, with SST reserved for hardtop and sedan.

The '68 Ambassadors were looking a tad different too: the front circular parking lights were replaced with slim rectangular ones integrated within the front bumper. The '68 Ambassadors also adopted AMC's new flush-fitting door handles, which looked cleaner and reduced Ambassador's width from 78.36 inches to 77.2 inches; length and height stayed constant at 202.5 inches and 53.6 inches respectively, for hardtop and sedan. However, the biggest news for '68 was Ambassador's adoption of standard air conditioning.

During this period AMC was receiving advice from ad agency Wells, Rich & Greene. Apart from humorous and creative ads, marketing executive Mary Wells Lawrence suggested a/c be standard on Ambassador, separating AMC from the herd. Air conditioning was standard on very few cars at the time, like Rolls-Royce; standard-issue a/c was unheard of in Ambassador-class vehicles, and in spite of the option's popularity on family full-size cars, it wasn't included in the advertised price.

To play it safe, Ambassador's a/c was made a "delete option," whereby if one lived in the colder parts of the country an Ambassador could be ordered sans a/c and a credit would be paid into the purchaser's pocket. It was common in places like Minnesota and Canada for very upscale domestic cars to be ordered with every gewgaw except a/c, so the delete option made sense.

Wells, Rich & Greene ads underlined the fact that AMC Ambassador made dollars and cents, in savings to the buyer. With so much standard, Ambassador could be compared to

Top: **SST trim level Ambassador hardtop and 4-door sedans, like this '69 car, were visually distinguished by a red rear taillight beauty panel (courtesy Jeff Limerick).** ***Bottom:*** **This '69 Ambassador SST 4-door has a/c and "Safe Command" power front disks. The 1969 model year was the first full year for the 390ci V8, a motor originally intended for Ambassador (courtesy Jeff Limerick).**

a Roller ... so it was. A 1968 AMC print ad had two brand-new burgundy (an awfully rich, expensive-looking hue) cars on display side by side. On the left was a $19,600 Rolls-Royce Silver Shadow, a very recent unitary construction design, touted as being the finest car in the world. On the right was the $2,918 AMC Ambassador DPL 2-door hardtop. The ad said it was unfair to compare a Roller with an Ambassador, but did so anyway! It was noted that both had a/c and unibody construction as standard, coil-sprung seats and deep-dip rust-proofing for no extra outlay. The Rolls-Royce also came with reclining front seats, an Ambassador option, plus less headroom than a Cadillac, even though Ambassador had more!

As a closer the ad stated, "The Ambassador is the finest car we make. And when you pay $2,918 for an automobile, we feel you have every right to all the comfort, luxury and value we can give you. Not everyone can afford a Rolls." Think more on the subliminal Caddy comparison. The '68 Ambassador still carried the option of a luxury houndstooth-upholstered interior with 2 throw pillows, which Ambassador DPL started. The Spirit of Ecstasy was safe, but Wells, Rich & Greene wanted you to wonder who really set the standard of excellence.

Move the mind down to Chevy Impala and Ford Galaxie, Ambassador's real rivals, to realize such cars didn't have a/c standard. In the '68 Roller/Ambassador ad, the Ambassador's federal side marker lights were very subtle, as were front headlamp body-color bezel surrounds. The Ambassador's taillight bezels were also in body color. If one chose an Ambassador wagon with optional third-row seating, a side-opening tailgate was included. This design, pioneered by AMC, allowed the additional 2 rearward-facing passengers to hop out, as per Rebel.

Ambassador was doing good business now, but was considered too similar to intermediate

AMC put styling distance between Rebel and Ambassador in '69, with the latter getting a Packard-like grille. AMC's design chief Richard Teague used to work at Packard. Ambassador also ditched the shared Rebel wheelbase, moving onto 122 inches of comfort (courtesy Jeff Limerick).

Rebel. Thus, AMC changed Ambassador's styling for '69 to distance their top car. Ambassador looked more imposing now, with a reworked front fascia composed of horizontal quad lights and black plastic grille, with a chrome bar connecting said lights. The rectangular parking lights were set in the front bumper under the quads.

The grille had a raised center section like yesteryear's Packard, Richard Teague influencing AMC from his days at that firm. The rear was jazzed up with thrusting fenders and ribbed rectangular taillights. SST level hardtops and 4-door sedans had a red rear beauty panel to complement the taillights. Between the new front and rear fascias Ambassador rode on a longer 122-inch wheelbase. The increase boosted weight, but not to worry; the 390ci V8 had been on hand since mid–'68 AMX introduction time, and was Ambassador worthy.

With Ambassador appearing so statesmanlike, many AMC dealers were ready to entice with a "Demonstration Ride." A uniformed chauffeur would turn up at a prospect's domicile, ready to impress with Ambassador SST ride comfort. And 1969 was also the year of the Ambassador Royale Stretch Limousine, built by Armbruster & Stageway, under the direction of Chicago automotive leasing mogul Robert Estes.

The 24-foot-long Ambassador RSL had the stock rear doors welded shut. A new center section was added just aft of the B pillar, and included a new large entry door. One RSL was even used by Wisconsin Governor Warren Knowles. With Ambassador on a roll, there was money to freshen things up for '70 too. Styling changes kept Ambassador in touch with '70 Rebel, involving rear panel alterations. Like Rebel hardtop, the Ambassador hardtop adopted the reverse angle C pillar window line.

This numbers-matching 304-powered Ambassador is one of only 986 SST 2-door hardtops built in 1972. When restored between August 2005 and April 2006, it was repainted C2 Stardust Silver (courtesy Wayne Macquarrie).

The sedan went with a slimmer C pillar, squared-off rear windows and a beltline that swept up beneath each rear window. The last trait was featured on Matador sedan through '78. In the rear full-width ribbed taillight panel were 2 square centrally located white backup lights. Common to all '70 Ambassadors was a freshened-up grille with several widely spaced horizontal chrome bars and one body-colored bar between the headlamps.

Styling was updated again for '71 with Ambassador's headlamps placed in separate chrome pods. The parking lights sat outboard of the headlamps, part of the front fender's leading edge. This meant front side markers weren't needed. The grille was decorated with a bright chrome surround and had rounded edges. In the center were cast metal grille insert and chrome vertical bars. At the rear, the twin backup lights were now outboard, plus the optional woodgrain appliqué on Ambassador wagons had more side coverage.

Wouldn't You Really Rather Have an Ambassador?

By this stage AMC's ad line asked, "If you had to compete with GM, Ford and Chrysler, what would you do?" The answer was equipment: Ambassador packed more standard stuff, and this quality was emphasized. Going forward to '72, Ambassador added power brakes to the auto, a/c and V8 that were its mother lode of stock items. In fact, in 1972 only two cars had more standard equipment than Ambassador: the Cadillac Eldorado and the Lincoln Continental Mark IV.

However, the Caddy and Lincoln didn't have Ambassador's reclining seats, nor its Buyer Protection Plan, which raised the question: Wouldn't you really rather have an Ambassador? Yes, if you could live without I6 economy. In the '71 model year the new 150 bhp 1bbl 258 I6 and Shift Command auto were included in the base Ambassador DPL sedan. SSTs got the 210 bhp 304 standard. Then, for '72, the V8 became Ambassador's only choice for the first time since 1964.

There was no DPL in the '72 Ambassador range; trim choices were now SST and Brougham alone. Horsepower ranged from the 304's 150 net ponies to the mighty 401's 255 bhp. It was the former motor *Consumer Reports* chose for its Ambassador SST 4-door in February 1972. This test showed the state of play concerning family cars. In the "5 Full-Sized Sedans" comparison, all cars were rear-drive V8s of domestic origin.

Representing the Big 4 were the Chevy Impala 350, Pontiac Catalina 400, Plymouth Fury III 318, Ford Galaxie 351 and Ambassador 304. *Comsumer Reports* purchased 4-door sedans with automatic, a/c, tinted windows, power steering, power disk brakes, AM radio, whitewall tires and vinyl roof. This spec approximated the average family car in America. However, within the similarity were differences.

In this group Ambassador was the nonconformist, as was AMC's wont. There were the good points; firstly, at 3,672 lbs, Ambassador was the only car on test under 4,000 lbs, an ominous sign concerning the pending fuel crisis. This allowed Ambassador SST to record the best acceleration/economy data of the group with 0–60 mph in 11.5 seconds, an 18-second quarter mile at 77 mph, and a normal use gas mileage range of 10–19 mpg.[9]

Such figures wouldn't have been possible on a mere 150 bhp with 2.87 final drive if Ambassador were as large and heavy as its rivals. This was also the first year Ambassador took advantage of the Chrysler Torqueflite Torque Command auto. Thus, there was no more efficient family

Top: The 304 V8 joined power brakes, a/c and automatic on '72 Ambassador's list of standard equipment. By now SST and Brougham were the only trim levels available (courtesy Wayne Macquarrie). *Bottom:* Equipped with HD suspension, front and rear swaybars, HD cooling system, Extra Quiet Insulation Package, lighting package, power steering and all-around Solar Glass tint, this Nova Scotia Ambassador SST was expensive at over $4,800 Canadian when new (courtesy Wayne Macquarrie).

This '72 Ambassador was also specified with sports steering wheel, AM radio and clock, but not power windows. Ambassador's extra length always came from the firewall forward, so there was no extra interior space compared to Classic, Rebel or Matador (courtesy Wayne Macquarrie).

6-seater than Ambassador, but there was an interior space disadvantage. *Consumer Reports* noted that although AMC marketed Ambassador as a "full-sized" car, it was 6–10 inches shorter than its rivals, and 2–3 inches narrower.

In truth this was a meeting of 4 full-size rides and 1 intermediate, explaining why Ambassador had 2–3½ inches less rear shoulder room. Being smaller and lighter, Ambassador came first in braking with the shortest stopping distance in the group. The optional power front disks cost $50 and showed negligible fade, producing straight panic stops with low pedal effort. In spite of Ambassador's substantial standard equipment, the car normally came with drums and the GM rides had power front disks standard.

Indeed, there were areas where AMC's budget shortfall against the Big 3 showed up. AMC made electric windshield wipers standard on all its '72 cars, but the 304 V8 needed alternate tankfuls of leaded and unleaded to deal with pinging and possible valve seat recession. So Kenosha wasn't quite up to speed with tighter emissions and low-lead living. The Ambassador SST tested had the optional $111 power steering, but all the other cars in the test carried this feature standard.

Handling was an Ambassador problem area; response and composure in emergency situations weren't up to the standard set by the top-rated GM cars. It was noted that the Ambassador test car had many front-end hardware and assembly defects, but whether this was due to act of God or the U.A.W. wasn't stated. However, the Ambassador's poor handling was also mentioned by *Motor Trend* in 1971: "It almost seems as if it's made in a foreign country — kind of a Mercedes with the handling qualities left out."[10]

Consumer Reports' $4,320 Ambassador SST had the optional $67 oversized F78–14 tires, but should have included the HD suspension pack with stiffer springs, firmer shocks, and rear swaybar. Corroborating *Motor Trend*'s left-handed praise concerning Ambassador quality, *Con-*

sumer Reports mentioned Ambassador's Frequency-of-Repair record had improved to "better than average," the highest of the 5 cars tested. So apart from *Consumer Reports*' atypical example, a new Ambassador would give its owners fewer problems than other full-size cars.

During restoration, this Ambassador's build sheet was found on top of AMC's trademark fiberglass headliner molding, sandwiched between said headliner and the roof panel (courtesy Wayne Macquarrie).

AMC's comprehensive Buyer Protection Plan was also discussed. Transferrable to a subsequent owner for $2, the warranty lasted 12 months/12,000 miles. A free loaner car was to be provided when warranty work saw the car tied up for more than one day. An AMC spokesman said around 98 percent of AMC dealers were participating in the no-charge loaner scheme, proving that AMC was your friend in need![11]

The 1973 model year was a difficult one for the enthusiast, because the 5 mph front/2.5 mph rear bumper law made many cars look front-heavy. On '73 Ambassador the 5 mph front bumper had a gap filling, flexible body-color trim panel, and prominent horizontal rubber guard strip that made chrome bumper guards unnecessary. The rear bumper had vertical black rubber bumper guards. For decoration, '73 Ambassador had grilles with heavier horizontal bars and blacked-out headlamp bezels.

In range rationalization, only the Brougham trim level was left for 1973's Ambassador hardtop, sedan and wagon. Now AM radio and tinted windows were included as standard equipment, but this wasn't enough to save the hardtop: 1973 would be Ambassador hardtop's last year. Sales were dwindling and AMC had a special new Matador Coupe due in '74, so they called it a day on the 2-door Ambassador. Substantial changes were on the way too for the remaining '74 Ambassador sedan and wagon 4-doors.

Ambassador Brougham grew 7 inches in length for '74, although the wheelbase remained 122 inches. The increase was due to redesigned front and rear fascias that incorporated recoverable 5 mph bumpers at both ends. The revision also brought Ambassador into line with Matador's new coffin-nose style, although it looked much different, and better, on Ambassador. Ambassador's grille had pairs of round lamps sitting in black bezels.

The inner rectangular amber parking lights were integrated into a decorative horizontal double chrome bar grille highlight section. The quad lamps, turn signals and additional rubber trim that broke up the massiveness of the new front bumper made Ambassador look very stately. Matador didn't have the hood ornament either! At the rear, new rectangular taillight surrounds existed, with now taller inboard white backup lights.

Ambassador's license plate moved from the rear bumper to between the taillights in

Ambassador finished up big, with 72 items of standard equipment in 1974 including 304 V8, pinstriping, new styling and 62-amp alternator. Ambassador always spelled value (courtesy The Rambler Ranch).

'74. The taillight/license plate complex of the Ambassador sedan was surrounded by chrome trim, and even the wagon's taillights were amended. In 1974, Ambassador really looked like a full-size, and a handsome one at that. The interior and dash took on '74 Matador's new setup with 3 square instrument pods, and much more.

AMC had gone to much trouble creating a coffin-nose Ambassador which required new hood and fenders among the revisions, but 1974 would be the nameplate's final year. Full-size sales nose-dived in '74 with the fuel crisis; folks went looking for family intermediates instead. A shame, because Ambassador sales had been good to that moment. Ambassador bowed out as AMC's top car with 72 items of standard equipment which included the 304 V8, 2-way tailgate and rear air deflector on wagon, new sound insulation, vanity mirror, pinstriping and even whitewalls.

The '74 Ambassadors even featured a larger 24.9-gallon gas tank and 62-amp alternator. The 401 motor was still around with AMX spec 255 horses, but sadly not the option of that car's 4-speed. So it was that the final Ambassador rolled off the Kenosha line in June 1974. To compensate for Ambassador's absence, AMC had available the Matador Brougham. Moving to midsize made sense in tough times, but what could replace hallowed Ambassador? Why have a car, when one could have an automobile?

Top: The Metropolitan small car represented an alliance between Nash and Austin. It was originally designated N.X.I. or Nash Experimental International (courtesy Marc Merkle). ***Bottom:*** By model year '58 the pillarless Rambler Cross Country wagon was gone. A 1959 Cross Country wagon is shown (courtesy Denny Schwartz).

Top: Apart from woodgrain accents, this loaded American Custom wagon features optional power steering, AM pushbutton radio, overdrive, backup lights, Twin-Grip differential, Spinner wheel covers and all-vinyl interior (courtesy Douglas Englin). ***Bottom:*** This two-tone Alamo Beige/Cinnamon Bronze '60 American Custom 2-door is one of 2,994 made that year. It has been featured on *My Classic Car* with Dennis Gage (courtesy Douglas Englin).

Top: This 1964 Ambassador 990, called "Rosie," is lavishly equipped, with features like Powerlift electric windows, AM-FM pushbutton radio with Vibra-Tone reverb rear speaker audio, front and rear seat belts, parking brake warning light and child-proof rear door locks (courtesy Mary Brancato). ***Bottom:*** The '66 Marlins, like this 4-speed car, were newly available with the Borg Warner T10 manual gearbox. This sports box was better able to exploit the 4bbl 327 specified within than existing 3-speeders (courtesy Phil Heitman).

Top: In 1967 AMC introduced a new 4 trailing arm link rear suspension on all senior cars. The torque tube was gone, and handling and roadability were much improved, on cars like this '67 Marlin with top-of-the-line 280 horse 343ci small-block AMC V8. AMC's new-design V8 was first seen in the '66 American Rogue (courtesy Isabell Montagu). ***Bottom:*** American Motors was never wasteful. By truncating the 109-inch-wheelbase Javelin into the 97-inch-wheelbase 2-seater AMX, presto. AMC had a Corvette competitor (courtesy George M. Stragand III).

Top: **With AMC languishing in 10th place in the '67 sales race, something had to be done. That thing was the 1968 Javelin pony car. Javelin gained the youth vote, and rid Rambler of its fuddy-duddy image (courtesy The Rambler Ranch).** ***Bottom:*** **With a 4.5-inch roof chop and hideaway headlamps, the sleek AMX-400 fueled dreams of what future cars would look like. As per the normal AMX, the AMX-400 had decorative sail panel fuel fillers (courtesy Mike Geary and Greg Ornazian).**

Top: Part of the Mark Donohue Javelin's mission was to homologate that rear ducktail spoiler, which the engineer/racer personally designed. ***Bottom:*** This is an SST car, but some MD Javelins were not, and some even came with column change autos. Like the '70 Trans Am Javelin, all items could be dealer-ordered and fitted. Thus, an original window sticker is necessary to verify authenticity (courtesy Wayne Davis).

Left: **The AMC Hornet incorporated the Project IV Cavalier showcar's body part commonality thinking into a stylish notchback sedan update of the 1964–69 American (courtesy Alexander Ortiz).** ***Right:*** **The AMC Hornet X that raced through Bangkok in the Bond movie *The Man with the Golden Gun* (1974). The hatchback is pictured in Britain's Beaulieu National Motor Museum, with the Bond speedboat from *Live and Let Die* (1973) (courtesy The Ian Fleming Foundation, www.ianflem ingfoundation.org).**

For anyone too young, or too poor, to have purchased a new prewar Cord, AMC helped realize dreams with their retro "coffin nose" 1974–78 Matador sedans and wagons. Much more enjoyable than prohibition (courtesy Pascal Cicchella).

This '77 Pacer wagon has the optional "Woody" exterior pack, and "Styled Road Wheels" with decorative center trim (courtesy Jim Williams).

Left: In 1974 came standard 5 mph recoverable bumpers, revised X "hockey stick" side decals and Gremlin's best sales result: 171,128 units in an extended AMC model year (courtesy Donnie Solomon). ***Right:*** Originally this '71 Gremlin with 258/Shift Command auto power team and pushbutton AM radio was purchased from a Seattle, Washington, AMC dealer for $2,478. It now wears 14 × 8-inch Cragar "Chrome Smoothies" with baby moon hubcaps and Grand Am Radial GT tires sized 205/70. This car has been nicknamed "Gremmie" (courtesy Jo Wilson).

Top: For '67, Ambassador adopted Rebel's new Coke-bottle styling, and suddenly the mailman looked very dapper. AMC ran an ad comparing the new Ambassador to Rolls-Royce, showing the great value offered over the Miserly 3. ***Bottom:*** Raced by Rambler Ranch Chief Mechanic Roger Scott, this Pacer sedan has a Clifford Engineering–tuned 232 I6 with Weber carb and AMC livery tricolor block (courtesy The Rambler Ranch).

Top: What's a Matador Coupe? Simply the best-styled new car of '74, according to *Car and Driver* magazine (courtesy The Rambler Ranch). ***Bottom:*** This '78 Concord AMX has been given the decal livery and Turbocast II rims associated with the '79 Spirit AMX. Trust the Economy Experts to liven up small cars (courtesy Jeff Limerick).

Left: AMC tried hard with Commando, masterminding the transition from C-101 to C-104. However, commercial success came with Commando's replacement, the 1974 Cherokee (courtesy Noah Gresham). ***Right:*** Note the extra rearward visibility afforded by reshaped rear windows. The 1981–82 Eagle Kammback was the final North American outing for the famous Gremlin shape (courtesy Jim Fracassa).

Spirit AMX leaping off the line at a 2008 SCSS heads-up street car comp in St. Louis. This car has appeared in a Napa commercial on the Speed Channel (courtesy Jim Landis).

Top: With straightforward body mods to improve axle articulation and approach angles and lift kit with special tires, the Eagle can live up to its go-anywhere Jeep heritage (courtesy Joshua Tulberg and Mick Stine). ***Bottom:*** A normal car that could be used where only 4×4 rigs had gone before? It took American Motors to think of it (courtesy Sean Weitzel).

Chapter 5

AMC — The Small Car Company

Pacer — Urban Vigilante

AMC's supremos Roy Chapin and William Luneburg were looking for a special new project car for the mid–'70s and beyond. With increasingly sophisticated buyer profiles, the firm utilized psychographics to pinpoint what the American buyer of the next decade really wanted, and the answer was utility. The car of the future would put substance before status, and eschew long, wide and low in favor of features that actually helped one get from A to B. AMC was going to start an urban revolution.

Shortlisted from 36 design proposals, the beauty contest winner was Project Amigo, a name from AMC's styling department. This decision at the end of 1971 gave rise to the 1975½ AMC Pacer. In AMC's own words: "Pacer, the first wide small car, has more of everything for everybody." AMC also liked to quote *Motor Trend* from February 1975: "Suddenly it's 1980—American Motors' new Pacer is the freshest, most creative, most people-oriented auto to be born in the U.S. in 15 years."[1]

The feeling was that this was the biggest domestic shake-up since the 1960 compacts arrived. More than that, Pacer would prove to mark the last time an American design would influence styling overseas. Rolls-Royce chief stylist John Blatchley originally did a modern version of the Silver Cloud after being influenced by the exciting new designs from Detroit after World War II. However, management chose the conservative route.[2]

It should also be noted that the '58 Auto Union 1000 SP was a mini 3-cylinder 2-stroke version of the 1955 Ford Thunderbird. Similarly the 1961 NSU Prinz and 1963 Hillman Imp were rear-engined, air-cooled, scaled-down knockoffs of the Chevy Corvair. Toyota's Celica was originally influenced by the Ford Mustang. Fast forward to the mid–'70s and Detroit was in a crisis; no one was looking to the Motor City anymore, but Kenosha wasn't in Detroit.

Porsche chief designer Tony Lapine admitted that the rear of the Pacer influenced the 1977 Porsche 928's rear end. There are strong similarities in the rear bubble hatch, doors and B pillar between the two, as AMC showed how to do a hatchback with a large glass area. The Pacer had a lot of glass, 5,615 square inches to be precise. Pacer's glass alone weighed 150 lbs at a time when a '75 full-size Imperial only had 4,145 square inches of glass. Detroit had been more concerned with a car shape's being visible, than having good visibility, until now.

AMC itself was critical of the poor rearward vision of fastbacks, so it was just as well Javelin was axed in '74! Contrary to Detroit thinking at the time, AMC felt it was better

Pacer was the world's first wide small car, bringing a comfort level heretofore unknown in this size class. The hatchback format was unusual for a domestic (courtesy Nolan Dehner).

to be round than square. Predating the Jell-O mold era by 7 years, the Pacer had some wind tunnel work, and according to AMC was 12 percent slipperier through the air than the typical compact. Apart from AMC's flush door handles, Pacer did without rain gutters and had hidden wipers and washer jets located on said wipers.

The left windshield wiper was articulated for better sweep clearance, and Pacer had an optional intermittent wiper setting. Answering the Gremlin/Hornet's difficult to see over high hood, Pacer had an unconventional front-hinged fast-fall-away hood. As part of the front fascia, Teague's people incorporated AMC's trademark tunnel port headlamps, with a squarish style this time. There was a hint of '74 Chevy Camaro about the Pacer's front and rear lights.

Functionality continued with Pacer's specially hinged asymmetric front doors. These heavy 80-pound units tilted outward at the top as they were opened, and used their weight to make opening and closing easier when, for example, a Pacer was parked on an uphill slope. Pacer's passenger door was also famously 3.6 inches longer than the driver's door. This was to aid rear seat passenger access, a problem with 2-door cars.

Pacer was the first domestic car with cab forward design, and a rarity in any era, for parking ease. One could see where the four corners were, no parking sensors required. The Pacer had quite a greenhouse, and Uncle Tom McCahill wasn't joshing when he said, "Belt lines are as low as a cricket's knee..."[3] This was so much the case that Pacer's inner door trim panel extended abnormally high, so as to conceal the side window when it was wound down.

One downside to the great glass area was that some folks felt privacy was at a premium. After years of sitting behind a big C pillar, a driver may find the Pacer to be awfully bright

Engineering-wise, Pacer was based on a truncated Matador base. It was only the second car in Detroit with rack and pinion steering and had an immense 5,615 square inches of glass, giving good visibility (courtesy Nolan Dehner).

and better suited to the Queen of England or the Pope than shy, retiring types. All that glass also made things warmer than usual. Thus, Pacer went against the grain of new car design and was available with optional $29.95 front window vent wings. Pacer's rear hatch glass was fixed, so the vent wings would boost through-flow ventilation.

For much of the country the only real solution was Pacer's optional $399.95 a/c. This was integrated with Pacer's pushbutton HVAC control panel, and with 4 outlets and adjustable slot vents was worth having. Pacer's dash was the most modern-looking in the AMC fleet, its curves and vent placement reminiscent of Humpster Javelin. And above the Weather Eye panel was Pacer's audio center.

At the top of the tree an AM-FM stereo radio 8-track cartridge combo costing $239 was available. In AMC brochure material a Barbra Streisand *People* cartridge was inserted as a serving suggestion. With Pacer a star was born: AMC was right to claim it was the small car everyone was talking about, and opinions were freely given about Pacer styling.

The public and press mostly warmed to the look. With the Apollo space program of recent memory, thoughts of moon buggies came to mind. Pacer's organic shape also suggested nature. *Consumer Reports* thought Pacer resembled a revolutionary tortoise.[4] *Popular Mechanics* were reminded of a box turtle,[5] and *Car and Driver* was one of many to bestow the description of fishbowl.[6]

Road & Track likened Pacer to a Toastmaster,[7] but they did seem to like Pacer and cared enough to do one of their "Styling Analysis" studies on the shape.[8] However, perhaps the most unusual description was the Goodyear "Martian" quote made in the 1977 *Goodyear*

Motorsports Club Magazine: "AMC Pacer ... new outlook. Built for 4ft Martians — grown taller to accommodate mere mortals! A great small car — fun to drive! Buy it! Show AM they're right!"

It was more enthusiasm than has ever been shown concerning a Prius, and people were indeed telling AMC they were on the right track. At Pacer's first customer clinic in Atlanta, Georgia, over February 3–6, 1972, Pacer scored 93 percent approval. AMC had considered a number of formats for the round one, including a radical mid-engined layout with rear-facing seats!

In keeping with the modern ways of GM's Olds Toronado and some Caddies, front drive had been considered. To this end, AMC took along a fiberglass Pacer mock-up to the Georgia clinic with disappearing headlamps and removable front seat console/driveshaft tunnel. People were asked if they would pay a premium for a front-drive Pacer with flat front floor. The participants, the majority of whom were typical domestic rear-drive sub-compact, compact and intermediate owners, weren't much interested in a front-drive Pacer, so AMC took it no further.

AMC carried out two further customer clinics in Denver and Dallas, confirming interest in a car designed around people. Pacer was touted as a vehicle designed around 4 bucket seats. As more evidence that American Motors was onto a good thing, there is the subsequent example of the Volvo 480 ES. Pacer's style was reflected on this rounded 2-door liftback front-driver designed around 4 seat placements, with lots of glass, a quickly falling-away hood and pop-up headlamps. Sounds familiar, and customer clinics also predicted this late–'80s coupe would do well in North America, where it ultimately was never sold.

Pacer started with soft-tune 232s and 258s making 90 and 95 bhp respectively. The glass bubble was an urban moon buggy, not a road rocket (courtesy Nolan Dehner).

Pacer utilized a truncated Matador chassis, making it in effect an intermediate with the ends cut off. In fact, early studies did use chopped-up Matadors, but driving results were less than stellar. It was obvious more work was needed to make a nice urban daily driver. Up front was traditional AMC independent unequal length control arm suspension with high-mount coils. At the rear was a Matador live axle, but with leaf springs, not coils.

From this base AMC went for refinement by mounting the entire front suspension on a crossmember with rubber mount isoblocks. This was heavy and expensive as methods went. Rear isoclamp bushings were used to attach the rear springs. Small car was code for buckboard ride, and AMC wanted to do something about that. For steering, AMC Pacer became only the second American car after the Ford Pinto to feature rack and pinion steering.

Pacer's rack and pinion steering was custom done for AMC by GM's Saginaw division; no GM car at the time used the system. Rack and pinion was associated with sporty steering, very direct about the center, but AMC's chief reason for using it was tight space. Non-boosted Pacer had a glacial 5.9 turns between locks, but the optional power steering cut this to 3.2 turns.

So Pacer's unibody used a quasi-front subframe and tricks to have a small face. For '75 AMC lowered the front-end accessory location (power steering, alternator, a/c belts) on all I6 cars. The Saginaw steering gear was mounted low in front of the crossmember, and Pacer would be the first AMC to get a low-profile crossflow radiator. A squat engine air cleaner also helped with the low hoodline. Pacer came with subtle-looking examples of AMC's "free standing" bumper design, incorporating bars with enough gap between themselves and the body to hydraulically move in and out under compression.

The gap between body and bumper wasn't noticeable unless one sidled right up to Pacer. *Consumer Reports* noted that Pacer's 5 mph bumpers were much more effective in their bumper basher test than the extended bumpers of the VW Rabbit. That spelled less damage and lower repair costs. Pacer's body also had a deep driveshaft tunnel to accommodate the high shaftline of the planned rotary engine. Rotary was seen as the future: fewer moving parts, high output for a given displacement, and very smooth operation at ultra-high rpm.

Many were working on the Felix Wankel–type rotary, but GM was designing one of its own, and it was thought Pacer would use this unit. Ultimately AMC wanted to create its own rotary too, and on February 7, 1973, took up a license to build rotaries of between 80 and 200 bhp from NSU licensees Curtiss-Wright at a cost of $1.5 million. The French-made Comotor rotary was also considered, but in the end there was no rotary.

The first fuel crisis saw GM pull the plug on rotary development. Rotaries are rather thirsty beasts and the prospect of 10 mpg suddenly wasn't appealing. Stricter U.S. emissions law was also a problem, given high rotary propensity for nitrogen oxide output. Rotor tip seal wear was an early Achilles heel that sullied the Wankel's reputation. NSU's having to provide free engine replacements for the Ro80 pushed that company to the brink. In the end only Mazda persevered with the concept after 1977.

In spite of the fuel crisis, AMC was still talking about doing its own rotary during 1975 and 1976, but it never transpired. Indeed, AMC adapted Pacer to accept the firm's long cast-iron I6, necessitating an engine bay firewall depression to cope with the length. To maximize I6 fuel efficiency, Pacer featured transistorized ignition as standard equipment. AMC also toyed with the idea of 4-wheel disks, but this was shelved due to cost.

Internally, Pacer also went by the project name "Urban Concept," and it was felt 4-wheel drums would be enough for city hopping. There were 10-inch front, as per V8 Gremlin and Matador, and 9-inch rear units. Front disks were optional and *Consumer Reports* said the non-power 10.7-inch front disks fitted to their Pacer gave good braking performance, and were preferable to the fade-prone all-drums or hard-to-modulate powered disks.

The Big Car Experience

It was true, small really was never this wide, and AMC summed up that full-size feeling when describing the Pacer wagon in the AMC '79 brochure as "compact with a big car personality." Giles Chapman also said the same when mentioning Pacer's positive aspects: "It's a roomy car with fantastic visibility, and it drives like a typically easy-going, full-size Yank even if it doesn't take up the same amount of roadspace."[9]

Pacer dimensions were 170, 77, and 52.7 inches for length, width and height. All this sat on a 100-inch wheelbase and meant Pacer defied classification. The measurements suggested the length of a subcompact, the width of an intermediate, and at 3,180 lbs, the weight of a compact. Pacer was indeed all of the above, and the luxury line was confirmed by a scene in the 1985 movie *The Mean Season*. In this film Kurt Russell was an investigative journalist tracking down a serial killer.

In one scene he went to interview someone who might have known the killer. This person claimed the two of them worked at Kenosha on the Pacer line in 1976–77. It was stated the alleged serial killer used to refer to the Pacer as a Kenosha Cadillac! Well, looking at the dash instrument cluster of a column-shift Pacer is somewhat reminiscent of a mid–'70s Caddy Eldo's dash. Plus, there was a spiffy rectangular analog electric dash clock in the optional Convenience Group that wouldn't have looked amiss in a Lincoln.

The chronology of affairs saw the Pacer production plan completed in January 1974. The body was to be Kenosha-built using new Gilman robots for some welding duties, like joining the upper shell to the underbody. The first Pacer body built was in July 1974, with the first car off the line in August. However, a September 1974 3-week strike caused Pacer to make a mid–'75 model year debut. Full Pacer production commenced in January 1975, with a dealer intro in February.

AMC was keen to avoid what happened with Hornet, where strike action resulted in no stock at launch. Pacer entered the fray with a starting sticker of $3,299, for which one received a 90 bhp 232 I6-powered Pacer sedan with all-synchro 3 on the tree and front split-bench seat. Five-inch-wide rims came with aluminum hubcaps and 14 × 6.95-inch bias ply tires; DR78–14-inch radials were optional. For $69 more, Pacer could have the 95 bhp 258, and AMC recommended this engine if one specified a/c. There was no early Pacer V8.

Other Pacer gearbox choices involved an overdrive version of the column-shift 3-speed manual. This overdrive was of the old style "add-on" Laycock de Normanville variety, like the type Rambler had in the '50s, but here overdrive operated only on top gear. A Pacer with the optional shorter 3.08 final drive, California's only Pacer choice, would be registering 2,630 rpm at 60 mph; with the overdrive 3-speed and standard 2.73 rear gears, revs would drop to around 1,700 rpm.

Sporty-minded owners chose a 3-speed floorshift manual, but this box wasn't available with overdrive. AMC's Torque Command auto was easier to use than either manual, and

Top: Pacer got an all-new dash molding with integrated HVAC that was shared with the Bricklin SV-1 sportscar (courtesy Nolan Dehner). ***Bottom:*** With the length of a subcompact, width of an intermediate and weight of a compact, the Pacer defied classification. American Motors broke the size mold—and this modified car breaks the Pacer mold (courtesy Rod Puckett).

was praised as a top-notch auto ideally matched to AMC's lazily tuned I6. In addition, the optional Torque Command auto, whether floor or column shift, allowed 49-state use of the taller optional 2.53 final drive for improved highway cruising.

Decorated Pacer, Trim Levels

In selecting trim level there was base, D/L or X. Economy-oriented base had a color-keyed rubber mat in the cargo area; it was no-frills. Pacer D/L was marketed as "The Plusher Pacer" and came with posh Basketry Print seating fabric in berry, black, blue or tan, dash woodgrain, custom padded steering wheel, door trims with fabric inserts to match the Basketry Print, plus door-pull straps and lower carpet trim. The cargo area was done in color-keyed carpeting. Wheel covers, color-keyed rubstrips, bright license-surround molding, and bumper protective strips were outside.

Starsky and Hutch types fancied Pacer X, billed as "The Racier Pacer." Pacer X was in the same performance vein as Gremlin/Hornet X. "X" marked the spot with non-reclining sports buckets available in 5 colors (berry, black, blue, tan or white), manual floorshift, dash woodgrain, sports 3-spoke steering wheel, Sof-Touch vinyl matching door trims with door-pull straps and lower carpet trim. Outside, D78 14-inch BSW tires covered sports slot rims (on X only); color-keyed rubstrips and bumper protective strips were in evidence.

So there was much commonality between D/L and X, and both came with AMC's Extra Quiet Insulation Package, as well as a front swaybar. Pacer wasn't available with a rear swaybar. Instead of D/L's front fender callout badge, there was a lower door "Pacer X" decal on the racer, plus a Pacer X badge on the hood's leading edge. The D/L and X packs retailed for $289 and $339 respectively.

According to release info, the D/L Basketry Print individual reclining seats could be ordered as a separate option on any Pacer; ditto the Sof-Touch vinyl buckets. With D/L one could exercise the Luxury Trim Option and upgrade from Basketry Print to Hyde Park fabric for seating surfaces and door trim inserts. The Hyde Park fabric was available in berry, black, blue and tan.

For Pacer's exterior there were 15 Luster Guard color choices, with 10 two-tone combinations. There were also 8 Bravado grain vinyl roof color choices, the same vinyl material available on Matador, but one couldn't order a two-tone color scheme with vinyl roof. Two mechanical combo packs existed upon Pacer's debut. Package 1 brought tinted windows and power steering for $139, while Package 2 grouped the front swaybar, power front disks and steel belted radials for $203.45.

For warranty, American Motors had a special offer from the start of December '74 to March 1, 1975, whereby the BPP was extended to 2 years for free. However, Pacer's delayed release meant the 12-month extension cost an extra $99. That Buyer Protection Plan was a strong selling point. According to a Boston University study, 68 percent of AMC purchasers at the time said the BPP was a major reason why they chose AMC.[10]

Pacer's solidity was shown in *Consumer Reports*' VW Rabbit versus AMC Pacer "Two New Small Cars" encounter. Rabbit chalked up a frightening 34 manufacturing and dealer-prep defects; Pacer had just 17.[11] Both were new release models, and VW, via Beetle, used to have an excellent quality reputation. However, in 1975 it was better to be made in

Pacer's wide engine bay was supposed to take a GM-designed rotary, but the fuel crisis saw that ship sail. In the '78 model year, AMC introduced the 304 to Pacer, but even before that, enterprising souls discovered: Pacer + V8 = heaven (courtesy Rod Puckett).

Kenosha than Wolfsburg. The test also stated that Rabbit was a subcompact, and Pacer was actually a compact.

The subjects of comfort and economy were up for debate. *Consumer Reports*' 4 adults said they were more comfortable in Rabbit than Pacer, but objectively a 3,200-pound compact does insulate a person better from road shock than a 2,000-pound subcompact. Pacer's Matador chassis did have intrusive wheel wells, limiting rear seat comfort, but still had more interior width space than any subcompact. *Consumer Reports* admitted Pacer had a very low interior noise level, quieter than many full-size cars they had tested.[12]

Tom McCahill concurred on Pacer's refinement: "In fact, it rides damn near as well as my Rolls."[13] This brings the eternal question, what's your vehicle size/economy trade-off? Forgetting about artificial EPA guides, *Consumer Reports* recorded city/highway figures of 19/29 mpg for their 4-speed 4-door Rabbit, and only 12/19 mpg for their automatic 232-cube Pacer. However, they found specifying automatic transmission on the VW worsened economy by 6 mpg, and judged Pacer's fuel efficiency good for an automatic compact.

VW Rabbit came with a 2-way catalytic converter, a troublesome device, whereas 49-state Pacer was no home for a cat. Pacer also worked out cheaper: even with the $119 power steering, front disks and $239.99 auto, the Pacer test car came in at $3,973 compared to Rabbit's $4,015. Whether it was VW Rabbit, Caddy Seville or Honda Accord, bigger price tags were affixed to smaller cars in the '70s. Where was the value?

Consumer Reports said they would recommend Pacer to anyone looking for a "fairly small car"; it scored reasonably. Rabbit tested out as the best subcompact to that point, but

Pacer wasn't a subcompact. Pacer also taught the Detroit lesson that a large-engined car can achieve economy if the revs stay low. Frictional losses are reduced, and holding a tall gear with ¾ throttle minimizes the loss of having to suck air past a partly closed throttle plate. An automatic car with big I6 and tall final drive achieves this.

There were some troubles in Pacer paradise—an early recall, for starters. All Pacers made in January and February 1975 were recalled for inspection by AMC concerning a possibly incorrectly routed fuel line that might leak and pose a fire risk. Some early cars may have been affected. There was also a greater strain placed on the rack and pinion steering of '75½ Pacers than anticipated. The AMC I6 was heavier than the proposed rotary. There were also power steering leaks on the '75½ and '76 Pacers, resulting in a redesigned steering unit. Pacer's specific I6 exhaust manifold also showed a propensity to crack.

Pacer X—Enthusiast's Choice

Teething problems arise, even on new cars using existing mechanicals. One interesting new Pacer item concerned aluminum expert Alcoa. In 1994, after 10 years' research, Alcoa's Pittsburgh engineers came up with a production process and 1994 factory to make Audi A8 aluminum spaceframes in Soest, Germany.[14] Twenty years earlier, Alcoa made the 14 × 6-inch cast alloy wheels optional on Pacer! These shiny rims were often seen in conjunction with the DR70–14-inch white-letter Goodyear Polysteel Radials.

Pacer X was one of the new wave of Detroit road cars, achieving a balance between ride and handling. Pacer X started with the D78–14-inch tire, whereas Gremlin and Hornet X came with the D70 14-incher. More sidewall compliance made for more comfort. These new balanced models, like the Pontiac Grand Am, navigated the divide between the old HD suspension teeth rattlers, and the soft-sprung land yachts that abraded the tread off their front tires while understeering off a precipice.

Computer-selected spring rates and tuning for radials produced good control and comfort. Pacer X was more ride-refined than Gremlin/Hornet X and turned in a sound skidpad figure of 0.653 g when tested in April '75 by *Road & Track* with Firestone Steel Radial 500s in DR70–14-inch size. Pacer X also made it through the cones with a slalom speed of 53.9 mph. *Road & Track*'s '73 Grand Am got 0.692 g on 15 × 7-inch rims with G70–15-inch rubber. These cars certainly "handled," and ride was good when the going was smooth, but there were common problems.

As with any live-axled Detroit car, the suspension got caught out on imperfect surfaces, and bottoming out, especially when loaded, was a distinct possibility. Pacer added in a few more wheelbase-related woes. Brake dive was particularly noticeable, as well as a delayed-onset oversteer due to the ride-compliant rear isoclamps. With 18 inches cut out of the Matador's wheelbase, Pacer's problems weren't unexpected. The 56/44 percent nose-heavy weight distribution was also something reminiscent of a V8 pony car. However, in its element Pacer X impressed.

With wide track and wide tires, Pacer felt secure, and could be pushed hard through a corner. Traveling with driver and one passenger, Pacer X easily dealt with gray flannel interstate. One of the AMC-supplied Johnson-brand CB radios was handy to keep tabs on Kojaks with Kodaks, or bears in the air. Cruising at 70–80 mph, you and your good buddy

Pacer's large rear hatch gave easy access to the cargo area, as seen on this heavily modified car (courtesy Rod Puckett).

riding shotgun could muse on how wasteful all those 6-seater full-size cars carrying just one person really were.

The 1bbl 258 seemed apt for the times. In '74 the 55 mph speed limit came to save gas, but stayed to save lives. With Pacer's standard 22-gallon tank, one could roll past those gas stations and watch OPEC weep! As per the new breed of performance road cars, the engine didn't seem to matter. The Pontiac Grand Am had racier 400s and 455s, but most were content with the 2bbl 400. The same applied to Mercury Cougar XR7; not much call to go beyond the 351 V8.

Thus, with people watching their savings, Pacer didn't overburden the consumer with engine choices they would drive past. Forget about engine cubes; could one even still see it now that a plethora of emissions plumbing had descended underhood? Forty-nine-state Pacers hummed around with EGR, gas tank vapor control, crankcase vapor control, and thermo-controlled air cleaner, with manual transmission cars carrying the additional burden of air injection. Plus, to keep the Golden State golden, California Pacers had a catalytic converter and air injection on automatics too.

By the '77 model year, California Pacers started with the 258 I6. Indeed, as part of regional fine tuning, AMC, like the Big 3, had a High Altitude Package. This pack could be ordered on a car even if it wasn't in a high altitude area (4,000 feet above sea level), in case Colorado mountain road driving was on the vacation agenda. The pack brought a special engine/gearbox/final drive combo, factory adjustments to carb fuel mixture, engine idle speed, and ignition timing and some changes to emission controls.

A shame AMC couldn't do something about their I6 cars' losing power on hard right-hand turns due to carburetor fuel starvation. To spice up highway living, AMC introduced a $99 2-barrel 258 engine option for '76. This engine was a Pacer exclusive for '76, probably because all the other model lines were available with the 2bbl 304 V8. This new 258 version sported a special intake manifold and made 120 bhp at 3,400 rpm and 200 lbs/ft at 2,000 rpm on an 8:1 compression ratio.

With less interest in V8s industry-wide, hotting up the six made sense. Chrysler did the same for '77, with a 2bbl version of their 225ci Slant Six to make the Aspen/Volare compacts tempting. The Holley 2bbl 258 did make a Pacer difference: *Car and Driver* found it improved the Pacer 258's ¼-mile showing from 20.4 seconds at 65.8 mph to 18.6 seconds at 71 mph. This moved Pacer X into contention with the Firebird Formula.

A Pacer fitted with X pack and 2bbl 258ci I6 cost $3,937, much less than the Formula's $4,566. The Formula's 49-state base power team was a 2bbl 350 V8/THM350 auto, good for 160 bhp and a highway EPA number of 21 mpg. Two-barrel Pacer X was only 1 second slower to sixty, but with an EPA highway figure of 25 mpg. GM's research showed pony car buyers were fickle, so a Firebird Formula and Pacer X might have been enthusiast alternatives.

Your Pacer X wasn't race-ready without the optional "Rally Pak" of auxiliary gauges.

Although an unlikely candidate for the drag strip, as this example shows, Pacers could be modified for unexpected purposes (courtesy Rod Puckett).

Family-type domestic cars weren't designed for full instrumentation, so Rally Pak added a 4-gauge console molding near the transmission tunnel, angled towards the driver. Readouts involved oil pressure, water temperature, ammeter and mini tach. Maybe the X get-up was too garish? If so, Pacer's HD suspension with stiffer springs, firmer shocks and front swaybar could be added to a normal Pacer for $15.

The value-conscious consumer sought out the '76 Pacer Sundowner, a limited-edition version with much additional equipment for a little over base. The Sundowner advert showed an Aztec-style Sun logo, and said Sundowner came with Custom interior, rear window washer/wiper pack, styled road wheels with whitewalls, remote control driver-side mirror and roof rack. A base Pacer cost $3,499, with Sundowner retailing at $3,599. With $300 worth of options, the buyer was ahead, but only if he visited an AMC showroom prior to Sundowner's final December 31, 1975, order date.

There was even more value available in 1976. In Bicentennial year, tall ships from around the world made the Atlantic crossing, a salute to America's 200th birthday. They could be seen at New York Harbor, at Newport, Rhode Island, and on the 4th of July parade up the Hudson River, but there was another fleet around in '76. That was when AMC introduced the fleet edition of Pacer, a no-frills version for sales reps to pound the highways in austerity. Perhaps said fleet wished to save gas too? If so, some teachers offered an ecological lesson.

Silent Running—Change of Pace

During the Pacer's currency, a group of Cleveland high school vocational teachers banded together to form Electric Vehicle Associates (EVA). EVA converted Pacers to electric power, and proceeded to sell such Pacer Volts to fleet buyers. The publicity picture showed a burgundy Pacer with crimson red vinyl interior, plain aluminum hubcaps, and an "Electric Car" callout decal on the lower part of the front doors.

The Pacer's open hood revealed that the normal I6 had been replaced by batteries and other electric car hardware. To emphasize the purity of it all, a rather fetching blonde stood by the electric Pacer in a dazzling white suit. EVA called their ecochariot the "Change of Pace," producing over 100 of the gas-shy devices. Of course, electricity is often generated using fossil fuel, but the Change of Pace would have been a boon to reducing tailpipe emissions, cutting noise pollution, and avoiding those pesky gas lines.

A '76 Pacer 258 1-barrel with 3-speed overdrive manual had nice EPA city/highway numbers of 20 and 31 mpg. This compared favorably with a car of equal intermediate comfort, the 6-cylinder manual '76 Chevy Chevelle Malibu sedan with 18/26 mpg EPA numbers. However, a Change of Pace offered infinite MPGs, making fleet operators gleeful. A burgundy Pacer one plugged into the mains may seem eccentric. This was a time when suburban pot parties were still in vogue, and the Carter administration was taking steps to legalize marijuana. One can speculate on the inspiration behind the Change of Pace, but they were undoubtedly creative times.

Wagons Roll!

If an electric moon buggy seems otherworldly, then a Pacer wagon is almost as normal as cornflakes and half a grapefruit in the morning. The company that gave us the Sportabout now had a Pacer wagon ready for 1977. Available only in a 2-door body style, so as to differentiate itself from 4-door Sportabout, Pacer wagon retained the famous or infamous asymmetric doors, and like Sportabout was of light-duty liftback configuration.

The popularity of small, maneuverable wagons continued through the '70s and encompassed such diverse things as the sober Toyota Corona wagon and Ford Pinto Cruising Wagon. Both had liftbacks, but the latter's panel van sides with small porthole windows was more passion wagon than grocery getter. Pacer wagon maintained the sedan's plentiful glass and was judged very attractive. Many felt this is what Pacer should have looked like from the start.

A Pacer sedan had 29.5 cu ft of luggage space with the rear seat down, but Pacer wagon had 24.9 cu ft with the seat up! With the rear seat folded, Pacer wagon's load capacity was a useful 48.3 cu ft, or over 5 times what a pony car measuring 20 inches longer could lug. Although, Pacer wagon wasn't as commodious as Sportabout, which had 56.4 cu ft, it did have a lower loading lip and was a foot shorter. Pacer wagon had length, width, and height measurements of 174, 77, and 53 inches, and was the world's first wide small wagon.

For singles and young couples with something to carry, Pacer wagon was a wiser choice, no less comfy than an intermediate V8 wagon, and only had a 76-pound weight penalty compared to Pacer sedan. The wagon also had a handling edge over the sedan, the extra length providing positive balance. The results can be seen by comparing *Road & Track*'s tests of sedan and wagon, both wearing the Alcoa 14 × 6-inch alloys and DR70–14-inch tires. Both turned in 0.653 g skidpad readings, and Pacer sedan's 53.9 mph slalom speed was improved to 56.1 mph by the wagon.

Pacer wagon braked better, with less dive, and eradicated the delayed oversteer to become a normal Detroit slow understeerer. For the public all this vehicle goodness started from $3,799; the cost to AMC was $12 million. That was the tab for converting Pacer sedan

This restored '76 Pacer D/L sedan shows the early fast-fall-away hood that aided driver road vision. One didn't have to park Pacer by ear (courtesy Charlie Cathcart).

into a wagon. Pacer sedan and wagon were identical from the B pillar forward, but the latter had new rear quarter panels, full-opening rear hatch, and a new roof.

Pacer's wagon roof had 5 longitudinal ribs running the roof's length, one inch wide and a half inch tall. They were stamped into the roof for strength and appearance. The public gave Pacer wagon its stamp of approval, with 37,999 sold in its debut '77 model year. Fitted with optional decorative side wood paneling, Pacer wagon also maintained the American tradition of the "Woody." In 1977, Pacer wagon made its movie debut in the successful comedy *Oh, God!*

In *Oh, God!*, God, played by George Burns, makes it rain and flood inside the red Pacer wagon owned by John Denver's mild-mannered supermarket manager Jerry Landers. AMC performed a few miracles of its own in '77 with Pacer revisions. Chiefly there was the "Quench" cylinder head for AMC's I6s. Benefiting Pacer and others using the AMC I6, Bob Petersen (AMC director of power plants and research) told *Popular Mechanics* how the Quench Head pushed the air/fuel mixture closer to the spark plug for more turbulence and a better burn.

AMC's I6s had been suffering pinging or misfiring, and QH made the engine able to run properly on no-lead gas. Because the engine ran better on lower octane gas, ignition timing could be advanced 2 degrees, improving efficiency and garnering 1 mpg more on the EPA urban cycle.[15] On the other side of the power team equation, AMC had a 4-speed floorshift available for '77, to replace the 3-speed manual with electric overdrive option that was expensive and seldom ordered.

Some felt the practical, good-looking wagon was the car Pacer should have been from the start. Here Pacer wagon (left) shares museum space with an early sedan (right) and a restyled '78 Pacer with a "Mercedes" grille (courtesy The Rambler Ranch).

The 4-speed was a conventional manual with 4th as the overdrive ratio. Technically it was released in mid–'76 model year on Pacer, and on '77 I6 Gremlins and Hornets. Combined with the optional 2.53 final drive, the economy gains were there for the asking. One didn't have to ask for so much in '77 because the Pacer came with 1976's Custom interior, front disk brakes and 232 / 3-speed manual floorshift as standard fare. With Pacer options it should be noted the Cruise Command cruise control was only available on automatic cars, and the Adjust-O-Tilt steering could only be specified on column shift automatics.

Promised as mid–'77 Pacer options were power door locks and locking gas cap. The '77 Pacer X now came standard with radial tires, DR78–14-inch BSW rubber on slot rims. Indeed, if radials were ordered on Pacer the optional front swaybar was now automatically included. In 1977, Pacer added an optional "Performance Package" that conveniently brought all the good stuff under one umbrella: 258 I6/4-speed floorshift, HD suspension, soft-feel sports steering wheel, instrument panel overlay, clock and the Rally Pak 4-gauge console group.

The only thing missing from the Performance Package was the Twin-Grip differential, something optional since Pacer's inception. The '77 Performance Package was mostly a renamed version of Pacer's '76 Rally Package. Pacer's Convenience Group brought a dome reading light, floor mats with carpeted inserts, electric clock, storage and litter containers, a second horn, "headlights-on" warning buzzer and illuminated sun visor vanity mirror.

By 1977 the Levi's seating material had gone beyond just Gremlin and Hornet to be available on more models. Pacer sedan was available with optional rear window shades, not unlike the rear sun visors of the Porsche 928. In both cases the aim was to protect rear riders from the glass bubble's sunlight. Pacer's Rallye Perforated vinyl sport buckets had lateral ribbing and shape similar to those in a Porsche 911, and indeed Pacer's face resembled that car's visage on account of the tunnel port headlamps.

Kenosha Porsche — CGE Pacer 401

AMC Pacer had front and rear bumpers from the same stamping, as introduced by Hornet. This meant it was hard to tell if Pacer was coming or going. It was also hard to see how one could customize a car that already looked like it was customized! Such a task would require the vision of Carl Green and his famous operation in Van Nuys, California. Hailing from Kansas, Carl Green had a number of creative highlights even before he set up his own firm, Carl Green Enterprises (CGE), in the early '70s.

Carl Green worked at Daryl Starbird's Custom Emporium in Kansas, and did metal work for Monkee Mobile stylist Dean Jeffries in the late '60s. The real Mecca for customizing was California, and that's where Green moved to. Prior to setting up CGE with Jon Jay, some interesting projects were engaged in by Carl Green in California. He was involved with Evel Knievel's custom Caddy pickup, and designed and built the first phase of the Porsche Chalon.

CGE restored vintage cars, did individual one-offs and commission design work, which included a 1931 Durant Fordor with raised roof and one-way mirrored glass that served as a novelty toilet inside a ladies' dress boutique! Strictly automotive, CGE soon became known for a flared bodykit that dressed up the Datsun Z sports car. This, plus a desire to work on the new Pacer, as well as to accommodate a 401ci V8 Pacer conversion, saw Carl Green do a flared bodykit for Pacer.

People who influenced Carl Green towards AMC were Gene Winfield and Spence Murray. Winfield was involved with movie and magazine car work, and had a soft spot for Kenosha's cars. Spence Murray was *Rod & Custom* magazine editor and had ties with AMC, plus was a motivator in getting the CGE Pacer shown to AMC management at a new car preview. Of immediate concern, Pacer needed flares to clear the big tires specified for Randall American's 401ci conversion.

Randall American of Mesa, Arizona, was known for hotting up AMCs, and here their subsidiary Randall Engineering worked out a V8 conversion process for the I6-only Pacer. This conversion was as straightforward as possible, and endeavored to use as many stock AMC/Pacer parts as possible for convenience. The original I6 engine mounts were kept, with 3 adaptor plates allowing the 401 V8 to be fitted. But there was interference from the front crossmember, and lack of clearance between the exhaust manifold and engine bay.

Randall Engineering's Marvin Johnson fixed the problems. The steering shaft, heater box and front crossmember were clashing, with the 401's oil pan fouling the crossmember. The solution was to tilt the V8 and cut a 9½-inch section out of the crossmember, rolling over to double thickness and welding for extra strength. Similarly, the right side of the floorpan was cut, welded and covered with insulating tape to clear and protect from the exhaust manifold. Finally, a mini air cleaner allowed the hood to shut!

The normal Pacer HD radiator was kept, as were Pacer I6 radiator hoses, fan and fan shroud. Because the V8 was shorter than the usual I6, AMC spacers were used to get the fan closer to the radiator. The Pacer I6 Delcotron alternator was used, not the Motorola unit used on V8 AMCs. Even the I6 power steering pump was retained, albeit using AMC's V8 power steering pump mount. In its original firewall position, the heater box would have to be removed each time the 2 rear spark plugs on the right bank of the V8 had to be changed.

The heater box was ultimately notched and placed towards the fender panel. A longer heater control cable and refrigeration line relocation allowed the Pacer's a/c system to be kept. The original CGE 401 Pacer to be converted started as an "X" car with HD suspension and power brakes. For the 401 conversion, Randall replaced the light-duty Torqueflite A904, used in all auto Pacers, with the larger and heavier A727. Drag racers do like to use light automatics to improve elapsed times.

The A727 casing could be fitted with A904 internals, and when the internals are replaced with custom aluminum parts, the result is an auto with internals ⅓ the weight of the original A727, but it costs money for the lightness of being. A lighter auto cuts vehicle weight, and lighter internals means more engine power reaches the rear wheels.[16] Between 401/A727 and live axle was a V8 Gremlin driveshaft shortened to 35¼ in, with the Pacer's I6 yoke present at the differential end, plus stock 2.73 rear gears.

Rolling stock was in the form of Western slot dish mags wearing GR50–14-inch B.F. Goodrich Radial T/As. The tires made the fender flares a necessity, not a luxury, and the monster radials were an initial size guide for Carl Green to work out said flares. On this first car, Green's work on the front spoiler and flares was all steel. The front spoiler was made up from 3 pieces of 18-gauge sheet metal.

In the interests of style, privacy and reducing interior heat, Green used hand lay-up techniques to make fiberglass window panels for the Pacer's rear side windows. These panels fitted inside the stock window frames, and Green also made a version with opera windows, even a panel for Pacer's rear window. One can see why the CGE Pacer was soon dubbed a hearse for midgets! The glass panes were still on the inside, so Carl Green mocked up interior padded upholstery panels to make things snug.

Some red-cast pearl and 2 coats of clear went over the factory powder blue exterior. Candy blue striping was added over the roof, coming down the B pillar and forward up and over the hood. The rocker panels were painted flat black. Jim Moser's striping shop added a double blue stripe for each fender flare and the front spoiler. Randall American and CGE logos were placed on the rear fiberglass sail panels, with a CGE Pacer logo on the lower door panel where it would normally say Pacer X.

This CGE Pacer 401 had the performance to match the looks. Weight in all-steel was 3,620 lbs, about what a mid–'70s Corvette weighed. The 401 crate motor was making 205 bhp net by '76, and combined with a 600 cfm Holley Model 6708, which had small primaries and big secondaries, the figures were impressive. The automatic car with driver and passenger aboard to record data clocked 0–60 mph in 7 seconds, 14.2-second ¼ mile at 96 mph, and city/highway economy of 11.6/18.6 mpg. Yes, Virginia, there really is a Kenosha Porsche.

Get past the unusual looks and the CGE Pacer 401 drove like one would expect a big-tired, big-motored and live-axled muscle car to fly: lots of grip, nose-heavy and with axle tramp under heavy acceleration and braking. However, consider this: in 1976 the $2,000 401 conversion and $1,500 CGE transformation saw one roll along in 9 grand worth of loaded V8 Pacer. Meanwhile a 4-cylinder 81 bhp Lancia Beta Scorpion listed for $9,943, sans options, and *Road & Track* timed it at 13.4 seconds for 0–60 mph and 19.1 seconds for the ¼ at 71.5 mph. And the Lancia didn't come with a Buyer Protection Plan.

With help from Randall and CGE, one could look bad-ass, not sad-ass. The blue all-steel CGE Pacer 401 was featured as a project car in the 1976 February and March issues of *Hot Rod* magazine. Carl Green, in unsolicited entrepreneurial fashion, took said Pacer to AMC's '76

This '77 Pacer "Woody" wagon has factory a/c and AMC's Styled Road Wheels. Note the Pacer sedan model on the dashboard (courtesy Jim Williams).

new car preview held at Lake Tahoe in July 1975. The car was a hit with AMC brass, dealers and invited press. The Van Nuys gate crasher was welcomed and a Texas AMC dealer bought the blue wonder there and then for $8,000.

Green then productionized the CGE Pacer kit, making molds of what was steel so fiberglass copies could be offered, and there was a promotional brochure created too. Carl Green sent a copy of the CGE Pacer brochure to every AMC dealer in the land. In the days before email and .pdf files, this act cost a pretty penny. Three to four kits had to be sold even before mailing costs were covered, but covered they soon were.

By March 1977, CGE had sold over 100 Pacer bodykits to interested dealers, and through 1978 that number climbed to 150 kits. This was the era of the DKM Macho Trans Am 400 and Dodge Lil' Red Express 360 pickup. Dealers wanted a positive attraction to draw crowds. An example was Lipman AMC/Jeep of Hartford, Connecticut, a dealer that also did V8 conversions.

Lipman marketed the Pacer Diablo, a car fitted with the CGE bodykit, turbine spoke rims and Diablo body graphics. This was a popular creation deliverable in 2 weeks, with the 360 V8 swap optional. Publicity pictures showed Pacer Diablo with Basketry Print individual reclining front seats and moonroof. In CGE's bodykit the flared front fenders and airdam spoiler, with provided attachment flanges, were bolt-on fiberglass items. To fit the rear flares, part of the rear fender metal was cut away, then the fiberglass flare was epoxied to the body with judicious use of filler for a neat finish.

Where chosen, CGE's fiberglass sail panels simply snapped into place over Pacer's stock glass. CGE kit parts were high-quality, hand-laminated items guaranteed to fit. To combat kit piracy, CGE items could only be obtained through AMC dealers, not CGE direct. Dealers from far and wide were interested in either getting kits, or requesting something even more unusual. Mention was even made of one AMC dealer from Vancouver, BC.[17] Further than that, one CGE Pacer went on tour in Europe, something not even Elvis managed!

CGE wasn't the only concern to cater to Pacer. KARVAN, a fiberglass van accessory maker, did a Porsche 911 Carrera-inspired front spoiler/nose piece for Pacer, as well as fender flares. However, KARVAN steered clear of a Porsche whaletail rear spoiler, on the grounds it would be too hard to attach. This challenge didn't daunt Carl Green. CGE did do a whaletail spoiler for Pacer, and one was affixed to the B.F. Goodrich Radial Challenge Series AMC Pacer pace car.

Pacer Sets the Pace—Trackside

CGE built 2 pace cars with turbo motors and side exhaust pipes. The Pacer itself was campaigned in IMSA racing, used by Amos Johnson's well-known Team Highball, an outfit closely associated with speedy AMCs. Pacer made its debut in the final race of the 1975 B.F. Goodrich Radial Challenge Series. That race, held on November 29 at Daytona, was a title decider between Johnson and Nick Craw in his BMW 2002.

Amos Johnson qualified his Pacer, with CGE bodykit, 4th. However, new-car teething problems saw him finish 7th. Craw finished 2nd, sandwiched between the 1st- and 3rd-placed Gremlins of Gene Felton and Steve Coleman, respectively. Robert Wood qualified his Pacer 47th, but failed to finish. Pacer did well in endurance events, especially the 1978 World Challenge For Endurance Drivers held on April 2 at Talladega.

A 1977 Pacer D/L wagon 258 with AMC's factory 14 × 6-inch aluminum rims, made by Alcoa. AMC spent $12 million developing Pacer wagon (courtesy Jeni Panhorst).

At this 6-hour race, Amos Johnson with John Mandeville finished 12th overall, but 1st in their Racing Stocks (RS) class in the Levi's Team Highball No. 7 Pacer (Johnson's racing number). Thirteenth overall and 2nd in class was the sister Levi's Team Highball No. 6 Pacer driven by Dennis Shaw and John Woodward. Third in RS was the Andy Vann team No. 21 Gremlin, with the Southwind Enterprises No. 99 Gremlin in 4th (RS). Thirtieth overall and 5th in RS was the Robert Wood team No. 79 Pacer, technically a finisher although its motor expired on lap 80.

Ahead of Amos Johnson's No. 7 Pacer, the 1st to 11th overall finishing positions were occupied by 9 Porsches and 2 Corvettes! Pacer was in fast company. Another good show was put on by Pacer at the 1978 6-hour race held at Daytona on July 2. Here the Levi's Team Highball No. 6 Pacer of Brad Frisselle and Dennis Shaw came 2nd overall, 2nd in RS. The Byron Wever No. 54 Pacer came 4th overall, 4th in RS. Legendary drivers Dick Barbour and Amos Johnson brought their Levi's Team Highball No. 7 Pacer home 5th overall, 5th in RS, one place ahead of the Gary Belcher No. 9 Gremlin.

In 1979's World Challenge For Endurance Drivers, a 6-hour race held at Talladega on April 1, Kal Showket and Phil Currin's No. 99 Pacer achieved 4th overall and 4th in RS. AMC Pacer was still out on the track in 1981, when at the 6 Hours of Daytona on July 2 the American Marine No. 76 Pacer of Art Yarosh and Bill Barber finished 26th overall and 26th in RS. So Pacer really had race pace, its wide track working with wide rubber to surprise those who thought it was just an urban turtle!

Pacer Pickup—Lil' Gopher

You need a vehicle to visit the races, carry the weekend-use dirt bikes and bring home what was bought at the hardware store—you need a pickup truck. Car-based pickups were rivaling the vibrant vans of the custom and street scene. There could have been a niche between the intermediate-sized V8 El Caminos and the small I4-powered Subaru Brat or VW Caddy. Carl Green thought of an AMC pickup the moment Pacer arrived.

Green mentioned the idea to Richard Teague when dropping off a CGE Pacer at Kenosha in December 1975. There were thoughts shared on the Pacer pickup, and Teague suggested the concept would work better if Green waited a little while and based the mini-truckster on the as-yet-unreleased Pacer wagon AMC was working on. Being longer than the sedan, Pacer wagon would have made for nicer proportions. To give an early start, Teague said Carl Green could have a dimensionally accurate, complete body in white (no trim or mechanicals) Pacer proto wagon to chop up.

Unfortunately, said body was accidentally scrapped by AMC in the interim! To make amends, Richard Teague arranged for Green to have a sparkly new, early production 1977 232-powered Pacer wagon with 3-speed floorshift manual in white, with a bare-bones spec eminently suited to Green's objective. Carl Green flew to Detroit, meeting Teague and taking delivery of the Pacer wagon, whose title was made out to CGE. Upon driving back to Van Nuys, Green removed the whole interior, rear windows, and liftback door, and proceeded to make markings and take measurements.

A Sawzall was then used to cut along the dotted line, and the rear wagon section made way for a new pickup bed. Sixteen-gauge sheet metal served as flooring and inner side panels, welded to tubing braces and the wagon's remaining rear lower ¼ panels. Central to this was a cut-down rear ½ cab section from a Chevy LUV pickup, turned back to front! In fact, the Chevy LUV interior light became the Pacer's cargo light. The Pacer pickup's tailgate was the lower half of the wagon's liftback.

Closed, the pickup bed had an area of 20 sq ft. This was good, but for more practicality, allowing longer loads to be carried with open tailgate as an extended floor, Carl Green increased the

Rated at 120 bhp and 200 lbs./ft., the 49-state 2bbl 258 I6 was a nice motor for a small wagon. However, California started with the 1-barrel version (courtesy Jeni Panhorst).

tailgate by 2 inches using box tubing, and used the same method to blend the pickup's sides with the raised tailgate height. The sides of the bed were raised 4 in, tapering down to the 2 inches of the higher shut tailgate. The tailgate used Ford wagon steel cables as a drawbridge-style lowering support, Chevy van hinges and the Pacer wagon's pushbutton liftback lock.

Carl Green's general philosophy at CGE was to create a quality modified vehicle that was objectively better. So it's no surprise that Pacer pickup looked like it was meant to be, and could have come off the Kenosha line. The level of finish and thoroughness was first-rate. The Pacer wagon's 5-rib roof was incorporated into the pickup in tapered fashion. The shape of the pickup bed, rear cab metal, and recessed rear LUV cab window implied little chance of cargo breaking glass.

The Pacer pickup's bed had a hinged panel allowing access to the spare tire, and each rear wheelhouse inner panel had a removable inspection door to get at taillights and wiring. Rubber scuff moldings protected the cab side metal from cargo-caused paint chips. Early pictures of the Pacer pickup worked on by Carl Green show a small, plain-looking little truck wearing the aluminum hubcaps that came with the base wagon. Richard Teague saw the pickup and was surprised there were no flames, nor the extrovert appearance associated with a customized car.

With this, and the fact most of the conversion changes were at the rear, Green went with a bright yellow exterior, candy flames, big wheels and his famous CGE Pacer bodykit. Wheels were huge 15-inch Cragars, 8 inches wide at the front and 10 inches wide at the rear. The rims had B.F. Goodrich T/A G50 and L50 radial tires front and rear respectively. These shiny rims and big tires were also used on the CGE Pacer sedan by this hour (1977). The Pacer pickup's color was AMC 6V Sunshine Yellow mixed with Gold Murano Pearl lacquer.

Flames and body pinstriping were entrusted to the steady hands of Van Nuys' Bob Bond. The pickup had the wagon's stock split front bench in brown vinyl, with the roomy area behind the seats custom trimmed by "Little John" Engelhardt in matching brown vinyl and carpeting. Carl Green thought of the Pacer pickup more along the lines of a 2-seater sports car than a utility vehicle. The purposely rakish roofline and bodykit added credence to this reasoning.

Two months' work and 300 lbs lost from the base wagon also brought efficiency improvements. When driving back to Van Nuys in the Pacer wagon, Green managed 16 mpg; on the return trip to AMC HQ, average mileage was 20.2 mpg. The journey back was done with 2 aboard, Green and Jay Storer, and included some spirited driving; and the new taller tires meant the odometer would underestimate the distance covered. Thus, figure 22 mpg, and Pacer pickup retained the stock 2.73 final drive.

Pacer pickup made its formal debut in Los Angeles in January 1977, scaring up a mighty amount of positive public interest. There was a lot of CB chatter and verbal high fives on Green's drive back to AMC; truckers and small kids seemed to like it. AMC liked the CGE Pacer pickup too, taking it on factory show tour in 1977 to drum up support and raise money from banks and investment companies. AMC evaluated the pickup, even updating it with the '78 model year "Mercedes"-style grille, but didn't actually put it into production.

With so much interest from regular folks and dealers, it was envisioned CGE would do low-volume conversions for dealers. CGE and the AMC network already had a good thing going. With the 401 engine swap, Randall American could do it, or a conversion kit could be obtained from CGE by a dealer so the 401 could be added to a stock I6 CGE Pacer locally.

Pacer's exclusive Basketry Print fabric seating, blue in this case, was also available in berry, black or tan. The rest of the interior was color-keyed to match (courtesy Jeni Panhorst).

However, it didn't transpire and many were disappointed like the chief of Argus Publications, Eric Dahlquist. He had an article about the CGE Pacer pickup called "The Great Green Hope" inserted into the middle of the AMC car section of the Argus *1978 New Cars* book.

The article wasn't exactly complimentary about AMC's managerial prowess. The Pacer pickup was featured in many magazines, looking slightly different each time but carrying the same license plate, 12M790. It was the same pickup, a one-off with appearance changes. AMC eventually returned the pickup to Carl Green, though by early 1978 it had the '78 Pacer grille and G/T side graphics with no flames. Green subsequently painted it red, white and blue and called it "Lil' Gopher," and it was used by Evel Knievel in his stunt shows.

Lil' Gopher returned to Green once more and for a while had the '78 grille and plain exterior with no flames. It was then given to a friend, and as of April 1984 it was stated that plans were afoot to make the Pacer pickup a 4×4 with 5-speed gearbox.[18] Fast forward to 2000 and the CGE Pacer pickup entered the National Rod & Custom Car Hall of Fame Museum. By 2007 Carl Green was planning to return Lil' Gopher to its original form.

When Pacer pickup was converted to 4×4 configuration, its body was jacked up into the air for greater ground clearance and wheel articulation. The big Cragars were gone and the vehicle appeared like it was on stilts. Green was going to put back the original undercarriage, restoring the 1977 look. Indeed, the chronology of CGE's Pacer work went CGE Pacer sedan, turbo AMC I6, pickup truck and flatnose conversion. The flatnose style gave Pacer sedan a slimline fiberglass front fascia with hideaway GM-sourced quad square lamps.

With the quad lamps closed the front resembled that of a flatnose Porsche 911. With the lamps revealed, the visage was similar to that belonging to the spotlamped tuner Porsche 928 by Strosek, 5 years hence! The Pacer slimline front was available from February/March 1977. CGE also had interesting side graphics, and rear fender flares for Pacer wagon. At the core, Carl Green wanted to give Pacer a sporty customized look. Making the front sleeker, he also expressed a desire to chop one foot out of the roof!

Artistic renderings resembled something aerodynamically worthy of NASCAR, and maybe that was because Pacer inspired like few other cars. Green mentioned that Pacer's asymmetric nature was a challenge. Different door lengths meant that, inside and out, nothing could be duplicated. Also, by the late '70s, customizing turned subtle to do Detroit's more restrained, downsized new models. Domestics and imports were increasingly being delivered with flared arches and spoilers from the factory, so a customizer finessed around all this. Carl Green even mentioned being interested in working on the look of the Mitsubishi-origin Challenger, Sapporo and Toyota Celica Liftback.

However, with subtlety comes blandness, and Carl Green stated why Pacer was a breath of fresh air: "On the other hand, they all look pretty much alike. That's why I like a design like the Pacer. It's different."[19] With its short length and character, Pacer was described as a latter-day hot rod. CGE also did a pickup version of the Gremlin, and bodykits for that subcompact as well as Hornet. With customizing, AMC provided an interesting start!

Later Pacers, 1978–80

Rocking into 1978, Pacer got its first major restyle, consisting of an upright grille. This had overtones of the '69 Ambassador, but was often dubbed the "Mercedes" grille. Detroit liked the Mercedes Compact's image and sales; small luxo sleds were on the rise through the '70s. Solution? Honor Janis Joplin and give your small car a Mercedes grille. It was the Rolls-Royce grille of the '70s and '80s! Many AMC fans prefer the purity of Pacer's original smiley face, which was less prone to dating.

For years it was assumed Pacer's '78 raised hood and grille were necessary to accommodate Pacer's newly available 2bbl 304 V8 option, but maybe not. Any fitment issues were cleared up by a modified air cleaner, that was used on subsequent Concords and Spirits. Plus, Randall American's 401 V8 conversions were performed on Pacers with the smiley face. To create a '78 Pacer 304, AMC merely followed Randall American's V8 conversion. However, a cogent argument can be made that the revised '78 hood was to give more clearance for the V8's larger radiator top tank. Plus, the I6 and V8 radiator core supports were different.

Pacer wagon had 24.9 cubic feet of load space with the rear seat up, 48.3 cubic feet with the rear seat folded. In the '70s, popularity of small wagons skyrocketed (courtesy Jeni Panhorst).

AMC said they introduced a Pacer V8 because the public asked for it. A total of 2,514 Pacer V8s were sold in model year '78, or 12 percent of that year's Pacer production. If AMC's official line is to be believed, that must have been some vocal minority! V8 Pacers were pleasant devices to drive, with no real-world gas mileage penalty compared to the 258. The 304 was the perfect companion for the Pacer wagon, and that comfy, torquey, rear-drive practical combo was a fast-disappearing American tradition.

AMC appeared to be pushing Pacer upscale, with less regard for gas mileage. The D/L was the new base, and the gas tank shrank in size from 22 to 20 gallons. To ensure one looked natty when filling up with gas, there were new exterior colors: Quick Silver Metallic, Claret Metallic, Khaki and British Bronze Metallic. Inside there was standard Reflection Print seat fabric, and optional Velveteen Crush upholstery one wouldn't find in a Honda Accord.

To keep up with naming fashion, Pacer sedan was rechristened Pacer Hatchback, which was code for sounding modern. The optional cruise control now went by the title "Electronic Cruise Command." That year one could option a 4-speaker integrated AM-FM stereo/CB radio, the dashboard head unit with a little L.E.D. window containing the CB channel. These units also carried the AMC A-mark logo, for that neat factory touch. CB radios were in vogue, but it appears the X pack had hit the end of the road.

The last year for Pacer X was 1977, but 1978 did have a "Sport Package" for Pacer. As with previous X, Sport Package was only available on Pacer sedan/hatch, and brought sport front buckets in Soft-feel vinyl, sports steering wheel (with optional "Soft-feel" sports steering wheel in black), DR78–14-inch BSW steel radials and sport slot rims. Optional choices included AMC's Styled Road Wheels or Alcoa alloys, and 1978 was the final year for the Alcoa rims.

Also around were 70-series white-letter Goodyear Polysteel radials, and the Rally Pak 4-instrument console cluster was still listed. Sport Package also included two-tone paint; Pacer was down to 7 combinations in that department by '78. Sport Package could only be chosen in Pacer if the 258 or 304 option box had been ticked, and had everything X ever had, minus the door decal. Moving into '79, the 304 V8 was still Pacer optionable—in fact, it was available across the AMC board—but Pacer was no longer sporty.

The Sport Package was gone and Pacer took on even more luxurious finery, leaving racing to the new Spirit hatch. A hood ornament arrived, as did Caberfae Corduroy seating surfaces, and the D/L title was simplified to "DL." Pacer also packed some exclusive features compared to Concord and Spirit, namely power windows and a Misty Beige Clearcoat exterior. The plushest Pacer had the "Limited" trim level that featured leather upholstery to go with Pacer's revised '79 interior door trim panels.

Heaven forbid Pacer DL be called spartan, it had individual reclining front seats in Caberfae Corduroy or Sport Vinyl, 12-oz color-keyed carpeting and seat belts, plus hood ornament and windsplit molding, electric clock and dual horns, with Velveteen Crush fabric an option. However, Pacer Limited was decadent, with 18-oz color-keyed carpeting, individual leather reclining front seats with corduroy trim accents, powered Adjust-O-Tilt steering, woodgrain 4-spoke steering wheel, power door locks and power windows operated via chrome toggle switches, AM radio, plus vinyl-trimmed folding center armrest and dual remote mirrors.

Amidst all this insulating opulence, the Rabbit diesel at the traffic lights could be seen, but not heard. The VW's engine rattle was of no concern to you: what benefit fuel efficiency if one arrives at a destination deaf? The Rabbit's sacred MPGs, or the Pacer Limited's Chelsea Leather, lighted front ashtray and Limited medallions? In 1979–80, bargains were to be had if one eschewed the fashionable front-drive econoboxes, and chose a rear-drive pre-downsized domestic.

The Iranian Islamic Revolution of late 1979 was a convenient opportunity to double the price of a barrel of oil overnight and return Americans to those long gas lines. Those lines provided plenty of time to consider the dilemma, pay way over list and wait to take delivery of aforementioned econocube, or choose attractively priced, overstocked I6 or V8 domestics and be at the mercy of OPEC. While one worked out how many miles of thrifty driving would have to be covered to work off the price difference, Vince Vance and the Valiants sang an amusing little ditty on the radio called "Bomb Iran."

In the economic despair of 1980, Vince Vance's reworking of the Beach Boys' tune "Barbara Ann" could almost have been an early Reagan '80 campaign song.[20] Pacer's standard 2bbl 258 and 4-speed manual overdrive power team helped redress the balance of payments, and the I6 Pacer's gas tank was back to 21 gallons, promising a good cruising range. Standard mechanical features by '79 were front swaybar, HD cooling and coolant recovery system. Manual air shocks were an option, as was HD suspension.

By 1980 the 304 V8 was out of Pacer life, but in Mexico it never arrived. In Mexico VAM introduced Pacer as a premium-priced luxury car in the 1976 model year. The VAM Pacer did get the 1978 restyle, but never received a V8. However, it was available with VAM's 282ci I6, and in '79, Pacer's final Mexican model year, this was part of a special edition version. 619 VAM Pacers were sold, including 250 '79 VAM Pacer Limited Edition X's. This version had the 282 I6, a/c, automatic and usually a sunroof.

The 1980 U.S. Pacer DL was available with Rochelle Velour and moonroof on the hatch, which helped with stargazing, but one didn't need an astrologer to see Pacer's future. Pacer sales had slowed appreciably from 1978, with the glassy one achieving just 21,231 and 10,215 unit sales in 1978 and 1979 respectively. Production splits were 7,411 hatch and 13,820 wagon in '78, and 2,863 hatch and 7,352 wagon in '79. Just 1,014 Pacer V8s were sold in 1979, and Pacer Limited was truly limited at under 2,500 units.

The '80 Pacers were held-over 1979 production cars, with 1,746 sold (405 hatch and 1,341 wagon) in the 1980 model year. Officially Pacer was withdrawn from sale midway through the model year. However, what appears to be an '81 Pacer with long VIN has been sighted in Houston, Texas. Pacer managed 280,858 sales in 4½ production years, and its early demise seems to have been due to outside influences, rather than any shortfalls in design or quality.

The Rise, Fall and Resurrection of Pacer

In the early days Pacer was getting a lot of positive exposure: it was headline news, and was even a 1975 Burger King promotional prize! Even the reigning Miss Winston, lovely Cindi Carson, sat in the *Car Craft* AMC Pacer with KARVAN bodykit that graced that magazine's cover in January 1976. So Pacer did the media rounds, which stimulated sales, helping the new model exceed its initial 70,000 target. Pacer actually hit 72,158 sales as a '75½ model year entrant. However, the issue of weight always hovered.

Pacer was up, running and being driven by AMC execs by the fall of '73, prior to the first fuel crisis. In the wake of the crisis, noises were made that Pacer should have been lighter. AMC's Director of Product Planning Dale Dawkins expressed that desire in early 1975, and it was hoped use of Libby-Owens-Ford's super-thin glass could cut 50 lbs from Pacer's 150 lbs of conventional glass. By mid '79 AMC said Pacer didn't meet its weight,

Moving into the '78 model year with a new grille and V8 option, Pacer was feeling the heat from new domestics, imports and even in-house AMC Concord (courtesy The Rambler Ranch).

cost or mileage targets during development.[21] However, this statement seems to have been made with the hindsight of the gas crisis.

When Pacer was on the drawing board, fuel economy wasn't a priority anywhere in Detroit; small dimensions yes, 40 mpg no. That was why Pacer and other new designs were being planned with thirsty rotary engines in mind. Pacer arrived at the weight expected of a pre-downsized compact with 5 mph bumpers, so it's hard to understand the criticism. The assertion that the 3,180-pound Pacer sedan was OK was confirmed by Richard Teague when he said Pacer wagon's small weight penalty over the sedan was because the wagon was done in early 1974.[22]

Weight wasn't an issue when Pacer sedan started being designed in late 1971, but it was when the wagon's turn came around, so AMC did something about it. The timeline of events also makes it hard to blame AMC's declining fortunes on Pacer. Apparently AMC was nearly bankrupt by early 1977, but Pacer had been a strong seller to that point. In model year 1976, Pacer amassed 117,244 sales, which was even more than Pontiac's Firebird, whose '76 model year total was 110,775. At the time both were available in a single 2-door body style.

Actually, in the '70s' teeter-totter of changing circumstances, small car sales faltered in 1976, and this played into Pacer's compact hands. The 1977 Pacer sales were also no slouch. The Kenosha Caddy managed 58,264 units in '77. Yes, the new winning wagon had undoubtedly poached sales from the sedan, but by now a quarter million Pacers had left Kenosha! Pacer sedan cost $60 million to develop, with $52 million of that being tooling costs. The design of Pacer wagon was a further $12 million. Not a big deal overall, and much was saved by using the Matador chassis.

The cost of coming up with new designs was increasing, and was getting burdensome for a company of AMC's size. To maintain high sales, new products were needed, and that meant big investment and advertising costs. Domestic car buyers were still used to the buzz

Top: A 1979 Pacer Limited wagon. American Motors introduced the Limited spec that year, upscale of DL. In all, 10,215 Pacers were sold in '79, and 7,352 of them were wagons (courtesy Nolan Dehner). ***Bottom:*** Pacer Limited included real Chelsea leather seating with corduroy trim accents, woodgrain 4-spoke steering wheel, vinyl-trimmed folding center armrest and 18-oz carpeting (courtesy Nolan Dehner).

of major restyles and new releases, and in 1977–78 there was front page news from GM and Ford that drew attention from Pacer. GM had possessed the thirstiest of the Big 4 fleets, and subsequently embarked on downsizing their lines.

GM had the cash and in 1977 unveiled their brand-new full-size line. These truly all-new models cost a fortune to develop, but reaped the sales rewards. Ford was jealous and told the public they kept LTD big ... for value. Full-size sales had been flagging and GM's smaller, lighter line meant it was safe for big car buyers to get back in the water. In 1978 GM did the same for their intermediates. Suddenly one could get a mid-size, rear-drive American car that was the same size as a Volvo 244. This was exactly what buyers wanted.

In 1978 Henry swallowed humble pie, and baked up a new compact line in the Ford Fairmont/Futura cars, small, boxy, efficient rear-drivers that would give rise to the new '79 Mustang. Then there was the rise of the novelty car. These weren't new models; they were returning, retrimmed or renamed fancy pre-downsized designs that proved extremely popular. For '77 the Camaro Z/28 reappeared, and together with its Trans Am sibling sold in the tens of thousands, sometimes even more.

Ford had a similar experience with their "Torino Terrors." These were gussied-up variants on the old Torino platform; examples included Ford LTD II, Mercury Cougar XR7, and the '77 Thunderbird. Regardless of whether a nameplate went up a platform size, or down, all paths led to Torino midsize, and voila! Ford had a trimmer, more fuel-efficient family car with a spirit of sport, and why would Henry lie to you?

Move from LTD to LTD II, and the gas hog problem is solved. Sales of these reborn intermediates were huge; compare 1971–76 full-size Thunderbird with mid-size 1977–79 Thunderbird: 299,146 versus 955,032 equaled no contest. A Torino T-Bird with base 302 was just right, but just to show how difficult tuning a car to changing domestic tastes was, the next smaller T-Bird bombed. Reducing length by 10 inches increased sales for '77, but the 1980–82 "Boxbird" T-Bird based on the Fairmont/Futura platform didn't fly, in spite of better MPGs.

At the same time the Japanese were cementing their position, with the newish Honda Accord and latest Toyota Celica. AMC also attacked Pacer from within with its new Concord luxo compact. Pacer was getting squeezed between the new domestic family cars, novelty rides and imports. All the newcomers had TV and print ads to woo the public; all Pacer had in '78 was a new grille and 304 option. The final harbinger of doom came in the form of the '80 GM X car. With a version for each division, what could Pacer do when the world's biggest automaker said X marked the spot on the small-car map?

There is some historic parallel between AMC Pacer and Pontiac Fiero. The Fiero was a short, wide sports car originally pushed as an urban commuter car. Fiero used mechanicals from existing models, GM T and X cars, putting most of the money into its futuristic body. Initial planned output was 75,000 units, and like Pacer, early sales and buyer interest exceeded expectations. Like Pacer, sales dropped off, with Fiero also getting to an approximate 300,000 total in a short 1984–88 period.

Reasons for the drop-off were different between the two. With Fiero early quality problems, like engine fires, quickly tarnished its reputation. Plus GM rediscovered the fact domestic buyers don't buy 2-seaters in volume. Pacer didn't have quality problems; it just got swamped by new releases. Common reasons for demise concerned fuel economy and niche marketing. By 1985–86 gas prices were falling and the public moved away from the small, light urban Fiero commuter, to a V8 Chrysler Fifth Avenue traditional sedan.

With Pacer, things swung the other way. The need for MPGs by buyers became pressing by 1979–80, and Pacer couldn't match a little Datsun on that score. Unlucky Pacer was designed with proposed strict federal crash safety laws in mind. There was even early–'70s talk of a federal visibility standard, to make it easier for drivers to see out of their cars. Pacer had all this covered, and even had more space available within its doors for heftier side guard beams, should legislation have required them.

Unfortunately for AMC, Detroit car industry lobbyists were able to persuade Washington to water down proposed laws, leaving Pacer with more safety and weight than necessary. Short-sighted Detroit couldn't see that slacker safety laws would make it easy for Japanese automakers to sell a ton of Hondas and Datsuns in America by the late '70s. The tiny front-drive 1977 Datsun F-10 5-speed hatch came with AM-FM radio, tach, reclining front buckets, fold-down rear seat, radials and EPA city/highway numbers of 29/41 mpg. The F-10 didn't stand a beer can's chance in Hades of passing a real crash test, but Pacer did. Where was Ralph Nader when you needed him?

The Fiero and Pacer episode also calls into question the possibility of niche products achieving volume sales over several years. AMC's Gerry Meyers didn't want to see Pacer as a quirky specialty machine, but it seems such devices are better accepted by the import crowd. All the domestic winners, like minivans, sport trucks and pony cars in their heyday, were plain products, no niche. The conservatism of domestic buyers ultimately sealed Pacer's fate, once the newness wore off. However, it was a pity the CGE Pacer pickup wasn't productionized, because sport trucks are as American as apple pie. The CGE Pacer pickup would have hit the oddball clean out of Pacer.

Standard '79 Pacer engine was the 258, with 304 optional. Over 1980–82 AMC gradually introduced its black box CEC ignition system on 258. In '81 this motor got a plastic valve cover, lighter block and crank (courtesy Nolan Dehner).

AMC Pacer seems to have something in common with James Dean. Pacer was with us for a short time, but its influence is long-lived. The round one has been featured in many films, often intentionally. Examples include *Car Wash* (1976), *Wayne's World* (1992), *Wayne's World 2* (1993) and *Starsky & Hutch* (2004). In the latter flick the Pacer served as a getaway vehicle for a wannabe assassin, albeit a very slow one! Pacer was also the subject of a bizarre makeover on the customizing TV show *Pimp My Ride*, and has been used in a Dell laptop computer ad.

Pacer's styling was undoubtedly an influence in creating the multi-colored Apple iMac, and the car has even been seen in a video game. Observe the 1999 Activision title *Vigilante 8 2nd Offense*. This game, for the original Sony PlayStation, had a number of '70s and futuristic vehicles. Although not actually referred to as an AMC Pacer, no doubt to avoid paying Daimler-Chrysler licensing fees, a round, glassy blue 2-door sedan with orange and green fluoro decoration is most certainly a '78 Pacer. While this virtual vehicle can't actually be driven by the player, it can be followed around on the gamefield.

Opinions about Pacer as a collector car have also changed. In the mid–'90s it was thought Pacer wagon would command the big money, because it looked more conventional than the wacky sedan. However, since then all Pacers have started to get serious money, as '70s cars have appreciated due to increased rarity. Pacer's unusualness has now become a selling point, as people rise against the cookie cutter! Commercially it may have been better to be a maverick in name rather than nature, but a small-car legend was never this wide.

AMC product-differentiated Pacer wagon from Sportabout by making the former a 2-door and the latter a 4-door. Pacer was discontinued midway through the 1980 model year (courtesy Nolan Dehner).

Don't Forget the Matador!

The tide of changing fortunes favored AMC by 1973, when its profits were 7 times the 1972 level. The reason was booming sales of small cars, once again AMC's economic savior. The figures didn't lie: AMC had 4.4 percent of the 3.9-million-unit small-car sector in 1971, and by 1973 owned 6.2 percent of the larger 4.8-million-unit small-car market.[23] In 1973, AMC sales were $1.7 billion, with net earnings of $44.5 million, and AMC's total North American market share was over 4 percent. It was a gain at the expense of the Corpulent 3, as any victory always was.

AMC was *the* American small car company, and showed a sneak Metallic Autumn Red Pacer front grille/headlamp preview pic as a teaser in their 1974 Annual Report. However, you would be wrong in thinking Big 3 conquest sales came from small cars alone. AMC said goodbye to the full-size Ambassador in '74, but still had faith in their intermediate. In 1974 came a major reworking of Matador, and one brand-new variant ... Matador Coupe!

AMC was well-known for small cars, but was finding it hard to register public family-sized car consciousness. The opposition was stiff in the 6-seater class: by 1973 Chevrolet could boast Impala had been the nation's most popular car for 13 years, selling over 10 million copies since its inception. Hence that '73 AMC ad campaign, "What's a Matador?" So AMC had to get noticed and go fancy with Matador Coupe.

AMC's existing Matador 2-door hardtop went by the sobriquet "Flying Brick," so was quietly shown the door at the end of the '73 model year. In came the '74 Matador Coupe, a genuine contender in the sports/luxo intermediate coupe arena, that shared no sheet metal with the contemporary Matador 4-door sedan, nor with the wagon. AMC's Gerry Meyers was VP of Product Development at the time, and Richard Teague said the original plan for a stand-alone coupe provided much creative freedom.

Matador Coupe would be directly competing with cars like the Chevy Monte Carlo and Pontiac Grand Prix, so style was of the essence. The result was an intermediate coupe that eschewed the upright grilles and '30s styling cues beloved of Detroit's designers. The closest rival was the G/P-related Pontiac Grand Am, which went antiestablishment with a futuristic rubber nose in '73. Matador didn't stop at the nose; it adopted the swoopy overall lines of the Ferrari Daytona, marrying this with AMC's tunnel port headlamps!

In charge of exterior styling was AMC's Robert Nixon, someone who was on the styling team of the tunnel port-headlamped '64 American. As AMC director of passenger car exterior styling, Nixon specially utilized round lamps on Matador Coupe front and rear. The rear fascia taillight effect was reminiscent of the Chevy Corvair. Although an original overall shape, Matador Coupe did steal Big 3 details, where beneficial. Thus, Matador Coupe avoided Pontiac Grand Am's louvered rear quarter windows, an unnecessary blind spot.

Unusually for this type of car, Matador Coupe had good visibility, the rear quarter windows and fastback glass being well sized. Pillars were slim and Matador Coupe had an integrated roof rollbar visible through the headliner. The federal rollover roof strength test involved a hydraulic ram stressing part of the roof's unibody, and measuring deflection. Matador Coupe had bulging fender wells, handy for NASCAR's big wheels. It was thought Mark Donohue dispensed advice to AMC concerning Matador Coupe's shape, but it seems any suggestions Donohue made were directed at the AMX/3.[24]

As a new vehicle, Matador Coupe had an appearance that was well received by the public and press. *Car and Driver* bestowed upon Matador Coupe their "Best Styled Car of 1974" award in the November 1973 issue. It seemed like all had been forgiven concerning Marlin. For 5 mph bumpers AMC didn't use Matador sedan/wagon's gap-concealing filler panels, going instead for "free standing" bumpers with rubber gaiters alone to conceal the retractable shock absorbers, avoiding the massive, blockish look of many mid–'70s cars.

Like other '74 AMCs, Matador Coupe had 2 vertical rubber bumper guards front and rear. Matador Coupe also had AMC's new '74 badge script font. Built on a 114-inch wheelbase, Matador Coupe was 4 inches down on Matador sedan and wagon's 118 inches. Exterior dimensions and weight were that of an intermediate coupe. Length, width, height were 209.4, 77.4, and 51.8 inches; weight came in at 3,643 lbs. Standard equipment on the 1974 Matador Coupe included 100 bhp 232 I6 and 3-speed column manual power team, non-boosted front disks, front swaybar and Extra Quiet Insulation Package.

In 1973 a mere 7,067 2-door hardtop Matadors were sold; in 1974, 62,269 Matador Coupes went to new homes! AMC had something different in Matador Coupe, and their tagline played on this: "This is one mid-size car you've never seen before...." They answered their own question too, "WHAT'S A MATADOR? THIS IS!" Matador Coupe was AMC's star at the '74 Chicago Auto Show, and a '74 Matador Coupe became the 6 millionth AMC vehicle built since the 1954 merger. America finally knew what a Matador was!

It was a good year for Matador — total Coupe/sedan/wagon sales were 99,586 in '74 — but there was some cost incurred too: AMC tooling costs for the Matador Coupe were $17 million. In 1974 AMC's capital expenditures and financing came to $123 million. Part was due to the revised '74 Matador range, but funds also went towards increasing manufacturing capacity and dealer facilities.

AMC was one of the few companies to turn a profit in the bleak fiscal pit of 1974, and VW was envious. If it weren't for strike action at the close of the fiscal year, things would have been even better. The strike cut AMC's net earnings by $13 million, to $27.5 million. However, sales for 1974 were $2 billion, and during 1974 AMC was able to pay semi-annual dividends for the first time since 1965.

Matador trim levels went from base, to either luxury Brougham or the sporty "X," the latter for Matador Coupe alone. Equipment ran against logic, with Matador sedan and Coupe getting a 24.9-gallon gas tank, whereas the wagon only had a 21-gallon tank. In addition, sedan and Coupe came with base I6 power, but heavier Matador wagon subsequently came with the 304, meaning more visits to the gas station. A 4,075-pound wagon needed that V8, and it was apt AMC provided Torque Command auto standard, instead of the 3-speed manual found on sedan and Coupe.

Family guy only wanted to handle loose change, not a shift, at the fast food drive-thru with kids in tow. There was plenty of room back there, 95.2 cu ft, which counted Matador's 8-cu-ft below-floor hideaway. Matador sedan and Coupe weren't too shabby with 19.1 and 14.3 cu ft respectively. However, the chief limiter on domestic family cars of the time was trunk floor shape, making soft luggage your best bet.

The Brougham package could be added to Matador sedan, wagon or Coupe. Outside there were chrome disk wheel covers with AMC logo in the center, "Brougham" script on the C pillar, tailgate air deflector and roof rack on wagon, hood paint stripes, bumper rub strips on Coupe, lower chrome rocker panel moldings on sedan, Coupe and wagon sans optional woodgrain paneling, back panel overlay on sedan, roll-down rear quarter windows for

A 1974 Matador Coupe X 304, the first year for American Motors' new sports coupe intermediate entry (courtesy Ettore Philip Demichele).

Coupe, full-length vinyl-filled protective side rubstrips, and fender lip, grille surround, rear hood and license plate surround chrome moldings.

Inside, Brougham brought standard individual reclining front seats. On sedan Custom Hyde Park fabric was standard, optional on wagon. The wagon came with crayon-friendly, hose-out Sof-Touch vinyl, an option for sedan and Coupe. Matador Coupe Brougham came standard with Hunter's Plaid fabric. Brougham's other interior appointments covered the expected custom door trim panels with assist straps and inserts, woodgrain instrument panel overlay, and full carpeting that included trunk or wagon cargo floor.

The term Brougham was a traditional domestic trim term for luxury, but "X" was an AMC exclusive. This sporty trim pack had standard double profile stripes, "X" front fender emblems, "Matador X" decal replacing the Matador nameplate on the hood and deck lid, complemented by Sof-Touch vinyl buckets and 14-inch slot rims. Matador Coupe X was the starting point for building a no-baloney performance machine. Richard Teague admired Pininfarina's flowing shapes, so consider Matador Coupe X a Ferrari sans the fancy label!

Thirty dollars for the handling pack was money well spent: apart from firmer shocks and springs, Matador Coupe X gained a rear swaybar to make its spec Grand Am equal. The most serious tires available were FR78 steel-belted radials. *Road & Track*'s Matador Coupe X generated 0.678 g on the skidpad, a good number for the time, and the AMC's overall feel was discernibly better than the Big 3. More wheel travel and less front-end float were unusual qualities, when domestic handling dictated holding a body parallel to the road at all times.[25]

Car and Driver's December 1973 comparo tables showed that Matador Coupe X delivered against Olds Cutlass Salon, Mercedes 450 SE and Pontiac Grand Am 400 sedan. Matador out-accelerated the bunch, being the only car in the 16s. Matador X was also the shortest-braking car, stopping from 70 mph to zero in under 190 feet. The AMC was also

The air filter decal never lies: 304 V8 power came standard on Matador Coupe X. The '74 Coupe engine choices ranged from 232 I6 to 401 V8 (courtesy Ettore Philip Demichele).

the cheapest car, which included an optional engine to smoke the G/A's base 2bbl 400. The Matador cost 4 grand, the Mercedes 14K!

Matador Coupe X 401—Performance Unlimited

The Matador Coupe X did register the highest decibel reading under full throttle, but that was because AMC was working harder for you. It was a question of value. Matador Coupe X came standard in '74 with the 150 bhp 2bbl 304 V8; nice, but you really wanted the top-line 255 bhp 4bbl 401 V8, the sort found in AMX. With this motor *Super Stock* magazine's Matador Coupe X 401 recorded 15.38 seconds for the ¼ mile at 94.26 mph. This was achieved in an unmodified a/c car, with self-shifting automatic, after a brake-torqued start, into a headwind![26]

It was a no-brainer getting the most out of Matador Coupe X 401; just put the shifter in "D" and floor the gas. Helping *Super Stock*'s Matador hook up was an optional 3.54 final drive, and the stock V8 ratio was 3.15 in '74. The 4-speed manual was reserved for Javelin AMX by this time, and a Matador Coupe V8 implied auto only, but no matter; a low-15s ¼ mile and sub-7-second 0–60 mph time weren't tardy in 1974.

AMC didn't like the meow of the 2-way cat, but the 401 had every other Christmas decoration hanging on it, like EGR, PCV valve, evaporative emissions control, electric-assisted quick-off choke assembly, environmental carb and distributor settings. As per GM cars, the transmission-controlled spark meant no vacuum advance in 1st or 2nd to curb nitrogen oxides, and the induction-hardened valve seats said no lead was no problem, but it didn't slow Matador.

By leaving the cat in the alley, AMC vehicles had the driveability and performance of yesteryear. Matador Coupe X 401 had the measure of a less tightly controlled '70 455ci GTO, and no one was prepping cars for mags by '74. Woodward Avenue was pretty quiet by now; just tumbleweeds blowing and Pintos prowling. It was child's play to blow off the kid's Mustang II Mach I V6. Matador Coupe X 401's driver felt guilty about taking the Mustang's pink slip, and with police sirens blaring, decided to keep the pedal to the 18-oz carpet and race off into the dark. The police put out an A.P.B. for a renegade Ferrari or a UFO because no one can see your badge at night!

AMC's performance-on-a-budget approach involved much bought-in componentry. AMC recalibrated the Chrysler Torqueflite auto to suit the torque curves of its engines. There was also Chrysler-sourced '74 seat belt interlock, Ford Motorcraft carburetion, GM Saginaw variable ratio power steering and GM collapsible steering column. The $473 a/c option on a '75 Matador wagon was also cheaper than that found on a Big 3 intermediate.

The Cassini-Coutured Matador Coupe

How could a comparably equipped Matador Coupe undercut rivals by $1,000? Economies of scale suggested that higher Big 3 production volumes equaled lower unit costs and lower prices for consumers, but as ever the most appealing window sticker belonged to little old AMC. Low price, not low quality, and for extra plushness one could option beyond Brougham to the Matador Coupe's Oleg Cassini Package. Mr. Cassini was a famous fashion designer; former first lady Jacqueline Kennedy was one of his patrons.

A Cassini Coupe was just the ticket to add that touch of class. Oleg Cassini did lend his name to the model, and publicity pics were taken of him with Matador Cassini Coupe. He was pleased with the finished result, considering the ride a swinging car. However, most of the Cassini Coupe's artistic element came courtesy of AMC's stylists. American Motors' Vince Geraci and team were responsible for the Matador Coupe's interior in general, and for this particular version.

Outside and in, some outlandish proposals were considered for Cassini. White top surfaces as per Ramblers of the '50s and '60s, not to mention psychedelic black and white patterns/decals and decorated '66 Rogue-style rear deck, were tabled for the exterior. Interior seating patterns ran from Battenburg cake to British Union (Jack) Flag and even checkerboard. In the end something much more restrained with copper eventuated.

Exterior color choices for Cassini Coupe were white, black or copper, with Bravado vinyl roof available in the same choices. Copper featured on the grille, headlamp bezels, protective profile rubstrips, rear license plate surround and even on the finned Custom wheel covers. "Cassini" script replaced the usual Matador front fender items.

Matador Coupe's dashboard was shared with '74 Matador sedan and wagon, but Cassini touches graced this molding and the rest of the interior. The main dash color was black, but copper was used for the overlay and dial faces. If one ordered the Visibility Group, a copper-faced clock would help pass the time. The steering wheel also carried copper accents. Since Cassini was predicated on Brougham, individual front reclining seats were a given.

Matador Coupe's dash was shared with '74 Matador sedan and wagon, and was considered a little boring after the snazzy Coupe exterior (courtesy Ettore Philip Demichele).

The Cassini Coupe's main interior color was black. Black Kasmir Knap Knit nylon material was employed on seating surfaces and door trim panels with their door-pull straps and fabric inserts, and copper buttons featured in both locations. Black Knap Knit was also on the sun visors and headliner, but thick 24-oz copper carpeting adorned the floor. Cassini medallions were embroidered on the headrests, and Cassini script also appeared on the glove box door.

Matador Cassini Coupe was popular on release; 6,165 were sold, compared to 10,074 Matador Coupe Xs. One example with copper exterior and black interior was used by James Bond's nemesis Francisco Scaramanga in the movie *The Man with the Golden Gun.* This famous Matador Coupe plane/car evaded Bond by flying from Bangkok to an island in the China Sea. However, the actual car could only do 500 meters, so a 1-meter-long radio-controlled model was used to depict the flight in the movie.

Racing with Matador Coupe

Matador Coupe was doing some real flying in NASCAR, where it replaced the so-called Flying Brick 2-door hardtop in 1974. Roger Penske still ran the show with AMC factory backing in red, white and blue livery, but Matador Coupe's victories all came from the deft touch of racer Bobby Allison. On November 24, 1974, Allison won the *L.A. Times* 500 held in Ontario, California; it was Matador Coupe's first win. Next came the Winston Western 500 held at Riverside on January 19, 1975, followed by the Rebel 500, which took place at Darlington on April 13, 1975. A final official Matador Coupe win also occurred at Darlington on September 1, 1975, as the Southern 500.

Team Teague overlaid a number of Big 4 styling cues on a loose Ferrari Daytona outline, to come up with a coupe that actually flew in the James Bond movie *The Man with the Golden Gun* (courtesy Ettore Philip Demichele).

Bobby Allison achieved a non-points victory in Matador Coupe at the Daytona 125 on February 13, 1975, coming in 2nd in the Daytona 500 three days later. It would seem Matador Coupe's aerodynamic shape lent a helping hand in NASCAR. Sadly, Mark Donohue never raced the Matador Coupe. After grabbing the '71 SCCA T/A title in the Humpster Javelin, Donohue won the 1972 Indianapolis 500 in a McLaren-Offenhauser for Penske Racing. In 1973 Mark Donohue was Can Am champ driving a Porsche 917 for Roger Penske.

After the Can Am success, the driver known as Captain Nice decided to hang up his racing gloves, becoming Penske Racing's team manager. However, Roger Penske wanted Donohue to drive in his new Formula One team based in Poole (United Kingdom). Mark Donohue was no stranger to F1: he achieved 3rd place in his first F1 outing, driving the Penske Sunoco-sponsored second McLaren entry in the 1971 Canadian Grand Prix.

For Penske's 1974–76 F1 operation, his own PC1 monocoque chassis, combined with Cosworth DFV V8 and Hewland gearbox, were utilized. On debut at the 1974 Canadian GP, Mark Donohue took this PC1 package to 12th place, and got a subsequent 5th-place finish at the 1975 Swedish GP. Halfway through the 1975 season, Penske F1 switched to a March 751 chassis, and Donohue used this to garner 5th place at the 1975 British GP.

In practice for the 1975 Austrian Grand Prix at the Osterreichring, Donohue crashed due to a tire blowout. Initially he appeared only slightly injured, but he subsequently died of brain injuries 3 days later on August 19 in Graz, Austria. It was a sad end for a great competitor with an AMC connection. Penske F1 returned for the 1975 U.S. GP with John Watson driving the PC1 chassis. Watson won the 1976 Austrian GP using the later PC4 design, but Roger Penske was through with Formula One. At the end of 1976 Penske said his outfit wouldn't contest the 1977 Formula One season. His Poole factory built the PC5 Indy car chassis.

Penske's time with Matador Coupe had drawn to a close as well. In spite of the car's racing success in 1975, AMC decided to withdraw factory NASCAR support at the end of '75. It had been a rough year for the auto industry and AMC, the company taking a $27.5 million loss in 1975. Penske Racing used the Matador Coupe once more, in the season-opening 1976 Winston Western 500, but after that, Penske and Allison campaigned a Mercury. However, Matador Coupe would return.

At the end of the 1976 racing season Bobby Allison stopped driving for Penske Racing ... and revived Matador! With AMC factory backing and finance sector sponsorship, the Matador Coupe was once again in red, white and blue AMC livery. Bobby Allison managed 5 top-5 finishes in the 30-race 1977 NASCAR racing season. The best was a 2nd place at the short track of the 1977 Nashville 400. In AMC showrooms things weren't so racy.

Traveling to Barcelona

In 1974, 312 Matador Coupe Broughams were chosen with 401ci power; 405 were happy with the base 232 that Matador Coupe Brougham came with; 315 people bought a 1974 Matador Coupe X 401. In the '75 model year it's believed 4 Matador Coupe X 401s were produced, with 85 Matador sedan/wagon 401s as well, even though the 401 was off AMC's official new-car power plant list. Officially the 360 was now top dog, but more folks chose 258-powered '75 Matador Coupes (4,537) than selected a 360 V8.

By '75 the 258, sporting 95 electronic-ignitioned pollution ponies like a Pacer, was Matador's new base engine, although California received the 120 bhp 304 V8 for starters. It was a year of performance decline industry-wide, because it was the day the cat came to town. The 2-barrel 360 V8 was now down to 140 bhp net, with the dual exhaust '75 4bbl 360 belting out 180 horses. As a guide, the 1975 Corvette with base L48 350 V8 had a mere 165 bhp.

In '75 the Matador Coupe X's new base motor was the 258 I6, but if one bought a left-hand-drive only, fully imported Matador Coupe with Cassini pack in Britain, it automatically came delivered with a 360 V8. There were fewer takers for Cassini Coupe in '75, 1,817 to be precise, part of the smaller 22,368 Matador Coupe total for the year. The 1975 model year was the last year for the X and Cassini packs on Matador Coupe. For 1976 luxury had a new name in Matador land: it was Barcelona.

The base price for a '76 Matador Coupe was a modest $3,621; this could still be upgraded to Brougham spec, and above that, Barcelona trim. The Matador Coupe Barcelona came with the following exterior embellishments: Barcelona hood ornament, Barcelona nameplate on hood and rear deck, Barcelona crest above the "Matador" plaque on the glove box, Barcelona crest alongside Matador fender script badges, and red and yellow body profile striping.

If the Matador Coupe Barcelona was chosen with tan interior, tan would feature on the Custom wheel covers, as accents around the front grille and rear license plate surround, and on the headlamp bezels. As per Cassini, since Brougham was a prerequisite, Barcelona had individual reclining front seats that were available in tan or black Knap Knit fabric, with matching 24-oz cut pile carpeting. Lower door panels had color-keyed carpet inserts, and the upper part of the door trim panel featured color-keyed Knap Knit material. The door-pull straps and headlining were also color keyed.

Matador Coupe Barcelona's loose-fit soft upholstery had horizontal decorative material bands of Mediterranean flavor. Given Barcelona was as luxurious as Cassini, and there was no licensing agreement required with Spain, the new trim pack was a good deal for the consumer and American Motors! Unfortunately, this didn't stop Matador Coupe sales from falling to around 10,000, or AMC from taking a $46 million loss for the year.

Roy Chapin's plan was to get annual production back up to 500,000. In the good times of 1973–74, production capacity upgrades were made, but these weren't fully utilized because AMC's 1976 output was only 332,900 units. Plant equipment could have produced 450,000 vehicles if required.[27] The Pacer was central to AMC at this time, so Matador Coupe changes were minor. Domestic automakers wanted their chariots to go further on a gallon, so taller final drives were featured. The stock Matador Coupe V8 rear ratio was now 2.87, and the 3.15 ratio joined the 3.54 on the options sheet.

Indeed, the build-up potential in '76 was still there, with careful optioning. It was possible to order a Matador Coupe with 4bbl 360, real duals, console Torque Command auto, HD suspension, Twin-Grip differential, FR78 white-letter steel-belted 14-inch radials and Sof-Touch vinyl buckets. Alternatively, 49 state fiends may have wished to try Matador Coupe in base 258 I6 form with 3-speed column-shift manual. Not sexy, but it came with a 3.54 final drive as standard. The solid manual connection and low gearing promised more pep and better economy than an intermediate coupe with base V8 and intergalactically tall gearing.

Engine options slimmed down to three for '77. The 258 gained 3 horses to reach 98 bhp, the 2bbl 304 was on 120 bhp, with the 2bbl 360 making 129 bhp. The 4-barrel, dual-exhaust 360 V8 had been discontinued at the end of the '76 model year. However, AMC had a new trim package to chase away the underhood blues. In November 1976 *Road & Track* declared, "Every respectable auto maker has to have a brougham these days." Well, not AMC; they ditched Brougham from the Matador Coupe at the close of '76.

For '77, if one wanted luxury in a Matador Coupe, the new "Barcelona II" trim pack option box was to be ticked. Barcelona II was like the original, except with more stuff in a

Achieving 62,269 unit sales on debut, the '74 Matador Coupe put American Motors in the driver's seat. Buckets were standard with the X pack (courtesy Ettore Philip Demichele).

stand-alone spec with exterior features like: two-tone Golden Ginger Metallic over Sand Tan, color-keyed bumpers and color-keyed sports slot 15-inch rims with wider GR78 whitewall radials. Helping with handling was a standard rear swaybar. Two color-keyed rearview exterior side mirrors were also in the deal, but what of domestic intermediate tradition?

Tradition foretold Barcelona II would receive a hood ornament and Landau padded vinyl roof with rear opera windows. The Opera Window and Padded Vinyl Roof Package had been a Matador Coupe Brougham option since January 1974. Apparently Richard Teague liked opera windows and felt Matador Coupe should have them available. These viewing apertures weren't standard on Cassini or '76 Barcelona packs. Engineering-wise, opera windows entailed regular Matador Coupe rear ¾ windows with fiberglass panel under the D/L Formal Window Package's trimmed roof, and a screw-in insert inside to partly cover the main glass.

With Landau and Opera, Matador Coupe was truly boulevardier, and its tan-only interior bore this quality out, handsomely. Actually, coming back down to earth, Barcelona II's interior, covered under the luxury interior trim group, was what one got in '76 Barcelona. Revisit the Kasmir Knap Knit interior fabric in "loose" trim effect, enveloping rake adjustable seats. This could all be enjoyed, except when freeway lane changing. That's when the reduced visibility brought by those stock opera windows wasn't so welcome.

If you couldn't see them, they could certainly see you! In 1978 the Barcelona theme color was a two-tone Autumn Red Metallic over Claret Metallic. However, was all that lux-

With a link to fashion designer Oleg Cassini and an accent on copper trim, Cassini Coupe added a touch of class to Matador (courtesy The Rambler Ranch).

ury a weighty problem? With '77 Barcelona II, AMC stated the 258 I6 was the base engine, but was "not recommended," suggesting the 304 would better lug the load. By '78 uprated engine choices for Matador Coupe were 120 bhp 2bbl 258 or 140 bhp 2bbl 360. The 360 had been moved from 245 lbs/ft at 1,600 rpm in 1977, to 278 lbs/ft at 2,000 rpm in 1978. AMC was getting better at emissions tuning.

This was enough to keep Matador Coupe humming on the highway and looking for Hardee's. The Barcelona interior was a comfy place to listen to David Soul on 8-track cartridge, but unfortunately it was AMC that was playing to an audience of one. Matador Coupe sales had fallen to 6,825 in 1977, and just 2,006 by model year '78. The market for sports/luxo intermediates wasn't what it used to be. AMC had once again come late on the scene, just like it had done earlier with Javelin and pony cars.

Matador Coupe had to fight it out for a slice of shrinking pie, with the likes of Chevy Monte Carlo, Chrysler Cordoba, and in '78 a new downsized Pontiac Grand Am. The success of the new midsize '77 Thunderbird also didn't help Kenosha. The public's desire for a smaller T-Bird ran contrary to the decline of this segment. The injustice was that 1977 Matador Coupe was swoopier and more advanced-looking than the blockish Thunderbird, but like Pacer, Matador Coupe suffered from not being new anymore.

The only major visual change to Matador Coupe during its run was a new grille for '76. The previous one-piece molding with round turn signals gave way to a two-piece rectangular grille insert with rectangular turn signals. New features like this and '76's interior hood release weren't enough to hold buyer interest. AMC was still backing Matador, though. Going into '77 model year the official line was that the range was being actively marketed, with a hope more would be sold.

In 1977 Matador picked up column automatic, power disk front brakes, power steering and individual reclining front seats as stock equipment. The first two items had already been standard on Matador wagon, which also came with the 304 V8. The Matador wagon was up-engined from sedan and Coupe, the latter using the 258/automatic power team as a base, whereas for '78, Matador wagon came with 360 V8 standard. Matador wagon was the only vehicle in its class with optional AM-FM radio accompanying a 6-speaker sound system. In 1978 the Barcelona pack became available on Matador sedan, and Coupe received the coolant recovery system as standard, but the end was nigh.

In August 1975 *Motor Trend*'s Tony Swan gazed into his crystal ball and correctly predicted that 1978 would be Matador's final year.[28] Somehow the 6-passenger, rear-drive, mostly V8-powered American family car had gone from mainstay normal to kitsch. As good an intermediate as Matador was, it was an unloved pre-downsized ride. The new 1977 GM full-size models, and 1979 Ford LTD sedan, wagon and coupe, were boxier, lighter and taller new models with exterior dimensions equal to or smaller than old intermediates.

These new designs had sharp, crisp lines, reduced chrome and less fussy styling. Compared to previous full-size models the statistical advantages were plain, but did a new GM full-size really give more than Matador? Let's see the figures. 1977 GM family cars had length, width, height, wheelbase, and weight stats of 213.8, 75.4, 53.9, and 115.9 inches and 3,802 lbs (with V8), front and rear headroom 38.8 and 38 inches, front and rear legroom 42.2 and 39.5 inches. Coffin-nose Matador sedan had length, width, height, wheelbase, and weight of 216, 75.7, 54.7, and 118 inches and 3,670 lbs (with I6), front and rear headroom 39.6 and 37.5 inches, front and rear legroom 42.8 and 39.6 inches.

The data reveal pre-downsized full-size cars didn't offer much more interior space than pre-downsized intermediates. The stats also show GM's new full-size line had similar dimensions to old Matador. Overall fuel economy and acceleration were equal too, which showed Matador wasn't carrying much fat. However, outside and in, Matador sedan and wagon were looking dated by the late '70s.

When Matador Coupe sales initially took off, conceptual drawings of sedan and wagon with the Coupe's sleeker styling were done. This rid the sedan of the grandpop image, and the wagon looked like a large Volvo 1800 ES sport wagon. Unfortunately, declining AMC intermediate sales meant the concepts were taken no further. Just as well for George Barris: with a metallic-green Matador, the Green Hornet might have had competition!

Taking into account the Matador Coupes assembled by VAM in Mexico as the "Classic AMX," and in Australia by AMI, the unusual 2-door topped out at approximately 95,000 units. Then there were all the other Matador body styles, not bad for something that started out as *Motor Trend*'s 1963 Car of the Year! Even at the end it was difficult for AMC management to accept the idea that come 1979, American Motors wouldn't be making a family car.

AMC director Andrew G.C. Sage II explained the management mindset that made it difficult to comprehend life without Matador: "There was an almost religious feeling about the car business, and particularly about having a standard-sized car—you were nothing without one."[29] Later, companies like Hyundai and Mitsubishi would have a product portfolio that covered cars, oil tankers, refrigerators, electric fans, etc. Similarly, at different times AMC had subsidiaries that made refrigerators, military vehicles, U.S. postal trucks, lawn and garden tractors, industrial engines and plastic parts.

For a large U.S. corporation, it was normal to have a 6-passenger family car among the goods manufactured. So Matador had important commercial symbolic importance. Would American Motors ever be the same without it? It allowed AMC's influence to extend as far as New Zealand! Campbell Motor Industries (CMI) located in Thames, like AMI in Australia, assembled a number of models for various car companies including AMC. CMI assembled right-hand-drive Ramblers using Canadian-sourced complete knockdown kits.

CMI assembled the Matador until 1975, with the company subsequently becoming Toyota New Zealand. AMI stopped assembling Matadors in 1976, so the British market received its final 1977 Matadors as left-hand-drive imports from America. Continental Europe was served by left-hand-drive AMCs assembled at the Belgian plant run by Renault. So it was that some of the Matadors in Spain came courtesy of American Motors.

Hornet 1975–77—Luxury, Economy and Sport!

The solidity of Hornet sales in its final 3 years was commendable, but one truth seemed inescapable: the small-car boom was over. After the momentous times of 1973–74, Hornet settled back to its original level of 85,991 for '75 and 71,577 in '76, finishing with 77,843 units in '77. It would seem that as in the '60s, general small-car interest wasn't sustained, causing AMC's fortunes to suffer.

In 1974–75, Hornet changes were minimal, AMC concentrating on the new Matador Coupe and Pacer lines. Hornet soldiered on and in 1977 was American Motors' top seller, which was cool because the competitive heat was on. Chrysler's revised compact line now went by the names Dodge Aspen and Plymouth Volare. This family valiantly procured the '76 *Motor Trend* Car of the Year title, and included a wagon that gave Sportabout its first domestic competition.

Chevrolet had recently introduced its sporty rear-drive Monza compact coupe. Along with its cousin the Buick Skyhawk, here were 2+2 hatches that could dent Hornet hatch sales. For 1976, AMC priced Hornet sedan and hatch keenly at the same $3,199 sticker, with Sportabout on a slight premium at $3,549. The big style change for this era was the adoption of a new vertical bar grille on the 1975 Hornet, like the trim piece on the 1966 Project IV Vixen fastback showcar.

Overseas Hornets

In Mexico they never saw a need to get rid of the "American" nameplate; that's what they called Hornet over there. In Australia AMI continued with the '72 Hornet through the 1973 model year. The local assembler got in synch with the U.S. Hornet in the 1974 model year, and carried on with the '74 style into 1975. Hornet sales peaked in Australia at 597 units in 1971. The model's popularity tailed off after 1972, due in part to GM subsidiary Holden's introducing a new, larger '74 Torana that looked a lot like the mid–'70s Hornet.

With a similar range of body styles there was even a Holden Torana hatchback that copied the Hornet hatch's camping-tent feature! Hornet hatchback's "Mini-Camper" option brought a weatherproof covering that fitted over the roof section from the B pillar rearwards, using the open liftback door, with 2 side windows and zippered rear tent opening. AMC's A-mark logo looked quite snazzy on the side too. Holden substituted their logo on the Torana's tent, but Hornet was the first sports hatch to explore the great outdoors!

In total 1,825 Hornets were assembled by AMI during 1970–75. The complete knockdown kits came by shipping container from the Brampton, Ontario, plant. To get around Australian import duty, the AMI Hornets used locally sourced seats, carpeting, headlamps, heaters and other items. AMI Hornets were available in one rationalized spec as a 4-door with power front disks, manual steering, V8 Hornet suspension settings and differential. Automatic transmission was the sole choice, although one or two manual gearbox Hornets may have been made.

AMI Hornets got by on 232/258ci I6 power; however, some 304 V8 cars were custom-done in the state of Western Australia (WA). In WA most AMI Hornets were sold through Premier Motors, with around 30 converted to V8 power by the sole Rambler/AMC service center run by Ben Ludlow. All Australian Hornets were sold under the Rambler marque, and Hornet was also assembled in right-hand-drive form in South Africa to escape that country's high import duty.

Hornet Luxury

AMC was busy fettling Hornet with '76 revisions like redesigned front door storage containers, larger sun visors and a new-style dome light. The 6-color-choice Bravado vinyl grain roof option was new to Sportabout too, which together with Hornet hatch could enjoy the Touring Interior. Touring trim brought individual reclining seats in Sof-Touch tan vinyl, with tan color-matched headlining, sun visors, and sports steering wheel. Wood-

Top: **Hornet, like this '74 Sportabout, continued to be a solid seller for American Motors until the nameplate's 1977 demise (courtesy Alan Wandrei).** ***Bottom:*** **Sales of Hornet dropped to 85,991 units in '75. In 1976 Sportabout got its first domestic wagon competition from Chrysler, when said corporation introduced their Aspen/Volare compacts (courtesy Alan Wandrei).**

grain instrument panel overlay, carpeted lower door panels, tan door-pull straps and AMC's Extra Quiet Insulation Package also came along for the ride.

The Touring Interior was tan only, and wasn't available on Hornet sedan. Correspondingly, the luxo D/L pack was restricted to Hornet Sportabout and sedan. This also had individual reclining front seats, but in Kasmir knit fabric; other equipment was the same as Touring Interior, but Sportabout D/L added exterior profile and rear-deck wood paneling. Sportabout D/L also came fitted with roof rack and rear window air deflector. Once again D/L implied a tan-only interior.

Stretching the Dollar

The mid–'70s was a time of much financial hardship: the auto industry had declined from a strong 11.8-million-unit 1973 total, to a weak 8.2-million 1975 level amid economic stagflation. The oddity about contemporary auto tastes was a desire to combine increased luxury with mile-stretching gasoline economy. EPA MPG numbers were writ large in ads and replaced the horsepower talk of yore.

AMC were firm followers of the Detroit MPG mantra of high load at low rpm. Keep an engine lugging a tall gear to minimize frictional and pumping losses. Low rpm cuts friction; having the gas pedal pushed further means an open throttle plate and an easier-breathing engine. The smallest-engined car isn't always the thriftiest. AMC had the best domestic numbers by having smaller-than-average cars, but atypically large motors.

A 258 Hornet wasn't straining in low like an I4 Pinto, so it drank little and that meant

This loaded '74 Hornet Sportabout was ordered with 258/column-shift auto, a/c, tinted glass, AM radio, individual reclining front seats, Visibility Group, Light Group, Extra Quiet Insulation Package and luggage rack (courtesy Alan Wandrei).

it polluted little. Thus, AMC was mostly able to meet emissions on 49 state cars sans catalytic converter, a potentially troublesome device at the time that most were forced to use come '75. AMC's method to avoid a cat was simpler than BMW's thermal reactors or Honda's stratified charge CVCC.

It was the little things that mattered, like an electronic choke for I6/3-speed manual power teams, new thermostat design, electronic ignition and proportional exhaust gas recirculation (EGR). The thermostat was part of getting the engine warmed up faster and off choke, and polluting less, as quickly as possible. Smart EGR, electronic ignition and Quench Head were about controlling a more thorough burn precisely.

Everyone was using their tricks. Chrysler pacified its V8's thirst and emissions with black-box-controlled Electronic Lean Burn (ELB) ignition. Volvo discovered that injectors squirting on closed intake valves reduced unburned hydrocarbons on their Bosch D-jetronic-fueled ohv I4s and I6s. GM favored the 2-way cat, with their man in charge of the program internally nicknamed "Captain Catalyst"!

With a smaller R&D budget, AMC tried a new-shape I6 carb air passage to good effect, and for '76, AMC had three-quarters of its fleet able to exceed 20 mpg in the EPA highway test without a downsized car in sight. Only the Matador V8s got under 20 mpg. Solution? Stick with Matador sedan and Coupe's base 258! A Hornet X hatch with 1bbl 258 and Torque Command console auto came with a 2.73 final drive standard, 3.08 or 2.53 axles as options.

The new floorshift 4-speed with 2.53 rear gears offered more economy and convenience than the 3-speed manual overdrive gearboxes of 1975 and 1976. Overdrive Hornets had the old-style piggyback, auxiliary OD add-on. Inside, Hornet's overdrive was activated via a turn signal stalk pushbutton. Overdrive was engageable in 3rd only, and automatically disengaged when Hornet slowed under 45 mph, the brakes were touched or the driver went for 2nd.

AMX Returns in Hornet Form

Things were looking up by 1976–77, as engineers got wise to the ins and outs of emissions power tuning. Power ratings were starting to climb again, modestly, and it was time to start enjoying driving again. So why not bring back AMX? The 1976 model year turned out to be the last year for Hornet X, still available on hatch and Sportabout. By the by, Hornet was proving itself a sporty number on the track. Bob Hennig's Hornet notched up several top-5 finishes in the IMSA Baby Grand series during 1973 and 1974.

On August 17, 1974, at Charlotte Motor Speedway, R. Nash, Bob McGraw and Max Sebba's No. 51 Hornet finished 2nd. In 1975, on May 10 at Riverside, Gene Felton's No. 96 Hornet finished 2nd, with Charlie Cook's Hornet following in 3rd. Amos Johnson took a Hornet to 2nd in class at the April 17, 1977, IMSA 100 Mile Road Atlanta race. At the February 5, 1978, World Championship 24 Hours of Daytona, Johnson, along with Dennis Shaw and Charles Woodard, drove their No. 41 Hornet AMX to 9th in GTO class.

For all the racing achievements, Hornet was more about a state of mind than impressing race fans. By the late '70s, "win on Sunday, sell on Monday" didn't exactly hold anymore. Hornet AMX was more attuned to taking a hot date to the Friday night disco, and that date wasn't pleased if one raced a Mustang on the way to said disco. Hornet AMX dazzled

Top: The air filter sticker declares the trusty 258 I6's presence, but one could still order the 360 V8 on '74 Hornet to sting the Big 3 compacts (courtesy Alan Wandrei). ***Bottom:*** AMC's Weather Eye HVAC is as much a part of the domestic-car lexicon as Endura bumpers and Cobra Jet V8s. This was the deluxe dash AMC liked to show in its sales brochures (courtesy Alan Wandrei).

in more subtle ways; in the words of AMC, "1977 Hornet AMX. The AMX comes on strong with a floor shift, console, sporty gauges, soft feel sports steering wheel, and more."

Hornet had honor in being chosen to represent the AMX tag, and the option of the 2bbl 5-liter V8 helped in that respect. Gremlin and Pacer were I6 only in 1977. However, the Hornet AMX's 49-state base power team held the most interest: it could be teamed with a 4-speed, but the V8 could not. The 2bbl 258 I6 had power and torque levels of 120 bhp at 3,600 rpm and 200 lbs/ft at 2,000 rpm; the 2bbl 304 V8's corresponding achievements were 120 bhp at 3,200 rpm and 220 lbs/ft at 2,000 rpm.

California made do with the 1bbl 258, and regardless of location the 304 was auto only. But what of the 4-speed? This wasn't the burly BW T10, but the lighter-duty BW SR4. This 4-speed box was essentially a 3-speed manual with an overdrive 4th added. It was a box found in Mustang II Cobras, and even in the much-vaunted '82 Mustang GT 5.0. The SR4 was a gearbox with a Ford connection: Henry made the casing whereupon the Blue Oval casting is visible.

The SR4 is also known as the "Pinto 4-speed" due to its popular presence in that Ford subcompact, as well as SROD (Single Rail Overdrive). Given that the engines of the era weren't exactly powerhouses, even that '82 Mustang "five point woe" was a 2-barrel 302. There's no point having a heavy-duty gearbox with a lo-po engine; that just makes the vehicle needlessly weighty. The SR4 could cope with around 220 lbs/ft of torque, which was what the 2bbl 5 liters of the era were making.

The 1979 model year was the only year the 2bbl 304 teamed up with the SR4 4-speed in AMC land. Anything hotter than the 304 and SR4's input bearings are likely to fail. In a time of high 17s and low 18s, the best equipment one could have was a sense of humor! That said, magazines showed that with a set of headers, readjusted distributor and carb re-jet, a second or more could be knocked off the elapsed times. So little Hornet AMXs and Mustang II Cobras have potential.

Fortunately, AMC had things well covered in the looks department. The '77 Hornet AMX had a color-keyed bodykit with front spoiler. Fender extensions front and rear blended into the front spoiler and rear valence panel. Along with color-keyed bumpers, this created a subtle, integrated, "hewn from the solid" look worthy of Carl Green! There were flat-black side rear-view mirrors, blacked-out grille and black bumper guard trim too.

The econoracer proudly wore "AMX" callout decals on the lower part of the rear fenders. Optional Hornet "super-graphic" oversized hood decal and deck-lid decal lit the AMX sportlight. Other standard '77 AMX touches were rear window louvers to cut glare, and 6-inch-wide slot rims for the D78 14-inch tires. The tiara on the whole deal was a brushed aluminum Targa roof band, to match the dashboard's aluminum trim. This roof band looked like the type seen on '70s Targa-topped Porsche 911s, which was probably why AMC referred to it in the AMX ad as being of "European style."

AMC's designers had gone to some trouble with the new AMX. Hornet AMX was a tad more special than '76's Hornet X; the '77 AMX package was limited to Hornet hatch, and the bodykit was delivered in "prime" form when ordered as spares. Inside, the fixed-back vinyl buckets were a bit of a drag, considering AMC had been so big on recliners, but at least the instrumentation was complete.

Hornet's extreme right dash gauge clock was replaced by a tach. The console 4-gauge "Rally Pak" had faces angled towards the driver, and from top right going clockwise there

For your comfort, Sportabout offered 35.6 inches and 37.4 inches worth of rear legroom and headroom respectively (courtesy Alan Wandrei).

were instruments for ammeter, oil pressure, water temp and a clock. The Hornet AMX ad showed this console gauge pak, and the ad line reworked boxer Muhammad Ali's old catch phrase. According to AMC, get ready to "Float like a butterfly ... Sting like a Hornet."

The Hornet AMX ad also baited with, "If you think it looks good, wait 'til you feel it perform!" Was there really more to an AMC AMX in '77? It all depended where one performed with AMX. Woodward Avenue wasn't the place for Hornet AMX; drag racing was best left to Scramblers. By this stage even Berry Gordy had moved Motown Records to the West Coast, and California's Highway One was calling AMX.

The coastal road section between Monterey and San Luis Obispo was more Hornet AMX's domain. Challenging twists and turns along with lateral G's were what AMX was about in '77. As horsepower diminished, so came the era of the "handling car." The term muscle car was no longer in circulation; the term "personalized transportation" had arisen to describe cars like Hornet AMX.

Hornet AMX 258 could have a 4-speed with 2.53 final drive, but the 304 option could not. Where had all the V8s gone? In 1975, 8,075 304-powered Hornets were sold; in '77 it was just 4,091 units, even though Hornet's total was stable. In practical times when every buck counted, more people were sliding with the six. In 1968, who could have foreseen an I6-motivated AMX with overdrive 4th, eking out every last drop of petroleum distillate from a huge 22-gallon tank?

It would seem there really was more to AMC in 1977! Hornet was chasing a unibody Toyota Corolla SR5 Liftback with 5-speed overdrive and "2.2 litre 20-R" I4. It was the AMX of its time. Image cars were especially popular in California, where ironically the weakest engine options existed because of the state's strict smog law. In this scenario one's medallion shone just as brightly when sitting in a 1bbl 258 Hornet AMX as in a Trans Am or Corvette. Those cars didn't come with AMC's 2-year/24,000-mile warranty, proving that AMC could at least still cover you like it was the '60s!

CHAPTER 6

Bricklin, Gremlin and Jeep

The Sports Car Malcolm Built ... with AMC Ingredients

Once upon a time there was an entrepreneur called Malcolm Bricklin who wanted to sell America an ultra-economy car. He suspected there were those who considered the Rambler American, and even VW Beetle, too large and wasteful. Thus, in 1968 he imported an initial 332 Subaru 360 microcars, and as a result is historically tied with the founding of Subaru of America. The Subaru 360 was a 2-stroke affair billed as a $1,297 econosavior, but it had some problems.

In Japan the Sube was perfect for congested, narrow city streets, but in America's big roadscape it was out of scale. The 360's speed capability was inadequate for U.S. urban usage; it also struggled with very cold winter weather. Plus, it was scary to drive such a small vehicle when one had to share roads with full-size cars.

The nail was struck into the 360's coffin when *Consumer Reports* stated that the Subaru 360 just wasn't up to snuff for safe American city motoring. That publication famously gave the 360 a "Not Acceptable" rating in April 1969. Bad luck, Malcolm: he parted company with Subaru, but not before taking 1,000 360s with him. However, that wasn't the end of the little Sube.

Fast-forward 5 years and the world was enduring a fuel crisis, with anything small like a Fiat 126 or Citroën 2CV soaring in European sales charts. In America the original Honda Civic was hot property as the '74 EPA gas mileage leader. It was at this hour that *Consumer Reports* discovered their old target, the Subaru 360, had been reactivated! "We hear that some of those early 360s, unused but weather-beaten, are again being marketed. Beware!"[1]

It would seem there's always someone around to take advantage of a crisis. In the mid–1980s Bricklin was at it again, this time with the small economy ride called Yugo. The Yugo was a vehicle made by the company Zastava in Yugoslavia. It was based on the old Fiat 127, with a body design by Zastava. Bricklin saw this as another opportunity to supply North Americans with very low-cost motoring. Although the Yugo had a low price as a new vehicle, objective tests by magazines concluded the consumer would get better value from a used car of more modern design.

In between the Subaru 360 and Yugo, Bricklin decided he would build a sports car, but not just any sports car ... a safety sports car! Being an economy car guy, he could rightly approach only one member of Detroit's Big 4 for some key parts: economy expert AMC! Yes, the Bricklin SV-1 was motorvated by AMC's still-potent 220 bhp 4bbl 360 V8 with duals. Inside, one would recognize the dashboard molding and automatic console shifter as being of AMC Pacer origin.

The Bricklin SV-1 (Safety Vehicle One) was like a forerunner of the DeLorean DMC-12: it was a Pantera with a conscience. The idea was to design a sports car that cared about the environment, the occupants it carried, and any pedestrians who might accidentally get run over. Thus, with SV-1 there was a choice of 5 exterior safety "day-glow" colors, and the body featured a soft nose cone. The interior was devoid of cigarette lighter or associated ashtray, because as you know, fire is dangerous.

The Bricklin SV-1 had fiberglass body panels using bonded acrylic and featuring futuristic powered electro-pneumatic gullwing doors. Body panels were made in a separate Minto, New Brunswick, Canada, factory. At a time when horsepower ratings were going south, the exceptional AMC 360 V8 was on Bricklin's list of passive safety items, providing ample passing reserves to avoid an accident in the first place. Malcolm obviously wanted to do the Cannonball Run in complete safety.

Unfortunately the Bricklin SV-1's financial plan was less secure. The sports car was put together in Saint John, New Brunswick, and things always get ugly when local politics are involved. The premier at the time was Richard Hatfield, and it transpired he funded the failing Bricklin enterprise to secure re-election. Local production, employment creation, kissing babies and all that jazz! It seems that the whole Bricklin SV-1 project was in dire financial straits from very early on.

The debacle has gone down in Canadian political history as the "Bricklin Election," quite infamous, something to scare small children with. Whatever happened to Bricklin's SV-1? Not a great deal: in 1974, 772 were produced, 137 with 4-speed manual. However, in 1975 and 1976, all SV-1s were automatics, and with AMC unable to contractually continue supplying V8s, Malcolm switched to Ford 2bbl 351 V8 power with a 175 bhp rating. Perhaps AMC was just too embarrassed to keep meeting Bricklin.

Early SV-1 ownership experience showed that the sports car wasn't as thoroughly engineered as it might have been. Bricklin enthusiasts today have remedies for the 2,854 SV-1s that were built. Money was lost on each SV-1 sold, and the car's demise and factory closure were sad indeed. With mid–'70s economic gloom, the only amusement left was watching a Pinto burn down in the street. That Yugo seemed ever so far away.

Return to the Planet of the Gremlins

Mirroring the fortunes of Hornet, Gremlin was having a hard time by the mid–'70s. In the '60s, Chairman Romney's false dawn of functionality left AMC in the wilderness until Javelin shot through. This time small wonders weren't a permanent solution, but at least AMC wasn't alone. The sales decline of '74 affected both big and small cars industry-wide; it just slugged the giants more so. Yes, the fuel crisis-sparked recession saw a 40–60 percent drop in full-size car sales compared to the record U.S. auto industry '73 harvest, but sales of subcompacts declined too.

Vega, Nova, Pinto and Maverick sales were also adversely affected by the downturn. Look closer and sales of all size categories were on a downer in the first half of '74; compacts and intermediates weren't immune.[2] The masses were pretty mad: cost-push inflation and

Gremlins could become dragstrip terrors with sufficient modification, as this 1976 model demonstrates (courtesy Eddie Stakes).

safety/pollution control federal dictates were producing more expensive new cars that didn't run that well, and were less economical on average. Truth to tell, the '73 family Impala didn't have desirable driveability either.

When placed between a rock and a hard place, people take desperate measures, like resorting to austerity. This explained how Plymouth Valiant sales actually rose 18 percent in the first half of '74. The 1974 model year would prove to be Gremlin's biggest result of all time, 171,128 units. However, AMC did extend the '74 model year to avoid catalytic converters, and the 1973 calendar year showed Gremlin's true sales peak (133,146) if one is looking for the fastest sales rate. In conclusion, the best of times were over by '75.

Sad to say, AMC was offering $200 rebate sweeteners to entice Gremlin buyers, and the austerity bug manifested itself by the falling popularity of the 304 V8 option. In 1975, 56,011 Gremlins were sold, including 52,601 I6 cars and only 3,410 with the V8. To help folks go further on less, AMC introduced Prestolite electronic ignition on its engines, and together with other tuning measures, plus taller final drives, improved its fleet average, with Gremlin 232 rising from 24 mpg to 30 mpg on the '76 EPA highway rating.

Electric overdrive was a new '75 Gremlin option for manual cars to stretch the gasoline. Style change was minimal in '75: AMC was focused on Pacer, with Gremlin getting a slight bumper revision, with more extensive changes for '76. The '76 restyle witnessed a change from circular to oval headlamp bezels, hexagon-shaped headlamp surrounds and stretched-hexagon front grille with round turn signals.

The Gremlin X's side stripe style also differed in '76, with amended, less curvy, spear-type stripe. The hockey stripes still swept onto the sail panel, but there was an extended spear base that included "Gremlin X" decal script, and went over the rear wheel well to the rear side marker. The front side marker lights were changed for '76, as part of the front restyle.

In 1976, Gremlin was available in a plusher Custom variant at $3,160. For $109 over base Gremlin, one received Custom split-bench front seats in Fairway pleated vinyl, full

AMC's 1977 Buyer Protection Plan II covered this Gremlin X for 2 years or 24,000 miles, whichever came first. The X pack's side decals were new for '77 (courtesy Robert Zabawa).

front and rear carpeting, Custom steering wheel and door trim panels, chrome drip rail moldings, chrome rocker panel moldings, Custom grille and spare tire cover. Optional was a Potomac Stripe fabric trim for seating, available in black, blue, green or tan. A "rally stripe" was also optional, and resembled the 1974–75 X hockey stripe decal.

In early Gremlin days, a Gremlin character logo was placed on the front fenders. Now base Gremlin could be distinguished from Custom by the Gremlin logo sitting on the sail panel, next to the canted vanes, as well as by an absence of brightwork. Gremlin sales weren't too bright in Bicentennial year, and AMC reduced prices for base and Gremlin Custom to $2,889 and $2,998 respectively. The 304 V8 option was dropped mid-year after just 826 Gremlin V8s had been sold. The Gremmy total for '76 was 52,941.

Gremlin Goes Racing

Emissions don't matter in racing, and fuel economy only counts in time-wasting pitstops. After the megabuck SCCA T/A series exploded with sponsors scattered to the four winds, the IMSA Baby Grand sedans treated race fans with down-to-earth grocery-getters. It was a series started in 1971 for small cars, with Class A covering cars with 1600cc ohc/2000cc ohv 4-cylinder motors. Class B dealt with larger-engined, more powerful small cars, which concerned Gremlin.

The track exploits of Gremlin had much to do with the racing activities of Amos Johnson and his Levi's Team Highball (LTH) operation. Johnson hailed from Durham, North Carolina; his teammate in early Gremlin times was Whit Diggett from Raleigh, North Carolina. Johnson raced the No. 7 LTH Gremlin; Diggett drove the No. 0 LTH Gremlin. The

This Hotscotch Orange '77 Gremlin X was specified with 258, console-shift auto, map light, a/c, power steering, power brakes and Rally rims. In mid-1988 Gary Bradley of Wahoo, Nebraska, did a 360 V8 conversion, which was followed by an early '90s 401 swap. The rear wheels and suspension as shown are nonstandard (courtesy Robert Zabawa).

racecraft was a 1971 Gremlin 232 3-speed manual that first socked it to 'em on June 10, 1972, at Donnybrooke when Johnson and Diggett came 1st and 3rd outright respectively.

On November 18 that year Whit Diggett finished 1st at Daytona International Speedway, with Johnson coming in 4th. A third Daytona LTH victory followed in the first event of the IMSA-sanctioned 1973 B.F. Goodrich Radial Challenge Series. The Citrus 200 saw a 1–2 result for Johnson and Diggett, but with some drama for the latter. Johnson led for most of the race on his way to 1st place, as Diggett came flying from 44th on the grid to snatch 2nd! It was a notable 1–2 that AMC mentioned in its Gremlin ad, proudly picturing Johnson's No. 7 Gremlin.

The ad stated Gremlin beat out a 52-car field composed of Capri, Pinto, Vega, Toyota, Opel and Mazda and said, "You may never want to race at Daytona. But it's kind of nice to drive a winner—AMC Gremlin—We back them better because we build them better." The opportunity wasn't lost to mention Javelin's Trans Am series triumphs and Matador's NASCAR Riverside win. So AMC cared about more than just the human race! AMC wasn't kidding about the diverse competition Gremlin was facing.

Pictured on the Daytona banking of an IMSA Baby Grand Sedan race were Ford Pinto, BMW 2002, Toyota Celica, Saab 96 V4, Mazda RX2, Datsun 1600, Chevy Vega and Opel, plus AMC Gremlin! In addition, concerning the Citrus 200, McCreary Tire & Rubber Co. ran an ad concerning the LTH 1–2 victory, mentioning how Johnson and Diggett were circulating on McCreary Radial road tires. It was also stated that Johnson's winning car recorded an average speed of 89.327 mph for the 202-mile February 16 event.

Baby Grand tin-top racing showed what was available for the economy/small car buyer, racers not far removed from showroom examples. Whether it was in the sales charts or on the track, the battle was fierce. In achieving a third consecutive LTH victory at Daytona on April 21, Amos Johnson tussled with the team of 2 Electrodyne Pintos and Mercury Capri. It was even piston versus rotary out there! On September 15 at Lime Rock, *Car and Driver*'s Patrick Bedard finished 1st in his Mazda RX2, John Morton 2nd in a BMW 2002 and Amos Johnson 3rd in a Gremlin.

Bedard also won in the RX2 on September 30 at Road Atlanta, with George Alderman's Gremlin placing 2nd. However, Amos Johnson's chief rival in 1973 was Nick Craw in the Miller & Norburn BMW 2002. Craw tied with Johnson on 34 points by winning the October 14 B.F. Goodrich Three Hour race at Indianapolis. In a technical result, team boss Russ Norburn had Craw down as driving both team cars. Craw partnered John Morton and Russ Norburn. Thus, even when Craw's car he was sharing with Morton expired, he was still the race winner as Norburn took the checkered flag in the sister BMW. Craw had done the minimum driving time in both cars required to claim victory.

Johnson and Diggett finished 2nd and 3rd respectively, which set everything up for the showdown that was the November 24 Daytona finale. In this night race, things got messed up for Amos Johnson, when Bob Hennig's race-leading Hornet spun out in front of his No. 7 Gremlin. In the skirmish, Hennig's Hornet clipped Johnson's Gremlin, causing the Gremlin to lose its headlamps. Whit Diggett stopped and handed his No. 0 car to Johnson, who went like a bat out of hell, overtaking Craw's BMW and winning the race!

Nick Craw's BMW expired during the race, so that would have made Johnson series champion, but there was a post-race protest. Craw questioned the timing of the Diggett to Johnson hand-over, and there was a problem. Unknown to Levi's Team Highball at the time, the hand-over occurred after the race's halfway point, so Johnson ended up getting no points. In the end Johnson and Craw, still tied at 34 points, were crowned joint champions, and shared the 1st and 2nd place prize money. The manufacturer's title went to AMC.

With 1978 came the final model year for Gremlin. Sales had fallen appreciably since the 1977 restyle, as smaller-engined imports and domestics put pressure on AMC's subcompact (courtesy Joe and Peggy Howard).

The B.F. Goodrich Radial Challenge continued into 1974, and the fuel crisis seemed to make small-car racing even more relevant. With a nod to the times, Carson Baird took his diminutive No. 8 Dodge Colt to victory on May 18 at Ontario Motor Speedway. Baird got his Class A Baby Grand sled through 180 minutes sans refueling! The thirstier, bigger-engined Class B BMWs and Gremlins had to pitstop for gas.

In a story reminiscent of the tortoise and the hare, Howdy Holmes' No. 10 Gremlin finished 2nd, 13 seconds behind Baird. Definitely a case of slower, but rock steady, wins the race. LTH was winning in '74 too; this time Amos Johnson was driving with Dennis Shaw. The pair won at Mid-Ohio on June 29, 1974, in lucky No. 7 Gremlin, finishing ahead of George Alderman and Brett Lunger in their No. 32 Gremlin. LTH won the 6-hour race by one minute!

Another strong showing for LTH came on August 10 at Talladega, with Shaw and Johnson finishing 2nd and 3rd respectively. However, Nick Craw won the race in his BMW 2002. On September 2 at Lime Rock, Craw won by 5 seconds from Johnson in 2nd and George Alderman in 3rd. This gave Craw a 17-point championship lead, but once again the outcome of the November 30 Daytona finale would prove championship decisive.

George Alderman recorded pole position for the 1974 Daytona finale; he won the race and the driver's title, but it wasn't that straightforward. Nick Craw retired from the race with a blown engine, Alderman passed Ray Korman's BMW, and next up was race leader Amos Johnson's Gremlin. Johnson couldn't improve his position in the driver's championship by winning the Daytona finale; he would still end up 3rd. However, he could affect the series in AMC's favor.

Johnson let Alderman through to win the race, which knocked Craw into 2nd in the championship, giving the driver's title to an AMC driver, and the manufacturer's title to AMC once again in 1974. Johnson said the decision to move over was sweet revenge in light of Craw's '73 Daytona finale protest, and was in no way the result of an order from American Motors. The teams fielding the No. 7 and No. 32 Gremlins were private outfits, but that didn't mean some informal AMC solidarity couldn't enter the equation!

Events started well for LTH in 1975, and there were good results during the year, but the gold medal just eluded Johnson. At the January 31 Daytona evening race, Johnson and Shaw finished 1st and 2nd respectively in their Gremlins. At the subsequent 24 Hours of Daytona on February 2, the No. 7 LTH Gremlin of Johnson, Steve Coleman and Dennis Shaw finished 17th overall. The only mod done on the car was using the wheels and racing tires of the Gremlin Radial Challenge Pace Car.

The No. 7 Gremlin was the highest-placed U.S.-built car at the 1975 24 Hours of Daytona. The Gremlin was mostly solid, Johnson just adding, "The clutch was slipping a little at the end," which was reported in the June 1975 issue of *Road & Track*. Johnson won at Road Atlanta on April 20, and on May 4 at Laguna Seca, LTH did another 1–2 victory, Shaw and Johnson finishing 1st and 2nd respectively on that occasion.

Dennis Shaw won again on May 10 at Riverside using the LTH Gremlin, and once again the driver's championship decider for 1975 would be the Daytona finale. Gene Felton qualified on pole and won the race, Nick Craw finished 2nd in the BMW 2002, with Steve Coleman in 3rd driving Gremlin that November 29 day. Amos Johnson decided to try out his new Pacer for the race, and he qualified 4th. However, the Pacer suffered newbie gremlins, so it finished 7th. This was enough to give Craw the 1975 driver's title. Johnson was runner-up.

That wasn't the end of the story for the LTH No. 7 Gremlin. The 5-time Daytona winner, which competed in IMSA RS (Racing Stocks) from 1971 to 1976, currently takes part in SVRA, HSR historic racing. It has been updated with 1977 Gremlin sheet metal and an uprated 258 I6. However, on the rear deck it still carries the Gremlin X style "3.8 litre" cursive typeface script on a white background, contrasting with the blue surround of an AMC red, white and blue color scheme!

1977—A Brave New Economy Car World

By the late '70s the VW Beetle was at an end. Dominant in the early '70s, VW was a couple of years late with its Rabbit replacement. The Super Beetle ended in '76 with lavish Detroit-style loaded limited editions like "The Sun Bug" and "La Grande Bug." By 1977 the standard Beetle Classic 1200 tallied just 12,090 U.S. sales; Rabbit was the new VW volume seller. However, the big sellers in the econobox league were now the Japanese firms, and they were offering a lot.

Remember when suddenly everyone owned Datsuns? The Datsun 710 range included power front disk brakes, unibody construction and reclining front seats as standard equipment. By 1976 one could buy a 710 2-door hardtop with color-contrasting "710" sidestripe

As economy fever rose, buyers were increasingly eschewing AMC's I6 in favor of the optional 2-liter I4. The four-cylinder versions went from 16.4 percent of Gremlin sales in 1977 to 29 percent in 1978 (courtesy Joe and Peggy Howard).

decal, 2-liter ohc I4 and 4-speed console shifter with EPA city/highway numbers of 23/33 mpg. The car had been National SCCA champ 2 years in a row. Nissan liked to say, "Datsun Saves — America's #1 Selling Import."

Honda's CVCC I4 1.5 liter Civic 5-speed Hatch had EPA city/highway figures of 35/47 mpg in 1976. With its transverse engine and front-drive power pack, '77 Civic could say it was the U.S. EPA gas mileage leader for the 4th consecutive year. Now that the economy car had moved on from air-cooled VW, what was Gremlin to do? Gremlin got smaller, for one thing. In 1977, Gremlin was restyled with a sloping nose that made it 4 inches shorter. The '77 Gremlin received a new hood with power bulge, shorter front fenders, less fussy bumpers and crosshatch grille with returned rectangular turn signals.

The round headlamps sat in square bezels with rounded edges. Front side marker lights were smaller, subtler horizontal units. Gremlin's rear fascia was reworked, too, with a larger, frameless liftback rear window like '77 Pinto. Larger, square, round-edged taillights accompanied a fuel filler that now lived behind the rear license plate. Previously there was the Gremlin cartoon character etched into the chrome filler cap. Unfortunately this arty item often got stolen, much as VW grille badges were purloined in the '80s by Beastie Boys fans.

Gremlin was looking like a small car again, and a pretty neat one in X spec. Gremlin's X sidestripe was redone for '77 into a spear with two-piece raised base. Base Gremlin was also given more bling with chrome wheel lip moldings and rain gutter trim, lockable and lighted glove box, extra interior carpeting and standard front disks. For another, Gremlin's revised Quench Head I6s were more economical, and with the V8 scratched, the subcompact came with Pacer line engine choices, including base 1bbl 232, and the optional 1bbl and 2bbl 258s. However, in 1977 people wanted more MPGs.

Back in '72, University of California researchers won a national Urban Vehicle Design Competition with a Gremlin designed to run on hydrogen. That said, AMC was looking for a more practical way to boost Gremlin economy: a 4-cylinder engine. AMC didn't have an I4 on their shelf, or the time and resources to cook one up, so they got the VW/Audi/Porsche EA827 2-liter I4 instead. In Gremlin's application that spelled an 80-horse 2bbl Holley carb version, with soft engine mounts to pacify 4-cylinder NVH.

AMC said the 2bbl Holley was the best-matched domestic carb for the 2-liter, especially when coping with the 50,000-mile emissions certification process, with its attendant good vibrations! AMC didn't have the resources to cope with the Bosch K-Jetronic fuel injection used by the Germans with this I4. The plan was to initially buy in the motor from VW, then assemble it at a newly acquired Richmond, Indiana, plant from January 1977. The Gremlin got the I4 as a mid–'77 model year option.

Optional the I4 was indeed: due to the expense of the licensing agreement, AMC couldn't make the 2-liter a base engine. The 232 I6 remained the standard power plant, with the 2-liter being present if one ordered Gremlin Custom. The standard Gremlin 232 3-speed floorshift manual came with a 21-gallon gas tank; the 2-liter Gremlin Custom had the 2 liter/4-speed manual floorshift power team and 13-gallon tank. The 4-cylinder Gremlin used the BW HR1 4-speeder.

The overhead cam I4 had a cast-iron block, crossflow aluminum head and quite some build-up potential. Observe the 1980–82 North American spec Porsche 924 Turbo with 3-way cat, Bosch K-Jetronic, KKK turbo version of the EA827 2-liter. This version of Gremlin's I4 had 143 horsepower and was 50-state legal. In European intercooled trim the 2-liter made over 200 bhp, and powered a Porsche to 6th place outright at the 1980 Le Mans 24 Hour race.

Voila! AMC instantly had a 4-cylinder subcompact with Gremlin Custom 2-liter. *Consumer Reports* pitted this Gremlin against 3 other ultra-misers in July 1977. The luminaries were Chevy Chevette, Dodge Colt M/M (Mileage-Maker), Subaru DL 2-door sedan and Gremlin Custom. All four came with 4 on the floor and price tags above 3 grand. Saving money had become an expensive business. With its new '77 duds, Gremlin looked very dapper pictured alongside the others, and equally modern.

These cars were all about fuel efficiency, and the new 2-liter put Gremlin in the economy ballpark. Gremlin recorded city/highway numbers of 17.5/29.5 mpg, which weren't far removed from the EPA figures of 21/33 mpg. Performance wasn't too shabby either. *Consumer Reports* matched *Motor Trend*'s 17.9 second 0–60 mph time, 3 seconds slower than a downsized GM full-size 5-liter V8 sedan, but 10 mpg better on average fuel consumption.

The extent some were prepared to go for economy was shocking. The Chevette Scooter was GM's price leader in '76, reviving the '50s no-rear-seat decontenting tradition. The U.S.-assembled pair, Chevette and Gremlin Custom, were less well-equipped than their Japanese counterparts, and the Dodge was a captive import. Thus, one had to pay even more for radials, or the Gremlin's $71 rear window defogger that shut off automatically after 10 minutes.

Look a little more closely, and Gremlin's compact-derived shortcomings were apparent. Gremlin Custom 2-liter was the only contemporary subcompact around that actually needed power steering, a $133 option. Plus, interior space efficiency wasn't as good as the front-drive Subaru's. *Consumer Reports* said Gremlin was so short on rear legroom that the rear seat could have passed muster as a modern-day iron maiden![3] In being converted to an I4 with aluminum intake manifold, Gremlin lost 250 lbs. However, even this reduction wasn't enough to match the best Japanese economy.

With 2bbl 258 Gremlin was something of a street sleeper, but midway through the 1978 model year, AMC introduced the GT pack for 258 extroverts (courtesy Joe and Peggy Howard).

With its small four, the Colt Mileage-Maker posted city/highway stats of 19/37.5 mpg. As a cut-down compact Gremlin, even at 2,660 lbs, was heavier than the opposition, which meant its I4 had to be a bit bigger than in cars like the Rabbit to maintain the same acceleration. However, technology of the day meant the trade-off in lost comfort, performance and safety to get better economy was severe.

The four-cylinder subcompacts were all cramped, acceleration was meager and crash safety was dubious. Gremlin easily had the strongest body in subcompact land, and its Hornet background promised some comfort for front-seat travelers. The engine showed up its non–AMC origin in driveability. Normally AMC I6s were good on emissions and driveability, but the 2-liter was unavailable in California and still needed a 2-way catalytic convertor as a 49-state engine. Even with cat it didn't run as well as AMC's I6.

The 2-liter had a reputation for being durable, but noisy. However, *Consumer Reports* found Gremlin Custom 2-liter tested out quieter overall than the I6 Gremmy they tried in 1975. The $34 Extra Quiet Insulation Package helped in that regard. If anything, Gremlin was starting to be like the old Beetle it once hunted. With a high, difficult-to-see-over instrument panel and foot-operated parking brake, Gremlin wasn't a user-friendly subcompact, but it did have quality.

A very low 15 sample defects were noticed by *Consumer Reports*, and in 1977 AMC introduced its upgraded Buyer Protection Plan II warranty. In the era of movie sequels like *The Exorcist II* and *Jaws 2*, a sequel sign was tacked onto many products to imply a sense of modernity and progress, like Mustang II. However, BPP II really was better. The original

This '78 Gremlin has Sunshine Yellow exterior, tan interior, 258/auto column shift, a/c, front buckets and Twin-Grip differential (courtesy Joe and Peggy Howard).

BPP had good things like comprehensive coverage, more carefully inspected vehicles, a loaner car if necessary, and toll-free hotline to AMC HQ. Now, for the first time since the '60s, AMC gave a 2-year warranty.

BPP II looked after all major drivetrain and engine components for 24 months or 24,000 miles, whichever came first. Service adjustments outside regular scheduled servicing were free, and then there was the new Trip Interruption Protection (TIP). There you were, tooling along in a Gremlin Custom 2-liter, or any new '77 AMC, on vacation, when you broke down 100 or more miles from home, and your friendly AMC/Jeep dealer couldn't fix the problem in a day. Have no fear, AMC was there, to pay up to $150 in food and lodging expenses.

BPP II and TIP also worked in Canada, honored by American Motors (Canada) Limited, so wherever you were, AMC was there with "the ONLY full new automobile warranty in America." The 2-year warranty was something VW was known for offering on Beetle, when the brand had a rock-solid reputation. This was another reason to choose Gremlin Custom 2-liter, and in the words of *Motor Trend* it was "as fun to drive as it is simple."

On the fun front, AMC displayed a Gremlin Custom 2-liter with optional X package in their 1978 catalogue. X pack had its sidestripes changed yet again for '78. In a radical move, a decal now ran on the lower third of Gremlin X's side. This was a coast-to-coast wide band decal containing "Gremlin X" script writ large. The decal color also adorned fender lips, and the whole shebang was like the new '78 Concord Sport's get-up.

In 1978 Gremlin was classed up with the new Concord's upscale square-dial dash, but many expected more from AMC. A new front-drive 2,000-pound hatch designed to fight Rabbit was the hoped-for home of the 2-liter/4-speed combo. Sadly, AMC lacked the cash for an all-new econoride, so Gremlin I4 had to do. Signs were that the public now mentally identified subcompacts with I4s exclusively. Four-cylinder Gremlin sales went up from 16.4 percent of the Gremmy mix in '77, to 29 percent in 1978.

AMC didn't ignore speed demons. Midway through the '78 model year American Motors introduced Gremlin GT. The GT pack was like Gremlin X on steroids; it was extreme. There was a fiberglass bodykit influenced by the '78 Concord AMX, featuring a deep front spoiler and all-around fender flares. The front airdam blended into the front flares, and 5-spoke sport wheels with trim rings were covered by DR70 14-inch outline-white-letter steel-belted radials.

Further functional GT items were front swaybar, Extra Quiet Insulation Package and standard 258 motor. All Gremlin GTs had the 258; the V8 was still absent. Inside, the Concord dash accommodated a tach, and the angled quad circular console instrument pack was just like Hornet/Concord AMX. Indeed, the GT's engine turned finish dash had more of the metal-look material than the '76 Gremlin X's early dash. Soft-feel vinyl buckets and sports steering wheel were Gremlin items of old.

Gremlin GT was completely color keyed. The bumpers and bodykit were in body matching color, and bumpers came with guards and protective strips. GT had a dechromed exterior, with blacked-out window line trim, side rear-view mirrors, front grille and even wiper arms because chrome was out of fashion. The outline of the front spoiler and fender flares were meticulously pinstriped, and Gremlin GT sported a profile mid-body spear stripe that recalled pre–'74 Gremlin X's.

With all the above in mind, no wonder AMC said, "Introducing Gremlin GT. If you want it any racier, paint a number on the door." It was enough to strike fear into the heart of any CAFE racer! AMC advertising suggested, "Take me to your highway," but fewer than 2,000 Gremlin GT purchasers did, making this model a rare collectible. Gremlin in general was getting rare on the road by this stage too.

The major reworking of '77 yielded 46,171 Gremlin sales, but this number fell to 22,104 in 1978. The public's idea of small car thrift had moved down a size. Back in 1970 less than 1 percent of Chevy Nova buyers chose a 4-cylinder engine, so the motor choice was dropped by '71. By the late '70s an I4 micro captive import like the new Ford Fiesta was notching up sales and helping Ford's CAFE fleet average.

So 1978 was the last year for Gremlin, although VAM in Mexico continued with the name in the 1979 model year. For creative production achievements, AMI in Australia even assembled one right-hand-drive Gremlin, with the car shown at the 1970 Sydney Motor Show. The vehicle was shipped to a U.S. collector after the year 2000. AMI didn't go on to assemble the Gremlin in Australia. With a total of nearly 700,000 Gremlins made in North America, AMI's omission was slight.

With that many made, Gremlin was popular on the street and in the world of entertainment. In the opening episodes of the *Planet of the Apes* 1974 TV series, a Gremlin is street-parked in what remained of the world the time traveling astronauts left behind. A Gremlin hung upside down on the capsized ocean liner of the movie *Beyond the Poseidon Adventure* (1979), starring Michael Caine.

An AMC Gremlin was also cheekily included in the 1984 movie *Gremlins*. At the start, character Billy Peltzer's inventor father buys the Mogwai creature called Gizmo as a present for his son. The cute Mogwai creature can turn into the evil, mischievous Gremlin! The Gremlin motor car was once again street-shown when Gizmo was bought.

Like Pacer, the Gremlin's impact has extended beyond the mere automotive world, and the period from which it came. Richard Teague didn't want Gremlin going stale, and the car's unusual looks and character certainly stopped that from happening. Actually, even in 1978 Gremlin wasn't quite done. AMC being the legendary recyclers that they were, they came up with something for *The Simpsons*' Hans Moleman to trade in on. Gremlin would be back in spirit!

Got Jeep?

In 1939 Joe Frazer became president and general manager of Willys-Overland, and he did an important thing. Frazer made it a priority that Willys-Overland get the U.S. Army contract to supply a general purpose (G.P.) vehicle. G.P. is where the Jeep name came from, a name Joe Frazer had the foresight to register as a Willys-Overland trademark, something that would be of value to several companies in the decades to come.

With the success of supplying vehicles in World War II and Korea, Willys-Overland wore the military Jeep contract as a badge of honor. Even in advertising its Aero Willys, the company added a small tag saying "Made by the makers of the world-famous Jeep — with billions of miles of tough service — production for Defense is our business." It's great being a defense contractor for Jeeps, jet engine parts and such when there's a war on, but what about peacetime?

Between 1941 and 1951 Willys-Overland concentrated on Jeep, and it niched itself into a corner. So along came Henry J. Kaiser to buy Willys-Overland for $60 million. Not subscribing

The Jeepster Commando was one of the off-roaders AMC gained when it purchased Kaiser Jeep in 1970. By the time of this '72 example the model was renamed Jeep Commando (courtesy Noah Gresham).

to the rational expectations of hypothesis thinking, Kaiser Corporation also heavily concentrated on Jeep, ceasing normal cars at the end of '55. Along the trail, all trace of Willys-Overland was lost. Willys-Overland Motors, Inc., morphed into 1963's Kaiser Jeep Corporation complex, which did ... well ... Jeep!

Next on the scene was American Motors, with an intention to buy Jeep. The intention mainly belonged to AMC boss Roy D. Chapin Jr., who had to conquer major internal AMC dissent. Jeep looked like a dead duck at the time, but Chapin saw something the others didn't. It proved to be historical redemption. On the subject of Pacer's relative failure, Chapin commented that it was "the bitterest pill I've had to live with," but buying Kaiser Jeep would prove great for Jeep and AMC.[4]

AMC paid $70 million to get Jeep in 1970, $10 million of which was in cash. For the money AMC got Kaiser's Toledo, Ohio, Jeep Universal factory and a model range that encompassed Jeep CJ-5/6, Wagoneer, Gladiator pickup and Jeepster Commando. In the '60s Kaiser Jeep had lost market share to domestic off-road competition from Chevy, Ford and International Harvester. Imports like the Toyota Land Cruiser and Nissan Patrol also took their toll. Jeep was no longer a license to print money. AMC would have to do something with the brand.

The AMCization of Jeep

The CJ-5 and CJ-6 correspond to what most people still think of as the classic Jeep. The '54 CJ-5 was a development of the 1953–68 CJ-3B, all with the Korean War Willys-

Overland M-38A1 as a design precedent. The CJ-5 had an 81-inch wheelbase, with the longer 1956 CJ-6 using a 101-inch wheelbase. AMC upgraded both with heavier-duty axles, bigger brakes and wider track. American Motors also re-engined the models with its own power plants.

Jeep adopted an optional 90-degree Buick Dauntless 225ci V6 in 1966 to answer criticism that I4 Jeeps were underpowered. This proved popular, so by 1968 75 percent of CJ-5s had the V6, which Kaiser Jeep was making under license in Toledo, Ohio. The Buick V6 was peppy but rough, and AMC wanted to use its own I6. Since the AMC I6 was quite long, the CJs were rebodied for '72 with a 5-inch nose stretch, which extended the hood and fenders. The CJ-5's wheelbase increased to 83.5 inches at this time.

So 1971 was the last year for the Dauntless V6 in CJ Jeep, and 1972 saw the choice of AMC 232/258 I6 or even 304 V8! That was all cool, but if CJ was Jeep's past, Wagoneer was Jeep's future. As with CJ-5, Kaiser was well in charge when Willys-Overland was working on the revolutionary Wagoneer. The 1963 Wagoneer designed by Brooks Stevens was quite simply the world's first SUV. It used the new modern Willys-Overland 1962 230ci overhead cam I6, front independent suspension, with the availability of power steering and automatic transmission.

With a 90 mph speed potential, the Wagoneer combined Jeep off-road prowess with road manners alien to any truck. The front independent suspension was subsequently replaced with a sturdier solid axle, but no matter; history had been made 7 years before the 1970 British Range Rover. That 230-cube overhead cam motor had some overheating troubles,

The AMCization of Jeep extended beyond simply popping an AMC logo onto the steering wheel. Over time AMC introduced its own engines, sturdier axles and a streamlined business model for the Jeep brand (courtesy Noah Gresham).

and in 1966 AMC's 232 I6 replaced the ohc I6 in Wagoneer. Already, in 1965, Wagoneer had gained the option of American Motors' 327 V8. Note that all these changes occurred under Kaiser's watch.

The V8 option further enhanced Wagoneer's on-road appeal, and it was quite a mover in its day. Whatever the terrain, have V8 will travel. Uncle Tom McCahill thought so: "Low low is rarely needed but when it is it comes on like Batman — pow." Using the 250 bhp 8.7:1 compression ratio 327 V8, the May 1966 *Mechanix Illustrated* report gave a 0–60 mph time of 13.8 seconds. Uncle Tom McCahill correctly predicted that a vehicle like Wagoneer could be all types of car to many people, rolled into one.

Another pointer to the future, also released at the same hour as Wagoneer, was the Gladiator-Series J. The J-thousand series pickup was produced in single-wall bed "Thrift-side," and double-wall bed "Townside" forms. A large vehicle from Kaiser times, it was incorporated into AMC's program of Jeep mechanical and trim pack changes. The pickup was known by its J10 and J20 trim tags as the '70s wore on.

The 327 V8 option on large Jeeps ended in 1967, since AMC switched to their new small-block V8. So in 1968–70 Jeep Wagoneer turned to the Buick 350 V8 for torque. Under AMC ownership Wagoneer was introduced to 360 and 401 V8 power from 1971 onwards. There were some power team bell housing changes that accompanied AMC's introduction of Chrysler's Torqueflite in 1972. The AMC V8 bell housing pattern also changed in the move from the old 327 V8 to the small-block V8.

In 1972 the AMC I6 bell housing pattern was altered to match the AMC V8's pattern. Previously the AMC 196/199/232 shared the same bell housing bolt pattern, with the older 196 having different dowel pin sizes. Such differences could be seen on Jeep models fitted with AMC motors in the Kaiser and AMC ownership eras. The last model AMC inherited from Kaiser Corporation was the Jeepster Commando.

The Jeepster was originally a rear-wheel-drive-only, more car-like Jeep, produced by Willys-Overland in 1948–50. The Jeepster was revived with all-wheel drive in 1966 as the C-101 Jeepster Commando. The Jeepster Commando had various body styles, including station wagon, convertible, pickup and roadster. In the C-101's final 1971 production year, Hurst Performance did a special Hurst Jeepster, in the style of the earlier Scrambler.

The rare Hurst Jeepster had a Champagne White exterior, plus red and blue stripes, along with Hurst logos. An 8,000 rpm rev counter was built into the back of the Hurst Jeepster's hoodscoop. Other visual items were a roof rack and Goodyear G70–15 inchers with raised white letters on wider steel rims. Manual transmission versions had the famous Hurst T-handle ergonomic shifter. Automatic Hurst Jeepsters had Hurst's Dual-Gate "His & Hers" console shifter. The obligatory sports steering wheel came along for the ride too!

A total of 57,350 C-101s were built before AMC revised the range into the 1972 C-104 Commando. AMC dropped the Jeepster name for '72, gave the model a conventional full-width grille and generally tried to normalize the Jeep Commando into a volume concern, but no dice. In spite of giving it the old college try, just 20,223 Commandos were sold in 1972–73. AMC hadn't found a lower-priced catch-all with Commando, and so turned their attention to another Kaiser-era device.

In 1963–68 there had been a 2-door version of the Jeep Wagoneer, but it wasn't a strong seller. In 1974 AMC made this 2-door rise from the fiery ashes as a phoenix called Cherokee. The 1974 Jeep Cherokee, that Wagoneer 2-door at heart, came with fixed rear side window and optional flip-out glass. The Cherokee was initially launched in base and sporty "S" guises, and it could be really sporty. With 120 mph speedo, optional 401 V8 and 3.08 rear gears around, Cherokee put the "Sport" in SUV.

Jeep Cherokee was a success, and had an option that was equally popular, bringing kudos to AMC-Jeep: Quadra-Trac. Quadra-Trac, which had been introduced in '73 on the Wagoneer, was a permanent or full-time all-wheel drive system that originally worked in conjunction with AMC's use of the GM THM400 automatic. No need to engage 4×4 mode when getting off the highway; Quadra-Trac adapted automatically with a Borg Warner 13–39 transfer case during 1973–79.

Quadra-Trac used Jeep's first transfer case made of aluminum and utilized chain drive. It had a built-in limited slip differential and vacuum-operated differential lock. The transfer case was placed just above the Wagoneer/Cherokee body frame, to avoid off-roading damage. The only remaining thing to do when communing with nature was to engage low range, which Uncle Tom McCahill found to be a complicated procedure on *Mechanix Illustrated*'s '66 Wagoneer.

Keeping Jeep Neat and Tidy

With Jeep, AMC were all about reducing complexity. To this end the number of Jeep permutations was reduced from 38 in 1970 to 22 in 1971, and just 9 by 1974! As part of the garage sale, AMC sold the Dauntless V6 tooling back to Buick in early '74. Less clutter, more refinement, so out went the unloved CJ-6, whose following was limited to South America and Sweden, and in came the 1976 CJ-7.

The CJ-7 was also a longer-wheelbase CJ-5 cousin, 93.5-inch versus 83.5-inch wheelbase respectively. The added length allowed for an automatic transmission, a first for a CJ, and therefore the option of Quadra-Trac. There were other physical changes from CJ-5. The CJ-7 had steel doors that weren't curved like those of CJ-5, plus a molded plastic hardtop. CJ-7 helped to almost double CJ sales overnight. AMC recognized that to expand sales, Jeep had to appeal to more than just the outdoorsman.

In 1977 all Jeeps came with front disk brakes as standard equipment. In 1978 AMC-Jeep claimed to have increased front legroom on Wagoneer, Cherokee and J-thousand series pickup by 2½ inches, and improved the heating and vent setup on CJ. AMC wanted Jeep owners to be comfy, and more luxury was a way to add value and go upscale. This dated back to the "Tuxedo Park" luxury trim CJ pack of 1961, and accelerated through the '70s with CJ, Cherokee and J-Series sharing the good stuff. In 1975 CJ and J-Series were both available with Levi's trim pack option.

In 1975 also came the arrival of the J-Series Pioneer pickup and the up-spec Cherokee Chief. The idea was to put popular options in one neat package, like the 1976 J-10 "Honcho" pickup and 1972–83 CJ-5 Renegade, a follow-up to the Renegade I and Renegade II of 1970 and 1971 respectively. In 1977 the CJ, Cherokee and J-10 could be optioned with the Golden Eagle package, which continued to be the case until 1983.

Above Renegade was the CJ Laredo pack introduced in 1980, with nicer seating, tilt steering wheel and bumpers, front grille, and side mirrors chrome pack. There was a J-10 Laredo from 1981, and Laredo could also be specified on Cherokee. In 1982 the even more upscale CJ-7 Limited was introduced, a luxury counterpart of the Wagoneer Limited, with a predecessor in the 1973 "Super Jeep" CJ-5. If ever there was a Jeep that personified luxury, it was the Wagoneer.

The Wagoneer was available in Tuxedo Park trim in the '60s. This carried special hubcaps and leatherette/fabric mix interior; it was the Jeep James Bond would drive, if he drove a Jeep. In May 1966 this version was superseded by the Super Wagoneer, which came with padded vinyl top, the AMC 270 bhp 327 HO V8, gold anodized aluminum body trim and bucket seats. So even in Kaiser times it was recognized there were some who didn't wish to get their rig dusty!

In 1978 AMC-Jeep replaced Super Wagoneer with the expensive, ultra-upscale $10,500 Wagoneer Limited. This iconic variant was loaded with standard a/c, power seats, power door locks, power windows, tilt steering wheel, cruise control, leather upholstery, full carpeting, simulated wood exterior paneling and more! Wagoneer Limited proved popular in spite of its high price, and the V8s were chosen so frequently that the sole I6 (258ci) was dropped. The 1978 model year was the last year one could specify 401 V8 on Jeep.

Think of Wagoneer Limited as satisfying a niche. AMC discovered there was a socioeconomic demographic difference between the typical Wagoneer purchaser and the average Cherokee buyer, in spite of the mechanical similarity. The Wagoneer set were rather country-club exclusive, so AMC introduced a 4-door Cherokee in 1977 for those who wanted to skip playing 18 holes and go rock climbing or bowling.

AMC-Jeep did more niche exploring with the 1981 Scrambler or CJ-8. The CJ-8 was a pickup cousin of the CJ-7, and could rightly assert that it was the only convertible pickup on the market. Obviously there was demand for a Jeep of this type, because 27,792 were produced between 1981 and 1986. Quadra-Trac was available on big Jeeps, trucks and CJ-7, but not CJ-8, although the Scrambler could be bought as an automatic.

A right-hand-drive CJ-8 with full-length hardtop and no pickup bed was used in Alaska for mail delivery. A version was also sold in Australia called the Overlander, which had full-length rear windows. The niche service continued with the 1981–85 CJ- 10, another CJ pickup mainly for export and use by the U.S. Air Force as an aircraft towing vehicle. The CJ-10 had square headlamps in its fenders, and as a tribute to World War II Jeeps, a 9-slot grille. Non-military Jeeps like CJ-2 and CJ-2A featured a 7-slot grille.

Carrying on the military theme, AMC's purchase of Kaiser Jeep Corporation brought the arrival of the famous AM General. AM General Corporation was a wholly-owned subsidiary of AMC at the time, that specialized in making military trucks and post office vehicles. It was a concern that could trace its origins back to Studebaker, when Studebaker General Products Division (SGPD) was a defense contractor.

SGPD was acquired by Kaiser Industries when Studebaker quit South Bend car production in '64. With the purchase of Kaiser Jeep, AMC then got the tactical military vehicle specialist AM General. The subsidiary brought in good money for AMC during 1970 and 1971, then cooled off as army and postal service budget cuts came into effect. In 1974 AM General entered the transit bus area, a province dominated by GM.

The thinking was that with the fuel crisis, public transport would be a long-term growth area. The bus route proved a tough avenue for AM General initially, but eventually showed promise. Plus, in October 1974, AM General received orders for 2½- and 5-ton trucks destined for Iran and the Philippines. Both countries were friendly with the U.S. at

Top: AMC-Jeep lengthened the CJ-5's nose to accept AMC's 232 I6. The longer-wheelbase CJ-7 permitted the introduction of automatic transmission and Quadra-Trac, new features for the CJ (courtesy The Rambler Ranch). ***Bottom:*** Jeep forged the off-roader template, with Suzuki Samurai looking like a little CJ-3B. Indeed, the "J" in the Samurai's LJ/SJ model code stood for Jeep (courtesy Mick Stine).

the time, ruled by the Shah of Iran and President Marcos respectively in those Cold War days. AMC also acquired Wheel-Horse Products, Inc., a manufacturer of lawn and garden tractors, in 1974.

AM General also received a substantial order for military vehicles in 1977. Between this and the rise of Jeep, AMC was pushed into the black. An overall $8 million profit accrued in 1977, rising to $37 million in 1978, with a $58 million profit produced in the first half of 1979. AMC was back in business! It was achieved by new AMC boss Gerry Meyers's reorganizing AMC activity towards more Jeep, less car. Factories that made cars, like the Brampton facility, were turned over to Jeep.

Car production was now the sole preserve of Kenosha, and Kenosha got involved in multitasking by doing car and Jeep components. The factory now made engines, forgings and axles for both lines. The strategy was hard to argue with, given Jeep's meteoric rise. Compared to 1970, Jeep sales doubled by 1974, exceeded 100,000 units in 1975 and totaled 168,000 in 1978. Indeed, by '78, 600 Jeeps were being built per day, or three times the 1970 level.

AMC couldn't keep pace with Jeep demand, and quality suffered in trying to do so. Signs of less car with AMC came in 1978, with Matador being limited to the 258 I6 and 360 V8 engine choices, plus dropping the line that year with no replacement for '79. However, with Jeep the gifts kept on coming. Big Jeeps got a '79 front fascia restyle with rectangular headlamps. Also, 1979 saw the limited edition "Silver Anniversary" CJ, commemorating 25 years since the first 1954 CJ-5 with a special metallic silver example.

Things were also hopping along for Jeep with overseas sales, distribution and production. For '75, AMC was setting up a new car/Jeep parts center in Swindon, England, that would help serve the 5,000 right-hand-drive Jeeps sold in the UK annually. At the time the Cherokee and Wagoneer were sold in the UK in left-hand-drive 360 V8 form. The right-hand-drive CJ-5 and CJ-6 were 232 I6-motivated. AMC was aiming for 20 percent of the UK 4×4 market within 2 years.[5]

As proven with established companies like McDonald's and R.J. Reynolds, increased sales come from overseas markets, and Jeep was no exception. In 1978, 60,000 Jeeps were sold overseas, and 50,000 units were assembled outside North America. For example, a local company in Venezuela switched from assembling Toyota to Jeep, doubling the capacity to make Jeeps in that country to 14,000. The change from Toyota was because Jeep was a more attractive product than the workhorse-only Toyota Land Cruiser. The Japanese vehicle lacked automatic transmission and permanent all-wheel drive at that stage; plus, there was no value-added luxury angle.

AMC built a new factory in Egypt at this time, with a capacity to make over 12,000 Jeeps. It should also be noted that the Cherokee was assembled under license in Brisbane, Australia, from 1981 to 1986. Jeep's postwar off-roader influence was immense, with the original Willys-Overland rig spurring the creation of the Land Rover, Toyota Land Cruiser, Nissan Patrol and lesser-known examples. There was the French Delahaye VLR, Italian Fiat Campagnola, a twin-engined English Mini Moke, and the wacky 1958 Citroën Sahara, which was a Citroën 2CV with a second engine in the trunk! Hotchkiss was a French licensee of Jeep as well. However, in spite of all the imitators, the American original was safe, because as you know, there's only one Jeep!

CHAPTER 7

The Spirit of Hornet Goes Off-Road

AMC '78—The Concord

Remember the Chevy Nova SS? Well, by 1975 the letters of interest were LN. In '75 the luxurious Nova LN, with reclining seats and six-cylinder engine serving suggestion, was the star. AMC's new boss Gerry Meyers wasn't kidding when he said the firm's new Concord compact was the hottest product going in '78. Small luxo cars were very popular, giving customers extra tinsel and hold-the-V8 option.

The Nova had been transformed into the Caddy Seville using GM's finest computer, and Peugeot 504s were filling affluent middle-class garages. So entered AMC's Concord, as mentioned by *Mechanix Illustrated*'s Bob Tripolsky in December 1977, "spelled without an e at the end, perhaps to differentiate it from the plane of the same name." True, George Kennedy never piloted an AMC Concord on the silver screen, but Concord outsold all other AMC car lines combined in 1978, so the Hornet replacement was certainly flying high!

Actually, the new Concord did appear on screen in the 1978 movie *The Betsy*, starring Tommy Lee Jones. In this film AMC's Kenosha line served as the factory of the fictitious Bethlehem Motors. Concords and other AMCs could be seen being assembled and painted. The Concord was also made at AMC's Brampton plant, as well as by VAM in Mexico City where it maintained the "American" moniker. The Concord also starred as the cover car of AMC's 1978 catalogue, and the mood was positive.

AMC's taglines for their 1978 cars in general were "The Value Americans Want ... The Size America Needs." They also said "AMC ... For The Comfort Americans Want." There was even mention about strength and weight being key for big-car ride comfort. AMC was having an each-way bet on the changing car scene. On the one hand they played on the fact small was in, but American-style. That is, they used some of Ford's anti-downsizing rhetoric, stressing strength and weight, implying that a Datsun or Honda small car wouldn't cut it on comfort.

AMC still had Matador, and along with Pacer and Concord could claim to cocoon occupants to a greater degree than a new Ford Fairmont or Plymouth Horizon. Concord had old-school Detroit plushness and style, minus the waste. The Hornet morphed into the elegant Concord on a budget, with a sloping nose facilitated by the use of 1977 Gremlin's front fenders, and more. A chrome 6-section egg-crate grille contained square white parking lights, and new windsplit hood with upstanding ornament marked Concord out as a solid American. The roof was also altered.

Concord represented Hornet plus suspension, noise absorption and styling refinements. Nevertheless, Concord AMX delivered the domestic pony-car experience enthusiasts expected in 1978 (courtesy Jeff Limerick).

Other detail changes ran to square metric spec headlamps and simpler bumpers. At the rear, Concord had large tri-color taillights and boxed central cavity for the license plate. The restyled rear had a passing resemblance to the rear fascia of the popular Datsun 610 (180B) sedan. Inside, Concord shared a new 3-square-dial face dash with Gremlin, influenced by Matador's revised '74 dash. AMC designers also managed to eke out more interior space, with one inch more headroom than Hornet and two inches more rear legroom.

Concord's front seat backs were contoured to create more room for rear passengers' knees. The Concord majored in comfort and refinement with insulation placed behind the dashboard and under the front floor, with sound-deadening material coating plastic-to-plastic contact surfaces. Like the '61 Rambler, Concord also featured a one-piece molded fiberglass headliner. Concord D/Ls went further with additional insulation padding for the rear floor and trunk.

So Concord registered fewer decibels on the move than Hornet, and with a smoother ride. Through the extensive use of rubber bushes, revalved shocks and reduced front spring rates, AMC's engineers gave Concord a ride befitting a Kenosha Cadillac. Indeed, Concord's excellent ride comfort was mentioned by several magazines. Concord was all luxury even in base spec, where it came with 232 / 3-speed floorshift manual, electronic ignition, front disk brakes, lower-level instrument panel vents, 22-gallon gas tank, interior hood release, chrome trim for rocker panels, fender lips, rain gutters, and hood edge, and that hood ornament.

Concord came fully equipped, but to truly savor the moment it was wise to choose the D/L pack. Concord D/L featured Landau vinyl roof and opera windows on '78 Concord

D/L 2-door sedans, color-keyed wheel covers, AMC's newly introduced Velveteen Crush fabric recliners, digital clock, woodgrain dash overlay, deluxe 12-oz carpet on the floor, outer seat bottoms and lower interior door trim panels. Concord D/Ls also came with larger-footprint tires, and D/L wagons had exterior woodgrain trim panels and standard perforated vinyl reclining front seats.

'78 AMX—AMC in Black

Concord came in 2-door, 4-door sedan, and wagon, plus hatchback, as per Hornet. Concord hatch couldn't have the D/L pack, but it could be ordered as the Concord Sport. This hatch exclusive featured sport slot rims and wide lower body "through-the-black-fender-arches" stripe decal, in the fashion of '78 Gremlin X. Beyond Concord Sport lay Concord AMX, AMC choosing to continue their ultra-sport tag after the success of '77 Hornet AMX.

With Concord AMX, expect the brushed aluminum Targa roof band, interior engine-turned trim, and ancillary console instrument pack of Hornet AMX, but with an accent on black. There was blackout trim for window frames, wiper arms, headlamp bezels, license plate recess, fiberglass front and rear fender flares, rear window louver and the soft-feel sports steering wheel. So anticipate all that on a standard '78 Concord AMX, and more if said AMX was ordered in exterior color code P1 Classic Black.

Concord had an optional 304 V8 with mandatory zombie shift, or the AMX buyer could stay with this standard 258/4-speed stick shift power team. This combination was more in keeping with sporty AMX (courtesy Jeff Limerick).

Classic Black Concord AMXs had a gold stripe for the AMX's standard color-keyed slot rims, black windshield reveal moldings and decorative gold decal from Targa band, over the front doors and finishing on the front fenders. Notable exterior points of difference between Concord AMX and regular Concord were the use of a unique grille, round headlamps and round amber parking lights on Concord AMX. AMX's open-mouth black insert grille had central "AMX" script, and the front fascia had a nostalgic angle. At a time when square lamps were in, Concord AMX recalled McQueen's Mustang, and that power-bulge hood came from Gremlin. No hood ornament on this Concord.

The black and gold livery was due to the popularity of the Bandit Trans Am from the 1977 movie *Smokey and the Bandit.* Ford's Mustang II King Cobra and Plymouth Volare Road Runner could be seen in the same colors, at a time when hood decals were as popular as medallions and open-neck shirts. However, Concord AMX was also available in Alpine White (G7), Firecracker Red (6P), Sunshine Yellow (6V) and Quick Silver Metallic (8C).

Inside, "soft-feel" vinyl buckets were standard and came in black, blue or beige hues. A Levi's Trim Package was an option shared with '78 Gremlin X, with that seat-of-the-pants sensation also available in black, blue or beige. Hardware-wise, 49-state Concord AMX was delivered with the 2-barrel 258 and 4-speed manual seen on Hornet AMX. With a rating of 120 bhp at 3,600 rpm and 210 lbs/ft at 1,800 rpm, the sturdy 258 was strong by late '70s standards.

In California, Concord AMX came with a 1bbl 258 and 4-speed at a time when Golden State Trans Ams were auto only. Concord AMX had a 304 option, which came with automatic only, wherever you lived. An indication of how this power team could move a Concord AMX was suggested by *Car and Driver*'s February 1978 test of a Concord 304 automatic, which did 0–60 mph in 10.4 seconds and reached a terminal velocity of 100 mph.

In February 1979 *Car and Driver* recorded 0–60 mph in 9.9 seconds and 106 mph top speed with a 4bbl 301 V8 Pontiac Grand Am auto, so Concord V8 was on par with the best domestic sport sedans going. AMC's 258 was sporting an 8.0:1 compression ratio, while the 2bbl 304 was still on 8.4 CR with 130 horses. This was in touch with the best 2bbl 302s Ford was fitting to Mustang II, but the Dodge Aspen R/T and Plymouth Volare Road Runner compact twins could still be had with 195 bhp 360s, so '78 401 Jeeps were observed by Concord AMX owners enviously.

With the dawn of CAFE, AMX handling was an asset that used stock DR78–14-inch steel radials and front swaybar to good effect. The sensible modified rapture that was '78 AMX came with the AMC declaration, "AMX: An exciting sporty car that makes driving come alive at an affordable price. With the exclusive AMC Buyer Protection Plan." It was muscle car meets consumerism!

The Concord AMX was very un–Concord-like: the underlying car sacrificed dynamism for comfort. Fifteen fast laps were done in the 258-powered Concord D/L 2-door sedan tested by *Mechanix Illustrated* in December '77, with the conclusion Concord wasn't really a handler, and buyers were advised to specify the HD suspension option. Similarly, *Consumer Reports* judged 4-door Concord DL 4-cylinder's accident-avoidance ability as being slow, but controllable.[1]

In the February '78 article on Concord V8, *Car and Driver* said, "You have the eerie feeling in steering the Concord down the road that somehow, something isn't quite right, isn't quite integrated." Part of this was anti-domestic sentiment common in journals at the time, but handling and ride comfort balance is a compromise. The flipside was that *C&D* judged ride comfort as nice, and *Consumer Reports* considered Concord DL as having the best ride in their group test.

A Concord was the perfect antidote to less-than-perfect road surfaces, but that wasn't to say Concord was a complete square. The comfort compact achieved some solid racing results. In 1979 the No. 61 Doell Associates Concord distinguished itself, starting with a 3rd place for Buzz Cason at the Champion Spark Plug 100 held at Daytona on February 3. On April 1 at the 1979 World Challenge for Endurance Drivers held at Talladega, Tom Waugh and Rick Knoop took the No. 61 Concord to 1st overall after 6 hours.

On July 1, at a 6-hour Daytona race, Tom Waugh, Lyn Saint James and Buzz Cason drove the No. 61 Concord to 2nd overall. In 1980, Kal Showket switched from Pacer to No. 69 Concord and with Durrell Kirkland and John Jones recorded 3rd overall at the 6-hour 1980 World Challenge for Endurance Drivers held on June 29 at Daytona. Finally, on June 14, 1981, in Portland, Oregon, at the G.I. Joe's Rose Cup, Buzz Dyer's No. 77 Concord qualified 48th and finished 11th, in the SCCA T/A series event.

In 1979 Concord sported a revised front fascia with quad square headlamps over slim, white-rectangle parking lights. The lighting flanked a waterfall grille with fine chrome vertical bars. The effect was even classier than '78, and Concord now had lighter aluminum bumpers. The Concord DL vinyl roof was redone so that it only covered the rear passenger section. The B pillar chrome integrated with the vinyl trim. In '79 DL was extended to

Compared to Hornet, the new Concord had large tricolor taillights, boxed central license plate cavity and a general rear-end look similar to the popular contemporary Datsun 610 (courtesy Jeff Limerick).

Concord hatch, where the AMX-style brushed aluminum Targa band blended with the half-vinyl top.

Concord DL hatch was compensation for the absence of a performance Concord in '79. The Concord Sport and Concord AMX were discontinued at the close of the '78 model year, and 1979 would prove to be Concord hatchback's Waterloo. However, eagle-eyed option buyers could still obtain a '79 Concord with a handling pack that included unique, bigger front and rear swaybars. Indeed, unlike Spirit and Pacer, the Concord could be bought with air shocks and associated compressor.

Mimicking Wagoneer, AMC introduced a '79 Concord "Limited" variant that was luxurious in the extreme. Concord Limited existed in 2- and 4-door sedan form, as well as wagon. Concord Limited brought Chelsea leather upholstery, 18-oz carpeting, body-colored wheel covers and AM radio. Full courtesy lighting was also included, and this Light Group entailed glove box and engine bay illumination, plus dome map lights.

A rather special year for American Motors, 1979 marked 25 years since the Nash and Hudson merger. To celebrate, a Concord Silver Anniversary limited edition with two-tone metallic silver-over-blue and wire wheels was released. It was only right that the optional finery of Rochelle velour upholstery should be introduced to Concord that year, but amid extravagance there was also thrift.

Concord — Consumer's Friend

Midway through the '78 model year it became possible to specify the 80 bhp 2-liter I4 Gremmy motor on Concords, except Concord wagon. With the 2-liter, AMC Concord sedan was decidedly Volvoesque. Indeed, the Concord's square-faced instruments weren't unlike the Volvo 244's arrangements of the era. To imbue Concord I4 with some pep, 4-cylinder Concord sedan and hatch column-shift autos had 3.58 rear gears. However, how quickly does one really need to race to reach the golf course?

With acceleration as leisurely as that of 4-cylinder imports, Concord 2-liter was a seldom-chosen option. AMC had a mind to shake up engine selection for '80. With a second gas crunch underway, the 304 V8 was retired at the end of '79, and closeness between the 232 and 258 saw the smaller I6 disappear at the same time. Thus, in 1980 AMC had the trusty 258, and a new I4 for Concord. The license agreement with VW had always made the 2-liter expensive, and therefore an optional Concord motor. To reduce this cost and gain torque, AMC switched to the GM 2.5-liter "Iron Duke" I4.

The 2.5-liter I4 was the new standard engine in a revised '80 Concord range. The front grille was changed again with a horizontal bar arrangement featuring "Concord" script on the driver's side. The rear fascia had wraparound taillights, and all Concord sedan body styles could now have opera windows. The 4-door DL and Limited now had triangular opera windows, which were no longer restricted to the 2-door sedan.

The 2-door Concord DL and Limited sedans went to a square opera window, with vertical strakes between the window and vinyl roof trim. Concord's vinyl roof trim covered the whole roof in 1980. The '80 Concord Limited wagons had blackout paint and chrome trim for the cargo windows. Power windows were also a first-time Concord option in 1980, but under all that glitter AMC was building Concord better, and that's what really counted.

The tach, AMC Rally Pak console gauges, 4 on the floor and disco dash overlays, underlined the AMX's sporting pretensions (courtesy Jeff Limerick).

Japanese imports were well made, but didn't much care for the harsh winters of North America. If one lived in parts with heavy snow, Mr. Plow and liberal use of salt to tame said snow, then AMC Concord was a wise investment. After a few winters the neighbor's Datsun had more holes than a Swiss cheese, but Concord was golden in a good way. AMC's primer, zinc primer, and wax sealer paint process was a start.

Rust-prone areas used galvanized steel, and special sealers and coatings were used in sensitive areas. AMCs were dipped above the door in primer, and for the lower body there was the Ziebart treatment. This material was applied to lower pillar areas, under doors, lower outer door inside surfaces, lower fenders and rear wheel openings. Concords, Spirits and Pacers also used plastic inner fender liners.

Because AMC really did build them better, their cars were better backed with a 5-year anti-rust-through warranty which wasn't affected by vehicle mileage, and could be passed to subsequent owners at no charge. If Ralph Nader were trapped in a snowdrift, he would want to be in an AMC, and not just Mr. Nader. Concord was a swell deal, and *Consumer Reports* said the 1980 Concord was a car of broad appeal with continually improving predicted repair incidence quality: "These days, you don't have to be an American Motors stock holder or the nephew of an AMC dealer to want to buy a Concord."[2]

In February 1980 the magazine put the Concord DL 4-door 2.5-liter up against much newer designs from GM and Ford, the Citation and Fairmont respectively, as well as Concord's contemporary, the Dodge Aspen. Concord maximized what it had to perform solidly on test with best ride, and braking rated as "good to very good." The 5 mph bumpers were also rated good to very good. CU felt the availability of opera windows on '80 Concord DL and Limited 4-door sedan was a boon to visibility.

Concord's I4 was judged as giving good driveability, with no typical 4-cylinder harshness. Concord and Citation both used the same motor, so put Concord's library quiet down to the extra sound deadening AMC engineered in. Concord also came with 12 sample defects, which was par for the course. However, the need to manually shut 3 upper dash outlets to get full heat to the floor showed Concord's HVAC system was from yesteryear. Plus, the headlamp dimmer switch was still in the footwell.

Vehicle heft was also a weighty problem. The 3,003 pound Concord was 100 to 300 lbs heavier than the more modern 4-cylinder Citation and Fairmont. The biggest gap was with Citation, the only front-driver in the group. With fuel economy being the order of the day, it was understandable why there was a 6 to 7-month waiting list for Citation I4. However, Concord held some MPG aces up its sleeve.

Concord I4 had the same 22-gallon gas tank as the 258-powered version. This gave Concord I4 a long cruising range at a time when gas shortages were as troubling as high gas prices. Consumer Union also found the 4-cylinder Concord tested got better gas mileage than the Concord I4 automatic's 20/25 mpg EPA figures.[3] At 90 bhp the Concord 2.5-liter was 10 horses stronger than Concord 2-liter. This hi-torque OHV engine didn't have to work so hard, permitting a taller 3.08 final drive and associated quieter operation with better mileage.

The Incredible Shrinking Range

The '80 Concord base price was $4,878, with the DL pack adding $299. In reality the 4.2/automatic power team proved the most popular on Concord and was EPA rated at 19/26 mpg city/highway in '81. Just so everyone knew it was a new '81, Concord's grille had its chrome horizontal bars more widely spaced and three vertical bars added, one in the center and two outboard. Concord DLs came with stainless steel "Full Styled Wheel Covers" and Limiteds with "Wire Wheel Covers" as standard. Also standard were galvanized body panels and aluminized exhaust; hence AMC's tagline "The Tough Americans."

The 14 × 7-inch "Turbocast II" alloy rims guaranteed a tough look. Turbocast IIs predated the A-Team van, and were associated with the '79 Spirit AMX. They were optional across the Concord line. There were 15 exterior color choices for '81 Concord and 3 interiors. Deluxe Grain Vinyl in black, blue, beige or nutmeg was standard, with Sculptured Rochelle Velour featuring on Concord DL in black, blue, wine, beige or nutmeg, and nutmeg-colored Chelsea leather on Concord Limited.

Tightening CAFE standards saw measures to raise gas mileage in '82. The new light-shifting BW T5 5-speeder was introduced in '82, along with a new version of Concord's Chrysler-sourced Torqueflite with wider-spaced economy ratios. Low-drag disk brakes were amongst incremental improvements, and '82 Concord I4 5-speed was EPA rated at 37 mpg highway, better than the 34 mpg of the '81 Concord I4 4-speed.

AMC was jettisoning the ballast in '82, the year Concord DL and Limited 2-doors did without opera window decorative strakes. At the end of the '82 model year, AMC axed the 2-door Concord, Limited 4-door and 2.5-liter engine. Going into '83 Concord was solely motivated by 2bbl 4.2 I6 power, in a range consisting of base and DL 4-door sedan, and 4-door wagon still available in base, DL and luxo Limited.

It would seem the essence of Sportabout sparkled to the end, and 1983 would prove to be Concord's final hour. Sales had been falling as more modern machinery came to the fore, including one emanating from Kenosha itself, born of a French alliance. It was only natural this newcomer should take sales from Concord. However, AMC was alive in Spirit!

Gremlin's New Get-Up

With Jeep on the rise and profitable, there were voices saying AMC should vacate the car business entirely and concentrate on off-roaders. AMC's new boss Gerry Meyers wasn't of this opinion. Not placing all the eggs into the one Jeep basket, he oversaw the $10 million investment program that witnessed the creation of the reskinned Concord and Spirit. Just as Hornet begat Concord, Spirit was a much-revised version of AMC's Gremlin, but that was sometimes hard to tell.

Gremlin was well known for its C pillar blind spot, and Richard Teague had proposed a second-generation Gremlin with more glass to solve the problem. The result was the 1974 XP Gremlin concept car. The XP was built on the chassis of a '71 Gremlin and had fiberglass body, grille and hood. It was a more delicate, lighter-looking shape, with prismatic, triangular *Dark Side of the Moon*–style rear glass area. The XP had Italian flavor and could have come from Innocenti.

The one red XP prototype was driven for a spell by Teague's daughter, and its influence wasn't seen until the '79 Spirit sedan arrived. This updated Gremlin had a normal, full rear window pane, greatly improving visibility. The rear fascia of Spirit sedan was the same as '77 Gremlin, but the front featured the classier visage of '79 Concord. There was also a blackout B pillar beauty panel with vertical ribbing.

Spirit sedan sported AMC's logo as a circular medallion, smack dab in the front grille's center, and aluminum bumpers with black end caps. Another upscale touch was having the AMC logo outline in chrome foil, in the center of the round rear red side marker lights. Spirit also incorporated the suspension refinements of Concord. We have the example of '74 Mustang II's front subframe with 6 rubber insulated mountings, the suspension of '75 Seville's motor on a steel subframe with Isoflex dampening cushions, plus comforting crossmember of Pacer. As the '70s went on, people wanted full-size comfort in smaller cars, and hang the horsepower!

Sitting behind the woodgrained Concord dash, a '79 Spirit Limited with leather seats felt like a Rolls-Royce compared to a '70½ Gremmy. Most would prefer the uptrimmed 2-liter I4 car to the raw '70½ Gremlin with big I6, and according to 1979 AMC brochure material, that 2-liter was standard Spirit equipment. Concord and Pacer commenced with 232 and 258 I6s respectively in '79.

The licensed 2-liter had been an expensive up-trim option, but its presence in Spirit spoke to AMC's renewed commitment to classy economy. Yes, it was possible to buy a $3,999 starter Spirit sedan, but Gerry Meyers said you couldn't find a stripper in an AMC showroom: "We never belonged in the beer-can market."[4] Standard gearbox for Spirit was 4 on the floor. Technically one could order an I6 Spirit with 3-speed manual, but it was a delete option.

Jim Landis's 1980 Spirit AMX drag racer has a 401 V8 stroked to 420 cubes by Barry Allen, with iron head, BIG roller cam and 13.5:1 compression. Using a Jerico 4-speed box and 12 × 30-inch street tires, this subcompact has done 9.42 seconds in the ¼ mile at 143 mph (courtesy Jim Landis).

Firing the Spirit's soul for the '80s was a new fastback, liftback coupe body style of commonly agreed handsome good looks. Was this really a Gremlin? Teague had struck again, with a fresh fastback that was thoroughly modern-looking with wide rear rocket-launcher taillights. Hard to believe the new Spirit liftback was just 0.2 inch longer than the 167-inch-long Spirit sedan, and that both Spirits still used the old Gremmy's 96-inch wheelbase! It all suggested comparison with the also new 1979 Ford Mustang III.

The Fox-body Mustang was a Fairmont-derived liftback or notchback with rear drive and live axle too, but lacked the flowing style of the Spirit liftback. Mustang was more notchback

Photographed by Bret Kepner on the winning cool-down straight at the 2008 Pinks All Out Event in St. Louis, this Spirit carries on the drag strip AMX tradition started in the '60s (courtesy Jim Landis).

than fastback. The Spirit and Mustang ranges stood comparison in engine options, with 2.0 I4, 3.8 I6, 4.2 I6, and 5.0 V8, and 2.3 I4, 2.8 V6, 3.3 I6, and 5.0 V8 from AMC and Ford respectively. Then there was the question of size. Mustang measured 179.1 inches in length on a 100.4-inch wheelbase, which only showed Ford had downsized to where the real small car company had been all along!

For weight, 4-cylinder Spirit liftback was 2,615 lbs, while I4 Mustang tipped the scales at 2,520 lbs, suggesting Spirit's unibody was a denser, sturdier structure. Echoing this sentiment was *Consumer Reports*' experience of '79 Mustang. They admitted to trying out only the 2.3 I4 and 2.8 V6, but expressed fears concerning the Foxstang unibody's ability to cope with the exertions of the optional 5-liter.

In the late '70s the public weren't concerned with torsional rigidity, and bought 369,936 '79 Mustangs. AMC sold a more modest number of Spirits, just under 35,000 units in 1979, representing a 57 percent improvement over 1978 Gremlin. In fact, the sound results for Concord and Spirit meant AMC's car side was close to the break-even point going into 1980. This served as insurance against falling Jeep revenues in the wake of the second gas crunch.

The Spirit of AMX Returns

For '79 AMC decided to leave Concord "all-luxo," and rest the AMX mantle upon Spirit. Being smaller and lighter with the same power teams promised action. AMC gave fair warning: "AMX. The styling says sizzle. The performance is nothing short of inspiring." Spirit AMX looked like an IMSA racer, decked out as it was with front spoiler, fiberglass flared fenders and rear spoiler. Spirit AMX was the granddaddy of the compact import ricer rockets! Front and rear black bumpers had guards and protective strips, should the owner have tired of piloting a hovercraft, and wanted to play bumper cars.

The fender flares were color keyed, and along with front spoiler and rear fascia panel, had an accent outline pinstripe. Large "AMX" callout decals appeared on the front doors, near the front fenders, and in the middle of the rear spoiler. A small chrome AMX badge was placed on the driver's side of the blackout front grille, and California-style dual remote side rear-view mirrors were standard. Body scuff molding strips were optional, as was the model's huge hood decal, a stylized AMX script surrounded by flames.

Filling the big wheel wells were AMC's 14 × 7-inch Turbocast II alloy rims, wrapped in Goodyear Flexten ER60–14-inch OWL (Outline-White-Letter) steel-belted radials. The '79 Spirit AMX was available in 6 exterior colors: Olympic White, Firecracker Red, Saxon Yellow, Morocco Buff, Wedgewood Blue and oft-publicity-pictured Classic Black. Choose Classic Black and the body profile, window line accent striping and blackout back panel standard with the other colors was deleted. If the car was black, one wouldn't be able to see the accent striping, obviously.

Little wonder AMC also said, "Meet AMX for 1979. Inside and out it's bold, commanding. Expect to be noticed." A word about advertising at AMC. Any small car maker finds advertising to be a greater percentage of overall costs than a large company does. However, AMC was beefing up in this area, thanks to some defections from GM. The confident Gerry Meyers had lured ex–Chevrolet director of PR James L. Tolley, who became AMC VP of PR.

In spring '79, former Chevy director of marketing Thomas A. Staudt became AMC

Top: A '79 Spirit DL liftback V8, the 304 was back again in AMC's subcompact line for the first time since mid–'76. The 1979 Spirit 304 and Mustang 302 made for an interesting 2-barrel V8 comparo (courtesy Mike Schaefer). ***Bottom:*** With the demise of the AMX tag, G.T. became the top Spirit performance pack for '81. This 1981 Spirit G.T. originally came with 2bbl 258/BW T4 4-speed power team, Turbocast II alloys and moonroof (courtesy Chad Quella).

VP of marketing. In addition, David J. Van Pearsem, ex–Oldsmobile director of marketing, became AMC general marketing manager.[5] These former GM people were interested in the challenge of being part of AMC's revival. American Motors' advertising plan had become befuddled in the years since Wells, Rich & Greene, so this was all to the good.

Inside Spirit AMX the disco dash aluminum effect overlays continued in a plush interior with 12-oz color-keyed carpeting and seat belts, and AMC's Extra Quiet Insulation Package. Leather-wrapped steering wheel and choice of Sport Vinyl or Caberfae Corduroy buckets were present, along with AMC's usual ancillary Rally Pak 4-gauge console instrument cluster. Spirit AMX had a rev counter in the extreme left dash pod, the place where less sporty Spirits had a digital clock.

The '79 Spirit AMX also had custom headliner, sun visors and AMX script badge on the glove box door, but for functionality also carried the G.T. Rally-Tuned Suspension Package. Consider the base Spirit sedan with bias ply tires, the only Spirit sold without front swaybar, as Spirit's handling start point. From Spirit sedan base camp, AMX was the summit, with handling brighter than its stock halogen headlamps. Rely on HD strut rod bushings, HD rear leaf spring isoclamp pads, HD Hi-Control leafs and more!

The G.T. Rally-Tuned Suspension pack had 27-mm front and 19-mm rear swaybars and adjustable Gabriel Strider shock absorbers, plus special steering gear. AMC's steering gear was made by GM's Saginaw division; therefore, AMX could utilize the spool-valve assembly (part no. 783 2057) from the Pontiac Firebird Trans Am's recirculating ball power steering. The Trans Am was acknowledged as having the most precise domestic high-effort car steering at the time, so Spirit AMX was guaranteed laser-like control.

Bottom: **This Spirit G.T.'s original 258 has been replaced with a later Jeep Cherokee–sourced AMC injected 4.0 I6. The 4-speed has given way to a BW T5, and non-standard dual exhausts are present (courtesy Chad Quella).**

G.T. Rally-Tuned Suspension also included upgraded brakes. Thus, Spirit AMX had 10.8-inch front disks with semi-metallic brake pads to stave off fading. Ribbed 10 × 1.2-inch rear drums were also present. AMC was employing old-school tech to keep the driver in charge, refusing to even use metric footprint tires! Meanwhile, Ford had gone full metric with Mustang, not just the footprint, but tire height and rim too!

The all-metric Michelin TRX wheel and tire system fitted to top '79 Mustang Cobras measured 15.4 inches tall, but only 5.9 inches wide. With 7-inch-wide Turbocast IIs, AMX gave more grip and 5-bolt hubs. Mustang was using a 4-bolt hub, which gave the fancy TRX more lipstick on a pig. When road cars are taken to the track, those lug bolts can shear clean off under strain. Having 5 bolts spreads the load and that's what AMX provided, plus serious 60 profile tires against Mustang's 65 aspect ratio.

Standard AMX power team was the trusty 258 I6 and 4-speed manual. This 2-barrel choice was rated at 110 bhp at 3,200 rpm and 210 lbs/ft at 1,800 rpm, or there was the optional 2bbl V8. The V8 had returned to Gremlin and Spirit land for '79. Although the AMC I6 and V8s still retained their respective 8 and 8.4 to one compression ratios, the 304 was now rated at just 125 net ponies. That year Ford had a 132 bhp 2.3 I4 turbo and 140 bhp 2bbl 302 V8 for Mustang, so Spirit was looking ghostly pale.

In reality the 2.3 turbo was better on paper than in practice, and was no threat to Spirit AMX V8. The Mustang 302 could edge out Spirit AMX in 0–60 mph by a half second, but all these V8 mini-racers sounded a lot better than their performance figures. A gasoline V8 of any kind was better than a diesel, or the wheezing 231 V6 resting under the hood of many a contemporary GM family car. Indeed, Spirit AMX V8s and manual transmission I6s came with "performance tuned exhaust sound."

So startup in an underground parking lot could be a stimulating experience. AMC's Twin-Grip differential was still around, and if specified on an automatic Spirit AMX V8, made a 2.87 final drive mandatory. The pop-up moonroof was a popular option on the 3,657 '79 model year Spirit AMXs made. Other proof Spirit was sporty could be found at the track, where the subcompact was incorporated into tin-top Racing Stocks like previous AMCs.

AMC Racing Tradition

Back in the glory days of SCCA T/A racing, one could even join the Javelin AMX Sports Car Club. Apart from a monthly newsletter, discounts on performance parts could be had. Club members could also watch racing films and engage in social events. At the end of the '60s, supporting organizations included Hurst Shifters, Engle Racing Cams, *Super Street Cars* magazine and the Javelin Racing Team, naturally.

By the mid–'70s the height of interest in such spectacles had passed, but Trans Am racing did continue, and examples from yesteryear still bellowed as they pounded familiar tracks. On June 1, 1975, at the Purolator 500 held at Pocono International Raceway, Jocko Maggiacomo finished 2nd in his No. 63 Javelin. In the 1976 SCCA Trans Am series Maggiacomo achieved three 1st-in-class finishes in Javelin.

The class victories were at the May 9 Jaycee GP (Pocono International Raceway), the May 30 Fifty Grand of Nelson Ledges (Nelson Ledges Road Course) and the September 5

Interior mods in this 1981 Spirit G.T. include Eagle Limited wagon-sourced deluxe armrests and a cup holder. Spirit made use of Concord's upscale dashboard (courtesy Chad Quella).

Mayor's Cup Trans Am Trois-Rivieres. Jocko Maggiacomo used 360 and 433ci displacements among the Javelin's V8 race engines through the year. However, major AMC racing interest focused on the I6 small cars by this stage.

Many teams raced Spirit, but the best-known outfit that did was Levi's Team Highball. It was LTH that recorded Spirit's first victory, and this represented Amos Johnson's first win in 2½ years! The event in question was the IMSA Champion Spark Plug Challenge Series' inaugural race season starter, the February 3, 1979, Champion Spark Plug 100 at Daytona. Sponsorship for the small car series had changed from the previous B.F. Goodrich Radial Challenge Series.

The race proved to be a 3-way tussle between Johnson's No. 7 Spirit, the Mazda of Jim Downing, and James Reeve's venturi-restricted Buick Skyhawk, which passed both the AMC and Mazda. The three cars broke braking rules 7 miles from the finish, going into an eventful turn 1 where they went off the course! Downing's Mazda was forced to retire, and Reeve made it back to the pits with a cut tire, leaving Johnson to take the checkered flag and victory!

Johnson's Spirit was followed home by the 2nd-placed Gremlin and 3rd-placed Concord of the Doell Associates racing team. It was a neat AMC 1-2-3 clean sweep! Success continued at the March 16 Sebring 3-hour race, where LTH had a 1–2 triumph, Dennis Shaw's No. 6 Spirit finishing 1st, with Amos Johnson 2nd in his No.7 Spirit. This was followed by some nefarious activity at the April 1, 1979, 6-hour World Challenge for Endurance Drivers.

At the tri-oval Talladega venue, Johnson was penalized for an illegal assist. Johnson used his No. 7 Spirit to "bumper car" Shaw's No. 6 Spirit into the pits for refueling, Shaw's car having run out of gas. Apparently this maneuver wasn't allowed. Everything was above board for the July 1 Daytona 6-hour race where Dennis Shaw, Don Whittington and Bill Whittington finished 1st overall in the LTH No. 6 Spirit.

The Team Highball Spirit also raced overseas, in West Germany at the infamous Nürburgring. The 1979 Spirit AMX V8 was already homologated for European FIA Group 1 Touring Car racing, so this model participated in the annual Group 1 24-hour race held at the "Old Ring." This long, 14.173-mile, densely forested, dangerous circuit originated in the 1920s. When first constructed it was a state-of-the-art road course circuit, but after Ferrari driver Nikki Lauda's brush with death, it stopped being used for Formula 1 in 1976.

Triple Formula 1 champion Jackie Stewart even dubbed the Nürburgring "The Green Hell." In spite of the extreme nature of the circuit, it is still used by car makers as a tester for new cars, and many have computerized Old Ring simulator chassis test rigs to theoretically put a new design through its paces. Tourists and locals alike can even try out the Nürburgring in their own cars for a fee.

The track has a number of sections, with the 14.173-mile layout involving Spirit AMX called the "Northern Loop." Preparation time for Team Highball was limited. Two stock 5-liter 4-speed '79 Spirit AMXs were supplied to Team Highball less than 3 weeks before shipping to Europe for the 24-hour race. In this time the cars were brought up to Group 1 specs. The two Group 1 AMXs were sponsored by AMC and B.F. Goodrich, using a 4bbl 304 and exterior livery consisting of blue, orange and yellow against a brilliant black base color.

Car No. 1 was driven by Team Highball principals Amos Johnson and Dennis Shaw, as well as Hollywood actor James Brolin. Car No. 2 was piloted by Mazda factory driver Jim Downing, Lyn Saint James and auto journalist Gary Witzenberg. Car No. 1 was set up for a fast lap, to qualify Spirit AMX high up the grid to help achieve a good overall finish. However, fog cut the qualifying session short, and cars No. 1 and No. 2 qualified 20th and 21st respectively.

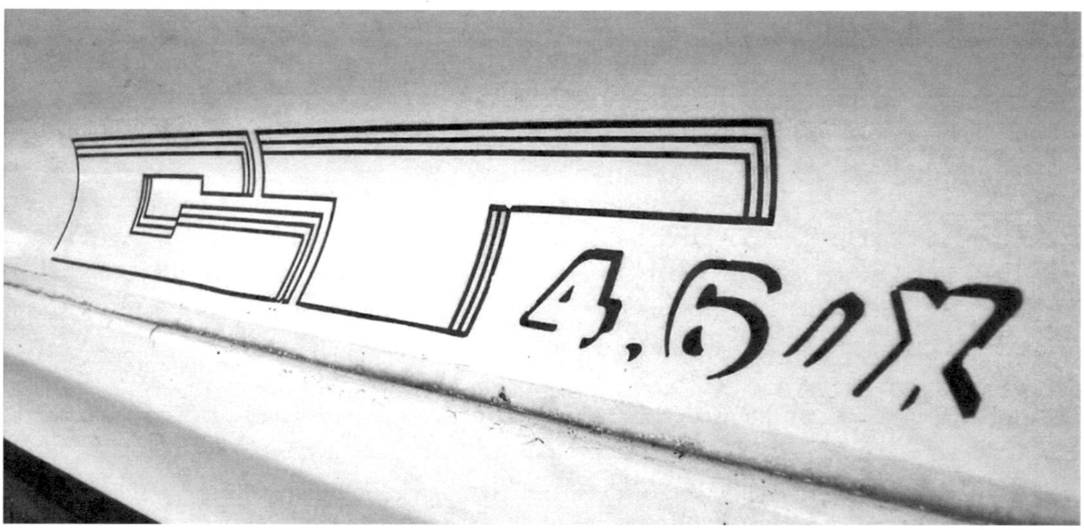

In Mexico the Spirit liftback was known as the Rally, with a special 1980–81 GT variant sitting above AMX with a 172 bhp 4.6-liter version of AMC's I6 (courtesy Mauricio Jordán Márquez).

Spirit AMX was up against less powerful but nimbler BMWs, Opels, Fords, VW Golfs, Audi 80s and even Spirit's AMC dealer stablemate, the Renault 5 (Le Car). So AMX would be hanging on through the twisties, and making up for matters on the straights where the car could touch 140 mph. Car No. 1 suffered broken front shocks, a slipping clutch, and an oil-burning 304. Both cars' brakes got a serious workout, and both cars also made it to the finish!

In the October 1979 endurance event car No. 1 finished 1st in class and 25th overall. The No. 2 Team Highball Spirit AMX registered 2nd in class and 43rd overall. In the field of 120 the Team Highball Spirit AMXs proved to be the fastest on street tires, the sponsor-related B.F. Goodrich T/A radials. B.F. Goodrich filmed Team Highball's Nürburgring experience from both ground and air, creating a documentary film titled *The Ultimate Challenge*. The race story has also been featured in the journals *Automobile Quarterly* (Vol. 19, No. 1) and *Road Test* magazine (March 1981).

The racing story of the No. 2 car didn't end there. It sat dormant until late 1980, whereupon it was used as a pace car at an IMSA Road Atlanta race. In IMSA-AC it used a hotter 304, sustaining damage during pace car duty. Team Highball was doing the IMSA-AC-Kelly American Challenge with Concords during this period. The Kelly American Challenge was an IMSA category for pony cars and Detroit iron in general.

Team Highball took the damaged No. 2 pace car and subsequently upgraded the mini-beast to IMSA-GT spec, fitting their IMSA-AC Concord front clip and a Penske Racing

From 1980 to 1983 VAM built their version of the AMC Spirit for Mexico. Equipment was rationalized to maximize local content. This '81 Rally GT's rear spoiler was standard fitment (courtesy Mauricio Jordán Márquez).

The 4-speed manual in this Rally GT was a Tremec 176-F unit, the only box available on this model. Note VAM's logo on the steering wheel hub (courtesy Mauricio Jordán Márquez).

NASCAR-derived dry sump 360 in the process. In chronology the Concord front clip fitment and hotter 304 occurred as Team Highball raced the No. 2 Spirit AMX prior to GT upgrade.

Amos Johnson drove the car in the 1981 Kelly American Challenge Series, with the No. 2 Spirit AMX used in that year's Daytona 24-hour race. In 1981–82 the No. 2 Spirit AMX was raced as a customer car, and was driven in late '82 at the Daytona Finale "Free for All" by a Team Highball employee. Both No. 1 and No. 2 Team Highball Spirit AMX racers survive, and have been restored back to their '79 Nürburgring look.

In 1982 a 258ci Eagle SX/4 Sport (an all-wheel-drive Spirit liftback) was raced in SCCA Pro Rally by Gene and Gary Henderson. Indeed, the 4.2-liter racing spirit of AMC was embodied by a special 1981 pace car. The Spirit liftback-based AMX Turbo was one of 4 official safety cars used in the PPG Indy Car World Series of 1981.

The sporty modified look came courtesy of Richard Teague, with the car built by Autodynamics of Troy, Michigan, under contract from PPG Industries. The coupe's 450 bhp turbocharged, fuel-injected 4.2-liter I6 was made by Turbo-Systems Inc. Transmitting all those horses to the road were a set of 16 × 8-inch Gotti aluminum rims wrapped in Goodyear Eagle GT 245/50 16-inch covers.

From AMX to G.T.

Changes to the regular Spirit were more mundane, but still important. For 1980, Spirit, like Concord, utilized the GM 2.5 I4 as a replacement for the VW/Audi/Porsche 2-liter. Spirit also sported the enhanced rustproofing ways of AMC, including aluminized trim screws and deep dip bath for the unibody up to the window line in epoxy-based primer.

These general changes applied to Spirit AMX too, and that version had some specific alterations for 1980.

Visually AMX's grille badge had moved to the center in 1980, the fender flares and front spoiler were in black, and there was just one black driver-side rear-view mirror standard. At the rear, AMX used to have a large mid-rear-spoiler "AMX" decal callout; this was replaced by a small, neat chrome AMX script badge. The 1980 AMX also sported a blackout license plate recess, or venturi, area, plus standard wheels and tires had changed to stamped steel 14 × 6-inch Spoke Styled rims with DR70–14-inch OWL Goodyear Flexten radials.

Turbocast II alloys on ER60–14-inch Flexten radials were now optional. However, in spite of the decontenting, AMX's range of exterior color choices expanded to 8! The choices were: Olympic White, Cardinal Red, Saxon Yellow, Cameo Blue, Cameo Tan, Medium Brown Metallic, Navy Blue and Classic Black. Inside things were much the same as in '79, with leather-wrapped sports steering wheel and "AMX" script badge on the glove box door, but there were no aluminum decorative overlay panels. Well, disco was on the way out by 1980.

One could still enjoy the *Thank God It's Friday!* soundtrack inside '80 AMX. There was a new optional Premium (stereo) audio system with amplifier, 4 high-fidelity speakers and fader control. Manual-transmission 4.2-liter AMXs still came with the "Deep-Throat" performance-tuned exhaust system. AMC reaffirmed that AMX was always hard-core, never soft-core: "AMX. For car enthusiasts only," and added, "For car enthusiasts, AMX is hard to resist. We planned it that way."

The VAM Rally always had a 4.6 I6, no I4s or the AMC V8. VAM's I6 engines were built in their Hidalgo plant, and were attuned to Mexico's low-octane gas (courtesy Mauricio Jordán Márquez).

There was no reason to doubt AMC's sincerity, but AMX was strictly moving to a six-cylinder beat in the '80s. The 304 V8 motor had been withdrawn from Concord, Pacer and Spirit lines at the close of the '79 model year. If one wanted a V8 in an '80 AMC vehicle, one had to order a Jeep. As things stood, AMX came with the same 110 bhp 2bbl 258 seen in '79, although its 210 lbs/ft torque rating was now at 2,000 rpm, hooked up to the usual BW SR4 4-speed.

The SR4 had different ratios when 258 teamed, compared to the 304 application. Automatic was still optional, and the G.T. Rally-Tune Suspension pack was still AMX standard. For '80, the 302 V8 had been replaced by a 119 bhp 255ci version, so in metric parlance '80 AMX and '80 Mustang Cobra both raced with 4.2-liter power!

In this paint-and-tape era one could jazz up base Spirit sedan and liftback with optional Rally Stripe body profile decals. Such decoration on the liftback closely resembled the two-piece split-tail profile stripe of 1977 Gremlin X. The two-tone paint option was unavailable on Spirit sedan, AMX, Rally Stripe or G.T. package cars. However, in 1980, two-tone paint was available on Spirit sedan DL, which retained its Dual Paint Stripe, whereas two-tone Spirit liftback lost the standard Dual Pin Stripe decals.

People were rightly concerned that tinsel had taken over. In 1980 AMX featured a 2.53 final drive ratio across the board, except for high-altitude automatics, which used 2.73 rear gears. But 1980 was a stricter year for emissions and CAFE. Less smog, more MPGs meant no 360 for Aspen/Volare in 1980, nor 400 for Pontiac, and a computer-controlled carb-fed 305 for Golden State Vettes. It was also the last year for AMC's AMX tag, but the G.T. pack continued in sporty Spirit.

AMC used the G.T. name 3 years before the '82 Mustang GT 5.0. The G.T. package was a '79 Spirit liftback option, in the style of the departed X pack. G.T. was available on '79 Spirit DL and Limited with the following items: steel belted BSW radials, Spoke Styled rims, Performance Tuned Exhaust Sound on V8s and I6 manuals, black full-length console with integral center armrest, black-leather-wrapped sports steering wheel, black steering column, black instrument panel with walnut burl overlays (which also featured on door trim panels), rev counter, black bumpers with protective strips and guards, dual black remote rear-view mirrors, black exterior trim moldings, black grille insert, black headlamp bezels, black wiper arms, black rear license plate recess and G.T. medallions.

Optional on Spirit DL and Limited liftbacks with the G.T. package was the G.T. Rally-Tune Suspension pack found standard on Spirit AMX, although this hardware upgrade was unavailable on 4-cylinder Spirits. G.T. was basically AMX without so much of *Smokey and the Bandit*. In 1979 it was possible to have a Spirit G.T. 5.0, although technically G.T. was an option pack, not a model in its own right. In 1980 the G.T. package was optional on base Spirit and Spirit DL. Once again the hardware upgrade pack, which included better brakes, was reserved for 4.2-liter Spirit liftbacks.

The Four Horses of the Apocalypse

By 1981 Spirit G.T. was the sole sports AMC variant, in a field that had seen better days. Mustang Cobra's 255ci V8 was re-rated up to 120 ponies, GM was fielding a 4.4-liter Chevy Camaro Rally Sport, with its Firebird Formula cousin boasting a standard 4.3-liter

V8. This quartet were all that remained of the pony-car crowd; even the rear-drive Aspen/Volare disappeared at the end of the '80 model year. AMC Spirit G.T. was the only car with an I6; the other 3 had V8s, but Spirit G.T. was also the only one with a real pre-econocrisis motor.

VAM unique Rally sports steel rims designed and made in Mexico, carrying the company's logo in the center. Alloy wheels were unavailable on Rally (courtesy Mauricio Jordán Márquez).

Ford reduced the bore of its 302 from 4 inches to 3.68 inches for the 255, Chevrolet's 262 was a smaller cousin of the economy 305 V8, and Pontiac's 265 was related to the already MPG-focused 301 V8. These chariots looked snazzy in their '81 clothing but wheezed through 2bbl carburetion. Only the 258-powered Spirit G.T. had real build-up potential. The AMX/G.T. 4.2s had two-thirds of the torque of a late '70s 6.6-liter Trans Am (210 lbs/ft versus 320 lbs/ft at 2,000 rpm), in a body that was 30 inches shorter with a vehicle weight three-fourths that of the Pontiac.

Unlike the Olds 403ci-powered Trans Am, the Spirit AMX/G.T. could have a 4-speed manual. The BW SR4's diaphragm-style clutch was light and user-friendly. A diaphragm clutch wasn't good at engaging and disengaging cogs with a high-horsepower, high-rpm engine, but that wasn't an issue in the early '80s. The '80 intro of the 85 mph speedo heralded an era when cars were getting so slow in North America that manufacturers were quoting 0–50 mph figures to look good, and forget about the ¼ mile.

In the slowly reviving performance era AMC made history in the '82 model year when Spirit G.T. became America's first pony car available with a 5-speed gearbox. The BW T5, made by the Warner Gear division of Borg Warner, was unavailable in Mustang, Camaro or Firebird until the following model year. The T5 was being used by AMC cars and Jeeps in 1982 to boost gas mileage. The T5 was created by putting a 5th gear where reverse would be on a BW T4. In 1982 the BW SR4, T4 and T5 were all available.

In '82 Mustang GT was stuck with the 3-speed plus overdrive box. GM cars were still using the heavy-duty BW T10, with long, narrow "H" gate and stiff action. The T5 was known for its light shift action, and its spec between Mustang and Spirit varied when Ford got the box in '83. AMC's ratios had wider 1–2 spacing, 4.03 for 1st and 2.37 for 2nd. That steep 1st gave pep off the line in the econo emissions era. In 1983 Spirit G.T. was a separate model, no longer just an option package.

In 1982 came the final curtain for Spirit sedan, all 2.5-liter versions and the base Spirit liftback. By 1983 Spirit's range was reduced to the $5,995 Spirit DL liftback and $6,495 Spirit G.T. liftback; the Limited trim level had departed at the end of the '80 model year. The above-mentioned prices referred to good-value-for-money, high-spec cars. Indeed, one only need compare '83 Spirit G.T. with the '82 Mustang GT that cost $8,965. By '83 Mustang

GT 5.0 had moved onto 4bbl carburetion and 175 bhp, and one would have to look south of the border for a comparable Spirit.

VAM's Gremlin and Rally

VAM's Mexico City operation had produced AMC-related and AMC-based vehicles since the '60s. Unusual variants included the VAM Lerma, a Concord-based car with Spirit liftback front and rear sheet metal, and unique locally tooled rear fender quarter panels. The Gremlin was a latecomer to VAM's local assembly program, arriving in 1974. Being still quite fresh on the Mexican scene, and minus the economy car overtones the Gremlin carried in North America, VAM saw no reason why the revised Spirit sedan couldn't continue with the Gremlin nameplate.

Thus, the Gremlin sedan lived on through to the end of the '83 model year in Mexico. However, of greater sporting interest was the 1980–83 VAM Rally. This was VAM's version of the AMC Spirit liftback. The Rally was exclusively powered by the VAM-engineered 282ci version of AMC's I6, with bore and stroke dimensions of 3.909 inches by 3.894 inches. VAM Gremlins never received this 4.6-liter motor. Outward appearance of the VAM Rally was much like that of the AMC Spirit liftback, but there were specification differences.

VAM had 3 Rally versions: the sporty AMX, extremely sporty GT and luxurious VAM Rally SST. The SST was only available in 1981, and the GT was around in 1980 and 1981, with Rally AMX produced throughout 1980–83. Motorvating AMX and SST was the regular 4.6 I6 with Ford Motorcraft 2bbl carb and 132 bhp on an 8.0:1 compression ratio during 1980–81. In 1982–83 this was revised to 129 bhp with 8.5:1 CR. The GT had the high-performance factory 282 with 8.5:1 CR, 172 net horses and Holley carburetion.

The "made in Mexico" VAM stamp of the I6's engine block. VAM's hi-po 4.6 has become a much-sought-after item on Stateside Gremlins and Pacers (courtesy Mauricio Jordán Márquez).

VAM engines were built in their Hidalgo engine plant. The VAM engineers were working to Mexico's mid–'70s to '86 constraint of low 80 octane gas, but less strict pollution laws meant more tuning freedom than in the U.S. Apparently the VAM I6 exhaust manifold is quite restrictive, so there is the possibility of even greater power. Given the potency of the high-torque 4.6-liter, the only manual used by VAM was the Tremec 176-F 4-speed. The BW SR4, T4 and T5 weren't too good at coping with hi-po engines.

The Tremec was the only gearbox fitted to the Rally GT,

and was the standard box on Rally AMX. Automatic was optional on Rally AMX, but standard and the only choice for Rally SST. The auto-only SST was luxury loaded with power door locks, power windows, power antenna, a/c, rear window defogger, center console with armrest, door armrests with integrated safety reflectors, chrome trim pack (chrome for fender lip, rocker panel, window frames, and bumpers), dual chrome door mirrors and passenger sun visor vanity mirror.

Underlining SST's luxo nature, no rear spoiler was available; neither was a rev counter. SST had the usual Concord dash with digital quartz timepiece. The Concord-introduced Noryl wheel covers found in America were SST standard issue, and Rally SST wasn't available with Rally AMX/GT's standard high-back front reclining buckets. However, all 3 Rally versions came with a 110 mph speedo and split folding rear seats.

Rally SST and GT came with full Light Group, which (as in America) entailed a dome map light, 2 underdash courtesy lights, glove box light, engine bay compartment light and liftback dome light switch. An interior dome light was optional on Rally AMX. AMX and GT both had the auxiliary Rally Pak instruments that SST avoided, and standard tachometer. The GT rev counter was just like the dashboard analogue unit found on U.S. 1979–80 AMXs. However, the Rally AMX featured a digital tach designed by VAM.

The VAM logo was found on AMX/GT's sports steering wheel, in the center of the VAM-designed sports spoke steel rims (Rally didn't feature mag or alloy rims), and was cast into the 4.6 motor. Mexico was strict on local content, and government legislation stopped some features from being factory fitted in 1982 and 1983. The Rally GT always came with rear spoiler: it was optional on AMX in 1980, standard in '81, and unavailable in 1982–83 because of the new regs.

In 1982–83 the electric trunk release was off the menu, as was the rear window defogger. The defogger was another GT standard fitting, optional on AMX. Its 1982–83 absence was compensated for by an optional rear window wiper. The Rally GT came with a standard AM/FM stereo radio, while AMX got by on mono. In 1982–83, Rally AMX could have an optional radio/cassette player with 4-speaker sound, 2 in the front doors and 2 in the cargo area.

The Mexican government's restriction on accessory importation made sure what was sold in Mexico was mostly made in Mexico. There was order to the organization of local vehicle manufacture, contrasting with the haphazard nature of same in other places like Australia, where car manufacture eventually had to be consolidated. This order flowed through what VAM offered too. A VAM Rally had important items like power brakes, power steering, inertia reel seat belts and HD cooling system standard. Four-speed cars came with a Hurst shift linkage and AMX/GT had sports pack exterior with solid colors, blackout portions and decals, but there was no V8.

The 2.0- and 2.5-liter I4s and 5.0 V8 were absent from VAM's Spirit, as were 3- and 5-speed manuals, cruise control, Turbocast IIs, blackout or aluminum-effect dashboard sections, or seats that wouldn't recline. VAM's Rally had all the bases covered without cluttering up the options list. Twilight style changes on Spirit/Rally were rare, though observant types spotted 1981's crosshatch grille with single crossbar part, and what about that Coventry Check fabric?

However, 1982 and 1983 VAM Rally AMX did adopt the shortened bumpers, protective strips and side caps of the U.S. AMC Eagle SX/4 Sport, with its associated blackout paint effect. Call it a Gremlin, Spirit or Rally, AMC's road to the rear-drive subcompact ended in Mexico and America in 1983. The hatchback concept would do an encore performance at Kenosha in 1984, but with a French accent.

Kenosha ... The Eagle Has Landed!

Back in 1978, AMC was looking for a new vehicle project. After the Pacer experience they weren't interested in another car, so Gerry Meyers said American Motors wanted an inexpensive Jeep-related model. Jeep was booming, so it would have been cool to get that Jeep feeling in a normal passenger vehicle. This became especially so when the '79 gas crunch started hurting Jeep sales. Meyers indicated in 1979 that smaller, lighter Jeeps would arrive for '84, but in the interim Eagle flew in.

Eagle was the marriage of Concord and a Jeep driveline by Jeep's chief engineer Roy Lunn. In traditional AMC "design-on-a-budget" style, Kenosha came up with the world's first crossover vehicle. In August 1979, AMC Eagle, the granddaddy of rides like Audi Allroad, Subaru Outback and Volvo XC wagon, introduced car-flavored off-road ability. The American/Hornet/Concord old-school early–'60s suspension allowed a lot of room for modification without a complete retool.

Lunn mounted the front differential on the engine block, with drive to the front wheels via universal joints and halfshafts. Eagle's all-wheel-drive system was a lighter, car-oriented development of Jeep's Quadra-Trac system. The Concord body was raised 4 inches to clear a "New Process" model 119, 42-disc, silicone-filled, LSD action, viscous coupling transfer case with 23-spline input. It was a single-speed transfer case with no low range.

As part of re-engineering Concord into Eagle, wheelbase increased 1 inch and Dana 30 and 35 model differentials were used. Eagle had 3 inches more ground clearance than Concord, which left some very open wheel wells. To solve this visual gap, Richard Teague took Concord hi-rise into the styling studio, and designed wheel-lip-extending plastic skirts. A plastic polymer material bearing the trademark name "Kraton" was used for the wheel well extenders, rocker moldings and lower door panel protectors.

Eagle also closed the gap on Concord by using 15-inch instead of 14-inch wheels. Other visual differences from Concord involved horizontal grille bars spaced slightly further apart, an Eagle script grille badge on the driver's side, and normal bumpers. Eagle was classified as a light truck by the EPA, an ominous development concerning future crossovers/SUVs and laxer CAFE targets, and was exempt from the 5 mph bumper law. Thus, Eagle's bumpers were closer to the body.

There were indeed 4×4 cars around, such as the lightweight Subaru sedans and wagons. However, the Japanese had part-time all-wheel-drive systems that could only be engaged off-road. There wasn't enough mechanical give in the system to use the 4×4 mode on hard road surfaces, where abnormal wear would have occurred. During 1980 Audi changed the world of high performance cars with its Quattro system, but this involved converting a front-driver to all-wheel drive, and diff locks were invoked.

AMC's 4×4 conversion had more in common with the Jensen Interceptor FF, and the 1980 Eagle made its debut with sophisticated standard features. The Eagle arrived in 3 body styles, 2- and 4-door sedan and 4-door wagon, exclusively powered by AMC's 4.2-liter I6.

Eagle represented the melding of Spirit/Concord and a Jeep 4×4 driveline, under the engineering watch of AMC's Roy Lunn (courtesy Sean Weitzel).

The '80 Eagle came with power steering, Chrysler TF 998-based 3-speed auto and independent front suspension. One didn't have to press any special buttons, or work any levers; Eagle was 4×4 made easy! Easy and luxurious travel was afforded by Eagle.

Gerry Meyers made it clear ahead of launch that Eagle was going to be priced high enough so it wouldn't clash with Jeep CJ or Cherokee.[6] As a result Eagle's base trim level was really DL, even though no DL badging was used. Thus, normal Eagle 2- and 4-door sedans rode around with luxo Concord hood ornament, vinyl roofs and opera windows as standard. AMC also had a Limited trim level for Eagle, complete with the Chelsea leather trim and 18-oz carpet found in Limited Concords and Spirits.

Eagle's Sport package had appearance items that made the crossover sportier. Available

The Eagle family started in '80 and was a hit, especially with AMC-Jeep dealers in colder climes. A 1986 Eagle wagon is shown (courtesy Joe Howard).

on 2-door sedan and wagon, Sport pack brought Durham Plaid interior seating fabric, leather-wrapped sports steering wheel, P195/75R Goodyear steel-belted all-season radials, front Marchal foglights, halogen highbeam headlamps, dual remote black sport side mirrors, 4×4 sport graphics, black bumpers and protective strips, black lower body moldings, blackout grille, rear fascia taillight-area blackout paint and profile side stripes.

Eagle Sport also had black moldings covering front and rear window surrounds, door frames and B pillars. Goodyear Tiempo tires were subsequently replaced by the updated Goodyear Arriva tire design. HD suspension and Trailer-Towing Package were $147 together in 1980. The tow pack included a weight-equalizing tow hitch, 7-connector wiring harness, additional wiring, auxiliary transmission oil cooler, and 3.54 rear axle ratio; plus, HD battery and automatic load-leveling rear shocks were associated mandatory options. Concord was the only AMC car available with an underhood compressor and rear air shocks, which was handy for Concord-bodied Eagle and the last item. The tow pack was rated at 3,500 lbs.

AMC was onto something special with Eagle. In June 1980, *Car and Driver*'s Don Sherman declared, "It has the most sophisticated power train Detroit has yet conceived: a full-time four-wheel-drive system that's smooth, quiet and compact enough to work in a car." Sherman also added that the base car happened to be plain old '60s-vintage AMC, but at a time when the public were experimenting with downsized, recall-ridden front-drivers, Chateau Sportabout had a more pleasant bouquet than 7-UP Escort.

AMC boss Meyers didn't bother with market research or customer clinics with Eagle, since time and money were in short supply. Gut instincts said Eagle would be a winner, and it was. Even though 1980 was a very depressed year for the auto industry, Eagle soared to 45,379 sales. Eagle wagon was the most popular version, accounting for 25,807 units. Snowbelt dealers in Colorado and New England were very pleased with the custom Eagle brought. So it was a given the range would be expanded for 1981.

The Spirit of Eagle

The '81 model year saw Spirit-based, all-wheel-drive Eagle variants coded Series 50, while Concord-derived Eagles were Series 30 cars. Old amigo Gremlin arrived in the form of the '81 Eagle Kammback, an all-wheel-drive Spirit sedan. At an entry-level price of $5,995 this was the lowest-priced 4×4 in the land! Then there was the snazzy Eagle SX/4, based on the Spirit liftback, which could also be specified with the Sport pack. The Eagle SX/4 Sport came with color-keyed vinyl sports steering wheel, floorshift console, dash parcel shelf and styled wheel covers, along with the blackout trim and medallions associated with Sport pack.

Series 50 Eagle brought power bulge hoods, and the 2.5-liter I4/4-speed as the Eagle's base power team for the challenging economic times. In all, 5,603 Eagle Kammbacks were sold, and 17,340 SX/4s, making the latter the most popular '81 Eagle. In 1981, Eagle offered optional alloy rims for the first time, and all versions got a new 24 square black plastic egg-crate grille. The Eagle script badge was moved to the grille header bar, still on the driver's side, and bumper end caps were smoothed into the Kraton side trim.

If you wanted to visit the videogame arcade in 1981 to play Berzerk or Pac Man, and it was snowing, AMC had you covered. A crowd of 37,429 people chose Eagle in the '81 model year, and by mid-year, Select Drive became available. Select Drive allowed the driver to switch

The wagon variant was the most popular Eagle version, to the tune of 118,819 units. A 1983 4.2-liter automatic example is at hand (courtesy Kyle Burnett).

to 2-wheel drive: a dashboard toggle switch was pushed left for 2WD and right for 4WD. To make the change, disengaging drive to the front wheels, the car had to be stationary.

With everyone on the better gas mileage trail, Select Drive boosted MPGs and made for sensational ad copy with the lines, "The Newest, Most Advanced Drivetrain in the World," and "Experience driving in the 4th Dimension." This tied in with changes for '82, when Eagle took on the low-drag front disk brakes and optional 5-speed manual or wide ratio automatic seen on Concord/Spirit. In still-depressed economic times, Eagle held steady on 37,923 1982 sales, but the 2-door sedan and Eagle Kammback were discontinued at the end of '82.

Both Eagle 2-door sedan and Kammback were slow sellers during '82, the Spirit sedan-based Kammback selling just 520 copies. That was effectively the end of the familiar Gremlin body shape in the U.S., although it did live on in Mexico for '83. It's probably no coincidence that Honda introduced their new 1984 Civic, which looked like a glassy '80s Gremlin, after AMC/VAM Spirit/Gremlin had been laid to rest, lest the public notice their plagiarism!

In 1981–82 a ray of hope shone on AMC fans, in the form of the Sundancer convertible. The Sundancer was a custom convertible conversion done by the Griffith Company of Fort Lauderdale, Florida. The base car was a Series 30 Eagle 2-door sedan, which was decapitated with reinforcement of the unibody and a steel targa rollbar welded to the door pillars to ward off body flex.

The front part of Sundancer's roof was a removable lightweight fiberglass hatch. The rear section was a foldable polyvinyl top, which could be concertinaed down and concealed by a rear deck trunk lid. Sundancers could be ordered through any AMC dealer. It was common at the time for convertible conversions to be made by specialist companies and

The success of Concord-based Eagle led to the 1981 intro of the Spirit-based Eagle Kammback, a go-anywhere Gremlin. This is an '81 2.5-liter automatic Kammback (courtesy Jim Fracassa).

sold through domestic dealers, because the Big 4 had stopped making factory ragtops for some years due to rollover safety concerns.

AMC's New 4-Banger!

In 1983 the Eagle wagon had the honor of becoming the official vehicle of the National Ski Patrol, but of even greater importance was the February 1983 introduction of American Motors' own 2.5-liter I4, replacing the GM Iron Duke used since 1980. AMC President W. Paul Tippett Jr. said that with the popularity of 4-cylinder engines in the energy-conscious '80s, it made sense to stop buying in I4s, and start making the firm's own design.

The Iron Duke had been in heavy demand during these years by GM's own X cars and subsequent Fiero. Supply and cost factors saw the creation of a real AMC I4. This new 150ci motor was of ohv configuration, with cast-iron head and block weighing 43 and 321 lbs respectively. It was derived from AMC's 4.2-liter I6; in basic terms, imagine that motor without the middle two cylinders. The 2.5-liter I4 also had a "Dual Quench" combustion chamber, a development of the Single Quench head AMC introduced on its I6s for '77.

Catering to the CB (Citizen's Band) radio craze of the mid–'70s to early '80s, AMC, and other domestics, offered optional integrated units for those times when one had to copy and get out (courtesy Jim Fracassa).

Dual Quench was even better at generating more turbulence and faster air/fuel mixture burn. The result was improved performance, economy and lower emissions. Jeep chief engineer Roy Lunn said usually passenger car engines are adapted for 4×4 and pickup applications, but the AMC I4 was specifically designed with Eagle and Jeep in mind. Engine development took 3 years with high power output and durability as key design goals.

Contemporary engine power/torque comparisons show the AMC I4 was well up to the grade. A 1987 Chrysler 2.5 SOHC TBI I4 made 101 bhp at 4,800 rpm and 136 lbs/ft at 2,800 rpm. On debut, AMC I4, with 1bbl carb and 9.2:1 compression ratio, knocked out 105 bhp at 5,000

AMC introduced the price leader $5,995 '81 Eagle Kammback as the cheapest 4×4 in America (courtesy Jim Fracassa).

In rear view, height was the main visual distinction of the Eagle Kammback as compared to the Spirit sedan (courtesy Jim Fracassa).

rpm and 132 lbs/ft at 2,800 rpm. In 1986–90 TBI fuel-injected form, those figures improved to 117 bhp at 5,000 rpm and 135 lbs/ft at 3,500 rpm. In the mid–'80s BMW was selling a port-injected 2.7-liter I6 targeting the CAFÉ-affected U.S. market; it made 121 bhp at 4,250 rpm and 170 lbs/ft at 3,250 rpm. With similar MPFI fuel management system the AMC I4 with 9.1 compression ratio was rated at 121 bhp at 5,250 rpm and 139 lbs/ft at 3,250 rpm.

Therefore, we could believe AMC's claim that their new I4 was a star of the econo-decade: "The new AMC 2.46 liter (150 CID) 4-cylinder engine is a unique engine designed for the '80s." As part of the performance attack the 150 I4 had larger intake and exhaust valve diameter sizes compared to the 258 I6. This was for better breathing, and given the final carb 4.2 motor made 112 bhp, the 2.5's high output per liter was in evidence.

High rpm engines characteristically have a large bore in relation to stroke, and Roy Lunn did say AMC tried to get as large an I4 as possible, given bore center tooling constraints. So to obtain 2.46 liters the bore was a large 3.875 inches, and the stroke a small 3.188 in. The 2.5 I4 was fitted with various types of fuel injection, the 4.2 never was, and power aside brought useful design attractions. A single-piece rear main bearing oil seal made for a better seal.

The 2.5's timing chain tensioner was designed to reduce timing chain noise and promote longer chain life. It also helped accommodate wear slack and maintain correct valve timing. A plastic cylinder head cover protruded 1/8 inch into the cylinder head, and used a factory-installed formed-in-place RTV gasket to combat oil leaks. A conventional gasket was available for situations where the cover had to be removed and replaced during cylinder head repairs.

The wagon and SX/4 variants were the two top-selling Eagles. The Eagle wagon was Sportabout related, with SX/4 based on Spirit liftback and selling 30,044 copies during 1981–83 (courtesy Joshua Tulberg and Mick Stine).

Accessory drive off the motor concerning power steering pump, a/c compressor, etc., could be via conventional V-belt or modern 1-belt-serves-all serpentine system. The 2.5 I4, like AMC's I6s, maintained the Kenosha tradition of having the intake and exhaust manifolds on the same side (driver's side). The 2.5-liter/5-speed power team in the Eagle Series 30 body was 1984 EPA rated at 24/32 mpg city/highway. In '83 Eagle offered 2.5 I4 economy as a base power plant, when Concord/Spirit were exclusively 4.2-liter I6 powered. However, you can lead a horse to water, but you can't make it sip.

Only 147 '84 Eagles were purchased with AMC's 2.5-liter. The AMC brand and Eagle line appealed to domestic car fans, who favor a large engine, but more than this, the tide was turning yet again away from fuel efficiency. An improving economy, falling gas prices and the heavier Series 30 Eagle made the 4.2 I6 a no-brainer. AMC had discontinued the SX/4 at the end of 1983, helping Eagle wagon sales to recover to 21,294 in '84.

In 1984 all the action was taking place in Brampton, Ontario. Eagle had gone completely Canuck, as Kenosha concentrated on the new Alliance/Encore front-drivers. The 4.2 I6 was mostly driving '84 Eagle, in a range reduced to 4-door sedan and wagon, with optional "Shift-on-the-Fly" (SOTF). With SOTF the driver could change from 2WD to 4WD without stopping the Eagle. SOTF was made standard in '85, along with 5-speed overdrive manual and the 4.2 I6.

The 1985 Eagle options included digital display radio tuners, and remote power door locks. A slight restyle saw the adoption of the Series 50 power bulge hood, and removal of the former hood ornament and grille header bar Eagle script badge. Winter starts were made easier with Eagle's exclusive use of a 56-amp alternator, replacing a 42-amp unit. Eagle sales in 1985 were down to 16,008, so there were no major changes for '86.

The '86 automatic Eagles no longer bothered with a torque converter lock-up for the 3-speed autobox, but window tinting was standard, along with 4WD emblems on the rear quarter panels. In 1986 Eagle changed to a Model 128 open differential transfer case, but changed back to the Model 129 unit for 1987. Eagle sales descended from 8,217 to 5,922 units between the 1986 and 1987 model years, prompting the 4-door sedan to be dropped. A mere 454 sedans were sold in '87.

A recently downsized Cherokee had taken a lot of sales from Eagle, and it had to be said this final Hornet vestige was aging by the late '80s. The 1988 model year was the final one for Eagle, and the 2,306 wagons retailed really reflected '87 carryovers. The '88 Eagle wagon had more standard equipment in the form of a/c, rear window defogger, halogen headlamps, AM/FM stereo radio, Light Group and Adjust-O-Tilt steering wheel. Options were power windows, power seats and mirrors, radio/cassette player combo, cruise control, rear window wiper, woodgrain side paneling, floor mats, headlamps-on warning buzzer and intermittent wipers. Some of the final Eagles even possessed aluminum engine valve covers.

And with that, Eagle said goodbye, cruel world — or should that have been adieu, monde cruel? Because in recent times AMC had concentrated on Jeep and a French alliance.

CHAPTER 8

Kenosha Serves Cafe au Lait!

That Riviera Touch

The see-sawing, peak-and-trough business fortunes of American Motors since the mid–'60s were well known. In 1979 AMC President W. Paul Tippett Jr. even made light of it: "We really have a three-word name. Nobody calls us just 'American Motors'— it's 'Struggling American Motors,' 'Ailing American Motors,' or 'Moribund American Motors.'"[1] The magic output that allows a car maker to make sufficient profit to plow back into R&D and retooling for new models was on the rise.

In 1969 a company like BMW made 145,000 cars and 5,000 bikes and was glad of it. It was enough in 1969, but not by the mid–'70s. In 1977 BMW made more cars than AMC for the first time in history, 290,236 versus 184,361. In 1978 AMC's car output fell to 170,739, and they weren't glad of it.[2] In truth the smaller car percentage in AMC's business was by accident and design. After the big losses of 1975 and 1976, the company was close to bankruptcy in early 1977 and restructured towards more Jeep under the new leadership of Gerry Meyers.

AMC was in the black in 1977 and 1978, but it needed to find a partner to ensure the continued manufacture of cars. A company couldn't be a volume automaker, achieving the necessary economies of scale, on Jeep alone. During 1977 a joint venture partner was sought, with AMC knocking on the door of Honda, VW and Peugeot, but to no avail. AMC then tried France's other car-making giant, Renault, and in Le Regie there was some hope.

Renault was founded by Louis Renault, but was subsequently nationalized in 1944. This act was done by Charles de Gaulle when he led the provisional French government in the immediate period (1944–46) after liberation from the Third Reich. However, Renault has behaved much like any private automaker, with an understanding it has always had to earn its keep. The French firm did have an early U.S. foray with the rear-engined Dauphine, but this proved less than stellar.

Dauphine is the female form of the French feudal title Dauphin. The small car was extensively tested, according to Renault, with pre-production models covering over 3 million kms in the mountains of Switzerland, the U.S., and Arctic and tropical African regions. The Dauphine made a 1956 press debut in Corsica with the claim it brought an air of "springtime, year in, year out."[3] The car was popular, and with production in France and other countries, it hit a grand total of 2,150,738 by 1968. But it wasn't all good.

The Dauphine journeyed to America to take advantage of the rising interest in small economy cars that accompanied the late–'50s recession, but wasn't that well received. *Road & Track* timed one at 32 seconds for 0–60 mph, and its quota of quality didn't cut it. In performance and reliability it wasn't a match for that other rear-engined rear-driver called Beetle. VW was still the king of small cars.

U.S. firm Judson Research & Mfg. Co. offered a $165 bolt-on supercharger kit for the Dauphine in 1958, but most looking for speedy small cars tried the I6 Rambler American or V8 Studebaker Lark. Renault's ad hoc, impromptu U.S. dealer network quickly dissolved with falling Dauphine interest. Renault's interest wisely turned back to places closer to home, and by the late '70s the company was a European star. Renault made its own machine tools, sophisticated robot assembly machinery and more front-drivers than anyone else.

The Japanese hadn't really adopted front drive yet, and outside Japan, Renault was the most efficient at producing the greatest number of cars, using the fewest people. Global expansion was in the cards, with Renault owning 10 percent of Volvo's Car Division and 20 percent of Mack Trucks by the early '80s.[4] Renault hooked up with Bendix to make electronic systems for cars in France, and was Europe's No. 1 automaker, and the 7th largest globally.[5]

There was some common history between AMC and Renault. The Dauphine was assembled by IKA in Argentina, which went on to make the Torino, a car using a Rambler chassis. AMC's '60s Belgium Rambler assembly factory was looked after by Renault, which sold the big U.S. cars through some of its dealers on the Continent as Renault Ramblers. In the early '70s, AMC and Renault even evaluated the joint development of a rotary that might have powered Pacer.

April in Paris

Two months of negotiation occurred between the companies in the winter of 1978–79. Felix Rohatyn was the original matchmaker, with a preliminary agreement signed and formalized in January 1979. Le Regie took a 22.5 percent stake in AMC in 1979. Renault's Chairman at the time was Bernard Vernier-Palliez, who had held the position since 1975. Of key importance to the joint venture was Renault's second in command, and subsequent boss, Bernard Hanon.

Executive deputy director Hanon had lived in the U.S. for 11 years, taught management at New York University, and was working at Renault when the Dauphine flopped in America 20 years earlier.[6] Gerry Meyers said the Renault people were close to U.S. business thinking, and that this would make for a smooth working relationship between AMC and Renault. Indeed, American Motors' top officers and staff started to make regular Paris visits to work on joint projects with Renault. The first quarterly planning and review meeting took place in April 1979.[7]

Renault had maintained an American presence even post–Dauphine. It was one of the Euro import brands, and in the '70s sold the 63 bhp 1,647cc Renault 12 America. By 1978 it had 320 dealers, and a tie-up with AMC would quickly expand the number of outlets for Renault vehicles. Renault's former U.S. VP of sales, James R. Fuller, started working for AMC as part of the dealership integration. There were other reasons, apart from the 1,300 dealers and manufacturing facilities AMC had at the start of the '80s, for Renault to hook up with American Motors.

Completely against the industry trend, AMC posted a $70.9 million profit in 1979.

With a debt-equity ratio of 14 and mid-year return on equity of 24.6 percent, AMC was doing better than GM! The stats were impressive: $3 billion worth of 1979 sales and $1 billion in assets made American Motors an attractive partner. And of course, there was the lure of Jeep. No wonder Gerry Meyers was pictured grinning at the wheel of a car transporter truck, with a pack of Beech-Nut Chewing Tobacco on the truck's dash, and a load of whitewall-tired Concords and Spirits. It was a time to be confident at Kenosha.[8]

Desperately Seeking Econocar—AMC Alliance and Encore

The first French model sold through AMC dealers during 1979 was the Renault 5. The Renault 5, or Le Car as it was called in America, represented the modern Renault started by the efficiently designed Renault 16. The Le Car was a front-drive hatchback, with North-South engine layout and very comfy suspension. It was Europe's first "Supermini," a class of larger, more advanced small family cars that went beyond the original 1959 British Austin Mini template.

Tragically, the Renault 5's young designer, Michel Boué, died at the age of 35, one year before the first of 5,471,709 copies of his work left the assembly line.[9] Apart from the R5,

The Renault 5, as the Le Car, was the first Renault sold through AMC dealers under the AMC-Renault alliance. A 1984 Renault 5 Gordini Turbo is displayed (courtesy Andrew Berridge, www.r5gordini.co.uk).

AMC dealers were also promised the larger Renault 18 for the fall of 1980. The R18 was a smooth-looking replacement for the Renault 12, and had been cooked up in just 18 months! It also had a North-South front-drive engine layout, and represented the first European market use of the new Renault 1,397cc Cléon I4, plus MacPherson strut independent front suspension on this size of Renault.

The R18 was a 5-passenger Euro sports sedan, sold in the class of upscale vehicles like the Saab 900, Audi 4000, BMW 320i and Cadillac Cimarron. In North America it was called 18i, and was joined by its wagon cousin the 18i Sportwagon at the same 1981 model year intro. Sportwagon was a lighter, upscale Euro equivalent of Hornet Sportabout. Note should also be made of the curvy, pear-shaped Renault 14 of 1976–82. This VW Rabbit class competitor had its unibody shell displayed in France's Pompidou Center, and had a transverse East-West I4 front-drive layout. The R5 and R18 were imported, and though the R14 was never even sold in North America, elements from all three were relevant to the AMC Alliance that was made at AMC's Kenosha factory.

The Alliance was the car, coded "model 142," that AMC-Renault planned to build in America, 200,000 units per year for the fuel-efficient '80s, starting in the '83 model year.[10] AMC's 1980 catalogue stated that AMC and Renault had the credentials to get the job done using an alliance of experience: "It unites the small-car pioneers of America and Europe." Renault also informed the American public that it had the answer for the '80s in a 1982 print ad. The first page displayed econo-competitors from Fiat, Honda, Ford, Toyota, Chevy, VW and Datsun.

At the top of the page was the question, "Quick, who has the most fuel-efficient car range?" Over leaf, on a two-page spread, the answer: "Voila, Renault." Renault's entire European fleet, from Renault 4 to Renault Alpine A310 V6, was shown in the desert, with a single palm tree and futuristic Renault factory in the background. Le Regie's diamond logo was prominently displayed, and the whole scene bathed in a sunset glow.

Renault wanted you to know this was more than a mirage. It had the science in the form of "EVE," a fuel conservation research laboratory in a car. As Renault said, to associate performance with fuel efficiency, simply say, "Voila Renault." Unlike VW and Fiat, Renault didn't have corporate aircraft. AMC didn't have chauffeurs for its management. Therefore, it was a safe bet that any car arising from the alliance wouldn't be wasteful.

In June 1981, Gerry Meyers made a formal statement that Renault would handle the cars, while AMC would take care of Jeep and Eagle from this point. Given the Alliance was an Americanized Renault 9, Europe's 1982 Car of the Year and a hot seller, the starting point was solid. AMC Alliance/R9 had a front-drive, transverse I4 engine layout, with MacPherson strut front suspension and trailing arm/torsion bar rear suspension. The I4 was the aforementioned cast-iron block/light-alloy head OHV Cléon motor, shared with the Renault Le Car.

Alliance's engine and transaxle were imported, featuring Bendix fuel injection and choice of standard 4 on the floor, with 5-speed overdrive manual or 3-speed auto as options. The 49-state Alliances had TBI (Throttle Body Injection), California cars had more efficient port injection to cope with stricter emissions. The Alliance harked back to the '57 Rambler Rebel with Bendix "Electrojector" injection. That car never went into volume production, and Kenosha never built a vehicle with 4-wheel independent suspension ... until now!

AMC Alliance also set a new standard for compactness. Even with 5 mph bumpers the new car was just 163.8 inches long on a 97.2-inch wheelbase, but with lots of interior space. A light weight of 2,030 lbs helped the 64 bhp car scamper to sixty in 14.3 seconds, and on to a top speed of 89 mph, when tested by *Car and Driver* in September 1982. This was equal to a late–'70s six-cylinder intermediate, but with much better MPGs. The stick-shift Alliance was EPA rated at 29 mpg city/37 mpg highway, enough to put OPEC out of business.

Apart from minor trim alterations and U.S. lighting law changes (Alliance had 4 head-lamps); this was authentic chateau R9 in spite of the different label. Rack and pinion steering was present, as were Renault's new and unusual "Monotrace" central frame front seats, which were mounted on a 9-inch-wide pedestal, and fully adjustable in fore/aft/recline variation. Rear passengers had more space to place their feet under the front seats compared to a normal car. High-spec Alliances permitted the seat to move on a convex radius for perfect tilt.

The Alliance handled and rode better than comparable Japanese cars, and the price was right. The debut announced base price was $5,907, with a loaded leather-and-stereo Alliance costing under 9 grand. An optional extra was an electronic "Systems Sentry" that warned the driver if engine oil, coolant, windshield washer fluid, brake fluid, power steering or transmission fluids were running low. A success with the public and critics, the '83 Alliance was a strong seller, and *Car and Driver* named it among their Top 10 cars of 1983.

Renault was also producing cars in Mexico, using the VAM operation. Renault had slowly made the transition from Torino to locally made Renaults with IKA in Argentina; in Mexico this transition was more rapid. VAM had been 6 percent AMC-owned, 94 percent Mexican government-owned. When Renault took a major interest in AMC in 1980, part of the aforementioned 6 percent automatically fell into Renault's hands.

The 1982 recession hit VAM mighty hard, and Renault was able to persuade the Mexican government to transfer complete VAM ownership to Renault. Privatization was very big in the '80s, and after the final AMC-related passenger car VAMs were gone at the end of '83, Renault started fresh in 1984! The VAM name was gone, the assembly operation was renamed Renault-Jeep or La Nueva Renault de Mexico. Renault retained Jeep, and added Mexican-produced Renault 5, 9, 11 and 18. However, the Renault Fuego coupe was never produced nor sold in Mexico.

This all seemed to be going according to Monsieur Hanon's plan. Hanon oversaw a process whereby Renault moved towards noncontentious front-drivers, in an era when automakers were searching for a "World Car," code for a one-size-fits-all markets vehicle. The Renault 18 was the first Renault about which critics claimed the Frenchness had been taken out. Apart from a competent, supple chassis and comfy seats, there was little about the AMC Alliance/R9 to indicate French origin.

Renault Gets Sporty with Fuego and Formula One

Combined with a middle-of-the-road, offend-no-one approach, Hanon energized high volume sales with racing, as any large manufacturer would. He pushed for Renault's involvement in Formula One racing. Renault entered Formula One in 1977 with a 1.5-liter V6 turbo of their own design, naturally, at a time when most teams used the normally aspirated

3-liter Cosworth DFV V8. It was the greatest avant-garde move since the French Revolution, and by the mid–'80s all Formula One front-runners used the 1.5-liter turbo format.

For Renault, or the French taxpayer, it was a $10 million per annum commitment, justifiable for Europe's No. 1 car maker. The quid pro quo was valuable R&D and PR for Renault. Thus, Renault could place a Renault Formula One car decal with the logo of Elf—France's national oil company and Renault tech development partner — on the rear hatch glass of R5s to excite the masses. Plus, on the 1982 Formula One Renault RE-30B Turbo V6, the cam covers carried "Renault Gordini." Sports Renault versions had the Gordini tag, another point of identification for the man or mademoiselle on the street.

That was the PR; the R&D flow-ons came in the form of the 560 bhp 1,492cc KKK twin turbo Formula One V6's Renix (Renault/Bendix) engine management electronics, that would subsequently benefit Jeep owners. Renault also offered turbo road cars in the '80s, with the top R9/R11 variants getting blown. In September 1985 CAR's R11 Turbo had Elf white-lettered insignia on its I4 turbo's red oil filler cap. The 1,397cc ohv Cléon made 105 bhp at 5,500 rpm and 119 lbs/ft at 2,500 rpm. For '87 that output was raised to 115 bhp.

The Renault 11 Turbo used a high 8.5:1 compression ratio with low boost to minimize turbo lag. Recorded stats for the 2,017-pound car were 0–60 mph in 8.6 seconds, 114 mph at 5,300 rpm in 5th and 30 mpg at 75 mph.[11] It seemed like Formula One had been a good teacher. The Renault 11 was the hatchback cousin of the R9 sedan. In 1983 the Alliance was introduced in 2- and 4-door forms, with the R11 joining Kenosha's production line for 1984 under the "Encore" nameplate. Supply wasn't readily available until the '85 model year.

In 1985 a convertible version of the 2-door Alliance was also released, Kenosha's first ragtop since 1968! The Alliance convertible came standard with the Alliance's new optional 78 bhp 1.7 liter I4. This was fancy enough, but during the Renault years the real glamour magnet at AMC dealers was the Fuego coupe. The Renault Fuego was derived from the R18 platform, although this connection was downplayed by Renault. The Fuego replaced the R15 and R17 coupes, which were Renault 12-based.

In Europe the Fuego, Spanish for "fire," took on the Ford Capri and Opel Manta, which were both rear-drive. The front-drive Fuego arrived in February 1980, and was the top-selling 2-door coupe in Europe during 1980–82. The car's designer, Robert Opron, had done the Citroën GS, and went on to do the Renault 25, and bestowed a rounded form

While the Alliance (Renault 9) and Encore (Renault 11) were made at AMC's Kenosha factory, the Renault 18i, Fuego and Le Car were imported (courtesy The Rambler Ranch).

upon the Fuego's wedge profile. The Fuego had the bulbous, high-waisted style of the Porsche 924, but avoided that car's slight awkwardness.

With a drag factor of 0.34 the Fuego was par for the course, and despite sedan underpinnings could inspire dreams. In a 1992 retrospective Fuego piece, *Autocar & Motor* magazine set the scene. It was Europe 1980, you were flying down a Continental autoroute during summer with Catherine Deneuve by your side in a new coupe. Not even her whiny agent in the back seat asking, "Are we there yet?" could spoil things. The Fuego looked special enough to make the whole reverie plausible.

The range topper was the Fuego Turbo, and in 1984 a marketing slogan described this version as "L'Aerodynamite!" The Fuego Turbo made its European debut in 1983, with a 132 bhp 1.6 liter turbo I4, top speed of 125 mph and 0–60 mph time of 9.5 seconds. However, Fuego Turbo appeared earlier in North America. The imported Fuego hit American shores in mid–'82 model year with a normally aspirated 1.6-liter I4, accompanied by an 11-grand 1.6 blown edition. The 1.6 turbo motor had arrived earlier in the 1981 Euro R18 Turbo, and the '82 U.S. Fuego Turbo used a smogged-down version of this I4.

They Call Him Le Hoff!

A Garrett T3 turbo puffed 12.8 psi max boost pressure, giving the 1.6 I4 107 bhp and 120 lbs/ft. Not enough to blow a turbo Mustang's house down, but work at the 5-speed stick and the U.S. Fuego Turbo could reach sixty in 10 seconds and a top speed of 110 mph. This was the same performance as a 4-speed 5-liter 145 bhp '82 Trans Am, but with 26 city/39 highway MPGs, and the interior had a boost gauge. Factor in the detuned 1.6 turbo and 365 mm system TRX rims and Michelin metric tires, and torque steer wasn't an issue. Visual changes for the U.S. translation involved larger bumpers, recessed headlamps with plastic surrounds, and interior and exterior color/trim differences, quite minor overall, with 0.35 cd registered.

Car and Driver's Rich Ceppos identified the Fuego Turbo as the suave handler that it was, and a tidy bit of product placement was managed when the Fuego Turbo made a cameo on television's *Knight Rider*. Here the Fuego Turbo rescued Michael Knight and did a handbrake turn that left the normally talkative K.I.T.T. speechless. *Knight Rider* was shown in several countries, including France, where it was dubbed into French. One can only imagine the nation's pride when a French-speaking David Hasselhoff entered the plush Fuego avec "Turbo" door decal!

Back to Bond

The Fuego also achieved a modern marvel in 1983 when it came out with the world's first infrared "PLIP" remote power door-lock control, a system subsequently seen on Eagle. The PLIP term was derived from the name of the device's French inventor, Paul Lipschutz. As if all this weren't enough, AMC-Renault returned to the realm of 007 in 1985 with the Bond movie *A View to a Kill*. Bond movies normally have a topical central theme. In *The Man with the Golden Gun* the 1973–74 energy crisis was plot-linked; in *A View to a Kill* the world of microchips was on show.

By the early '80s the entrepreneurial exploits of companies like Apple and Atari had shone a light on the computer hardware and software entity that was California's Silicon Valley. Therefore, what could be a better story for the high-tech '80s than Bond battling the evil Max Zorin, hell-bent on destroying Silicon Valley? This was the tale of *A View to a Kill*, filmed in a number of international locations, as per usual Bond franchise practice.

Some filming took place in France, where Renault's automated factory was used as Zorin's microchip warehouse, and Paris was the setting for stunt work featuring the AMC Encore/R11. Bond, once again played by Roger Moore, steals a 1984 Renault 11 TXE Electronic from a Paris cab driver, so as to give chase to assassin May Day. The stunt sequence was coordinated by famous French stunt man Remy Julienne, and saw the R11 jump onto and off a sightseeing bus, lose its roof, and get chopped in two by a subsequent collision!

Bond was able to continue driving the front half, given the Renault's front-drive nature. Three cars were used for the sequence: a complete car, one with the roof removed, and a further one in two halves. The complete car has appeared in various Bond displays over the years, including the Edinburgh launch of the movie *Quantum of Solace*, starring Daniel Craig as 007. Going back to *A View to a Kill*, it was a case of déjà vu to see Moore's Bond purloin an AMC-related vehicle to chase a bad guy, or gal. Some things just never change!

Thank Heaven for Little Jeeps!

AMC's late '70s success rested on Jeep, so when the energy crisis and recession of 1979–80 arrived, there was just one thing to do: get more MPGs! To rescue stagnant or falling sales, AMC introduced economy changes to boost mileage. For 1980 the base Jeep CJ-5 power team was the 2.5-liter Iron Duke/4-speed manual, the first time a CJ had seen an I4 under AMC-Jeep ownership. American Motors got an Isuzu diesel C240 unit from GM. Isuzu was a GM subsidiary, and the 2.3-liter I4 was fitted to export CJs built at the Jeep plant in Toledo, Ohio, during 1980–82.

CJs also used a more efficient Dana 300 23-spline input transfer case with aluminum tail housing over the 1980–86 period. Freewheeling CJ/SJ hubs and modest 1981 aero body changes, along with dropping the CJ-7's rear axle ratio to 2.73, conspired to lure people back to Jeep. AMC even revised the trusty 258 motor for '81 with a weight-loss program. The low-carb 4.2 I6 featured a plastic valve cover, lighter block and redesigned crank, all of which added up to 50 pounds off the scales.

The 258 also got smarter with AMC's CEC (Computerized Emission Control) system. A black-box computer-controlled ignition system along the lines of Chrysler's ELB (Electronic Lean Burn) or GM's ESC (Electronic Spark Control), CEC had an exhaust-mounted oxygen sensor, coolant temperature switch and microprocessor to calculate optimal ignition timing. The system was fitted to all 258ci California '80 AMCs, 1981 Jeeps and 49-state AMCs by 1982.

CEC and automatic torque converter lock-up all went towards raising AMC's CAFE credentials. Economics was even putting the squeeze on rich folks who liked Wagoneer. This full-sized Jeep was very popular in V8 form, but the 258/4-speed manual returned as the standard power team in 1980. Indeed, in the general economic malaise, 1982 was the first year one couldn't get a 304 in CJ. All the austerity measures were OK up to a point,

As a downsized replacement for the 1974–83 SJ, the new XJ Cherokee became a popular basis for extreme off-roading machines (courtesy Kurt Buresh).

but more was needed. Although Wagoneer sales held steady thanks to its upscale buyer demographic profile, CJ and SJ Cherokee sales needed Jeep-aid.

New, lightweight big Jeeps were needed, and Gerry Meyers promised they were on the way for '84.[12] Jeep's lifesaver was the 1984 XJ Cherokee, a downsized off-roader for the '80s. The XJ's genesis was in 1978 with initial sketches, and clay models that used SJ Cherokee as a starting point. XJ Cherokee was also the first new AMC design that was part of the AMC-Renault joint design venture, and benefited from Renault money. Indeed, in the aforementioned movie *A View to a Kill*, Bond-girl character Stacey Sutton drove a crisp white XJ Cherokee, to go with the stunt Encore/R11 hatch as product placement.

The XJ was Jeep's first unibody design, although the term "Uniframe" would be more precise. Uniframe implied a light base frame welded to the floor panels. The strength of full frame, the lightness of unibody! The XJ rig was 1,000 lbs lighter, 21 inches shorter, 6 inches narrower and 4 inches lower than SJ. One was looking at dimensions of 165.3 L, 70.5 W, and 63.3 H for a 100.4-inch-wheelbase 2-door Cherokee, with an AMC 2.5-liter I4/4-speed manual-equipped starting weight of just 2,716 lbs. The 2.5/BW T4 power team was only around in '84. Cherokee was also available in a 4-door wagon, a response to Chevrolet's new 2 door S-10 Blazer.

XJ Cherokee Team Teague styling was of a minimalist, blockish, sans-chrome, '80s nature. It was the sort of 4×4 the clay animation character Gumby would be happy to own, but beneath that small, toylike exterior, XJ was all Jeep. Live axles were used front and rear, with a new Roy Lunn designed "Quadra-Link" front suspension. Quadra-Link involved 4 control arms, two below the front axle and two above. The front suspension also featured a Panhard rod, coils and gas shocks.

Rearwards XJ Cherokee had two longitudinal leaf arm sets, each with 4 leaves. There were also gas shocks and a mild rear swaybar, if the optional "Up-Country" off-road enhancement package wasn't specified. With Up-Country the rear swaybar was omitted and the following were included: skidplates for the front suspension, transfer case, and gas tank; different front and rear springs to allow a one-inch increase in ride height; two front and one left rear tow hooks; uprated gas pressurized shocks; and 15 × 7-inch rims with P225/75R radials.

XJ Cherokee used Dana 30 and Dana 35 differentials front and rear respectively, and chain-driven transfer cases with aluminum tail housings. All-wheel-drive systems available on XJ were part-time Command-Trac and optional full-time Selec-Trac. The 8.5-inch semi-floating Dana 44 differential with HD iron housing is reputed to have been XJ's finest hour. The Dana 44 was fitted during 1987–88, and featured on U.S. XJs with manual gearbox and tow pack.

Renault engineer François Castaing designed the XJ's drive train around the little AMC 2.5 I4 motor; this was, after all, a downsized design. A sign XJ would be a hit came in 1980 when excess CJ/SJ stocks existed, but there was a waiting list for Eagle. In '84 XJ Cherokee delivered the modern, frugal off-road experience people sought, and sales were over 100,000 units per annum once XJ got in the groove. XJ proved a critical success too, picking up a number of 4×4 magazine awards, which AMC-Jeep was happy to point out in advertising.

Options to consider included a rear window vent. Normally 2-door Cherokee's extended length rear windows were fixed. Also optional during 1984–86 was the GM 2.8 V6, and in 1985–87 Renault's 2.1-liter intercooled turbodiesel lent Gallic agricultural charm. The OHC 2,065cc I4 used a Garrett turbo, making 85 bhp at 3,750 rpm and 132 lbs/ft at 2,750 rpm. Renault's hookup with AMC allowed the sale of Jeeps through Renault outlets in Europe. Later on came the Italian 2.5 VM turbodiesel-powered European, South American and Australian XJs.

Some European markets even had a commercial panel-van version of the 2-door Cherokee. The Cherokee van attracted a lower level of road tax and had the rear windows replaced by sheet metal. There was also no rear seating, and a flat cargo area to help deliver croissants and suchlike. Indeed, XJs were not only exported overseas, they were made overseas. During the Tang Dynasty, cast iron, gunpowder and printed paper were all Chinese inventions. Therefore, the manufacture of XJs in Beijing, China, represented a return to form.[13]

Under the post–Chairman Mao free-market reforms, economic zones were set up, and manufacturing joint ventures between overseas companies and local Chinese partners started. AMC got in on the ground floor with a 1983 agreement to manufacture the 1984 4-door XJ Cherokee by the Beijing Jeep Corporation. An attempt was even made to make the XJ in Australia. A local Brisbane, Australia, operation had been turning out SJ Cherokees between 1981 and 1986.

The 258/360-powered SJs found it tough to achieve sales against more frugal diesel Toyota Land Cruisers and Nissan Patrols. The XJ could have changed Cherokee fortunes down under. However, attempts to assemble the XJ in Australia were denied by the Button Plan. This Australian federal government model tried to streamline local car production into a smaller number of larger manufacturers better able to achieve economies of scale. Under this directive, small operations that assembled AMC cars and Jeeps wouldn't be encouraged.

Around this time America was ready for more powerful Jeeps, since gas was getting cheap, so AMC-Jeep introduced their multi-point fuel-injected ohv 4.0 I6. A mix of 258 and 2.5 liter dimensions, this modern version of the 4.2 had bore and stroke of 3.875 inches × 3.414 inches, displacing 242ci. The 4.0 made an '87 model year debut with 173 bhp at 4,500 rpm and 220 lbs/ft at 2,500 rpm. This represented a 50 percent power and 47 percent torque improvement over the outgoing 2.8 V6.

The 3,959cc motor used Renix engine management electronics, which had an octane knock sensor and was advanced for the time, but had no permanent memory for a diagnostics system. Once the ignition was shut off, all codes were lost. However, the 4-liter was well received and Cherokee weight with the new engine was still just 3,228 lbs. No doubt Cherokee benefited from the new program-timing committee organized by President W. Paul Tippett Jr. in 1979. Under this, AMC's top 10 company officers and Tippett would manage new projects from start to finish with a keen eye on weight, cost and economy targets.[14] So Cherokee held no nasty surprises.

Accompanying the new 4.0 was the use of the Aisin-Warner 30–40LE 4-speed automatic. This '87-introduced box, jointly developed by Borg Warner and a Toyota subsidiary, came with torque converter lock-up on the overdrive 0.75 4th, plus power and comfort bias electronic shift programs. Earlier than this, XJ's range expanded to include the up-spec '85 XJ Pioneer 4 door, and many more trim packs would ensue. For '86, Cherokee became available in 2-wheel-drive form, with attractive 2-door Cherokee bait price of $9,195. AMC also liked to point out Cherokee offered 2 "shift-on-the-fly" 4WD systems, while Blazer had just one and Bronco none!

The Wagoneer and Wagoneer Limited were upscale XJ Cherokees with a 4-headlamp front fascia; the lamp pairs were vertically stacked. The Wagoneer Limited had vinyl decorative side wood trim, and by '87 possessed Michelin self-sealing tires, automatic and "English Walnut" side panel trim as standard equipment. A second XJ spinoff was the 1986

This extensively modified 1996 XJ Cherokee 4-door 4.0 automatic has a front axle with Dana 60 high pinion 5.13 gear ratio and OX Locker, plus rear disk brake conversion. The transfer case is a New Venture 231 unit with slip yoke eliminator kit (courtesy Kurt Buresh).

MJ Comanche pickup. The ad said, "Easy to be a truck. Hard to be a Jeep," but the XJ base promised true Jeep off-roadability.

Replacing the CJ-8 pickup, the Comanche had an XJ wheelbase stretched to 119.6 inches, and 7-ft-5-inch bed. From the doors forward it was pure XJ, and reminded one of Pacer's transformation into CGE Pacer pickup. Seventy-five percent of pickups are ordered in 2WD form, so it was handy that MJ became the first Jeep truck with a 2WD option. There were 43.8 inches between wheel wells and standard payload capacity of 2,205 lbs. Like XJ, MJ Comanche was a commercial and critical success, picking up *Four Wheeler* magazine's "4 Wheeler of the year" award.

In 1988 the arrival of the "Eliminator" package made Comanche an overtly sporty off-roader. Available on the 2WD shortbed variant, Eliminator brought MJ's optional 4.0 I6, new 10-hole aluminum 14-inch rims with 215/65 HR radials, special exterior graphics, color-keyed grille, fender flares and front airdam. The interior featured buckets, tach, sports tiller, upgraded trim and standard 5-speed stick. With Renix 4.0 in 3,000 lbs of mini truck, the "Eliminator" bed decal aft of the passenger cab wasn't just for show.

Amid all the new stuff, SJ Wagoneer soldiered on. In 1983 the 258/automatic power team and Selec-Trac 4WD were standard with associated EPA figures of 18/25 mpg city/highway. In 1984 the SJ Wagoneer Limited was renamed Grand Wagoneer to avoid confusion with the smaller XJ Wagoneer Limited. Mid–'84 saw a decontented "Wagoneer Custom" debut at $15,995. Wagoneer Custom jettisoned woodgrain paneling and took on steel wheels with humble hubcaps, along with part-time 4WD.

BDS suspension parts feature, along with a custom rear mono-link with polyperformance 1 in uniball. Tires are 39.5 × 16-inch Super Swamper IROKs on 16 × 8-inch Eaton beadlock rims. This Cherokee has a 16-gallon RCI aluminum fuel cell, and custom exocage made out of 0.120-inch wall tubing (courtesy Kurt Buresh).

In spite of a 3-grand discount from Grand Wagoneer, Wagoneer Custom wasn't popular. Too many questions at the country club, asking if one's family had endured a financial hardship, you understand? But Grand Wagoneer wasn't just surviving, it was thriving! So move from the soup kitchen to the wine cellar, and savor vintage '86 Grand Wagoneer's new instrument panel, grille and taillights, plus '87's revised woodgrain panels. In Finland the SJ Wagoneer's main motor was a 4.4-liter Valmet 411 Diesel, with an aftermarket turbo proving popular. In mid–'80s America the 360 had regained favor with SJ buyers who no longer feared the MPGs.

Don't let the plushness fool you: whether it was an old Willys or the latest XJ, Jeep could always master the terrain. In the inaugural 1973 Snow Drift Rally, SJ Wagoneer finished 1st and 2nd. In a February 1985 *Autocar* off-roader group test a 258ci CJ-7 Renegade showed its efficiency by providing the most torque at the lowest rpm, 199 lbs/ft at 1,600 rpm, and conquering the off-road course while delivering 0.5 mpg better fuel economy than the 1-liter I4 Suzuki SJ 410 also tested.

The *Autocar* test showed where off-roaders were going. The CJ-7 Renegade was expensive (the importer charged $28,883), and 9 out of 10 were sold in the city of London, England. This is not a place that really needs a 4×4 to visit the Queen. The CJ-7 was the only 4×4 in the test open to the elements, thanks to a canvas top. An old-school wartime Willys Jeep outperformed all the modern rigs — Range Rover, Nissan Patrol, Mercedes G-wagen, even the CJ-7! The off-road mystique of Jeep and the romance of the great outdoors were making premium Jeeps a luxury car alternative for affluent buyers.[15]

The Civilian Jeep had the most history of any 4×4; former President Reagan even had two. A CJ-6 and blue CJ-8 were personal transport on his California ranch. The blue CJ-8 had the license plate "Gipper," which was Reagan's nickname, after the 1920s star football player George Gipp that the President played in the 1940 movie *Knute Rockne All American*. On his deathbed Gipp urged Notre Dame coach Rockne to inspire the team when the odds were against them, by asking them to "Win one for the Gipper."

Ronald Reagan used the Gipper line when campaigning for president in 1980. There can't be a more iconic combination than Reagan, Jeep CJ and the Gipper! The CJ's historic influence extended overseas to licensees that assembled CJs. These included Mitsubishi, which made the CJ-3B until 1998. Indian company Mahindra started making the CJ-3B in 1954, carrying on into the 21st century with the CJ-5 as a companion model. The CJ-7 Renegade famously featured as the transport of Mindy McConnell in the TV sitcom *Mork & Mindy*. Alien Mork from Ork arrived home at the start of each episode, sitting upside down in the CJ-7's passenger seat.

In spite of the CJ's evolutionary refinements it couldn't last forever. The CJ-5 left the building in 1984, with all remaining CJ North American variants being discontinued in 1986. The CJ's replacement was the XJ platform related YJ Wrangler, an all-new model, but with much of the CJ's spirit. The Wrangler was solely sold in Canada as the YJ, since Chevrolet had the rights to the Wrangler name for a pickup truck trim level in that neck of the woods.

The Wrangler was a lower, wider, and comfier Jeep that sat on a 93.4-inch wheelbase with dimensions of 153, 66, and 68 inches for length, width, and height. YJ had a squarer galvanized steel body with square headlamps, rubber mounted to a steel chassis. There were plastic wheel arch flares and padded roll arch, with weight starting at 2,902 lbs for a 2.5 I4 manual. From 1987 to 1990 YJ's base motor was the electronically injected 2.5 I4, with the carb 4.2 I6 and Chrysler 999 3-speed auto as options. In '87 the Wrangler's 4.2 was rated at 114 bhp at 3,000 rpm and 209 lbs/ft at 2,000 rpm.

The CJ-5 took some heat in 1984, at the hands of investigative journalism TV show *60 Minutes*. The show aired claims the CJ-5 was easy to roll over. Lawsuits against Jeep failed, but attention was paid in the YJ's development to improving handling. The YJ still used traditional 4×4 rigid axles and leaf springs, but said springs were wider, and trackbars and swaybars were judiciously used to make YJ a tidy handler.

Although still very capable off-road, Wrangler had slightly less ground clearance, a larger windshield and more attention to a/c. The Jeep was growing up, and designers recognized that in modern times it would be spending much time on-road.

Two GTAs, Medallion and Premier

After years of abstinence the public indulged its desire for high-performance cars by the mid–'80s. If it was fast and sporty, it was popular, and we were back to quoting 0–60 mph, not 0–50 mph! Therefore, it seemed appropriate to import the Renault Alpine sports car as a head-to-head rival for Corvette, Nissan 300ZX Turbo, Porsche 911 and Ferrari 308

GTB. The Alpine was a 2+2 rear-engined exotic with fiberglass GRP body on a steel backbone frame, an Alpine specialty.

The specs said the right thing. In Euro trim the Alpine had 200 bhp (DIN net), weighed 2,600 lbs, had 4-wheel vented disks, 4-wheel independent double wishbone suspension and something the Corvette didn't: decent ride comfort! The engine in question was a 2.5-liter V6 with Garrett turbo and Renix ECU. This was a smaller version of the PRV (Peugeot Renault Volvo) V6 found in the DeLorean, but the Alpine only came with a 5-speed stick and manufacturer performance figures of 0–60 mph in 6.6 seconds and 147 mph top speed.

Pedigree was assured with Alpine. The company was started by Jean Redélé. Redélé's family owned a Renault dealership, and started racing the very humble Renault 4CV. He went on to make performance specials using custom chassis and Renault hardware. This creativity led to the famous A110 and A310 rally cars. Alpine became enveloped by Renault, like tuner Gordini, and oversaw Renault's motorsport activities. Alpine also made the mad mid-engined, wide-body Renault 5 Turbo that notched up almost 60 rally victories by 1982 and was featured in the movies *Trail of the Pink Panther* (1982) and *Never Say Never Again* (1983).

The Alpine had been getting slightly larger, comfier and more refined over the years, making the A310's replacement an ideal North American debutante. Interesting features included sunk-in reinforcing tubes for the fiberglass body, excellent Renault sedan-derived HVAC and powered self-opening doors. Believe in Le Regie's tagline: "There's More to Life with Renault." The plan was to expand daily Alpine production from 12 to 25 cars, with half exported to America.

In the UK the Alpine was called the GTA. Peugeot Talbot owned the rights to the Alpine name in the UK, having acquired same when buying the English Rootes Group as part of Chrysler Europe. Remember the red English Sunbeam Alpine Maxwell Smart used to drive? In any case, if an Alpine could be called GTA, it might also be dubbed AMX in America. The Alpine could have revived AMC's old nameplate, and served as a serious '80s showroom magnet.

U.S. media were showing publicity pics of Alpine under the banner "AMC for '86." There were still solid plans to export the $30K Alpine to America for '87, with approximately 3,000 unit sales per year. Alpine said emissions were no problem; they could engineer a smog version with catalytic converter and 175 bhp SAE net.[16] Unfortunately the thing never came to fruition, and the GTA America actually received in AMC showrooms for '87 was a sportified AMC Alliance!

Once the initial disappointment of no Alpine subsided, the realization dawned that Alliance GTA was quite the funster. After the turbo 1.6 I4, Fuego had been re-engined with Renault's normally aspirated 2.2-liter (2,165cc) injected I4 for two years, but was now gone. Zender of West Germany was contracted to do a special color-keyed bodykit consisting of front and rear spoilers, side skirts and fender flare extensions. The front fascia slat grille was also color matched.

Alliance GTA was a zero-chrome zone with window frame, headlamp surrounds and door handles all in black. Sports suspension included the upgraded 4-torsion bar rear suspension of Euro Renault 9/11 Turbos. The 15-inch alloy wheels wore P195/50 VR tires, even more serious than the 195/55 VR 15-inch tires on the new 140 mph Euro spec Renault 21 Turbo.

The Alliance GTA power team was the 95 bhp Renault F series ohc 2-liter and 5-

speed manual. AMC-Renault claimed 0–60 mph in 9.9 seconds, with GTA front fender insignias just behind the wheel wells, sports seats and Euro Renault range-sourced small leather-wrapped sports steering wheel as cake icing. The Alliance GTA was available in the 2-door sedan and convertible body styles, making for a very distinctive Alliance.

At some point AMC-Renault would have to complete its North American range with a family-car flagship. In 1984 Renault launched two successful models in Europe, the big Renault 25 sedan and the Matra-built Renault Espace. The Espace was a minivan that set a new benchmark for car-like handling. So impressive was the Espace that even F1 designer Gordan Murray was a fan.

It was speculated in the media that the Espace would be a more suitable "feel good" flagship for North America than the R25, once the U.S. economy picked up.[17] This thinking was fueled by the success of Chrysler's minivans. However, it was an R25-based sedan called the Premier that would prove to be AMC-Renault's real big car project, coded X58.

X58 was a joint design venture between AMC and Renault engineers, that commenced in 1982 and used the R25 as a starting point. Thus, Premier was a large front-drive sedan with North-South engine configuration, power rack and pinion steering, and all-independent suspension. For styling AMC sought the advice of its in-house team, as well as submissions from a number of design firms. In the end the angular, wedge look of Giugiaro's Ital Design company won out over the more rounded proposal of Teague's people.

Premier had a 0.31 drag factor, a 106-inch wheelbase and a large body for its class. Its measurements were 192.8, 70, and 53.3 inches for length, width and height, making Premier

Premier's roomy interior, with unusual "up-down" mode button dash controls, represented the last design work done by Richard Teague prior to his 1984 retirement (courtesy Ian Dagenais).

a mite longer than the Ford Taurus. Weight started at 2,862 lbs for a 4-cylinder Premier. Base power team was the AMC 2.5-liter I4 and a 4-speed automatic co-developed by Renault and Volkswagen called the AR-4. AR-4 had mechanical lock-up on 3rd and 4th. In Premier application the I4 with TBI was rated at 111 bhp at 4,750 rpm and 142 lbs/ft at 2,500 rpm.

The starter 4-door Premier LX with bench seat front and rear, Pinstripe Velour Fabric and column-shift auto, retailed for $12,474. Premier I4 came with more power than rival family cars with a base engine, but for $14,079 one could have a Premier ES which automatically came with a 3.0 V6. The PRV 3 liter, of all-alloy construction, with 9.3:1 compression ratio and hemispherical combustion chamber made 150 bhp at 5,000 rpm and 171 lbs/ft at 3,750 rpm. Premier ES was also up-trimmed with Sport Velour Fabric.

Both engines used a single serpentine engine accessory belt drive and Renix ECU. AMC's 9.2:1 compression ratio all cast-iron I4 had the Double Quench combustion chamber design. Premier performance figures were 0–60 mph in 11.5 and 10 seconds for the I4 and V6 editions respectively. The V6 motor used the German ZF 4HP18 4-speed auto with split torque, semi lock-up 3rd and mechanical lock-up on 4th. François Castaing was in charge of Premier's drive train and general engineering. The Renault influence included the North-South front drive layout, plus suspension.

At the front there were MacPherson struts, 26 mm front swaybar and zero-offset geometry to keep Premier tracking straight, even when the front wheels encountered different surfaces. At the rear, trailing arms and 4 transversely mounted torsion bars were employed, along with a 22 mm rear swaybar. Torsion bars were used to create a roomier interior, since coils are more intrusive on a unibody.

The styling of this '89 Premier ES V6 was by Ital Design. Giugiaro's company won out over an in-house AMC proposal (courtesy Ian Dagenais).

There were 6 different front coil stiffness levels, depending on the Premier's power team and exact spec. An "Enthusiast Group" sports suspension pack included firmer shocks, spring settings and bigger 28 mm front swaybar. AMC suspension chief Bob Batchelor and his team fine-tuned Premier to North American road conditions and ride tastes.

The interior was also AMC's work, apart from the Renault-style turn signal flipper. Richard Teague's roomy Premier interior had 2 binnacles with an unusual "up-down" mode button. The binnacle to the left of the steering column did lights; the one on the right covered HVAC functions. HVAC settings were illuminated.

The Premier was to be built in a special new 1986 Bramalea factory, near AMC's existing Brampton, Ontario, operation in Canada. Wagon and coupe versions of Premier were also in the works. The coupe, featuring pop-up headlamps, was to be called the Allure. AMC saw Allure as a way to officially return to NASCAR, for the first time since Matador Coupe days. With a competent chassis and Premier's initial power vent 265 mm front disk and 225 mm rear drums, the Allure V6 promised satisfaction.

Hummer—The One That Got Away

In 1978 AMC's AM General exited the transit bus building business; it wasn't making much dough. Tactical military vehicles were AM General's specialty, and the subsidiary started working on an historically significant new model in 1979. The M998 Series High Mobility Multi-Purpose Wheeled Vehicle (HMMWV — Humvee) was a new 1.25-ton truck replacement for the M151 and some other light tactical vehicles.

AM General with its M998 was a latecomer to a 3-way tussle for the contract to build and supply a truck for the U.S. Army. Rival competitors were Teledyne and Chrysler Defense. The rivals had proposals that were well advanced in their planning, but that was their downfall. Being late to the party, AM General was starting fresh, and were better able to meet the requirements the Army actually wanted.

AM General came up with a rig that best met the goal of a light-armor, deep-water-fording, Arctic and desert dueler in just 10 months.[18] The U.S. Army gave AM General a contract based on this submitted prototype in 1981. Subsequent development and operational testing was completed during a 5-month period in 1982. In March 1983 AM General got a $1.2 billion 5-year contract to make 55,000 Humvees. This request was then upgraded to $1.6 billion and 70,000 Humvees.

One could count on an AM General vehicle with full-time 4WD, independent suspension and 16 inches of ground clearance to have the right stuff, but AMC wouldn't be paid Army scrip. Unfortunately 1983 was when AM General was sold by AMC to LTV Corporation, becoming a wholly-owned subsidiary of LTV Aerospace and Defense Company. National security was part of the reason for the sale. Renault had 46 percent of AMC by this stage, and it was considered risky for a U.S. Army defense contract supplier to be linked to a foreign government.

Renault was 91.5 percent French government-owned, with the remaining 8.5 percent held by Renault employees, and this didn't sit well with Uncle Sam.[19] The other major reason for selling AM General was that AMC-Renault needed the cash. Renault greatly expanded its holding in AMC in 1980, because the Jeep sales decline and bad economy inflicted on AMC a $197.5 million loss that year.[20] There was also a need to fund the development and tooling costs associated with the new '80s Jeeps and cars AMC-Renault was working on.

In 1984 AM General's HQ moved from AMC's Amtek technical center to Livonia, Michigan. On January 2, 1985, the first Humvee rolled off AM General's assembly line at its new South Bend facility. Charting the historical continuum, 1989 saw AM General cease manufacture of its medium-size truck line, when it closed its factory on Chippewa Avenue in South Bend, Indiana. This operation had been acquired by Kaiser Corporation in 1964, when that corporation got Studebaker's General Products Division, the defense contract supplier that became AM General.

AM General enjoyed further U.S. Army contracts in August 1989, 1994 and 2000, but what really put the company in the spotlight was 1991's Operation Desert Storm, a.k.a. Gulf War I. In this conflict the Humvee became a star as the Patriot missiles rained during live TV coverage of the warfare. Suddenly a lot of folks wanted their own Humvee, and 4 months after the war ended, production of the Hummer was announced. The Hummer was the civilian version of Humvee, still designed and built by AM General.[21] Hummer production commenced in 1992, and in April that year AM General was purchased by the Renco Group, Inc., of New York, from LTV.

The Business of Renault

Humvee and Hummer were a missed opportunity for AMC-Renault, but of more pressing concern was the decline of AMC Alliance. Alliance sales stabilized halfway through 1984.[22] By the start of 1985 calendar year Kenosha shut down for two weeks because of surplus Alliance/Encore stocks.[23] For '86 the Encore name was dropped and all variants were simply called AMC Alliance. By the end of the '86 model year Alliance sales had slowed dramatically.[24] So what caused the Alliance's reversal of fortune? A clue came from another car in *Car and Driver*'s 10 Best Cars of 1983.

Apart from Alliance, the Mustang GT 5.0 with EPA rating of 17 mpg was also *Car and Driver* selected. Popularity of this V8 funmobile rose continuously; its fuel efficiency couldn't compare to that of Alliance, but this didn't seem to matter anymore. With each passing day after President Reagan's 1983 State of the Union address, an improving economy and falling gas prices saw people return to living large. Alliance wasn't suffering alone; the 1981 U.S. Ford Escort was losing popularity by the mid–'80s.[25]

Lee Iacocca also said why Chrysler persisted with its rear-drive 318ci remnant from pre-downsized days: "We're now almost 100 percent front-wheel drive. The only reason we still have one rear-wheel drive, which is our worst gas guzzler, is that it is also our hottest seller." Highlighting how the changing energy picture affected buying patterns, Iacocca added, "Once it appeared that everyone would buy little boxes that got 50 miles per gallon; now we can't give them away."[26]

Ford decided the downsized rear-drive 1979 LTD-related models like Crown Victoria and Mercury Marquis Brougham would continue into '86 and perhaps through 1990. The company acknowledged that buyers seemed to like the size, comfort and presence of a traditional rear-driver. Echoing this sentiment, Cadillac's John Grettenberger said the luxury

E29 MTP

E29 MTP

brand would persevere with rear-drive Brougham into the 1990s, since sales during the 1986 model year rose 40 percent.[27]

With money to be made from being big, the Reagan administration gave in to lobbyist groups and decided CAFE's 27.5 mpg goal was no longer necessary. AMC-Renault discovered in the mid–'80s what AMC alone experienced in the mid–'60s and '70s: that the demand for MPGs could be fleeting. What the Big 4 captured with Chevette, Escort, Omni and Alliance was the swing voter. This group of individuals cast their vote in favor of economy in tough times, returning to old habits when the economy lightened up.

The core market for smallish, economy cars had been growing since the late '50s, but it still wasn't big enough to support all comers. The core was now dominated by the Japanese automakers, who inherited Mr. and Mrs. Thrift from VW Beetle. In 1980, 25,417 Renaults were sold in North America, and with local production at Kenosha, it was hoped the total for AMC-Renault cars would be 250,000–300,000 by the decade's end. Was there something wrong with the cars?

The most talented model was the Renault 5 or Le Car. This small car received a 5-door body style in 1982, but still no automatic. However, the Le Car made the best of the gas crunch years, and achieved niche cult status in America during its currency.[28] The R18 was a mixed bag; worldwide it notched up millions by selling a little here and there in many countries, but in America it wasn't special enough to make an impression. The 1981–82 18i sedan imports were short-lived, but the wagon version carried on to 1986.

Opinionated magazine *CAR* declared the R9 to be the definitive boring car, and said its R11 hatch cousin was vin ordinaire. Whilst acknowledging the efficiency of the R11 Turbo's engine, *CAR* still thought it sounded like a vacuum cleaner. Was it fair to describe '80s Renaults as white good household appliances, when that was Toyota's forte? Renault was, after all, a mass production automaker, and didn't the Fuego have a greater sense of style than the Celica?

There were also noises made about how Alliance and imported Renaults didn't match Japanese quality standards. Renault has never been known for flawless build quality, but the Alliance was a quantum leap forward from Dauphine. Kenosha had its problems when it came to making a high-tech car for the '80s. It was a large plant with old equipment and traditionally high labor costs, which were the result of concessions to the U.A.W. when Rambler was running hot in the late '50s.

By the time Alliance arrived, the wage disparity had diminished, and Renault had plans to replace Kenosha with a modern factory containing shorter distances between work stations. The Bramalea plant was a sign of that thinking. However, Kenosha's inadequacies didn't stop Alliance from being a sales winner in '83. Shortfalls in character or quality were less important than the fact the tide had turned against economical rides.

Things weren't easy for Renault back in Europe either. In 1980 Le Regie sat on the Continental throne, but by the mid–'80s, European rivals were storming the Bastille. The Renault 5 was France's best-selling car during 1972–82, and in 1980–82 it was also Europe's

Opposite top: **There were strong plans to export the Renault Alpine GTA turbo V6 to North America and sell it through AMC dealers (courtesy Ashley George and www.renaultalpineownersclub.com).** ***Opposite bottom:*** **As a fibreglass-bodied rear-drive exotic, the Alpine was promoted under the "AMC for '86" banner. It was a chance to revive the AMX tag and challenge the Corvette again (courtesy Ashley George and www.renaultalpineownersclub.com).**

No. 1 seller. However, in 1983 a revived Fiat, its labor relations settled, introduced its new small family car called the Uno, Europe's Car of the Year 1983. Stodgy French rival Peugeot also surprised with their new, exciting Pininfarina-styled Peugeot 205.

In a role reversal, Peugeot was France's new small-car champ and Renault's new R25 unseated Peugeot to become master of big French cars, so long a Peugeot bastion with its 504 sedan. VW/Audi, Opel and Ford of Europe were also putting Renault under serious pressure in France. Ford of Europe took 7.9 percent of the French market in 1984, with the help of the Ford Sierra and newly reskinned Ford Fiesta.[29]

Europe's automakers were engaging in a destructive price war, where overproduction was dealt with through major discounting. Renault launched a price-leader version of the next generation "Supercinq" R5 in Italy that undercut the Uno by 15 percent, garnering many sales for Renault, but the road to hell was paved with discounts. Renault was amassing significant red ink in the mid–'80s. Le Regie lost $2.75 billion in 1984, and the same amount again in 1985.

For many years the Renault 5 and 18 had been France's two top-selling cars, and were in need of replacement. Last of the R5s and R18s went by the grandiose titles of Laureate and Deauville respectively, while Renault poured just over $1 billion into developing the Supercinq or new R5. The new Renault 5 was based on the East-West layout and underpinnings of the R9. It was a larger car that tried to retain the general styling cues of its Le Car predecessor, but it wasn't going to be exported to America.

Renault's rise and fall was symbolized by its Formula One exploits, a trailblazer with the François Castaing and Bernard Dudot–designed 1977 turbo 1.5-liter V6, but in the end it just didn't quite get there. In 1982 the F1 Renault was fast but inconsistent: René Arnoux and Alain Prost managed 10 pole positions from the season's 16 races.[30] Prost won the first two races of the year, in South Africa and Brazil, but had 7 DNFs. Prost was even rear-ended by Didier Pironi's Ferrari in a German Grand Prix practice session, on a rain-soaked Hockenheim circuit. The '82 driver's title was won by Keke Rosberg in the slow but steady Williams Cosworth V8.

Friction between French drivers Arnoux and Prost was there from the start, and for 1983 Prost got American Eddie Cheever as a new teammate. With the Renault RE-40 F1 car, Alain Prost very nearly became 1983 World Champion, but was beaten by Nelson Piquet in the BMW turbo I4-powered Brabham, the first turbo to get the F1 driver's title. Prost was trying hard to become France's first F1 champion, and there were severe recriminations in the aftermath.

Brazilian Piquet had beaten Prost by just 2 points, with Brabham overtaking Renault in the final few races. Prost felt Renault Sport had been too conservative in the RE-40's development, and mismanaged the pressure placed by Brabham in those final races. Renault blamed Prost, who was fired and moved to McLaren for 1984. It was downhill for Renault in F1 from that point; 1985 proved a most disastrous racing season. In 1986 Renault was merely an engine supplier, and pulled out of F1 altogether at the end of the year.

Bernard Hanon, the Renault boss at the center of the AMC-Renault alliance and F1 advocate, was behind plans to get 1984 F1 World Champion Nikki Lauda to drive for Renault in the 1985 F1 season. Lauda had just become champion for the third time in 1984, beating new McLaren teammate Alain Prost by half a point. However, there was a media leak on how much Lauda was going to be paid to race for Renault. This huge fee wasn't in

Series 30 Eagles, like this 1986 4.2 auto with a/c, represented the last vestige of the wholly-AMC-designed passenger vehicle (courtesy Sean Weitzel).

good taste considering Renault's red ink and job cuts, so Lauda remained at McLaren and Hanon was replaced by new Renault chairman Georges Besse in 1984.

Georges Besse wasn't really a racing enthusiast; he was a hard-edged executive from the chemical industry. Another notable 1984 departure was AMC's long-time design supremo Richard Teague, who announced his retirement in August.[31] Gerry Meyers had left much earlier. Meyers signed a 4-year contract with Renault during 1981, but left AMC in January 1982. Renault's commercial director Jose Dedeurwaerder became AMC's new boss.

Renault's global expansion wasn't exactly going to plan, either, with its subsidiaries in Mexico and South Africa taking losses. The former VAM operation in Mexico lost over $11.7 million in 1985.[32] La Nueva Renault de Mexico stopped making the Renault 5 and Renault 18 in 1986, as well as Jeep; 1987 was the final year for the Mexican-made Alliance and Encore models, with Renault leaving Mexico completely at the end of the year. Mexico and South Africa both like big-engined cars. It seemed like Renault's fuel efficiency was best appreciated in Europe, at a time when a barrel of oil was getting pretty cheap.

New models like the Supercinq, R25 and Espace slowly pulled Renault back to respectability. In 1986 Renault reduced its losses to half the 1985 level, and received money from the French government equal to this amount. Halfway through 1987 calendar year a modest $220 million profit was forecast, aided by Renault's new medium-sized family car the Renault 21. The R21 succeeded the R18, and provided hope for AMC-Renault's North American car line, which consisted of Alliance sedan and hatch, Renault 18i Sportwagon and Eagle cross-over in 1986.

The R21 was Renault's latest front-drive design, available in sedan and wagon forms, and to be sold in America as the '87 Medallion. The Medallion wasn't assembled in North America; it was a large-engined R21 export version with slight cosmetic differences, coming from Renault's Maubeuge factory in Northern France. Looking very modern in the late–

Contemporary magazine opinion was that Eagle's dashboard was more back to the '60s, than back to the future. However, that interior had something '80s Taurus and Cavalier didn't have: character (courtesy Sean Weitzel).

'80s idiom, the Medallion sedan and wagon sported respective cd drag factors of 0.34 and 0.35. So anxious were AMC-Renault dealers to get new product sales that a free phone line was established so interested prospects could get the latest on the Medallion.

R21s with engines under 2 liters stayed with the R9's East-West layout. R21s with larger motors, like Medallion, chose a North-South configuration to combat torque steer. Medallions used the 2.2-liter I4 seen in the Fuego, teamed with a standard 5-speed overdrive manual or optional electronic-controlled 3-speed auto. The 2,165cc ohc I4 was rated at 103 bhp at 5,500 rpm and 124 lbs/ft at 3,000 rpm. Automatic transmission was standard on the wagon.

The Medallion's engine bay was designed to take the PRV V6 motor. With the changing energy picture and renewed U.S. interest in larger engines, R21 V6 compatibility was a design requirement. The V6 and auto would have been a great power team for the wagon, but Medallion stayed with the 2.2 I4 exclusively. Medallion's 5 mph U.S. bumpers were color keyed and had a black protective stripping. Body dimensions for sedan were a trim 183.2, 67.5, and 52.8 inches for length, width, and height. Medallion sedan sat on a 102.4-inch wheelbase; the manual sedan's starting weight was 2,650 lbs and trunk capacity was 15.2 cu ft.

Trim levels consisted of base DL and upscale LX. The former came with Accent Stripe Velour upholstery. Medallion LX had a Pinstripe Velour interior, standard side-bolstered front buckets, and a tach, and for the exterior body, accent stripes, dual-powered remote-control black side mirrors and full-width taillights with red inboard upper lens segment. Specify the optional Touring Group and a leather-wrapped steering wheel would be included, along with cast aluminum rims fitted with P195/60 HR 14-inch BSW "High-Speed" steel-belted radials.

Medallion had expected European items like rack and pinion steering, 4-wheel independent suspension and power front disk and rear drum brakes standard. In Europe the high-level R21s would have 4-wheel disks; even so, magazines were agreed that Medallion was a nice car to drive. The Medallion sold quite well in 1987, especially given the limited funds AMC-Renault had for media promos. The larger Premier would soon join Medallion. However, the cloud on the horizon was Renault's commitment to the North American market.

Surviving in the '80s

At Detroit's zenith, 1 in 6 U.S. workers' income was related to the auto sector. In the 1978 movie *Blue Collar*, a Goodyear electronic billboard informed highway drivers of the Motor City's rising 1977 output. But all was not well: Detroit was under pressure from Japan. In 1960 Japan exported just 7,000 cars, 942 of which were U.S.-bound. In 1965 Japan exported 100,716 cars, and the number was rising. In 1970 the American car market was 8.4 million units in size, with 84.8 percent provided by the Big 4 and just 3.7 percent by Japanese automakers.

Gulliver GM wanted Lilliputian AMC to succeed, because it feared government. Any large corporation occupying a monopolistic position, or engaged in associated activities, has reason to expect federal attention. An antitrust case was filed by the U.S. Justice department against IBM. The legal case *U.S. versus IBM* lasted from 1969 to 1982, and concerned the anticompetitive launch timing of IBM's 360 and 370 "Fighting Machines." The federal government eventually dropped the case, and judicial opinion said the government's case was flimsy and without merit.[33]

The Series 30 4-door sedan was the third most popular Eagle variant, with 27,501 sold over 1980–87. From '85 onwards, Eagle flew on 4.2 I6 power exclusively (courtesy Sean Weitzel).

More recently, action has been directed against Microsoft, regarding its attempts to keep Windows and Internet Explorer software numero uno. Thus, GM was always happy to tell the feds that Detroit contained the Big 4, not the Big 1. Plus, it was sending Saginaw steering gear and THM automatics Kenosha's way, as a good neighbor should. However, as the '70s wore on, GM became more concerned with actually being dominant than with the perceptions of federal regulators.

By 1982 the U.S. auto market rested at a recessionary 7.98 million total, with Detroit and Japanese shares posted at 72.2 percent and 22.6 percent respectively. The balance of power had changed.[34] In 1980 Japan made more cars than America, and America had made more cars per year than any other country for 76 years! Also in 1980, Datsun declared itself the highest EPA-rated gas mileage brand in the land. Never mind; in Detroit's freefall there was still time for art.

After the second gas crunch, L.A. artist Dustin Shuler impaled a '59 Caddy with a 20-ft spike, took a picture and cut the car up into 59 pieces. Each Caddy piece had the photo affixed, autographed and dated October 23, 1980.[35] There were warnings of Japan's steady rise through the '70s. The 1973 Datsun 610 range carried a lot of standard equipment that was usually optional. More importantly, prior to the first fuel crisis, Datsun started its "Datsun Saves" jerry or gas can ads in America.

Quoting U.S. Bureau of Highway figures, Datsun stated the average gas mileage was 13.5 mpg, whereas its new Datsun 1200 got 30 mpg. Therefore, the 1200 could save one a gallon of gas per day. The ad had the text and picture of the cute 1200 superimposed on a spare gas can, which was neat since, in 1973, a barrel of oil cost 3 bucks, and by 1980 it was $32![36] In 1977 Toyota proudly stated it had 1,000 dealers across the nation, and Honda had licensed its CVCC tech to Ford, Chrysler, Toyota and Isuzu in 1973.

Honda's 1972 CVCC I4 impressed by being able to pass proposed 1975 emissions regs without a catalytic converter. By 1978 the company was mentioning terms like "environmental protection" and "natural resource conservation." Datsun audaciously reworked Ford's old "Total Performance" slogan into "Total Economy" and "Total Quality" for its ads. Examples abound on how America relies on the automobile, like the Reverend Robert H. Schuller's Garden Grove Community Church in Orange County, California, offering a Drive-In "Worship in Your Car" Sanctuary. For a drink on the run, one couldn't go past Vince Bruner's Robinson's Cruz-Thru with draft beer to go in Fort Walton Beach, Florida.[37]

If people rely on their cars a lot, and the price of feeding said cars goes through the roof, those folks will seek out the most cost-efficient manner of maintaining personal transport. The result was lots of new imported Japanese cars on the docks of Long Beach, California, in the early '80s. Japan's reach didn't stop there; in 1986 Japan's auto companies took 13.15 percent of the West German market. By the late '80s they were putting the bite on Peugeot in its stronghold African markets. Even France was under attack with Renault seeking trade barriers. Renault's Jose Dedeurwaerder said, "All we want to do is fight on an equal basis with the Japanese."[38]

VW used to be the world's third biggest car maker on Beetle power. By the mid–'80s, third place belonged to Toyota, showing the Japanese had taken VW's title of econocar producer for the globe. At this time Toyota wasn't shy to state it was going to overtake Ford and GM to become number one, one day.[39] Japan's secret for success was high productivity, low labor cost, high quality and a low Yen, most of which Renault is still struggling with in Australia.

Finding itself at a $4,500 price disadvantage against equivalent Toyotas and Hondas, Renault Australia boss Rudi Koenig mentioned a supply change to the Korean-built Renault Fluence and Turkish-made Renault Megane for 2010. Lower labor cost compared to French factories would allow items like Bluetooth and Sat Nav to be included at no extra cost. To make up for competitive shortfalls, Western countries resorted to import quotas to keep the Japanese at bay. There was no written agreement, but it was accepted Japan would restrict exports to 10 percent of the European car market.

U.S. restrictions on the sale of Japanese imports were very loose, being laissez faire in the '70s, followed by a 1981–85 1.85-million-unit quota limit, or more accurately a voluntary export agreement.[40] To beat a quota system, just make the cars in the export country. In the '80s Nissan famously set up shop in England and America. Starting in the fall of 1986 a new factory in Washington, Tyne and Wear near Sunderland, issued forth British-made Nissan Bluebirds exempt from European trade barriers. A target of 80 percent local content was set, with component suppliers chosen on quality.[41]

Stable industrial labor relations were seen as key for the UK operation's success, and was the reason Nissan built its U.S. plant in Smyrna, Tennessee. It was a locality alien to the Detroit-focused U.A.W., and nontraditional car-making regions with unemployment would become the areas of choice for foreign companies making cars in America. The Smyrna plant started making small pickups in June 1983, with the Nissan Sentra (Sunny) added in 1985.[42]

Local content on the pickup was 50–55 percent; the Sentra started at 47 percent, since Nissan wanted to get the quality right first. Factory forklift driver Dot Faulk summed up the situation. "Nissan was a Godsend," said Dot. "I was unemployed when they came along to build the plant.... I don't belong to a union; I don't think we need one." Any problems were addressed to the lead technician or supervisor.[43]

When the Sentra came online, 5,000 people worked at the very modern factory. Nissan planned to increase that number to 8,000 in 1986. Employees also enjoyed benefits, like Dot Faulk's company-lease 300ZX. By the spring of 1984, Honda, Nissan, Renault and VW were all making cars in America, although the Japanese were enjoying the most success. Nissan's Sentra was turning up the heat on AMC-Renault's Alliance.

The irony is that in 1999 Renault would take over a troubled Nissan and restructure the company for success. However, in the '80s it was the Land of the Rising Sun that was on the up. In 1984, 133,000 Japanese cars were U.S.-made. The leading Japanese import that year was the Honda Accord, which was already being made in Maryville, Ohio. Under the U.S. quota system, if you made more, you could import more, and they did. In 1987 Honda sold 738,306 cars in North America.

European brands that used to have a steady U.S. presence were being driven out. Fiat had given up its official dealer network by the mid–'80s, and by '86 was only represented in America by the infamous Malcolm Bricklin's dealer network.[44] Aside from the "Fix-It-Again-Tony" factor, Fiat boss Vittorio Ghidella offered another explanation for Japan's victory over Europe in America: "The Japanese operate particularly in relation to the American market: they produce essentially small American cars, not really small European ones."[45]

The figures speak for themselves: in 1983 Europe exported 420,000 cars to America, while Japan nudged their quota limit on 1.86 million.[46] A year after Mr. Ghidella made his statement, a movie was released that featured Japan's new dominance of the American auto scene. The 1986 comedy *Gung Ho* starred Michael Keaton and was about a fictitious Japanese corporation, Assan Motors, that took over an inefficient U.S. auto plant. The irony was that the Japanese cars made in the movie were mostly Fiat Regatas!

At the top end of town, upscale European brands were wooing buyers that used to choose Lincolns and Caddies. Saab was doing great business, with 360 dealers and 45,000 sales per annum in the U.S. by the mid–'80s.[47] For yuppie baby boomers, quirky became a feel-good factor. A lot of buyers just didn't want to own the brands or types of cars their parents or grandparents had. A generational switch occurred as Saab, Volvo and BMW sales rose against a background of a changed mindset where Detroit was unwell. As Blake wrote in his *Songs of Experience* poem "London," "The mind-forg'd manacles I hear."

Car Wars—Detroit Strikes Back!

According to Ford VP of design Donald Kopka, who worked under Virgil Exner, the legendary Chrysler stylist Exner didn't even like the tailfins he was credited with starting.[48] Zora Arkus-Duntov wasn't happy with the nose-heavy consequences of inserting the big-block Chevy V8 into the C2 Corvette. Richard Teague wasn't wild about Javelin's Humpster restyle, but in every case marketing won out ... until now. The '80s would prove a time for frippery to be pared down, as Detroit got back to basics.

Donald Kopka predicted there would be no grilles by 2000. GM took a front-drive, fuel-injected Buick 3.8 V6 route to '86, where V8s exited and touch-screen displays entered. Some 500 to 700 pounds were lost, and Bonneville was no longer rear-drive. While GM,

A 1987 AMC Eagle wagon. For '88 the model was renamed American Eagle, but still carried door plaques with the AMC logo. The '88 Eagle build sheets also sported AMC's A-mark logo (courtesy Sandy Busque).

Ford and Chrysler designed the right thing, they weren't immune to using captive imports to smooth things out. Ford brought the new European Fiesta to America in the late '70s. Sales were 40,549 in 1977 and 76,145 in 1978.

Sell 3 econoboxes, and you get to offload one 460ci gas guzzler, squaring things with CAFE. However, rule changes meant that for 1980 captive imports couldn't contribute to CAFE, which made the new U.S. Ford Escort very timely. To overcome the economic difficulty of making a small car in America, GM turned to the Suzuki SA310, which it sold as the Chevy Sprint. By doing this, they incurred the wrath of regulators. GM wanted Japan's quota limit lifted, so it could import cars like the Sprint and concentrate design and production resources towards more value-added vehicles.

The Reagan administration was OK with lifting the quota, but Ford, Chrysler, AMC and the U.A.W. were not. Ultimately GM back-door imported a Korean-made Opel (Daewoo), which was sold as the Pontiac Le Mans. Ford did the same with their Festiva, which was a Mazda 121 made by Korean firm Kia. Chrysler had brought in the Dodge Colt from Japan for many years. The economics were simple: Korean workers got one-sixth the pay of their U.A.W. counterparts, or $7,500 per year in 1986.

To fill in the blanks, GM and Ford tried captive imports at the top end of town too. GM would try to lure luxo import buyers with the 1990s Caddy Catera, an Opel Omega. In the '80s Ford imported the German-made Ford Sierra XR4i and Scorpio under the Merkur moniker (German for the winged god). Lincoln-Mercury chief Bob Rewey thought 100,000 Merkurs could be sold annually by the end of the decade. Both Merkur and Catera failed to meet sales expectations.

In 1986 Hyundai introduced their Excel hatchback for $4,995; it sold 264,000 units in its first full model year, 1987. Malcolm Bricklin's Yugo was a budget compatriot. At this time the $5,499 Dodge Omni America was the lowest-priced new domestically made car. To get serious about small cars, and address the East-West wage disparity, GM started Project Saturn, a plan to profitably build a small car in America. Following the Japanese example, Saturn was made in Spring Hill, Tennessee, on a greenfield non–U.A.W. site.

Ford powered up Alpha Project, where every aspect of their global operation was examined for efficiency improvement. Ford of Europe engaged in dialogue with Fiat in the mid–'80s to avoid unnecessary competition. As king of the Jell-O mold, Ford's Ghia-built Probe V research vehicle had large doors that moved outwards and back, plus a cd of just 0.137.[49] In 1986 GM was at the cutting edge of computer-aided design. Using aero work on a screen (Autoscope), a complete car could be imaged up in high-resolution color in 11 hours. In the '80s AMC was caught between well-resourced Detroit giants and hungry import brands that were also made in America.

Pentastar Blues

Chrysler wasn't in a happy place at the close of the '70s. Its state of health was exemplified by *Consumer Reports*' 1980 Dodge Aspen. The top-rated Chevy Citation was calculated as using an estimated 655 gallons over an annual 15,000-mile usage, while Aspen was at 955 gallons.[50] This was in spite of using the 3-speed Torqueflite auto with 3rd gear lock-up torque converter, later shared with AMC cars. Citation was faster as an I4 than Aspen

Eagle's 4.2 I6 carb motor is shown. Eagle never got the '87 introduced 4.0 injected AMC I6. Note the Light Group–included engine bay light (courtesy Sandy Busque).

was with its standard 225ci I6. To draw level, Aspen had to be 318 V8 optioned; unlike AMC Concord, an I4 was unavailable. There was a 6 or 7-month Citation waiting list. Buyers ignored Aspen by 1980.

Ford Fairmont recorded a low 8 delivered defects; Aspen came with 26! In *Consumer Reports'* words, "Our Aspen was a mess."[51] But Lee Iacocca was already here, and major change was taking place. Iacocca, the man allegedly fired from Ford for being too successful, descended upon Chrysler in 1979 to polish the Pentastar. Thirteen out of Chrysler's 47 plants were shut, and an answer to GM's front-drive X car was in the works. Chrysler's I4-powered ecoblock front-drive K-car would replace its Aspen/Volare compacts in 1981.

The K-car was essential to secure federal loan guarantees, and was shown to legislators well in advance, according to Ron Wakefield.[52] Seeds of the CAFE-friendly Special K were sown in France. In 1978 Chrysler became the first member of the Big 4 to offer small U.S.-built front-drivers. Those cars were the Dodge Omni and Plymouth Horizon twins, 5-door hatchbacks that originated with French car maker Simca.

Simca was half of Chrysler Europe; the other half was the British Rootes Group of Sunbeam Alpine/Tiger fame. Simca was doing a modern replacement for their 1100 family car. The result was the 5-door hatch with front drive and transverse engine layout called Horizon of 1977. Unfortunately, this was a time when Chrysler was retreating. Apart from losses at home, Chrysler Europe was also in the red and there was major industrial relations unrest in its UK operation.

Chrysler sold Chrysler Europe to Peugeot in 1978, who promptly resurrected the Talbot marque. Thus, as of July 10, 1979, Chrysler-Simca became Talbot-Simca. In 1979 there was the odd parallel situation of the Horizon hatch being sold as a Simca in France, a Talbot in the UK and a Plymouth in America. A world car indeed, but Chrysler had left the building. Chrysler Australia was sold to Mitsubishi in 1982, its locally designed I6 and V8 rear-drive Valiants no longer anyone's cup of tea, given high gas prices.

The Horizon and Fifth Avenue both had torsion bar front suspension, showing the influence of Chrysler ownership while Simca was working on the Horizon. A major part of Chrysler's '80s renaissance was its handling of industrial relations. Union employee participation was encouraged. Take shares in the company one has a stake in, rather than a pay increase. Indeed, cooperation between management, unions, parts suppliers, dealers and government was claimed to be behind the $5,499 '87 Horizon that Chrysler said was cheaper than comparably equipped Japanese cars. They called it the Import Fighter!

Iacocca also used show-biz buddies to help the Pentastar shine. In 1981 Chrysler launched the Imperial. This rebodied Aspen/Volare, with sleek imposing grille and hideaway headlamps, was the equivalent of GM's turning Nova into the Seville. Imperial was a name associated with luxo Chryslers, and the computer-controlled, fuel-injected 5.2 V8 was the smoothest 318 in a long spell. Cadillac was the only other domestic with electronic injection at the time.

Eagle opened the car door to off-roading without diff locks or low range. Just flip a toggle switch between 2WD and 4WD and go (courtesy Sandy Busque).

The Imperial's interior was either Kimberley Velvet or Mark Cross leather. In fact, the Imperial FS Edition came with a collection of Frank Sinatra cassette tapes in a Mark Cross case. Print ads had a conversation between Old Blue Eyes and Iacocca, one chairman of the board to another, about the merits of Imperial's technical features. Putting the sincerity of this discourse about fuel injection and digital tuners aside, Imperial hit a bum note in the sales charts.

Buyers looked more fondly upon the new '80 front-drive razorback Seville than the rear-drive Imperial. The recession, and the fact Chrysler's reputation was still in the toilet, did Imperial no favors. The model was withdrawn at the end of the '83 model year.[53] Imperial may not have reached the top of the hit parade, but TV audiences were enjoying the dulcet tones of Ricardo Montalban, extolling the virtues of rich, Corinthian leather.

Chrysler turned a 1979 $1.7 billion loss into a 1982 $170 million profit.[54] K-cars and minivans were putting a smile on Mr. Iacocca's dial. The mid–'80s saw the Chrysler Fifth Avenue luxo sedan steal the Detroit limelight. With a design basis still traceable to Aspen/Volare, Fifth Avenue didn't look as adventurous as 1981–83 Imperial, and didn't have fuel injection, but the public and cops loved it! The gussied-up, expensive, 3,753-pound, 206.7-inch-long leviathan handsomely outsold its plainer Plymouth Gran Fury and Dodge Diplomat siblings.

Buyers liked the traditional, boxy Fifth Avenue more than the wedge-shaped front-drivers GM was peddling in '86. Rich Corinthian leather has more ambiance than a vacuum-formed plastic dash with a microchip living inside. The Fifth Avenue's decorations went well with mid–'80s affluence, but Chrysler had something truly worthy of Dynasty: the Chrysler-Maserati.

Sophia Loren Meets the Le Baron

J.R. Ewing's semi–Italian-made Cadillac Allante had more style than one could shake a Stetson at, and Chrysler had an answer. Lee Iacocca was friends with Alejandro de Tomaso of Pantera fame, owner of Maserati at the time. Chrysler had a 15 percent stake in Maserati and gave de Tomaso $5.5 million in 1984 to develop a 2-seater convertible.[55] This 3,033-pound ragtop was Italian built, featured front drive and possessed 8- and 16-valve editions of the familiar Mopar I4.

The 2.2 I4 turbo was a more enthusiastic motor than Allante's 4.1 V8, and Chrysler-Maserati's $25,000–$30,000 projected price undercut the Allante's planned 50-grand sticker. Chrysler-Maserati's C pillar porthole window etched with Chrysler's Pentastar was reminiscent of a '50s T-Bird, and was no doubt Iacocca's one-fingered salute to his former Ford corporate masters. Iacocca described the new convertible as "the best-looking Italian to come over since my mother."[56]

The Dodge Daytona sports car also put on a fine show when Frank Sinatra used it to overtake Sammy Davis Jr. and Dean Martin's C4 Vette in the 1983 movie *Cannonball Run II*. Ain't that a hole in the boat for GM? Chrysler had record sales and profits in 1985. The company got $275 million from the sale of Peugeot shares, a legacy from the disposal of Chrysler Europe. The coming Dodge Shadow and Plymouth Sundance were promising P cars, but all wasn't pleasant at Chrysler.

Gaps existed in Chrysler's portfolio. In the post-energy crisis era its passenger car engine range basically consisted of 2.2/2.5 I4 and 318ci V8. Chrysler happily received Mitsubishi's 3-liter V6 for its '87 Dodge Caravan and Plymouth Voyager minivans. Chrysler was also lacking in off-road recreational vehicles. Meanwhile, AMC was at a loose end. A sleepy Kenosha was contracted to assemble Omni/Horizon, as well as Fifth Avenue and its relations for Chrysler in 1986.

Dangerous Liaisons

Renault's talks with Nissan to use AMC's Brampton, Ontario, plant collapsed at this time. The proposal was eerily similar to the movie storyline of *Gung Ho* (1986). Jose Dedeurwaerder made the ominous statement, "We have never hidden the fact that we want a partner for AMC."[57] Renault man Dedeurwaerder had stepped down as AMC boss, replaced by Joseph Cappy. However, amidst all the uncertainty, Renault affirmed its commitment to AMC. AMC had sold subsidiary Wheel-Horse Products, Inc., and its American Center Detroit headquarters building in 1984.

Behind closed doors Lee Iacocca was sweet-talking Renault out of its 46 percent holding in AMC. In August the formal announcement of Chrysler's takeover of AMC occurred, and it wasn't a surprise. Renault hadn't managed to make as many Renault-based cars in America as hoped, and like Fiat abandoned weak markets to concentrate on strong ones. The success of the XJ Cherokee and Bramalea plant became more of a reason to sell AMC than to keep it. Chrysler did the math: to come up with a respected off-road brand like Jeep would have cost them a lot more money than simply buying AMC. It was the ultimate no-brainer.

It wasn't until 1985 that things turned bad for the AMC-Renault alliance, and there were signs Renault's decision to get out was a quick one. Apart from plans to sell the Alpine sports car in America, and the new Wrangler with Renault motor in Europe for '87, just check the actual cars. The '88 Eagle wagon continued with build sheets and door plaques bearing the AMC logo. Documents said American Motors Sales Corporation Ltd. built the Eagle wagon.

The American Motors Sales Corporation entity was also marked at the top of the '88 Premier's Vehicle Ordering Guide and Price List, along with the new "Eagle" brand name. American Motors Sales Corporation referred to AMC Canada, formed in 1956 for the production of AMC vehicles in, and distribution from, Canada. By this hour the Eagle crossover was solely Canadian Brampton-built, with Premier made nearby in Bramalea. Technically AMC Canada didn't exist post-takeover, but the paperwork still carried AMC's impression.

All '88 Premiers had the AMC format VIN, and the AMC logo continued to appear on many Premier parts, like radiator hoses, throughout the sedan's 1988–92 run. Early '88 Premiers even carried the Renault rhombus logo, Alliance style. As part of the Chrysler takeover the Eagle brand was created. Iacocca promised to retain the AMC name early on, but went with Eagle and its new eagle-head logo subsequently. Bramalea was renamed Brampton Assembly, and Chrysler got the marketing rights to the Jeep brand in Germany, Austria, Switzerland, Scandinavia and the Benelux countries.[58] Renault met its Waterloo, when it encountered Iacocca the Invincible!

Epilogue

August 5, 1987, was the date of Chrysler's takeover, but if you thought AMC's influence ended there you would be wrong. Jeep J-Series pickup production ended in '88, and on December 14, 1987, the last Eagle wagon, renamed "American Eagle," left Kenosha. However, August 1987 was the takeover date, as well as the first build date of the new AMC-designed Premier sedan! One could find an AMC build plate on the Premier driver's door, as well as an emissions certification underhood decal on 1988–89 Premiers that still stated American Motors Corporation.

Chrysler didn't pursue the proposed Premier wagon, Allure coupe, or even the planned 5-speed manual with AMC 2.5 base power team. Only the Premier sedan made it through, and yet the Renault rhombus on 1988–89 Premier's stereo, plus various AMC signage, must have irked the Mopar masters, so they had a 1990 makeover. The '90 Premier was restyled, losing the "design giugiaro" front fender badges previously present. The 2.5 I4 was shown the door; with fuel crisis days fading, most Eagle Premier buyers had gone for the 3.0 V6.

Chrysler replaced Renix engine management with its own ECU hardware and software. An upscale "Limited" trim level was introduced above ES as well, and yet the Chrysler gods on Mount Michigan were still displeased. If one worked in public utilities, emergency services, the military or forestry management in '80s Europe, it was possible to encounter a Renault-badged Dodge 50 Series 4x2 cab/chassis. The Renault logo on a black plastic grille could be found with Dodge lettering still hood present.[59]

Renault Truck Industries used the Dodge 50 Series because the vehicle suited their needs. However, Renault's dealings with Chrysler concerning Medallion and Premier were forced. On the derriere of the 1989 Medallion it said "imported for Eagle"; under the AMC buyout conditions, Chrysler had to sell some Renaults in America. Apart from revised grille slatwork, replacing Renault rhombus with Eagle's head, the Medallion looked like it did in '87. However, when it came to captive imports, Chrysler preferred them to come from long-time partner Mitsubishi.

The AMC Alliance departed at the end of '87, and in its place came the Mitsubishi-sourced Eagle Summit. Chrysler was also more interested in the Normal, Illinois, car production hookup with Mitsubishi that was Diamond Star Motors. However, Chrysler was contractually bound to make Premier at Bramalea for 5 years, and use 260,000 Renault V6s. To accelerate Premier production, and use up the alloy SOHC V6s, Chrysler introduced the low-rent Dodge Monaco-badge-engineered sister sedan.

Premier's final build date was December 1991, and when the dust had settled, 139,051 Premier/Monacos were made during 1988–92. Meantime, 1989 was the final year for Medallion. Chrysler VP Robert Lutz said Medallion and Premier were unsellable in his 2003 book *Guts*, but Chrysler bought AMC for Jeep, not for those two sedans. Not much marketing money or effort was put Medallion's way. The Renault 21 was a good car, but not part of Chrysler's plan. Premier was unlucky to come after the 1986 Ford Taurus. The Taurus, with its industry-standard supersize cup holder, set the Jell-O mold for aero front-drivers. By coincidence, Richard Teague's son Jeff was a Team Taurus designer.

The Premier's design basis was chosen over a family car proposal Chrysler itself was working on. Premier gave rise to the next generation of modern Pentastar family cars known as LH models. Bramalea was rejigged to produce the '93 Eagle Vision, and Premier bodies

The YJ Wrangler replaced the long-running CJ-5/CJ-7 family. A 1991 Wrangler Renegade is shown (courtesy George M. Stragand III).

were used as test mules for the LH drive train. The Eagle Vision was joined by Chrysler Concorde and Dodge Intrepid cousins. The LH clan's north-south front-drive engine layout was alien to Chrysler Horizon/K-car east-west practice.

As the ultimate parting shot, Premier's subsequent rear disk-brake system was included on the Dodge Viper! Eagle Vision ended in 1997, although the Concorde and Intrepid were made over for '98 and continued to 2004. A planned redesigned '99 Vision became the Chrysler 300M, the front-drive revival of the halcyon Chrysler Letter Car series. Thus, Premier influenced Chrysler family cars until the Mercedes tie-up brought rear-drivers, based on a defunct E class platform. The Eagle brand wasn't nearly as long-lived.

Dodge was already Chrysler's sporty brand, and this combined with wasteful badge engineering saw to Eagle's death. Upon Chrysler's takeover, AMC dealers became Jeep/Eagle outlets. AMC got out of the car business with Concord's '83 demise, so by 1988 remaining AMC dealers were Jeep/Eagle 4×4 focused. Their expertise and resources were geared towards the off-roaders, so Medallion and Premier weren't a great fit. Speaking of good fits, Chrysler discontinued the Jeep Comanche pickup at the end of the '92 model year, just because it stole Dodge Dakota sales!

With Medallion and Premier gone, Eagle didn't offer anything car-unique as a brand. Chrysler also had a long-term goal to offload Plymouth, and class up Chrysler, so that only Chrysler/Jeep and Dodge would remain. So it was that in November 1997 Chrysler announced the end of the Eagle brand, and its headquarters in Auburn Hills, Michigan. Jeep's luster remained undimmed; in 1988 XJ Cherokee contributed one-third of Chrysler profits. The Mopar moguls rewarded brave Cherokee, by bestowing upon it a Chrysler 8.25-inch rear differential.

In 1988 Cherokee was available in a Pioneer Olympic Edition; recall the Seoul and Calgary Games. In 2001, the XJ Cherokee came in "60th Anniversary" guise, commemorating the Willys-Overland Jeep's birthday. This would also be the XJ's final year. The arrival of Mercedes hastened the XJ's end as MB cost-cutter Wolfgang "Whirlwind" Bernhard cleared Chrysler's decks. XJ Cherokee production ceased in mid–2001, and the South Assembly part of the Toledo factory that made XJ was torn down.

The old SJ Wagoneer weathered Chrysler's presence in fine style. In 1989 the big Jeep purloined an overhead console from Chrysler's minivan range, and a standard rear window wiper/washer facility. There were new SJ paint colors for '90. Recessionary times once again threatened sales of high value-added rigs: 1991 was supposed to be SJ's final year, with the last 1,560 Grand Wagoneers bearing a "Final Edition" dashboard badge. However, 4 1992 Grand Wagoneers were produced and sold too.

In 1993 the SJ's place was taken by a ZJ Grand Cherokee-based Grand Wagoneer. This fancy version of the new ZJ design came with the 220-horse "Magnum" 318 V8 and Quadra-Trac as standard equipment. This modern Grand Wagoneer was a critical success, but a commercial failure, so it was discontinued at the end of model year '93. Buyers no doubt felt it too close to a Grand Cherokee, and lacking the special woodland/golf club/sportsman quality of the old SJ.

It had been Chrysler's intention to replace both the ancient SJ and small XJ with the ZJ Grand Cherokee, two Eagles slain with one stone. However, strong XJ demand, and a pressing need to revise Chrysler's minivans for '91, saw ZJ Grand Cherokee placed on the back burner. The ZJ's tale started way back in 1983, when even AMC conceived it as a larger, more refined XJ successor. Larry Shinoda, Adam Clenet and Giorgetto Giugiaro were contracted to come up with design proposals, but ultimately AMC decided to go in-house.

The public's first glimpse of the clean slate came in the form of 1989's Jeep Concept 1 show car. The next time was when Bob Lutz, with Detroit Mayor Coleman Young riding shotgun, tore up the steps of Cobo Hall and smashed through a plate-glass window in the new ZJ at the 1992 North American International Auto Show. The ZJ Grand Cherokee, the last AMC-designed Jeep, was produced at the specially built Jefferson North Assembly plant in Detroit, Michigan, between 1993 and 1998.

The ZJ used adapted versions of the XJ's 4×4 systems, but permanent all-wheel-drive Quadra-Trac was a ZJ exclusive, and a feature remarked upon by *CAR* magazine's Russell Bulgin in 1994. QT's full-time 4-wheel-drive system had selectable low ratio, a rear differential with 66 percent locking action, and that well-known center viscous coupling. A sophisticated system without differential locks, according to Bulgin, it handled tough terrain with aplomb: "Unpredictable Iceland presents a serious off-road challenge, but fails to faze the Jeep Grand Cherokee, which just keeps lumbering on regardless."[60] European market ZJ Grand Cherokees were assembled by Magna Steyr in Austria.

In the Iceland Grand Cherokee Limited article titled "Jeep Freeze," the engine present was Chrysler's 318 V8, but most ZJ buyers stuck with the base 4.0 I6, keeping this rig 100 percent AMC. AMC-era terms like Quadra-Trac lived on, as did Jeep's rugged off-road ability. However, in '96, ZJ had its front fender "Grand Cherokee" script badge typeface changed from AMC to Chrysler style. Both ZJ Grand Cherokee, of which 1,428,095 were made, and its 1999–2004 WJ successor had solid axle suspension. The WJ Grand Cherokee continued to use AMC's 4.0 I6.

The YJ Wrangler was another AMC creation that traveled into the Chrysler era. This Jeep was made at Brampton until the famous old Canadian AMC plant was closed on April 23, 1992. Continuing the tradition of lavish CJs, in 1991–94 special YJ Wrangler Renegade had a pricey $4,266 "Renegade Decor Group" options pack. In 1991 exterior color choices were white, black, or red; in '92 an added color was blue, and bronze featured for '93.

Wrangler Renegade had custom 8-inch-wide 5-hole alloy rims, color-keyed body flares, a center console with cup holders, leather-wrapped steering wheel and full carpeting. To create a Wrangler Renegade, a normal Jeep was factory-sent to Auto Style Cars in Detroit. The Wrangler Renegade with the option pack fitted was then returned to the Jeep factory, and was in turn sent to a dealer. Dealers loved the Jeep: a complete Renegade with their cut factored in was almost $20K in 1991! High price and fixings not suited to off-road living kept Wrangler Renegade exclusive.

The 1987–95 YJ Wrangler notched up 685,071 sales, and its TJ replacement had an intentional retro resemblance to the AMC era CJ-7. American Motors terminology even crept onto the TJ and later JK in the form of a respective sports-oriented and bare-bones pack denoted "X." AMC influence also continued with its engines, the 2.5 I4 becoming a long-standing Wrangler base motor. In 1991 the 2.5 gained multi-point fuel injection, and in '93 this was upgraded to sequential injection. For '97 AMC's I4 adopted hydraulic lifters, a "Quarter-Wave" tuning chamber in the intake duct, and a Helmholtz resonator atop the throttle body. The last two additions produced a nicer, more refined sound.

At the same time the 2.5 I4 was helping the environment with a 3-way cat and dual heated oxygen sensors. The AMC I4 finished up in 2002; in 2003 Wrangler's new base engine was the Dodge Neon's DOHC 2.4 I4. With AMC's 4.0 I6, the first revision under Mopar management was freer-flowing injectors, boosting outputs to 177 bhp and 224 lbs/ft in 1988. A more serious workover came in 1991 when Renix engine management was replaced with Chrysler equivalents, and old-fashioned hotrodding created the "4.0 Litre High Output" motor, as the AMC I6 became billed.

The new 4.0 HO had intake port size increased one-eighth inch, a larger throttle body, new less restrictive intake and exhaust manifolds, higher flow injectors and sportier cam for 190 bhp and 225 lbs/ft. With the efficiency improvements and smarter underhood electronics, EGR was surplus to requirements and junked! The 4.0 held to this spec and output between 1991 and 1996. In 1995 there were small head changes, and in '96 the block was strengthened with more block webbing and a stud girdle for the crankshaft's main bearings.

Things went a bit downhill with smaller exhaust port "enviro" heads in '98, compensated for in mid–'99 by a freer-flowing intake manifold. In 2000–1 distributorless "coil on plug" ignition and better exhaust porting set the balance of power in favor of sport. Thus, a 2004 WJ Grand Cherokee 4.0 impressed with 190 bhp at 4,600 rpm and 230 lbs/ft at 3,000 rpm. That was the final year for the AMC 4.0 in North America, its place taken by Chrysler's 3.8 V6. However, both 2.5 and 4.0 AMC motors lived on in China.

When Mercedes came on the Chrysler scene the Chinese-Jeep partnership was renamed Beijing-Benz Daimler Chrysler Automotive. The Chinese-assembled XJ Cherokee evolved with cosmetic Grand Cherokee-like changes for this market, and was produced as the Jeep 2500 through 2006 using the AMC 2.5 I4. The Chinese outfit also bought the tooling for the 1999–2004 WJ Grand Cherokee when that model was discontinued in North America at the close of the 2004 model year. It was then introduced to the Chinese market as the Jeep 4000 and Jeep 4700 in 2006. The model names represented the AMC 4.0 I6 and Chrysler quad cam V8 engines respectively.

Richard Teague worked briefly at Chrysler when Packard's design team moved to Chrysler. After Packard's demise, Teague subsequently left Chrysler due to conflicts with management. Ironically the friendly people in Chrysler's '90s neighborhood were often ex–AMC folk! Chrysler's Neon was the work of former AMC staff. Chrysler's Director of Small Car Operations, who oversaw development of the successful PT Cruiser, used to be an AMC guy.

By the end of the '80s Chrysler was in trouble again, because man cannot live on K-car and minivan alone. AMC brought the Grand Cherokee, a Ford Explorer challenger. Eagle Premier inspired the LH cars, and with them Chrysler had something to rival Taurus. AMC culture taught Chrysler cab-forward design, and how to do niche models. The Dodge Viper, Prowler V6 hot rod and aforementioned PT Cruiser come to mind. Chrysler had been like a mini–GM, with design carried out in fragmented, rigid department fashion. AMC influence showed a work team could see a new model through from drawing board to fruition with a more cohesive result. Be organic, not bureaucratic!

One interesting figure who made the move from AMC to Chrysler was François Castaing. The ex–Renault man moved with his family to Detroit in 1980 while working in the AMC-Renault alliance. It's not often that someone has a hand in designing a Formula One turbo V6, and one of the world's most successful off-roaders of all time (XJ Cherokee). In 1988 Castaing became Chrysler's Chief Engineer, and was part of the team that created the Dodge Viper. In 1996 François Castaing became executive VP for Chrysler International Operations.

After the '98 merger with Mercedes, Castaing was technical advisor to Chrysler CEO Bob Eaton, and retired in 2000. Indeed, it might be said the creative ways of AMC's people made Chrysler attractive to Mercedes merger-wise. AMC certainly made Jeep the modern "more than Willys" company it is today. Chrysler discovered AMC's Jeep legacy the hard way, with Hummer.

In December 1999 AM General got into a deal with GM, whereby the latter exploited the popularity of Hummer. Through this hookup GM got exclusive ownership of the Hummer name globally, plus associated marketing and distribution rights. AM General began assembling the Chevy Tahoe-based H2 at the new Mishawaka factory in 2002. The original Hummer was redesignated H1, and in 2006 the baby H3 came along. AM General retained ownership of the Humvee name. There was an intellectual property legal battle between Chrysler and GM over which brand had the exclusive rights to the traditional 7-vertical-slot Jeep grille.

With the Humvee/Hummer being historically linked to Jeep, and no discernible dilution of Chrysler's intellectual property suffered, Chrysler couldn't stop Hummer from using that distinctive front fascia. Ultimately Hummer became a casualty of the 2007–8 global financial crisis. GM failed to offload the Hummer brand to Chinese company Sichuan Tengzhong in 2010, not even for a paltry $150 million.[61] The Humvee and AM General continue on.

Reproduction specialist Year One used to have an AMC parts listing, but with limited demand this was withdrawn. However, there are smaller outfits that still supply AMC/

Top: **The Rambler Ranch, located in Elizabeth, Colorado, is the destination to visit for all things AMC/Rambler. Started by Terry Gale, it showcases cars and memorabilia associated with American Motors (courtesy The Rambler Ranch).** ***Bottom:*** **The Rambler Ranch's '50s-style cafe harks back to the decade when American Motors made the economy car par excellence known as Rambler (courtesy The Rambler Ranch).**

Eagle/Rambler parts, and have even got into the reproduction business too. Of course a trip to Pikeville, North Carolina, might yield similar results. This is the location of what is reputed to be the world's last AMC dealer, putting aside those operations that became Jeep/Eagle outlets at Chrysler takeover time. Collier Motors is different, very different.

Collier Motors sits frozen in time with a lot of new and used AMCs, plus a stock of pre-loved non–AMC trade-ins. Some of the "new" AMCs still carry window stickers, and some are marked with prices. The dealer, with AMC A-mark logo still atop, is in a derelict, rather than museum state, with zero-miles AMCs exposed to the elements and grass growing around. The dealership has always been in the ownership of the Collier family, selling Ramblers and AMCs since the '50s. Robert Collier shut it down in 1979 when Renault bought a chunk of AMC. Today Collier Motors will sell parts, but prefers to sell complete cars.

Traveling down Route 66 requires an iconic American like Rambler, and Chantel the mannequin agrees (courtesy The Rambler Ranch).

If you want to see shiny Ramblers and AMCs, head out on the trail to the Rambler Ranch in Elizabeth, Colorado. Here one can find a '67 Marlin with 4bbl 343 V8 sitting next to a Bricklin SV-1. There is the one-of-a-kind Pininfarina-bodied Nash Ambassador, and the 34th (out of 104 made) 1951 Nash-Healey sportster. Such mint examples sit in a 5-building complex filled with period memorabilia and mannequins! An in-house restoration shop carries out the auto refurbishments, and '50s-style Rambler Café is the perfect venue for club meetings, special events, parties or Sha-Na-Na!

The Rambler Ranch was started by Mr. Terry Gale, with just one '50s Nash Ambassador his father bought second-hand in 1969. On site is also a Pacer sedan racer with Clifford Engineering-tuned Weber carb 232 I6, that can pull 135 mph on straights. The car was campaigned by Rambler Ranch Chief Mechanic Roger Scott during 1990–96 in Silver State Classic race events. The Pacer racer's exterior, and its motor, are decorated in AMC red, white and blue livery.

It's fitting that individuals and clubs keep the spirit of AMC alive, because when Mr. Iacocca came to Kenosha, AMC parts depots and archive material were junked. Then again, isn't AMC still going? In 1977 AMC management decided they would only concentrate on Jeep/off-roaders, and not develop any new regular passenger cars. When Chrysler arrived they let the AMC Jeep crew do their thing: produce existing designs and introduce new work AMC cooked up during the Renault era. In 1988 Jeep was AMC, so all that's required is revival of that A-mark logo!

Appendix A. Selected American Motors Model Specification Tables

1956 Rambler Custom 4-door Hardtop Sedan

Price: $2,025 (delivered)
Length/Width/Height/Wheelbase: 191.14/71.3/58/108 (inches)
Weight: 2,890 lbs
Engine: OHV 3.2-liter (196ci) 7.47:1 I6, cast-iron head/block, 1bbl Carter AS-2349S
Power/Torque: 120 bhp @ 4,200 rpm / 170 lbs/ft @ 1,600 rpm
Gearbox: 4-speed Borg Warner Dual-Range Hydra-Matic automatic (3.58 final drive)
Suspension: Front — Independent, unequal length control arms, coil, damper
Rear — Coil, damper, live axle
Brakes: Drum front (9 inches), drum rear (9 inches)
0 to 60 mph: 16 seconds (*Car Life*, April 1956) (a/c fitted)
Economy: 20+ mpg highway (manufacturer claim)

For model year '56 the Nash/Hudson American Motors combine released their first new design. A moderately sized, frugal family car with efficient OHV I6, unibody construction and the comfort of all-coil suspension. Custom represented the highest trim level. These high-quality, no-nonsense, value-for-money cars made the Rambler name, and for '57 there would be a V8.

1969 SC/Rambler

Price: $2,998 (msrp)
Length/Width/Height/Wheelbase: 181/70.8/55/106 (inches)
Weight: 3,095 lbs
Engine: OHV 6.4-liter (390ci) 10.2:1 V8, cast-iron head/block, 4bbl Carter AFB 4664S
Power/Torque: 315 bhp @ 4,600 rpm / 425 lbs/ft @ 3,200 rpm
Gearbox: 4-speed Borg Warner T10 manual (3.54 final drive + Twin-Grip differential)
Suspension: Front — Independent, unequal length control arms, coil, damper, swaybar
Rear — Semi-elliptic leaf springs, damper, live axle, traction bars
Brakes: Solid disk front (11.2 inches), drum rear (10 inches) — power assisted
¼ mile: 14.3 seconds @ 98 mph (AMC/Hurst figures)
Economy: 9–11 mpg (premium gas) (*Car and Driver*, May 1969)

AMC and Hurst cooked up a 1,320 ft F/Stock class special named SC/Rambler with AMX model ingredients. On board were "AMX 390" motor, plus top AMX brakes, suspension and even steering wheel. Quarter-mile fans call it the Scrambler, collectors call it a classic. Just 1,512 were made in its one and only model year of 1969.

1970 AMC Rebel Machine

Price: $3,475 (msrp)
(Red-White-And-Blue Machine Package standard on 1st 1,000 cars, $75 thereafter)
Length/Width/Height/Wheelbase: 199/77.24/54.41/114 (inches)
Weight: 3,817 lbs
Engine: OHV 6.4-liter (390ci) 10:1 V8, cast iron head/block, 4bbl Autolite Motorcraft 4300
Power/Torque: 340 bhp @ 5,100 rpm / 430 lbs/ft @ 3,600 rpm
Gearbox: 4-speed Borg Warner T10 manual (3.54 final drive)
Suspension: Front—Independent, unequal length control arms, coil, damper, swaybar (0.94 in)
Rear—Coil, damper, live axle, swaybar (0.95 inch)
Brakes: Solid disk front (11.2 inches), drum rear (10 inches)
¼ mile: 14.57 seconds @ 92.77 mph (*Road Test*, May 1970)
Economy: 11 mpg (premium gas—ave. with 4 speed + opt. 3.91 final drive)
The Machine represented AMC's, and Detroit's, final intermediate Super Car hurrah before insurance, emissions, economy and other forces of doom impinged upon the enthusiast. Machine came with standard features like HD suspension and front non-power disks, but had more options than Scrambler. The year was 1970, and we would never race like this again.

1971 AMC SC/360 Hornet

Price: $2,663, Go-pack (includes 360 4bbl + Ram Air) = $199
Length/Width/Height/Wheelbase: 179.3/70.6/52.48/108 (inches)
Weight: 3,215 lbs
Engine: OHV 5.9-liter (360ci) 8.5:1 V8, cast-iron head/block, 4bbl Autolite Motorcraft 4300 (Ram Air on test)
Power/Torque: 285 bhp @ 4,800 rpm / 390 lbs/ft @ 3,200 rpm
Gearbox: 3-speed Borg Warner Shift Command automatic (3.15 final drive)
Suspension: Front—Independent, unequal length control arms, coil, damper
Rear—Semi-elliptic leaf springs, damper, live axle, traction bars (opt.)
Brakes: Vented disk front (10.9 inches), drum rear (10 inches)
¼ mile: 14.8 seconds @ 94.63 mph (*Hot Rod*, December 1970)
Economy: 13 mpg (city), 17 mpg (highway)—(regular gas)
The final in AMC's high-performance car trilogy, the SC/360 Hornet was intended to circumvent the evil insurance company performance premium. The base price bought a 245-horse 2bbl 360 and 3-speed manual power team, but a 4bbl 360 was optional. SC/360 Hornet came standard with D70 14-inch Polyglas tires on 6-inch-wide slot rims, HD suspension was in the Go-pack. The model drew fine praise for its excellent handling.

1973 AMC Javelin AMX 401

Price: $3,191 (base Javelin AMX msrp)
401 Go-pack = $476.25, 4-speed = $188.05
Length/Width/Height/Wheelbase: 192.3/75.4/51.5/110 (inches)
Weight: 3,830 lbs
Engine: OHV 6.6-liter (401ci) 8.5:1 V8, cast-iron head/block, 4bbl Autolite Motorcraft 4300 (cowl air induction optional, and fitted on test)
Power/Torque: 255 bhp @ 4,600 rpm / 345 lbs/ft @ 3,300 rpm (net figures)
Gearbox: 4-speed Borg Warner T10 manual (3.91 opt. final drive on test)
Suspension: Front—Independent, unequal length control arms, coil, damper, swaybar (0.94 in)
Rear—Semi-elliptic leaf springs, damper, live axle
Brakes: Vented disk front (10.9 inches), drum rear (10 inches)—(power assist opt.)
¼ mile: 15.4 seconds @ 91 mph (*Road Test*, June 1973)
Economy: 9.4 mpg (city), 11.6 mpg (highway)—(regular gas)

By '71 AMX was a special spec Javelin. In 1972–74 the 255-horse Javelin AMX 401, along with the SD 455 Trans Am and 454 Vette were the 3 fastest domestic cars money could buy. The 401ci Go-packed AMX had the abilities of a bygone age. AMC had built the smogger to end all smoggers. The '74 model year was the final year for Javelin, but AMX would return.

1976 AMC Pacer X

Price: $3,499 (base), 2bbl 258 $99, X pack $339
Length/Width/Height/Wheelbase: 170/77/52.7/100 (inches)
Weight: 3,190 lbs
Engine: OHV 4.2-liter (258ci) 8.0:1 I6, cast-iron head/block, 2bbl Holley (no catalytic converter)
Power/Torque: 120 bhp @ 3,400 rpm / 200 lbs/ft @ 2,000 rpm
Gearbox: 3-speed Chrysler Torque-Flite A904 automatic (3.08 final drive)
Suspension: Front — Independent, unequal length control arms, coil, damper, swaybar (X pack)
Rear — Semi-elliptic leaf springs, damper, live axle
Brakes: Vented disk front (10.7 inches), drum rear (10 inches) — power assisted
0–60 mph: 13.4 seconds (*Car and Driver*, May 1976)
Economy: EPA 25 mpg highway
The "Small Was Never This Wide" Pacer brought a new dimension in comfort to American small cars. The unusual lifestyle-oriented Pacer combined an advanced futuristic body with AMC intermediate mechanicals. For '76 American Motors spiced up Pacer with an optional 2-barrel version of the 258 I6.

1977½ AMC Gremlin Custom 2-liter

Price: $3,248 (base sticker)
Length/Width/Height/Wheelbase: 166.6/70.6/51.5/96 (inches)
Weight: 2,660 lbs
Engine: OHC 2-liter (121ci) 8.2:1 I4, aluminum head/cast-iron block, 2bbl Holley-Weber 5210 (has catalytic converter)
Power/Torque: 80 bhp @ 5,000 rpm / 105 lbs/ft @ 2,500 rpm
Gearbox: 4-speed Borg Warner HR1 manual (3.31 final drive)
Suspension: Front — Independent, unequal length control arms, coil, damper
Rear — Semi-elliptic leaf springs, damper, live axle
Brakes: Vented disk front (10.27 inches), drum rear (9 inches) (non-boosted)
0 to 60 mph: 17.9 seconds (*Consumer Reports*, July 1977)
Economy: 17.5 mpg (city), 29.5 mpg (highway) — (unleaded gas)
In the wake of the fuel crisis AMC searched for more MPGs and found the VW/Audi/Porsche 2-liter I4, which it used under license in selected Gremlins and Concords during 1977–79. Due to the expense of the licensing agreement, the 232 continued as the Gremlin's base motor. The Custom trim level opened the door to 4-cylinder economy!

1988 Eagle Premier LX

Price: $12,474 (debut msrp)
Length/Width/Height/Wheelbase: 192.8/70/53.3/106 (inches)
Weight: 2,862 lbs
Engine: OHV 2.5-liter (150.5ci) 9.2:1 I4, cast-iron head/block, Double Quench combustion chamber, TBI (Throttle Body Injection)
Power/Torque: 111 bhp @ 4,750 rpm / 142 lbs/ft @ 2,500 rpm
Gearbox: 4-speed electronic (Renault/Volkswagen) AR-4 automatic (3.85 final drive)
Suspension: Front — Independent, MacPherson struts, coil, 26mm swaybar, (28mm — Enthusiast Group), zero-offset geometry
Rear — Independent, 4 torsion bar (26mm), trailing arms, gas dampers, 22mm swaybar

Brakes: Vented disk front (10.4 inches), drum rear (8.9 inches)—power assisted
0–60 mph: 11.5 seconds
Economy: 26.6 mpg city / 41.5 mpg highway
The Eagle Premier was a large front-drive family sedan, which used the Renault 25 as an engineering starting point. It was the last AMC-designed passenger car, an '80s Matador if you will, featuring American Motors' own 258 I6-derived 2.5-liter I4 in a Renault-style North-South engine layout that influenced future Chrysler LH cars.

Appendix B. AMC Organizations

The International AMC Rambler Car Club

amcrc.com

Founded in 1980 by Frank and Elaine Wrenick to aid the preservation, collection and restoration of AMC-related cars. Maintains printed AMC archive material and publishes the quarterly *Rambler Reader*, monthly *Ad Release* and annual *Parts Source Guide*.

The Rambler Ranch

ramblerranch.com

Started in 1993 by Terry Gale, The Rambler Ranch restores and displays vehicles associated with the AMC and Rambler brands.

Terry Gale
Rambler Ranch
P.O. Box 1487
Elizabeth, Colorado 80107
U.S.A.

American Motors Forum

amccars.net

The central AMC forum for all models.

The Pacer Page

www.amcpacer.com

The world's number-one Pacer information website, started in 1995 by Jeni Panhorst.

Planet Houston AMX

www.planethoustonamx.com

Established 1983 by Eddie Stakes. The place for rare AMC parts, memorabilia, and information, and to register your SC/360 Hornet.

Eddie Stakes
1902 Wycliffe
Houston, Texas 77043
U.S.A.

The AMX-perience

www.amx-perience.com

Website containing information concerning AMX-related coupes, forum, parts vendors and classifieds sections.

The Coupe Coop!

www.matadorcoupe.com

Run by Craig Bond, this is the most complete 1974–78 Matador Coupe information resource on the net. Fly in for a visit! Register your coupe today!

Gremlin Community

www.gremlinx.com

Founded in 2000 and run by Donnie Solomon, this is the world's biggest Gremlin online resource.

Kennedy American, Inc.

kennedyamerican.com

Dealing in AMC car parts (includes reproductions) from 1936 to 1988. Founded by Jeff Kennedy in July 1992 from initial bought-up AMC parts inventory.

Kennedy American, Inc.
7100 State Route 142 S.E.
West Jefferson, Ohio 43162
U.S.A.
(614) 879-7283
sales@kennedyamerican.com

The AMC Eagle Nest

www.amceaglenest.com

A website established in 2003 with historical information, a forum and parts store concerning the 1980–88 all-wheel-drive Eagle variants related to AMC Concord and Spirit.

Evolution 4x4

www.evolution4×4.net

An off-roading performance specialist that caters to Eagle & Jeep. Founded by Mick Stine.

459 North Lowell
Casper, Wyoming 82601
U.S.A.
(307) 472-5779

Colorado AMX

www.coloradoamx.com

The AMC Javelin and AMX-related website and workshop (Davis AMC) of father-and-son team Wayne and Aaron Davis. The Big Bad colors shine especially bright in Colorado!

AMC Hornet.com

amchornet.com

A resource forum concerning the AMC Hornet started by Alexander Ortiz in 2002.

Chapter Notes

Chapter 1

1. Graham Robson, *The Illustrated Directory of Classic Cars* (London: Greenwich Editions, 2004), p. 146.
2. Noel Grove, "Swing Low, Sweet Chariot!" *National Geographic* (July 1983): p. 24.
3. Quentin Willson, *Great Car* (New York: Dorling Kindersley, 2001), p. 485.
4. Michael Sedgwick, *Classic Cars of the 1950's and 1960's* (Twickenham, England: Tiger Books International, 1997), p. 30.
5. David E. Davis, Jr., "Paris by Trans Am," *Car and Driver* (January 1979): p. 40.

Chapter 2

1. Sedgwick, p. 197.
2. Barney Sharratt, "Lord of Austin," *Thoroughbred & Classic Cars* (June 1992): pp. 86, 89.
3. Barney Sharratt, "The Austin Atlantic Sports Saloon," *Thoroughbred & Classic Cars* (October 1992): p. 94.
4. Paul Wager, *BeetleMania* (London: Bison Books, 1995), p. 14.
5. Liz Turner, "Us and our cars," *Autocar* (17 and 24 December 1986): p. 39.
6. Peter Homola, "Red Giant," *Autocar* (12 June 1985): p. 61.
7. Klaus Freund, ed., *Auto Katalog 1980 (Ausgabe* Nr. 23) (Stuttgart, Germany: Vereinigte Motor—Veriage, 1979), p. 52.
8. AMC Rambler CLUB, "America's first diecast aluminum engine 1961–64," *Rambler Reader* 14, no. 2 (1993): p. 22.
9. Mike Taylor, "From the Ground Up," *Thoroughbred & Classic Cars* (September 1989): pp. 69, 70.
10. *Ibid.*, p. 70.

Chapter 3

1. *Autocar*, 23 July 1986, p. 6.
2. Graham Robson, *A–Z of CARS of the 1970s* (Devon, England: Bay View Books, 1993): p. 12.
3. Tom Stewart, *Ultimate Autos: The Kings of Bling* (Edison, NJ: Chartwell Books, 2007): p. 115.
4. Ralph Guldahl Jr., "Hornet SC/360," *Hot Rod* (December 1970): p. 38.

Chapter 4

1. *Motor Trend*, "Aiming Straight" (September 1971): p. 46.
2. Christy Campbell, *The VW Beetle: A Celebration of the VW Bug* (London: Hamlyn, 1990): p. 60.
3. Eric Dahlquist, "1970 Gremlin," *Motor Trend* (March 1970): p. 72.
4. *Consumer Reports*, "The Little Cars" (January 1971): p. 13.
5. *Ibid.*, p. 8.
6. Steve Collison, "Street Sweeper," *Car Craft* (May 1972): p. 43.
7. *Ibid.*, p. 43.
8. *Consumer Reports*, "The Little Cars," p. 15.
9. *Consumer Reports*, "5 Full-Sized Sedans" (February 1972): p. 95.
10. *Motor Trend*, p. 47.
11. *Consumer Reports*, "5 Full-Sized Sedans," p. 89.

Chapter 5

1. Karl Ludvigsen, "Suddenly It's 1980," *Motor Trend* (February 1975): p. 35.
2. Martin Buckley, "By Royal Dis-appointment," *Thoroughbred & Classic Cars* (November 1999): p. 67.
3. Tom McCahill, "We Test AMC's Pacer," *Mechanix Illustrated* (August 1975): p. 30.
4. *Consumer Reports*, "Two New Small Cars" (July 1975): p. 406.
5. *Popular Mechanics*, "AMC Pacer Station Wagon Is a Styling Coup!" (October 1976): p. 96.
6. Don Sherman, "The Flying Fishbowl," *Car and Driver* (May 1976): p. 70.
7. *Road & Track*, "AMC Pacer Wagon: Ke-

nosha's small wide car grows up" (February 1977): p. 46.

8. *Road & Track*, "American Motors Pacer: The world's biggest small car?" (April 1975): p. 39.

9. Giles Chapman, *The Worst Cars Ever Sold* (Gloucestershire, England: Sutton, 2006), p. 15.

10. *Business Week*, "AMC gambles $60-million on a new compact" (20 January 1975): p. 78.

11. *Consumer Reports*, "Two New Small Cars," p. 408.

12. *Ibid.*, p. 408.

13. McCahill, p. 30.

14. Dennis Adler, "European Impression: Audi A8 Quattro," *European Car* (August 1994): p. 44.

15. *Popular Mechanics*, p. 176.

16. Marlan Davis, "904 Versus the World!" *Car Craft* (June 1998): p. 56.

17. Art Spinella, "Carl Green: Sculpting Rolling Stock," *Automotive Age* (February 1978): p. 89.

18. *Pickup, Van & 4WD*, "Little Orphan AMC: Two lovable little pickoupes" (April 1984): p. 55.

19. Dean Weston, "Carl Green: West's Best Customizer," *1001 Custom and Rod Ideas* (March 1977): p. 55.

20. George Johnson, "Plugging into the Sun," *National Geographic* (September 2009): pp. 35, 38.

21. Charles G. Burck, "A Fresh Start — Again — for American Motors," *Fortune* (16 July 1979): p. 72.

22. *Popular Mechanics*, p. 96.

23. *Business Week*, p. 76.

24. Patrick Foster, "1974–78 AMC Matador Coupe: Kenosha's Question Marque," *Collectible Automobile* (December 1996): pp. 52, 53.

25. *Road & Track*, "American Motors Matador X: Sleek & fast, but oversize & thirsty" (March 1974): pp. 44, 45.

26. Jim McCraw, "Matador X 401: It's the Real Thing!" *Super Stock* (February 1974): p. 67.

27. Burck, p. 68.

28. Tony Swan, "AMC's Mystery Wagon," *Motor Trend* (August 1975): p. 67.

29. Burck, p. 68.

Chapter 6

1. *Consumer Reports*, June 1974, p. 453.

2. Roger Huntington, "Detroit Notebook," *Autocar* (31 August 1974): p. 44.

3. *Consumer Reports*, "Four Economy Subcompacts" (July 1977): p. 396.

4. Burck, p. 68.

5. *Autocar*, 31 August 1974, p. 24.

Chapter 7

1. *Consumer Reports*, "Four Compact Cars" (February 1980): p. 118.

2. *Ibid.*, p. 118.

3. *Ibid.*, p. 114.

4. Burck, p. 80.

5. *Ibid.*, p. 72.

6. *Ibid.*, p. 80.

Chapter 8

1. *Ibid.*, p. 67.

2. Freund, p. 242.

3. Sedgwick, pp. 144, 160.

4. Grove, p. 33.

5. Robert Ball, "Renault Takes Its Hit Show on the Road," *Fortune* (4 May 1981): pp. 275, 276.

6. *Ibid.*, p. 280.

7. Burck, p. 72.

8. *Ibid.*, p. 66.

9. Giles Chapman, "Style of the '70s," *Autocar & Motor* (5 April 1989): p. 69.

10. Burck, p. 76.

11. *CAR*, "Eastern Most" (September 1985): p. 142.

12. Burck, p. 74.

13. Simon Worrall, "Made in China," *National Geographic* (June 2009): p. 122.

14. Burck, p. 72.

15. *Autocar*, "All Weather Contenders" (6 February 1985): p. 22.

16. *Autocar*, "The French Connection" (23 July 1986): p. 29.

17. *CAR*, August 1984, p. 45.

18. Stewart, p. 93.

19. Ball, p. 280.

20. *Ibid.*, p. 275.

21. Stewart, p. 95.

22. *CAR*, August 1984, p. 45.

23. *Autocar*, 6 February 1985, p. 9.

24. John Lamm, "Seasonal Changes," *Autocar* (1 October 1986): p. 36.

25. Edouard Seidler, "Turning Point," *Autocar* (5 June 1985): p. 47.

26. Grove, pp. 28, 29.

27. Lamm, p. 38.

28. *Motor Sport*, "Supercinq Comes to Britain" (March 1985): p. 263.

29. *CAR*, September 1985, p. 64.

30. Tamiya News Editing Room, *1984 Tamiya Catalogue* (Shizuoka City, Japan: Tamiya Plastic Model Co., 1984), p. 22.

31. Patrick R. Foster, *American Motors: The Last Independent* (Iola, WI: Krause Publications, 1993), p. 275.

32. *Autocar*, 3 September 1986, p. 7.

33. Walter Nicholson, *Microeconomic Theory: Basic Principles and Extensions*, 5th ed. (Texas: Dryden Press, 1992), p. 613.

34. Grove, p. 13.

35. *Ibid.*, pp. 34, 35.

36. Kenneth F. Weaver, "Our Energy Predicament," *Energy: A National Geographic Special Report* (February 1981): p. 2.

37. David Jeffery, "America's auto mania," *Energy:*

A National Geographic Special Report (February 1981): p. 29.

38. *Autocar*, 1 October 1986, p. 4.

39. Ben Oliver, ed., *The Best of CAR: The '70s and '80s* (London: Portico Books, 2008): p. 111.

40. Edouard Seidler, "Turning Point," p. 47.

41. *Motor*, "The Washington file" (17 August 1985): p. 22.

42. Stuart Birch, "Family affair," *Motor* (17 August 1985): p. 24.

43. *Ibid.*, p. 25.

44. *CAR*, September 1985, p. 83.

45. Edouard Seidler, "Miracle Man," *Autocar* (31 July 1985): p. 39.

46. *Autocar*, 6 February 1985, p. 9.

47. Mark Wheeler, "Upwardly Mobile," *Autocar* (17 and 24 December 1986): p. 18.

48. Mark Gillies, "Design for Today," *Autocar* (10 December 1986): p. 55.

49. Gordon Wilkins, "Looking Ahead," *Daily Express Guide to 1987 World Cars*, p. 48.

50. *Consumer Reports*, "Four Compact Cars," p. 114.

51. *Ibid.*, p. 120.

52. Ron Wakefield, "Chrysler's H-car," *Motor* (16 May 1984): p. 24.

53. Bill Vance, "Revived Imperial a victim of early '80s recession," *The London Free Press* (Friday, 9 May 2003): p. E4.

54. Grove, p. 9.

55. *CAR*, August 1984, p. 39.

56. Graham Jones, "Shaping Up for a Fight," *Autocar* (3 September 1986): p. 30.

57. *Autocar*, 1 October 1986, p. 4.

58. *CAR*, April 1988, p. 9.

59. *Off Road and 4 Wheel Drive*, July 1988, p. 5.

60. Russell Bulgin, "Jeep Freeze," *CAR* (August 1994): p. 108.

61. *The Telegraph* no. 971 (3–9 March 2010): p. 35.

Bibliography

Adler, Dennis. "European Impression: Audi A8 Quattro." *European Car*, August 1994.

AMC Rambler CLUB. "America's first die-cast aluminum engine 1961–64." *Rambler Reader* 14, no. 2, 1993.

Autocar, 31 August 1974, p. 24.

_____. "All Weather Contenders." 6 February 1985.

_____. "The French Connection." 23 July 1986.

_____. 3 September 1986, p. 7.

_____. 1 October 1986, p. 4.

Ball, Robert. "Renault Takes Its Hit Show on the Road." *Fortune*, 4 May 1981.

Birch, Stuart. "Family Affair." *Motor*, 17 August 1985.

Buckley, Martin. "By Royal Dis-appointment." *Thoroughbred & Classic Cars*, November 1999.

Bulgin, Russell. "Jeep Freeze." *CAR*, August 1994.

Burck, Charles G. "A Fresh Start — Again — for American Motors." *Fortune*, 16 July 1979.

Business Week. "AMC gambles $60-million on a new compact." 20 January 1975.

Campbell, Christy. *The VW Beetle: A Celebration of the VW Bug*. London: Hamlyn, 1990.

CAR, August 1984, pp. 39, 45.

_____. "Eastern Most." September 1985.

_____. September 1985, pp. 64, 83.

_____. April 1988, p. 9.

Chapman, Giles. "Style of the '70s." *Autocar & Motor*, 5 April 1989.

_____. *The Worst Cars Ever Sold*. Gloucestershire, England: Sutton, 2006.

Collison, Steve. "Street Sweeper." *Car Craft*, May 1972.

Consumer Reports. "The Little Cars." January 1971.

_____. "5 Full-Sized Sedans." February 1972.

_____. June 1974, p. 453.

_____. "Two New Small Cars." July 1975.

_____. "Four Economy Subcompacts." July 1977.

_____. "Four Compact Cars." February 1980.

Dahlquist, Eric. "1970 Gremlin." *Motor Trend*, March 1970.

Davis, Marlan. "904 Versus the World!" *Car Craft*, June 1998.

Davis, David E., Jr. "Paris by Trans Am." *Car and Driver*, January 1979.

Foster, Patrick R. *American Motors: The Last Independent*. Iola, WI: Krause Publications, 1993.

_____. "1974–78 AMC Matador Coupe: Kenosha's Question Marque." *Collectible Automobile*, December 1996.

Freund, Klaus, ed. *Auto Katalog 1980* (*Ausgabe* Nr. 23). Stuttgart, Germany: Vereinigte Motor — Veriage, 1979.

Gillies, Mark. "Design for Today." *Autocar*, 10 December 1986.

Grove, Noel. "Swing Low, Sweet Chariot!" *National Geographic*, July 1983.

Guldahl Jr., Ralph. "Hornet SC/360." *Hot Rod*, December 1970.

Homola, Peter. "Red Giant." *Autocar*, 12 June 1985.

Huntington, Roger. "Detroit Notebook." *Autocar*, 31 August 1974.

Jeffery, David. "America's auto mania." *Energy: A National Geographic Special Report*, February 1981.

Johnson, George. "Plugging into the Sun." *National Geographic*, September 2009.

Jones, Graham. "Shaping Up for a Fight." *Autocar*, 3 September 1986.

Lamm, John. "Seasonal Changes." *Autocar*, 1 October 1986.

Ludvigsen, Karl. "Suddenly It's 1980." *Motor Trend*, February 1975.

McCahill, Tom. "We Test AMC's Pacer." *Mechanix Illustrated*, August 1975.

McCraw, Jim. "Matador X 401: It's the Real Thing!" *Super Stock*, February 1974.

Motor. "The Washington file." 17 August 1985.

Motor Sport. "Supercinq Comes to Britain." March 1985.

Motor Trend. "Aiming Straight." September 1971.

Nicholson, Walter. *Microeconomic Theory: Basic Principles and Extensions*. 5th ed. Texas: Dryden Press, 1992.

Off Road and 4 Wheel Drive, July 1988, p. 5.

Oliver, Ben, ed. *The Best of CAR: The '70s and '80s*. London: Portico Books, 2008.

Pickup, Van & 4WD. "Little Orphan AMC: Two lovable little pickoupes." April 1984.

Popular Mechanics. "AMC Pacer Station Wagon Is a Styling Coup!" October 1976.
Road & Track. "AMC Pacer Wagon: Kenosha's small wide car grows up." February 1977.
_____. "American Motors Matador X: Sleek & fast, but oversize & thirsty." March 1974.
_____. "American Motors Pacer: The world's biggest small car?" April 1975.
Robson, Graham. *A–Z of CARS of the 1970s*. Devon, England: Bay View Books, 1993.
_____. *The Illustrated Directory of Classic Cars*. London: Greenwich Editions, 2004.
Sedgwick, Michael. *Classic Cars of the 1950's and 1960's*. Twickenham, England: Tiger Books International, 1997.
Seidler, Edouard. "Miracle Man." *Autocar*, 31 July 1985.
_____. "Turning Point." *Autocar*, 5 June 1985.
Sharratt, Barney. "The Austin Atlantic Sports Saloon." *Thoroughbred & Classic Cars*, October 1992.
_____. "Lord of Austin." *Thoroughbred & Classic Cars*, June 1992.
Sherman, Don. "The Flying Fishbowl." *Car and Driver*, May 1976.
Spinella, Art. "*Carl Green: Sculpting Rolling Stock*." *Automotive Age*, February 1978.
Stewart, Tom. *Ultimate Autos: The Kings of Bling*. Edison, NJ: Chartwell Books, 2007.
Swan, Tony. "AMC's Mystery Wagon." *Motor Trend*, August 1975.
Tamiya News Editing Room. *1984 Tamiya Catalogue*. Shizuoka City, Japan: Tamiya Plastic Model Co., 1984.
Taylor, Mike. "From the Ground Up." *Thoroughbred & Classic Cars*, September 1989.
The Telegraph, 3–9 March 2010, p. 35.
Turner, Liz. "Us and our cars." *Autocar*, 17 and 24 December 1986.
Vance, Bill. "Revived Imperial a victim of early '80s recession." *The London Free Press*, Friday, 9 May 2003.
Wager, Paul. *BeetleMania*. London: Bison Books, 1995.
Wakefield, Ron. "Chrysler's H-car." *Motor*, 16 May 1984.
Weaver, Kenneth F. "Our Energy Predicament." *Energy: A National Geographic Special Report*, February 1981.
Weston, Dean. "Carl Green: West's Best Customizer." *1001 Custom and Rod Ideas*, March 1977.
Wheeler, Mark. "Upwardly Mobile." *Autocar*, 17 and 24 December 1986.
Wilkins, Gordon. "Looking Ahead." *Daily Express Guide to 1987 World Cars*.
Willson, Quentin. *Great Car*. New York: Dorling Kindersley, 2001.
Worrall, Simon. "Made in China." *National Geographic*, June 2009.

Index